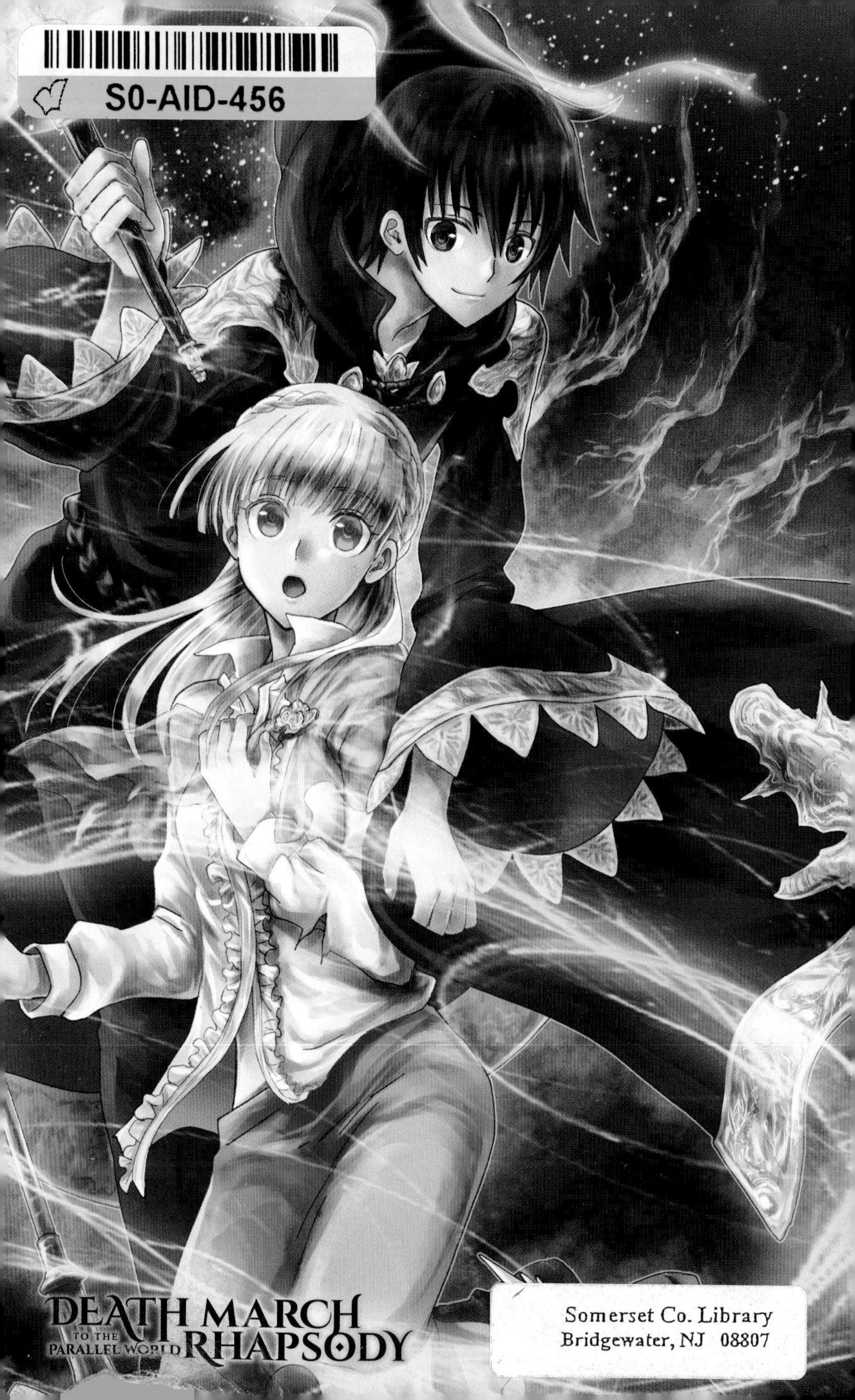
DEATH MARCH
TO THE PARALLEL WORLD RHAPSODY

CONTENTS

CHAPTER 7: Labyrinth

005

CHAPTER 8: Commence Assault

023

CHAPTER 9: Exploring the Labyrinth

045

CHAPTER 10: Assault Climax

071

CHAPTER 11: Boss Battle

099

CHAPTER 12: Back to the Surface

129

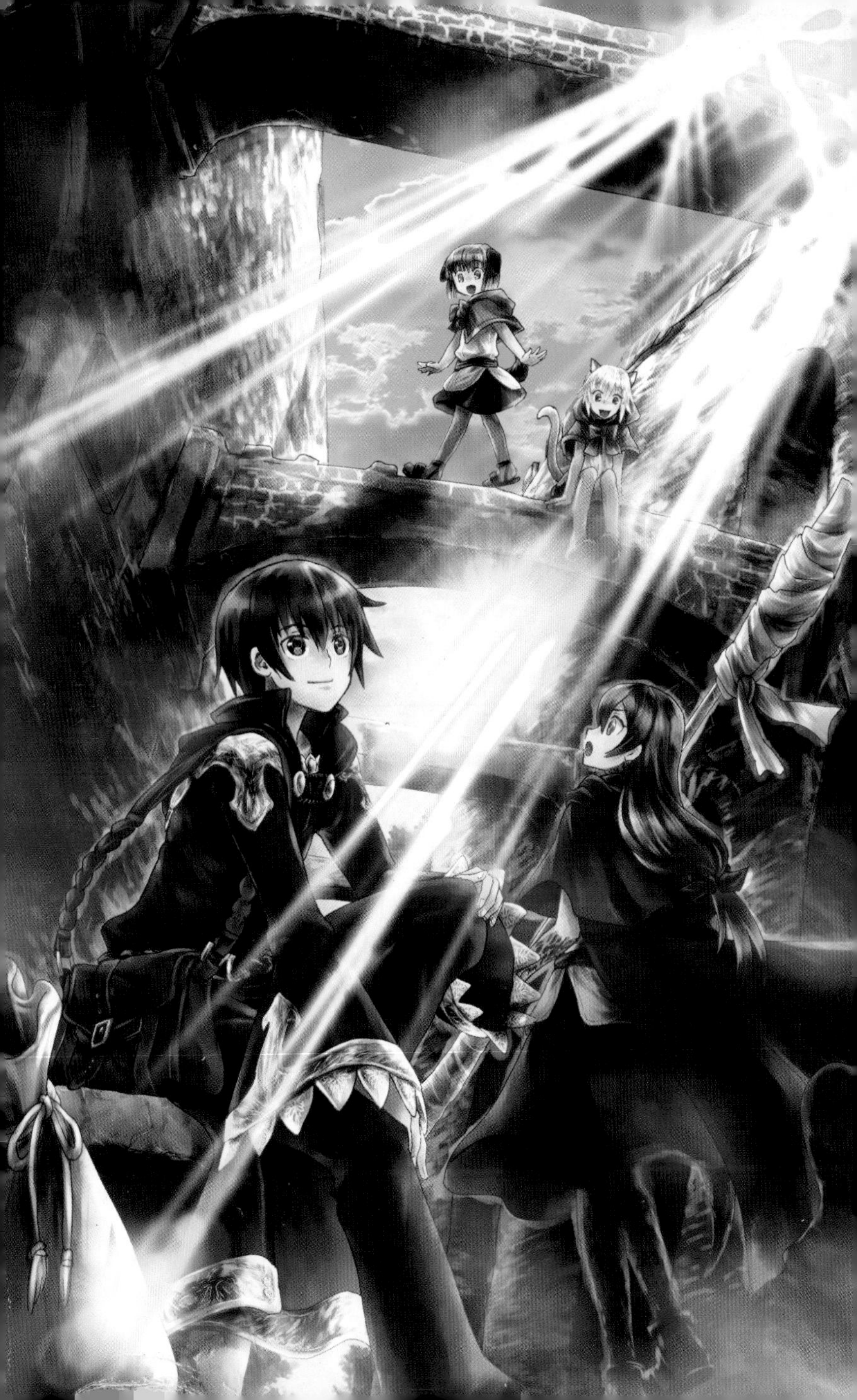

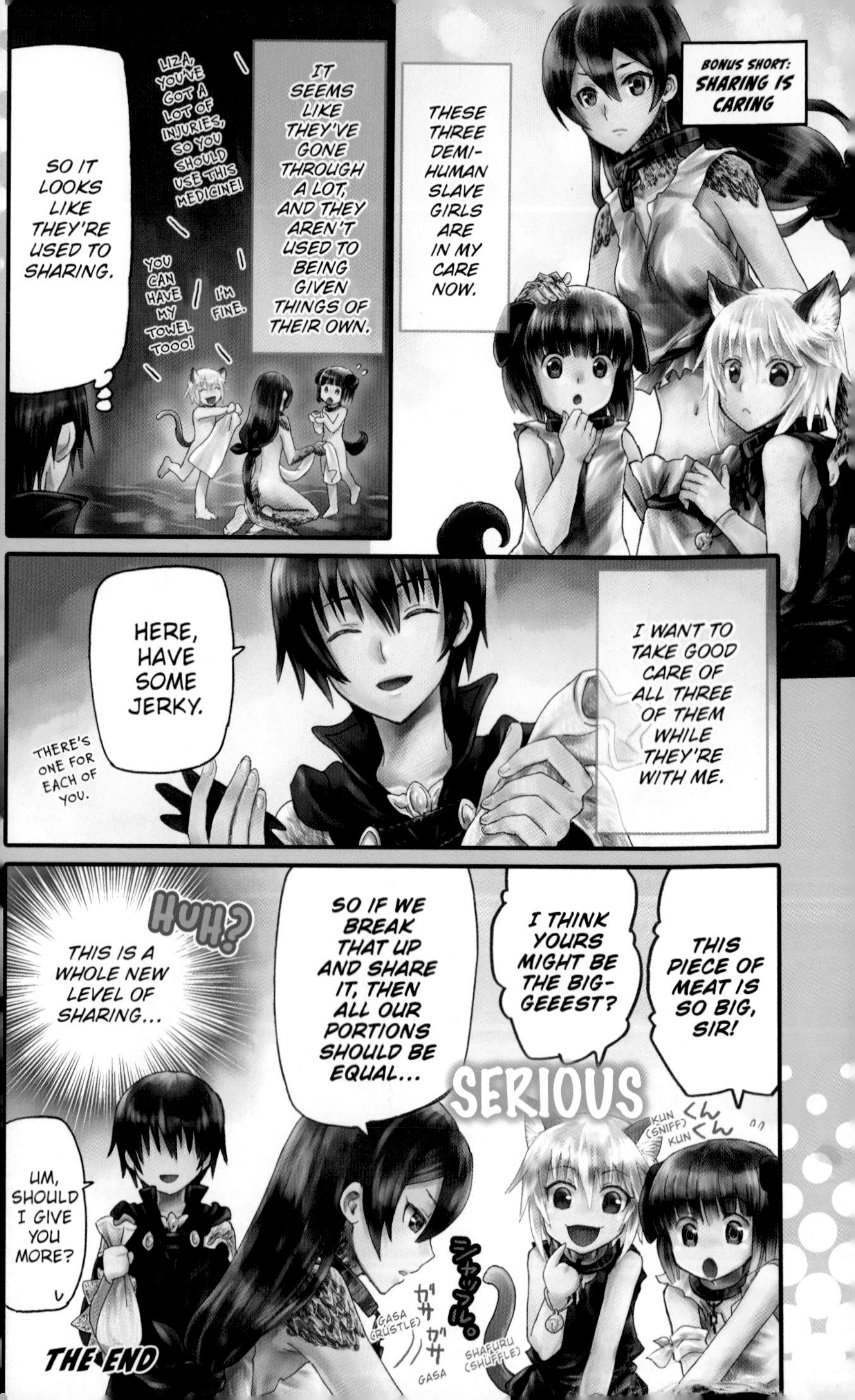
BONUS SHORT: SHARING IS CARING
THESE THREE DEMI-HUMAN SLAVE GIRLS ARE IN MY CARE NOW.
IT SEEMS LIKE THEY'VE GONE THROUGH A LOT, AND THEY AREN'T USED TO BEING GIVEN THINGS OF THEIR OWN.
LIZA, YOU'VE GOT A LOT OF INJURIES, SO YOU SHOULD USE THIS MEDICINE!
I'M FINE.
YOU CAN HAVE MY TOWEL TOOO!
SO IT LOOKS LIKE THEY'RE USED TO SHARING.
I WANT TO TAKE GOOD CARE OF ALL THREE OF THEM WHILE THEY'RE WITH ME.
HERE, HAVE SOME JERKY.
THERE'S ONE FOR EACH OF YOU.
THIS PIECE OF MEAT IS SO BIG, SIR!
くんくん
KUN (SNIFF) KUN
I THINK YOURS MIGHT BE THE BIG-GEEEST?
SERIOUS
SO IF WE BREAK THAT UP AND SHARE IT, THEN ALL OUR PORTIONS SHOULD BE EQUAL...
シャッフル。
SHAFURU (SHUFFLE)
ガサガサ
GASA (RUSTLE) GASA
HUH?
THIS IS A WHOLE NEW LEVEL OF SHARING...
UM, SHOULD I GIVE YOU MORE?
THE END

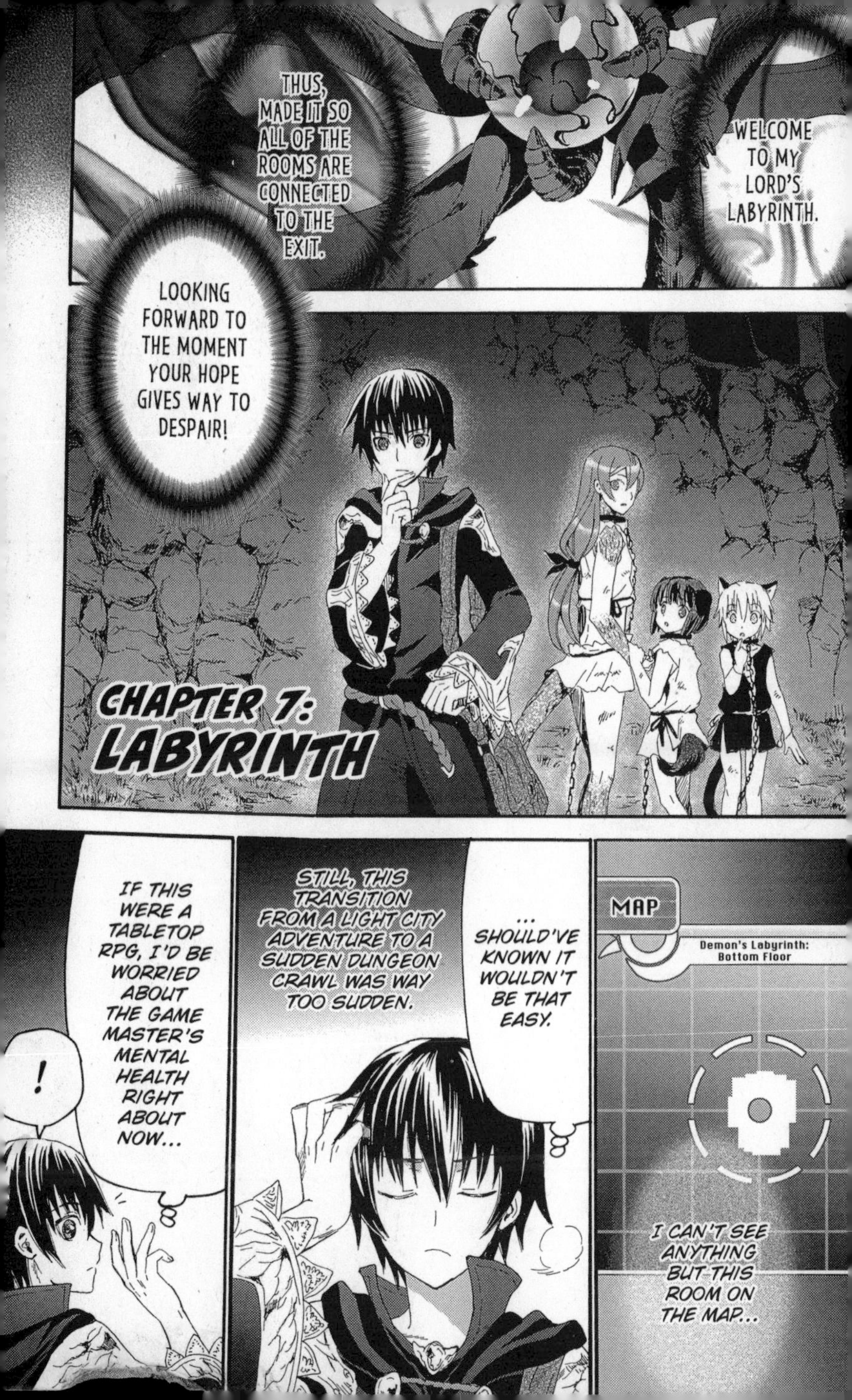
WELCOME TO MY LORD'S LABYRINTH.
THUS, MADE IT SO ALL OF THE ROOMS ARE CONNECTED TO THE EXIT.
LOOKING FORWARD TO THE MOMENT YOUR HOPE GIVES WAY TO DESPAIR!
CHAPTER 7: LABYRINTH
MAP
Demon's Labyrinth: Bottom Floor
I CAN'T SEE ANYTHING BUT THIS ROOM ON THE MAP...
...SHOULD'VE KNOWN IT WOULDN'T BE THAT EASY.
STILL, THIS TRANSITION FROM A LIGHT CITY ADVENTURE TO A SUDDEN DUNGEON CRAWL WAS WAY TOO SUDDEN.
IF THIS WERE A TABLETOP RPG, I'D BE WORRIED ABOUT THE GAME MASTER'S MENTAL HEALTH RIGHT ABOUT NOW...
!

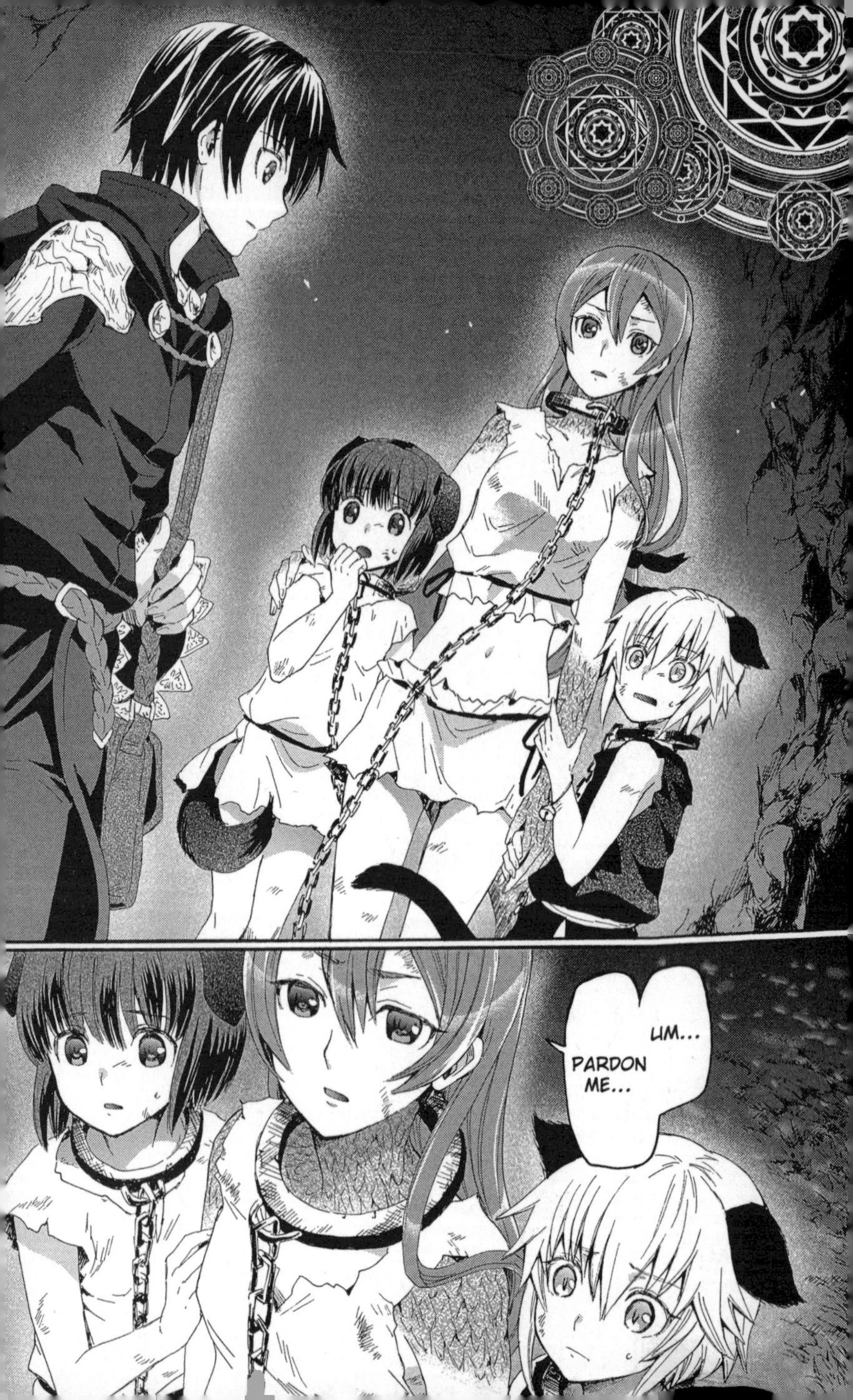
UM... PARDON ME...

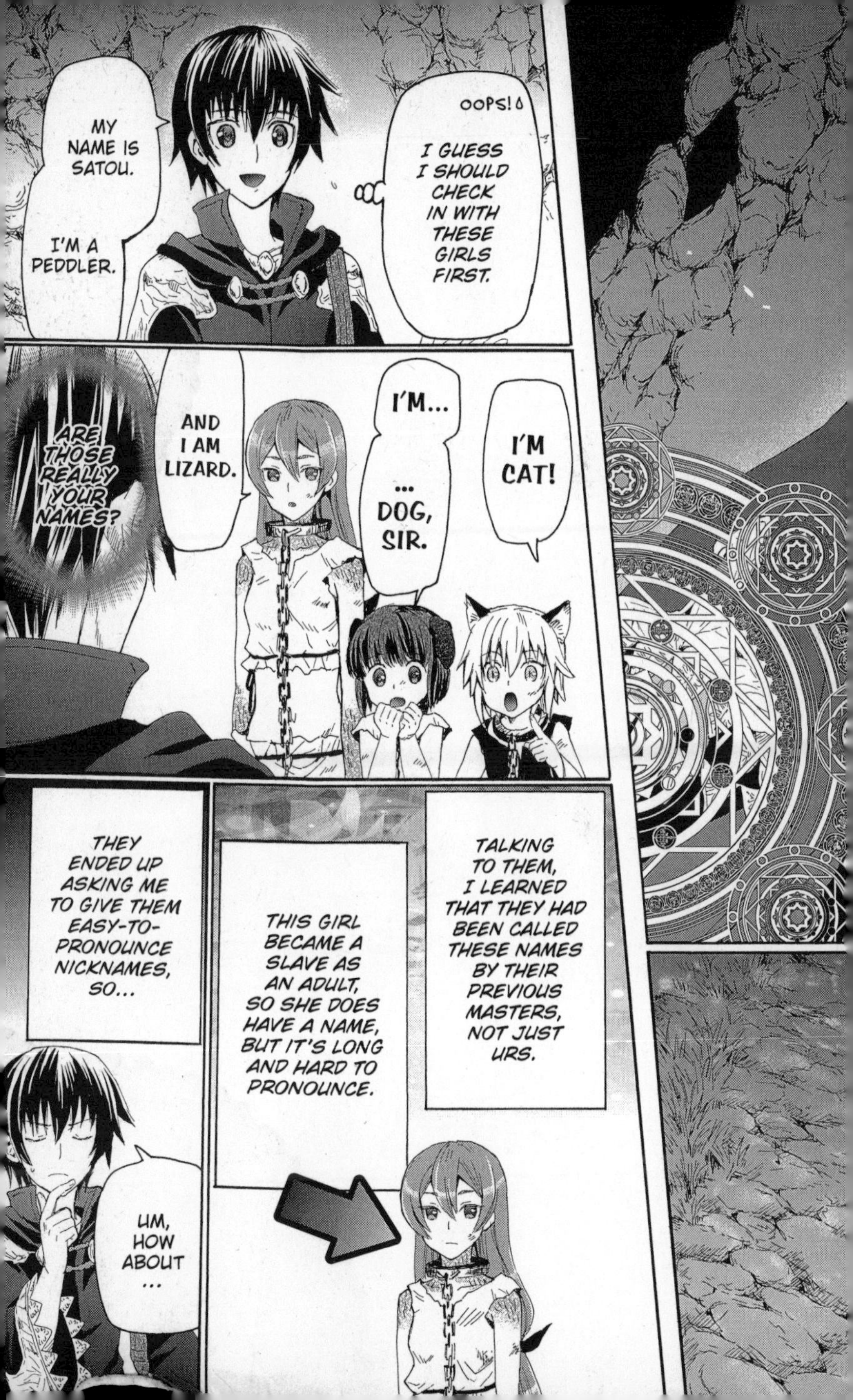
OOPS!
I GUESS I SHOULD CHECK IN WITH THESE GIRLS FIRST.
MY NAME IS SATOU.
I'M A PEDDLER.
I'M CAT!
I'M...
... DOG, SIR.
AND I AM LIZARD.
ARE THOSE REALLY YOUR NAMES?
TALKING TO THEM, I LEARNED THAT THEY HAD BEEN CALLED THESE NAMES BY THEIR PREVIOUS MASTERS, NOT JUST URS.
THIS GIRL BECAME A SLAVE AS AN ADULT, SO SHE DOES HAVE A NAME, BUT IT'S LONG AND HARD TO PRONOUNCE.
THEY ENDED UP ASKING ME TO GIVE THEM EASY-TO-PRONOUNCE NICKNAMES, SO...
UM, HOW ABOUT ...

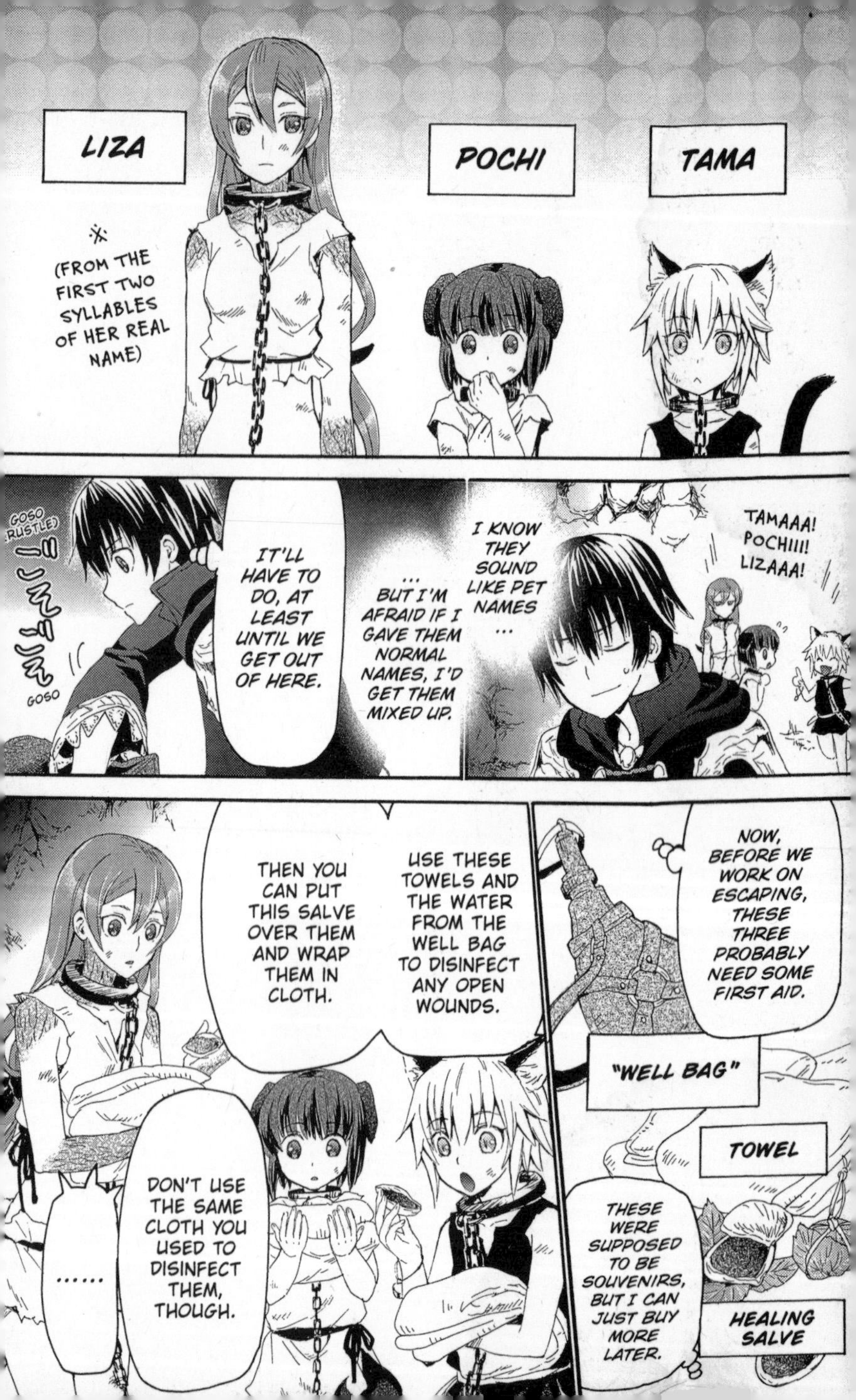
TAMA
POCHI
LIZA
※ (FROM THE FIRST TWO SYLLABLES OF HER REAL NAME)
TAMAAA! POCHIII! LIZAAA!
I KNOW THEY SOUND LIKE PET NAMES...
...BUT I'M AFRAID IF I GAVE THEM NORMAL NAMES, I'D GET THEM MIXED UP.
IT'LL HAVE TO DO, AT LEAST UNTIL WE GET OUT OF HERE.
GOSO (RUSTLE)
GOSO
NOW, BEFORE WE WORK ON ESCAPING, THESE THREE PROBABLY NEED SOME FIRST AID.
"WELL BAG"
TOWEL
THESE WERE SUPPOSED TO BE SOUVENIRS, BUT I CAN JUST BUY MORE LATER.
HEALING SALVE
USE THESE TOWELS AND THE WATER FROM THE WELL BAG TO DISINFECT ANY OPEN WOUNDS.
THEN YOU CAN PUT THIS SALVE OVER THEM AND WRAP THEM IN CLOTH.
DON'T USE THE SAME CLOTH YOU USED TO DISINFECT THEM, THOUGH.
......

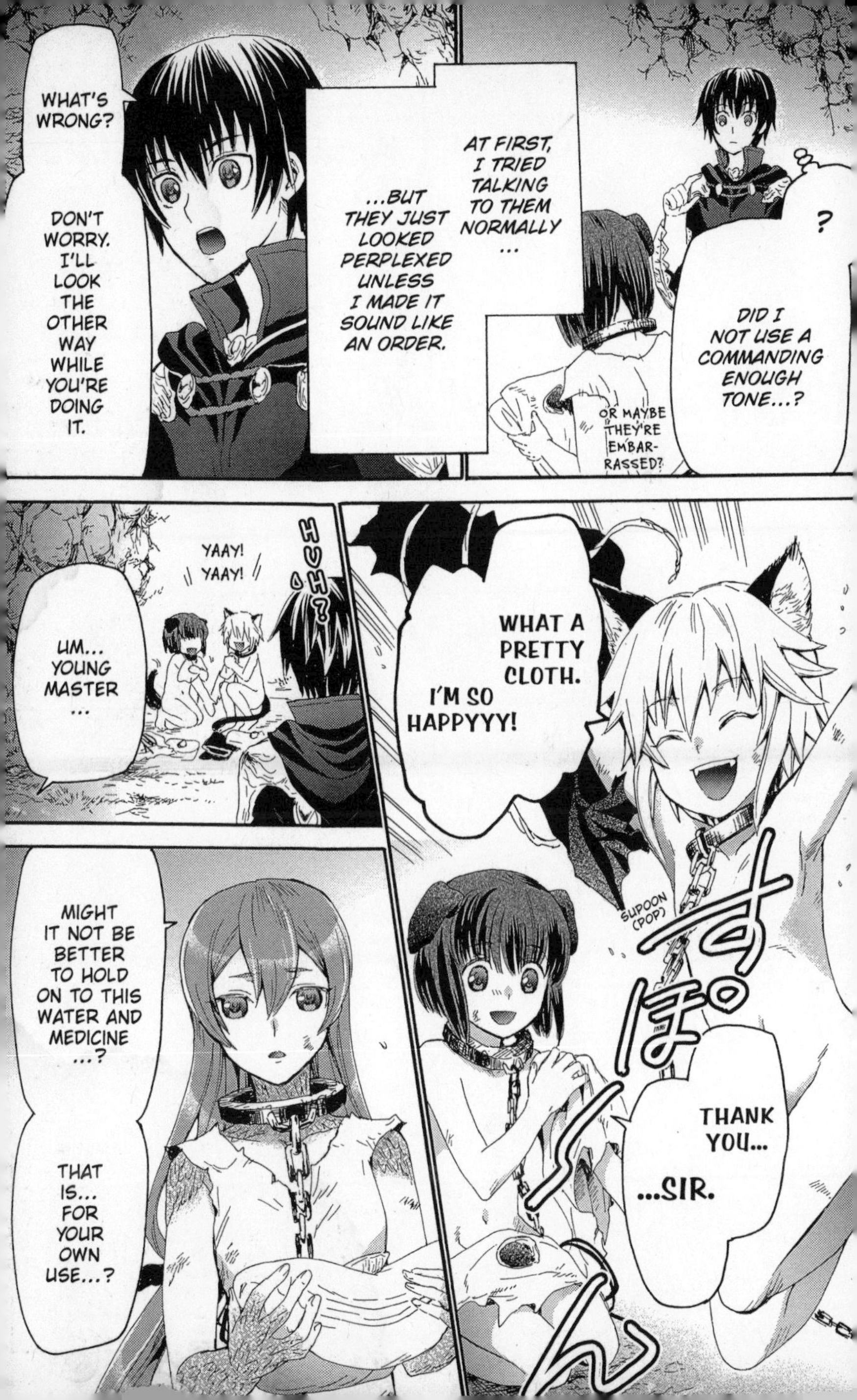
?
DID I NOT USE A COMMANDING ENOUGH TONE...?
OR MAYBE THEY'RE EMBARRASSED?
AT FIRST, I TRIED TALKING TO THEM NORMALLY...
...BUT THEY JUST LOOKED PERPLEXED UNLESS I MADE IT SOUND LIKE AN ORDER.
WHAT'S WRONG?
DON'T WORRY. I'LL LOOK THE OTHER WAY WHILE YOU'RE DOING IT.
WHAT A PRETTY CLOTH.
I'M SO HAPPYYY!
SUPOON (POP)
すぽん
THANK YOU...
...SIR.
YAAY! YAAY!
HUH?
UM... YOUNG MASTER...
MIGHT IT NOT BE BETTER TO HOLD ON TO THIS WATER AND MEDICINE...?
THAT IS... FOR YOUR OWN USE...?

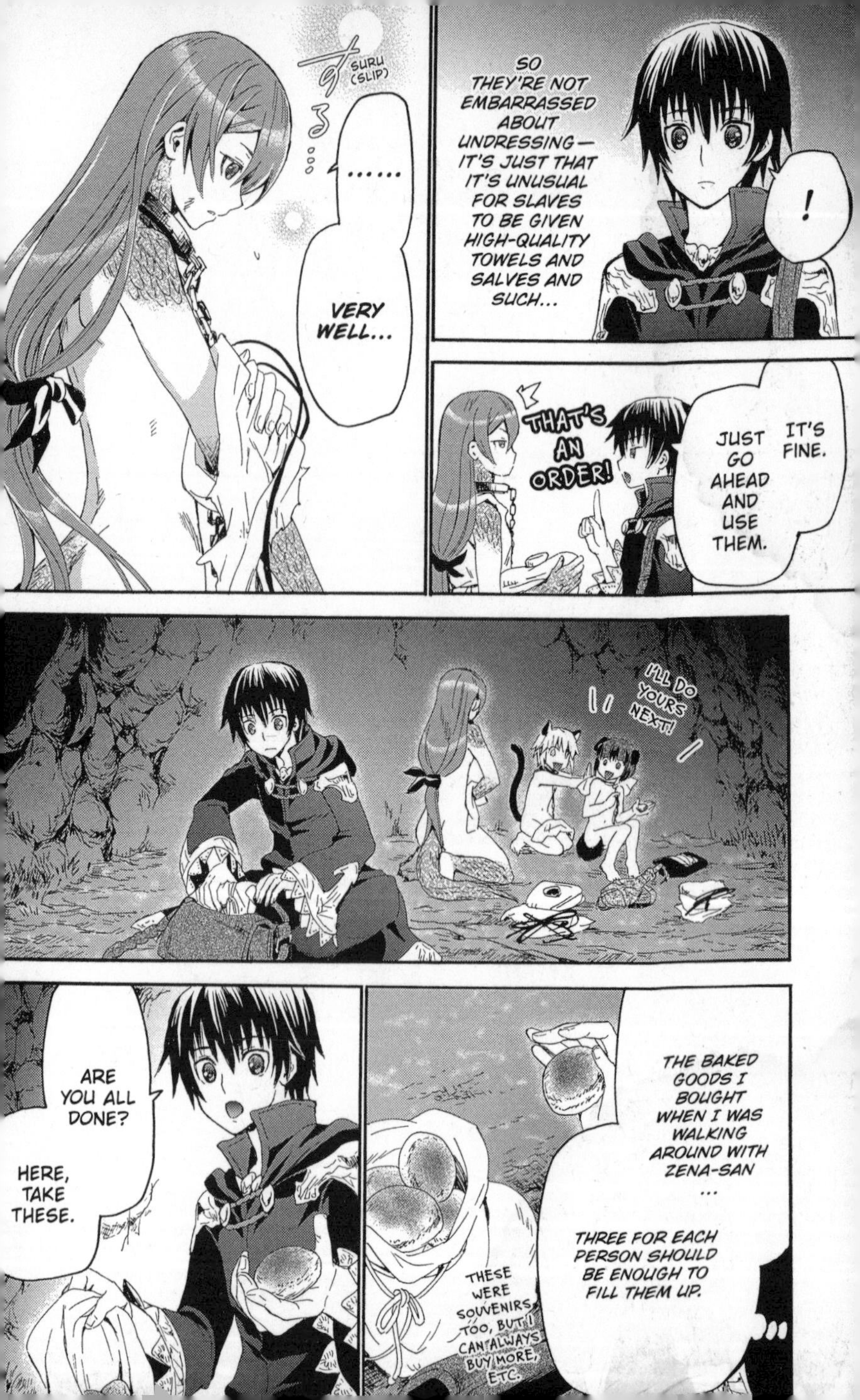
!
SO THEY'RE NOT EMBARRASSED ABOUT UNDRESSING—IT'S JUST THAT IT'S UNUSUAL FOR SLAVES TO BE GIVEN HIGH-QUALITY TOWELS AND SALVES AND SUCH...
IT'S FINE. JUST GO AHEAD AND USE THEM.
THAT'S AN ORDER!
SURU (SLIP)
......
VERY WELL...
I'LL DO YOURS NEXT!
THE BAKED GOODS I BOUGHT WHEN I WAS WALKING AROUND WITH ZENA-SAN ...
THREE FOR EACH PERSON SHOULD BE ENOUGH TO FILL THEM UP.
THESE WERE SOUVENIRS TOO, BUT I CAN ALWAYS BUY MORE, ETC.
ARE YOU ALL DONE?
HERE, TAKE THESE.

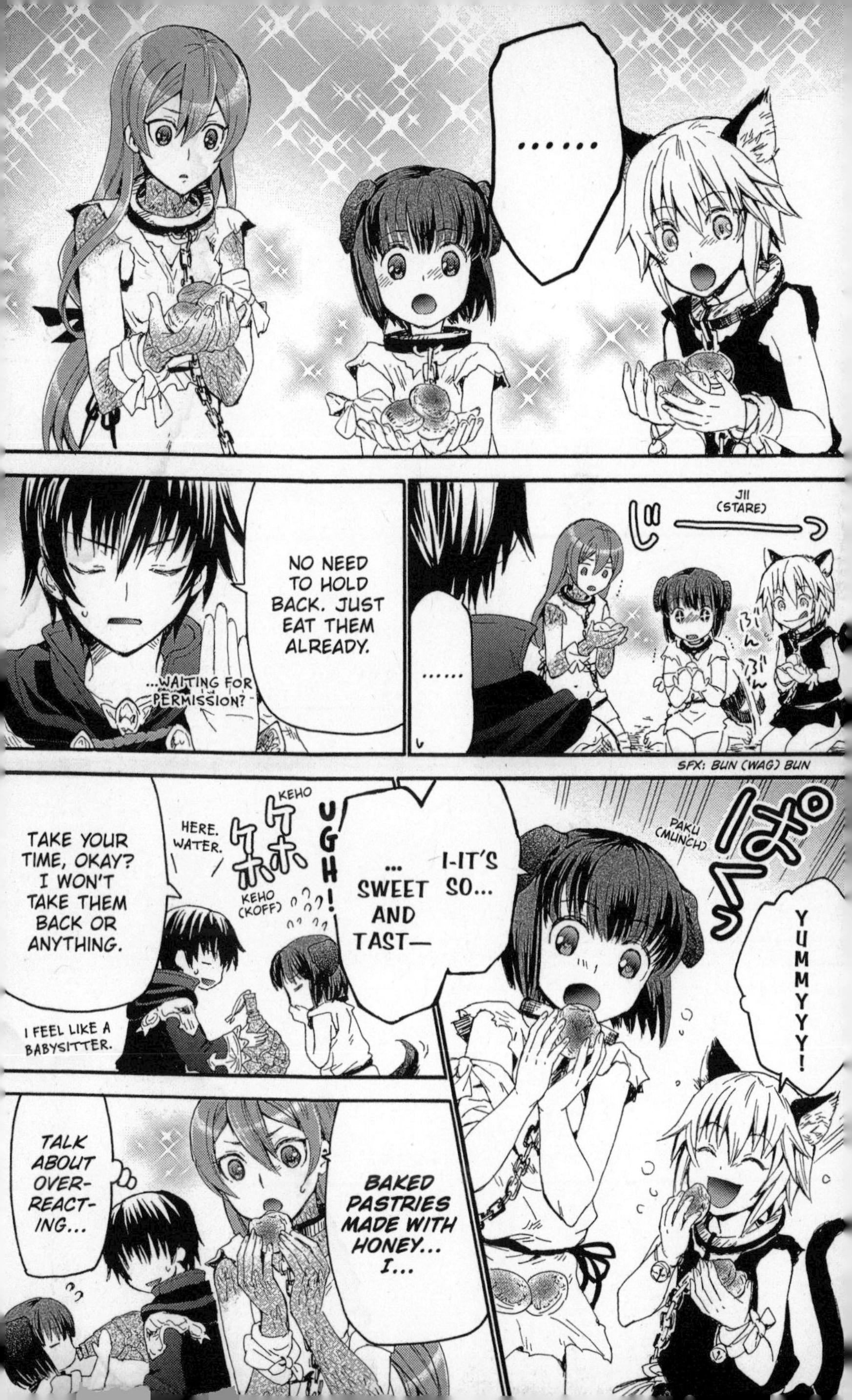
......
JII (STARE)
......
SFX: BUN (WAG) BUN
NO NEED TO HOLD BACK. JUST EAT THEM ALREADY.
...WAITING FOR PERMISSION?
PAKU (MUNCH)
I-IT'S SO... ...SWEET AND TAST—
UGH!
KEHO
KEHO (KOFF)
HERE. WATER.
TAKE YOUR TIME, OKAY? I WON'T TAKE THEM BACK OR ANYTHING.
I FEEL LIKE A BABYSITTER.
YUMMYYY!
BAKED PASTRIES MADE WITH HONEY... I...
TALK ABOUT OVER-REACTING...

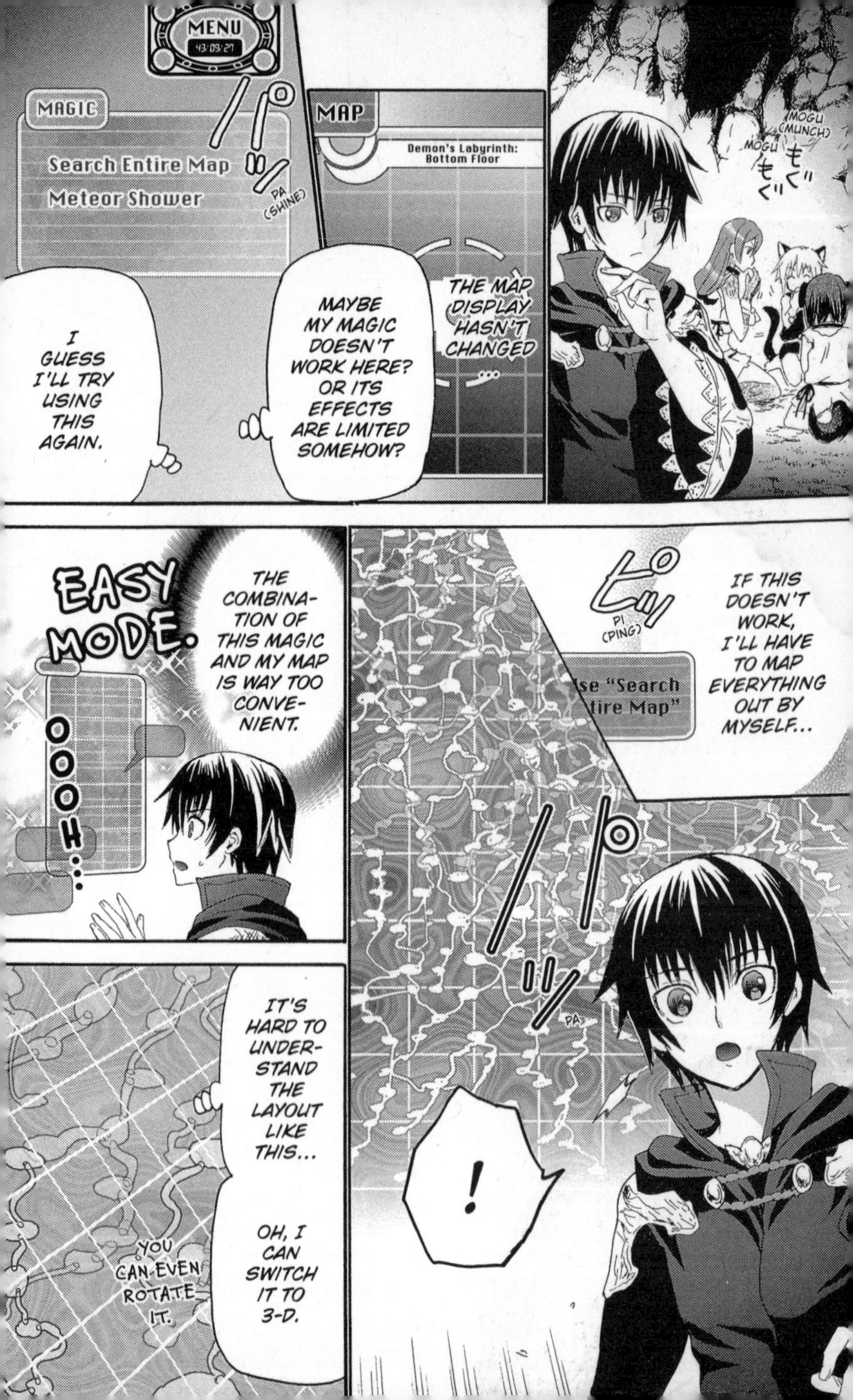
MOGU MOGU (MUNCH)
MAP
Demon's Labyrinth: Bottom Floor
THE MAP DISPLAY HASN'T CHANGED...
MAYBE MY MAGIC DOESN'T WORK HERE? OR ITS EFFECTS ARE LIMITED SOMEHOW?
MENU
43:09:27
MAGIC
Search Entire Map
Meteor Shower
PA (SHINE)
I GUESS I'LL TRY USING THIS AGAIN.
PI (PING)
se "Search
tire Map"
IF THIS DOESN'T WORK, I'LL HAVE TO MAP EVERYTHING OUT BY MYSELF...
PA
!
EASY MODE.
THE COMBINATION OF THIS MAGIC AND MY MAP IS WAY TOO CONVENIENT.
OOOOH...
IT'S HARD TO UNDERSTAND THE LAYOUT LIKE THIS...
OH, I CAN SWITCH IT TO 3-D.
YOU CAN EVEN ROTATE IT.

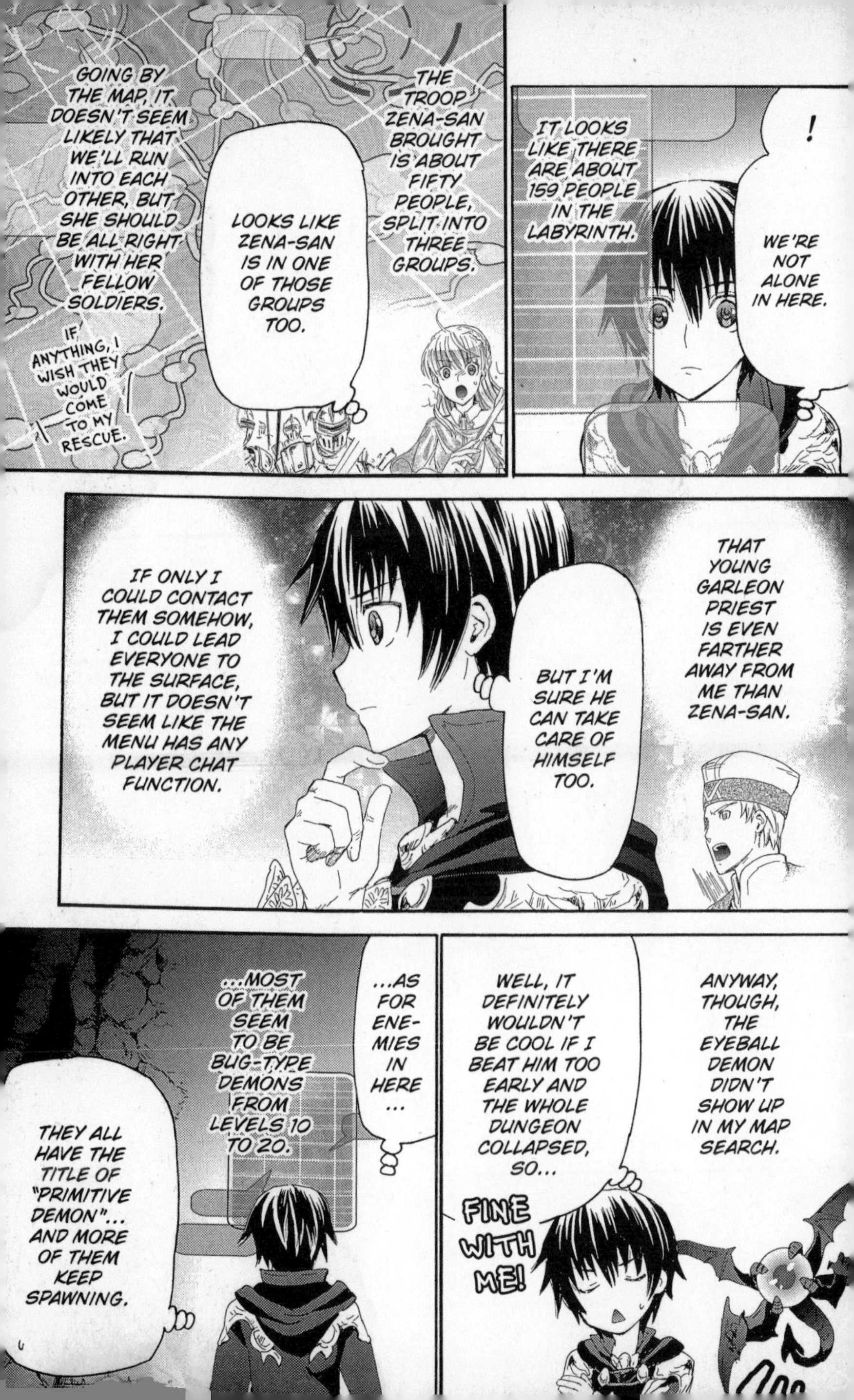
!
WE'RE NOT ALONE IN HERE.
IT LOOKS LIKE THERE ARE ABOUT 159 PEOPLE IN THE LABYRINTH.
THE TROOP ZENA-SAN BROUGHT IS ABOUT FIFTY PEOPLE, SPLIT INTO THREE GROUPS.
LOOKS LIKE ZENA-SAN IS IN ONE OF THOSE GROUPS TOO.
GOING BY THE MAP, IT DOESN'T SEEM LIKELY THAT WE'LL RUN INTO EACH OTHER, BUT SHE SHOULD BE ALL RIGHT WITH HER FELLOW SOLDIERS.
IF ANYTHING, I WISH THEY WOULD COME TO MY RESCUE.
THAT YOUNG GARLEON PRIEST IS EVEN FARTHER AWAY FROM ME THAN ZENA-SAN.
BUT I'M SURE HE CAN TAKE CARE OF HIMSELF TOO.
IF ONLY I COULD CONTACT THEM SOMEHOW, I COULD LEAD EVERYONE TO THE SURFACE, BUT IT DOESN'T SEEM LIKE THE MENU HAS ANY PLAYER CHAT FUNCTION.
ANYWAY, THOUGH, THE EYEBALL DEMON DIDN'T SHOW UP IN MY MAP SEARCH.
WELL, IT DEFINITELY WOULDN'T BE COOL IF I BEAT HIM TOO EARLY AND THE WHOLE DUNGEON COLLAPSED, SO...
FINE WITH ME!
...AS FOR ENEMIES IN HERE...
...MOST OF THEM SEEM TO BE BUG-TYPE DEMONS FROM LEVELS 10 TO 20.
THEY ALL HAVE THE TITLE OF "PRIMITIVE DEMON"... AND MORE OF THEM KEEP SPAWNING.

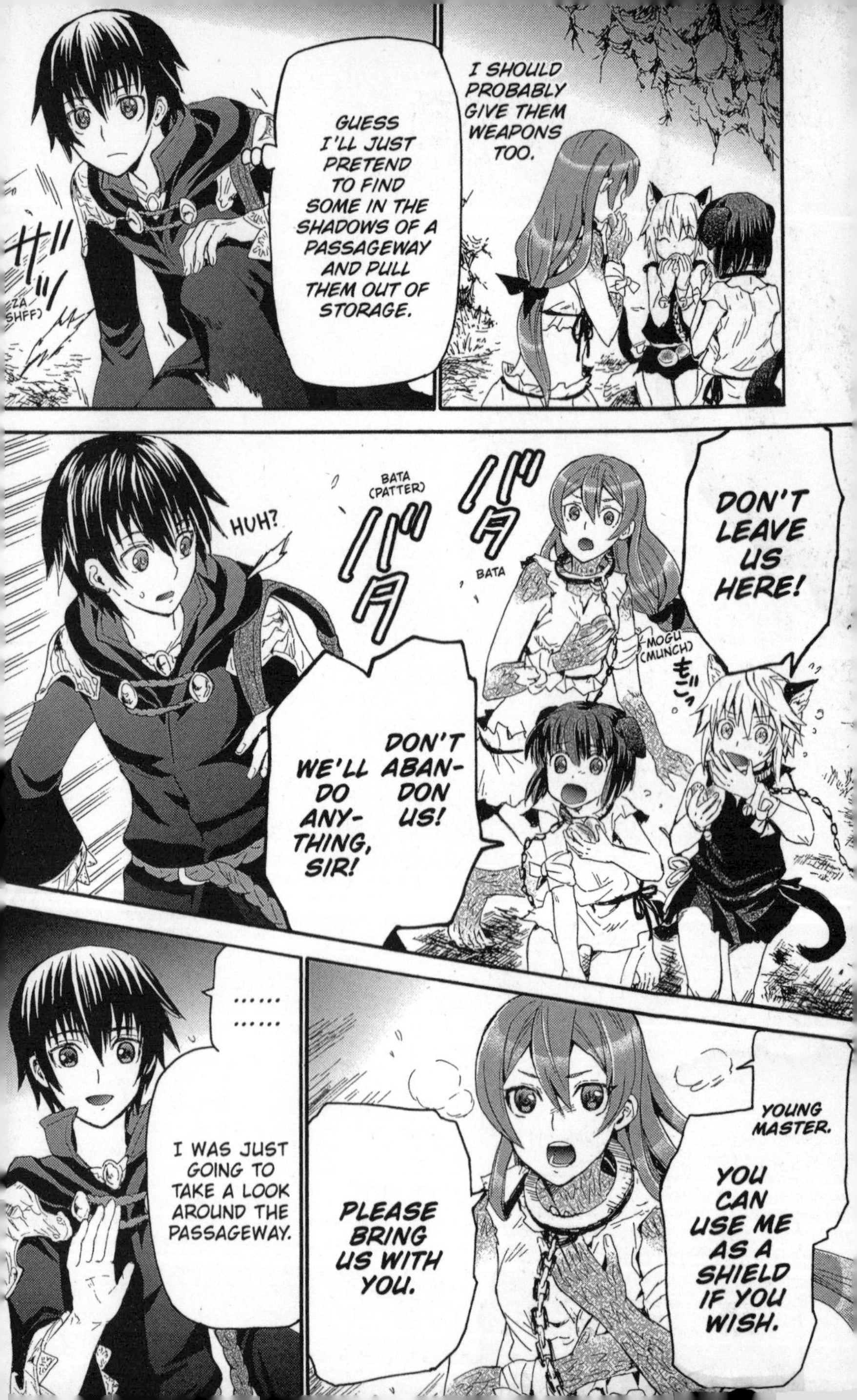
I SHOULD PROBABLY GIVE THEM WEAPONS TOO.
GUESS I'LL JUST PRETEND TO FIND SOME IN THE SHADOWS OF A PASSAGEWAY AND PULL THEM OUT OF STORAGE.
ZA SHFF)
DON'T LEAVE US HERE!
MOGU (MUNCH)
BATA
BATA (PATTER)
DON'T ABAN-DON US!
WE'LL DO ANY-THING, SIR!
HUH?
YOUNG MASTER.
YOU CAN USE ME AS A SHIELD IF YOU WISH.
PLEASE BRING US WITH YOU.
....
I WAS JUST GOING TO TAKE A LOOK AROUND THE PASSAGEWAY.

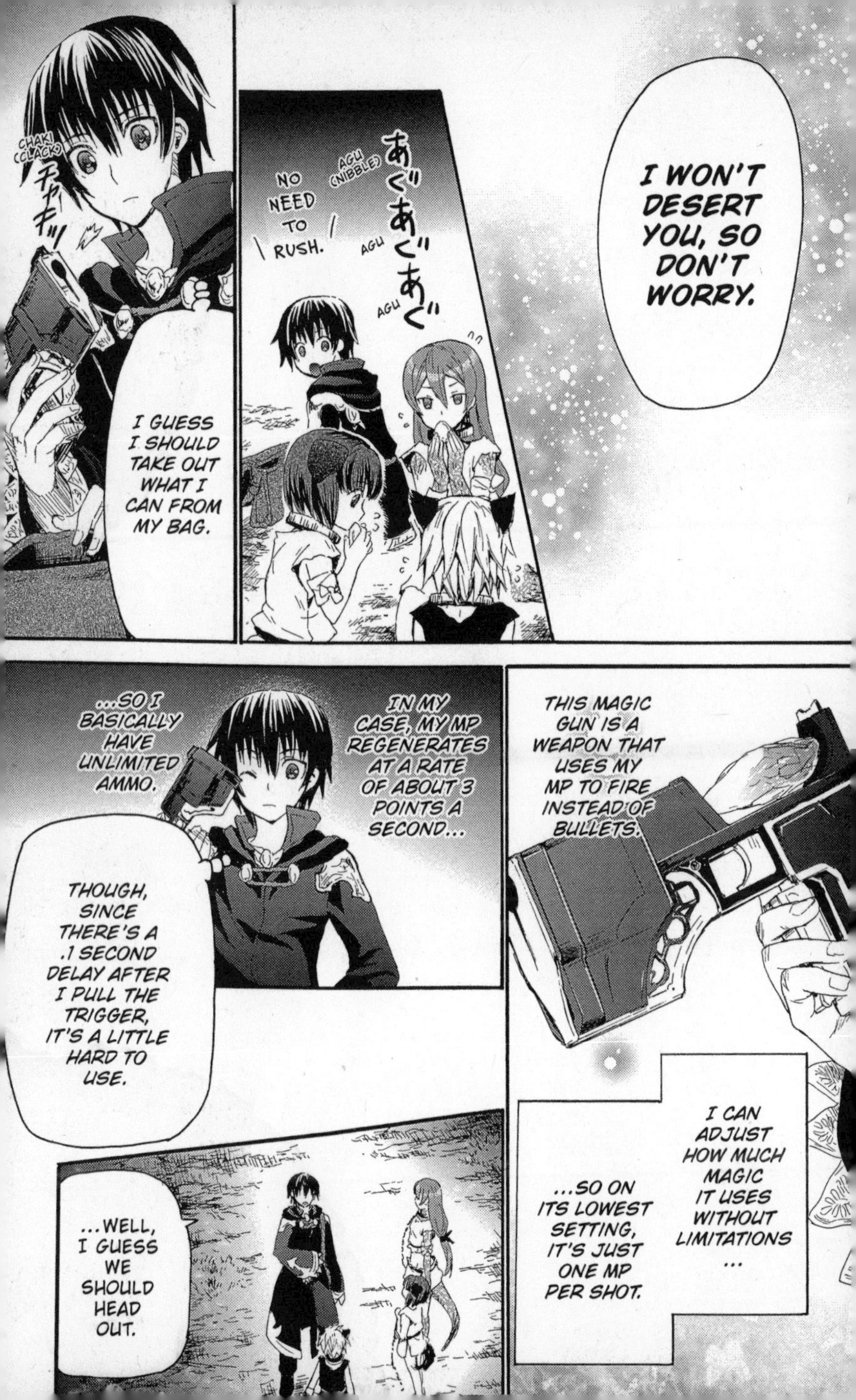

I WON'T DESERT YOU, SO DON'T WORRY.
あぐあぐ
AGU (NIBBLE) AGU AGU
NO NEED TO RUSH.
チャキッ
CHAKI (CLACK)
I GUESS I SHOULD TAKE OUT WHAT I CAN FROM MY BAG.
THIS MAGIC GUN IS A WEAPON THAT USES MY MP TO FIRE INSTEAD OF BULLETS.
I CAN ADJUST HOW MUCH MAGIC IT USES WITHOUT LIMITATIONS...
...SO ON ITS LOWEST SETTING, IT'S JUST ONE MP PER SHOT.
IN MY CASE, MY MP REGENERATES AT A RATE OF ABOUT 3 POINTS A SECOND...
...SO I BASICALLY HAVE UNLIMITED AMMO.
THOUGH, SINCE THERE'S A .1 SECOND DELAY AFTER I PULL THE TRIGGER, IT'S A LITTLE HARD TO USE.
...WELL, I GUESS WE SHOULD HEAD OUT.

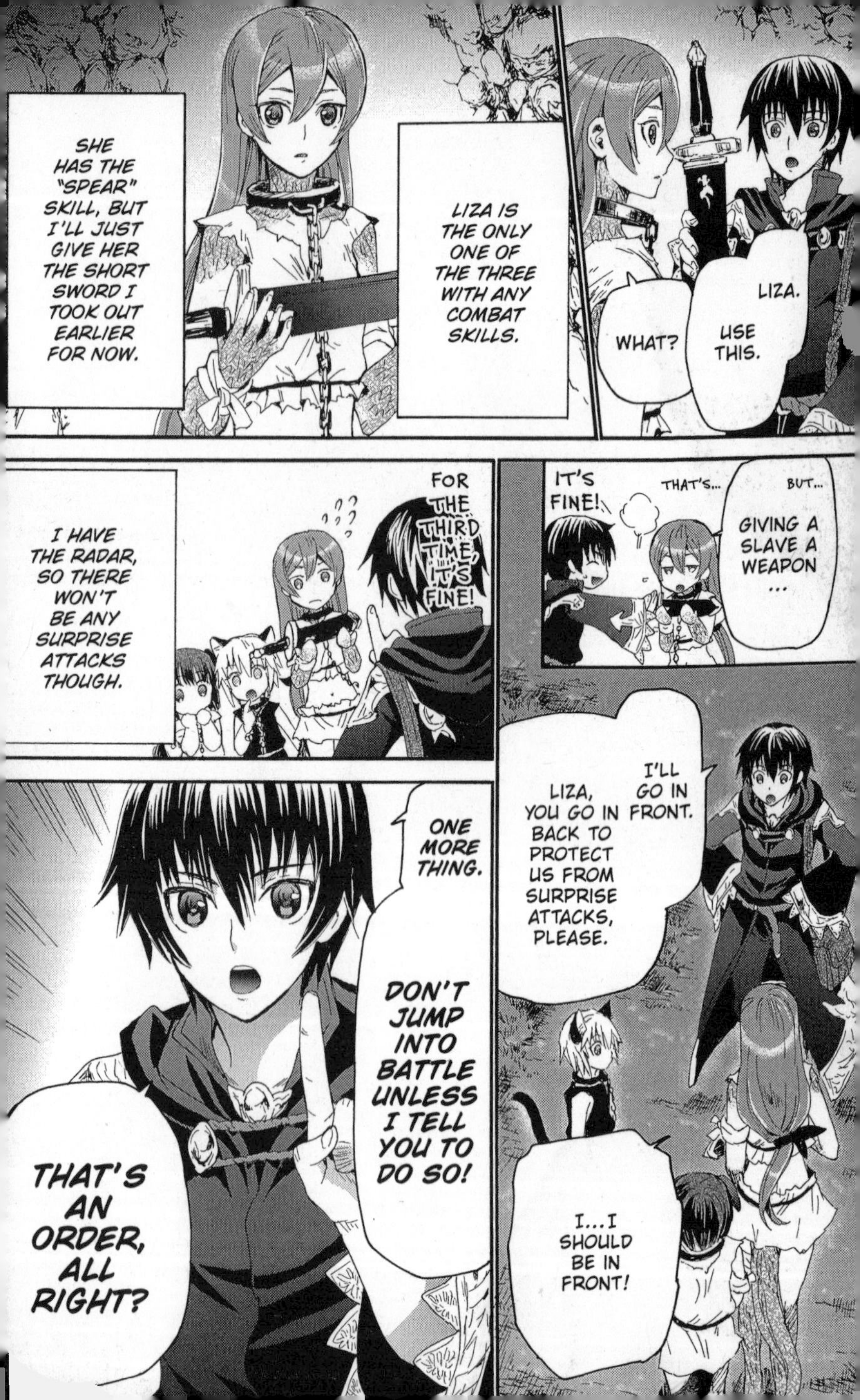
LIZA. USE THIS.
WHAT?
LIZA IS THE ONLY ONE OF THE THREE WITH ANY COMBAT SKILLS.
SHE HAS THE "SPEAR" SKILL, BUT I'LL JUST GIVE HER THE SHORT SWORD I TOOK OUT EARLIER FOR NOW.
BUT... GIVING A SLAVE A WEAPON...
THAT'S...
IT'S FINE!
FOR THE THIRD TIME, IT'S FINE!
I HAVE THE RADAR, SO THERE WON'T BE ANY SURPRISE ATTACKS THOUGH.
I'LL GO IN FRONT.
LIZA, YOU GO IN BACK TO PROTECT US FROM SURPRISE ATTACKS, PLEASE.
I...I SHOULD BE IN FRONT!
ONE MORE THING.
DON'T JUMP INTO BATTLE UNLESS I TELL YOU TO DO SO!
THAT'S AN ORDER, ALL RIGHT?

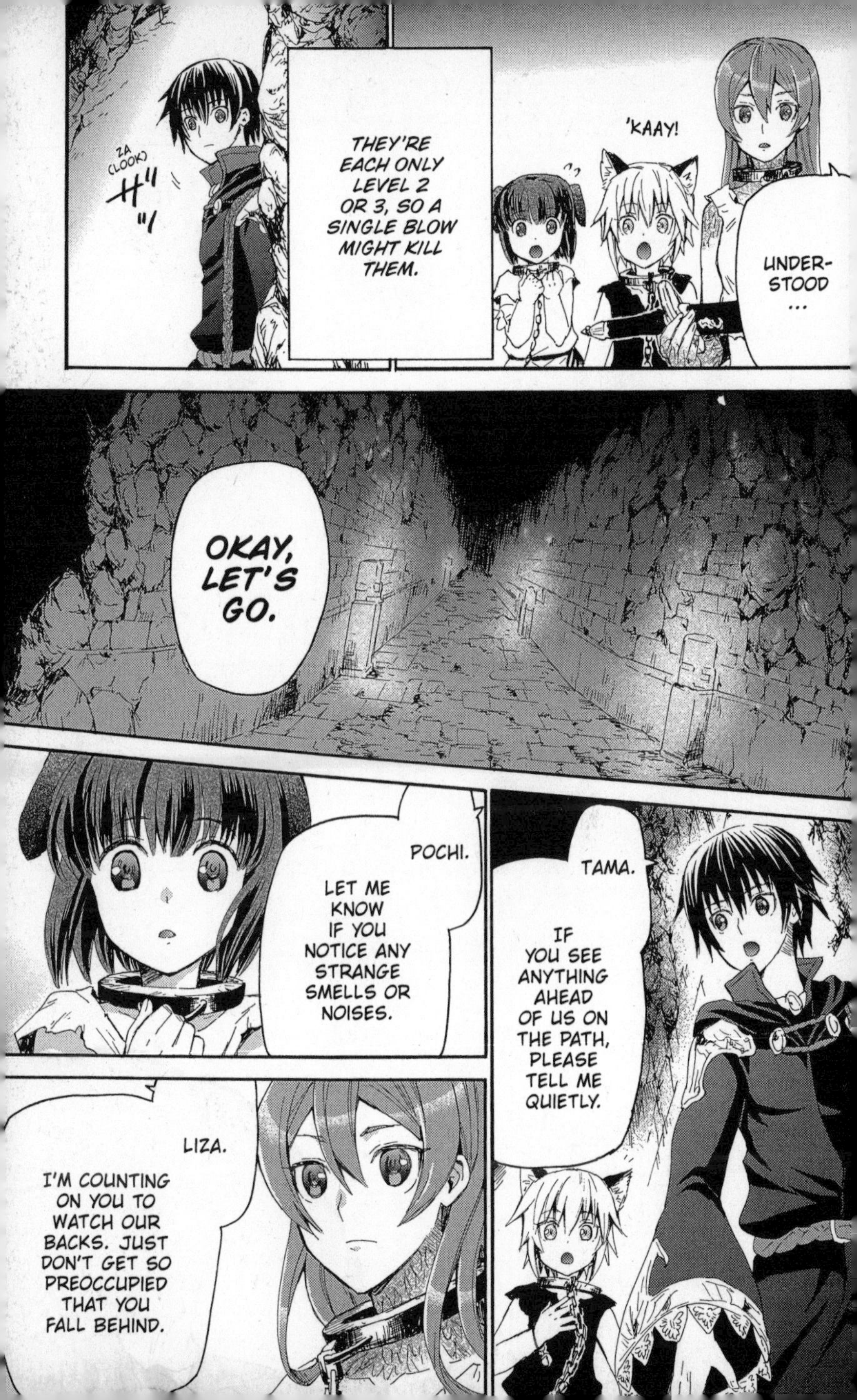
'KAAY!
UNDER-STOOD...
THEY'RE EACH ONLY LEVEL 2 OR 3, SO A SINGLE BLOW MIGHT KILL THEM.
ZA (LOOK)
OKAY, LET'S GO.
TAMA.
IF YOU SEE ANYTHING AHEAD OF US ON THE PATH, PLEASE TELL ME QUIETLY.
POCHI.
LET ME KNOW IF YOU NOTICE ANY STRANGE SMELLS OR NOISES.
LIZA.
I'M COUNTING ON YOU TO WATCH OUR BACKS. JUST DON'T GET SO PREOCCUPIED THAT YOU FALL BEHIND.

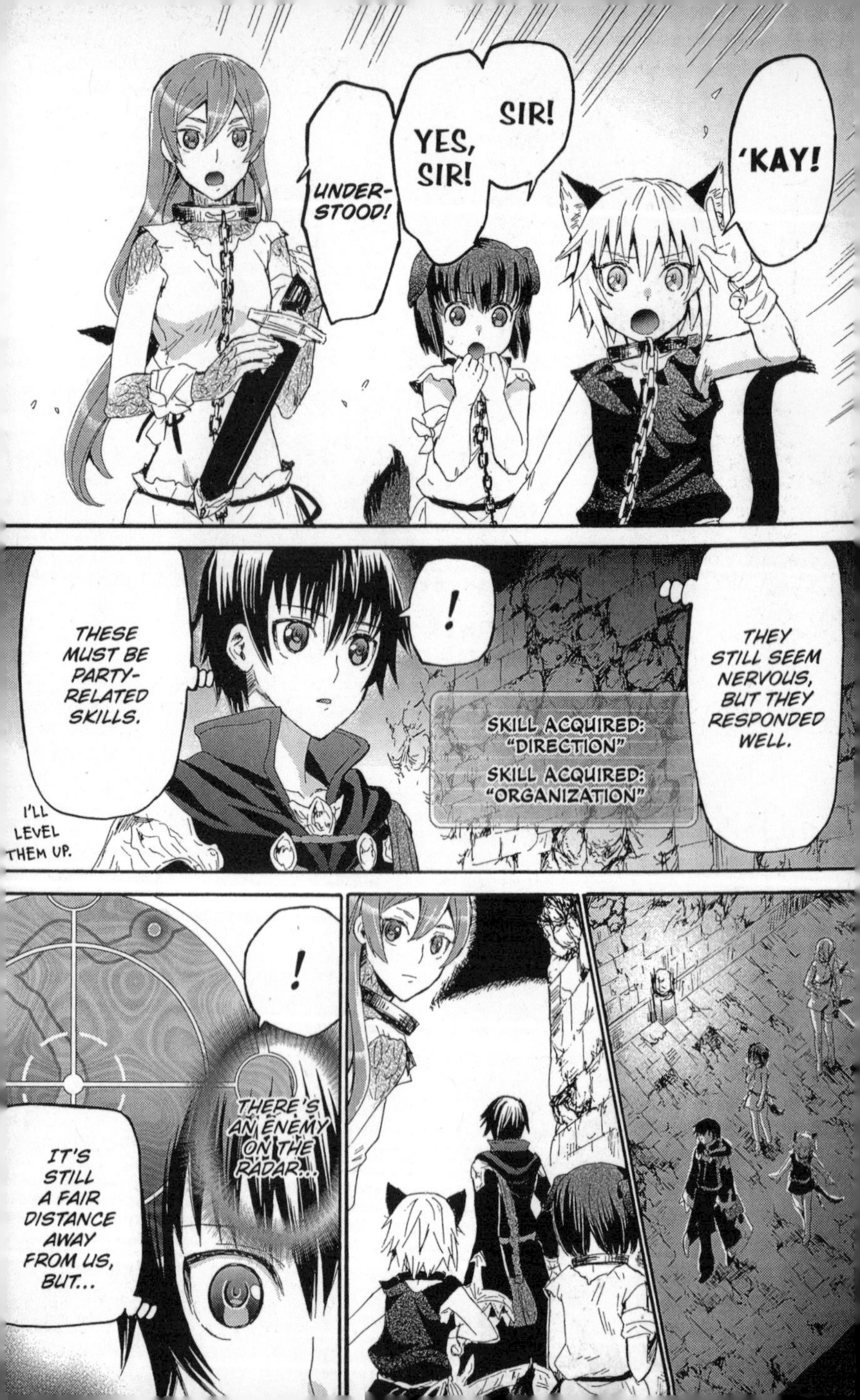
'KAY!
SIR!
YES, SIR!
UNDERSTOOD!
THEY STILL SEEM NERVOUS, BUT THEY RESPONDED WELL.
SKILL ACQUIRED: "DIRECTION"
SKILL ACQUIRED: "ORGANIZATION"
!
THESE MUST BE PARTY-RELATED SKILLS.
I'LL LEVEL THEM UP.
!
THERE'S AN ENEMY ON THE RADAR...
IT'S STILL A FAIR DISTANCE AWAY FROM US, BUT...

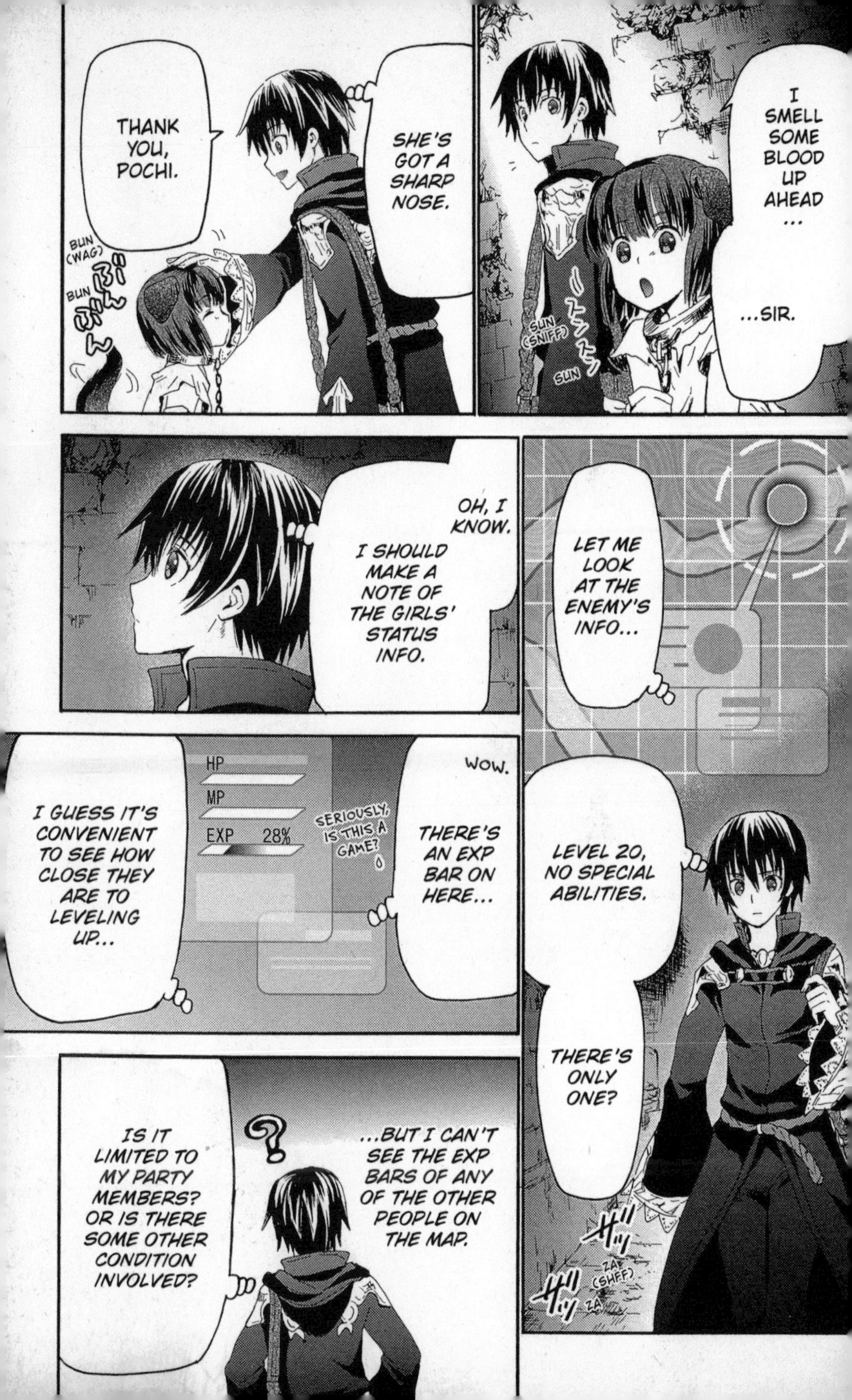
I SMELL SOME BLOOD UP AHEAD ...
...SIR.
SUN (SNIFF) SUN
SHE'S GOT A SHARP NOSE.
THANK YOU, POCHI.
BUN (WAG) BUN
ぶんぶん
LET ME LOOK AT THE ENEMY'S INFO...
LEVEL 20, NO SPECIAL ABILITIES.
THERE'S ONLY ONE?
ZA (SHFF) ZA
OH, I KNOW.
I SHOULD MAKE A NOTE OF THE GIRLS' STATUS INFO.
WOW.
THERE'S AN EXP BAR ON HERE...
SERIOUSLY, IS THIS A GAME?
HP
MP
EXP 28%
I GUESS IT'S CONVENIENT TO SEE HOW CLOSE THEY ARE TO LEVELING UP...
...BUT I CAN'T SEE THE EXP BARS OF ANY OF THE OTHER PEOPLE ON THE MAP.
IS IT LIMITED TO MY PARTY MEMBERS? OR IS THERE SOME OTHER CONDITION INVOLVED?

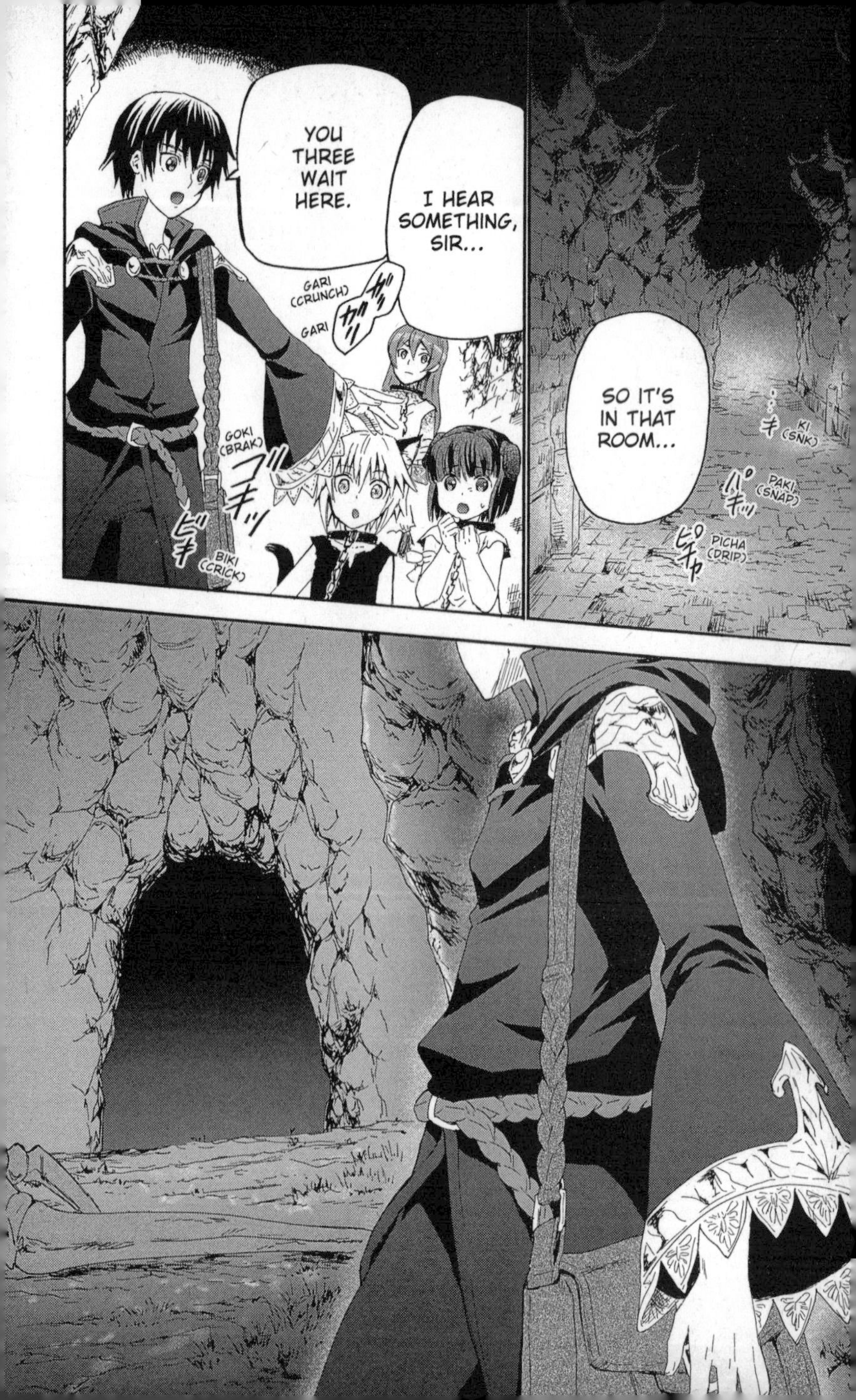
SO IT'S IN THAT ROOM...
KI (SNK)
PAKI (SNAP)
PICHA (DRIP)
I HEAR SOMETHING, SIR...
YOU THREE WAIT HERE.
GARI (CRUNCH)
GARI
GOKI (BRAK)
BIKI (CRICK)

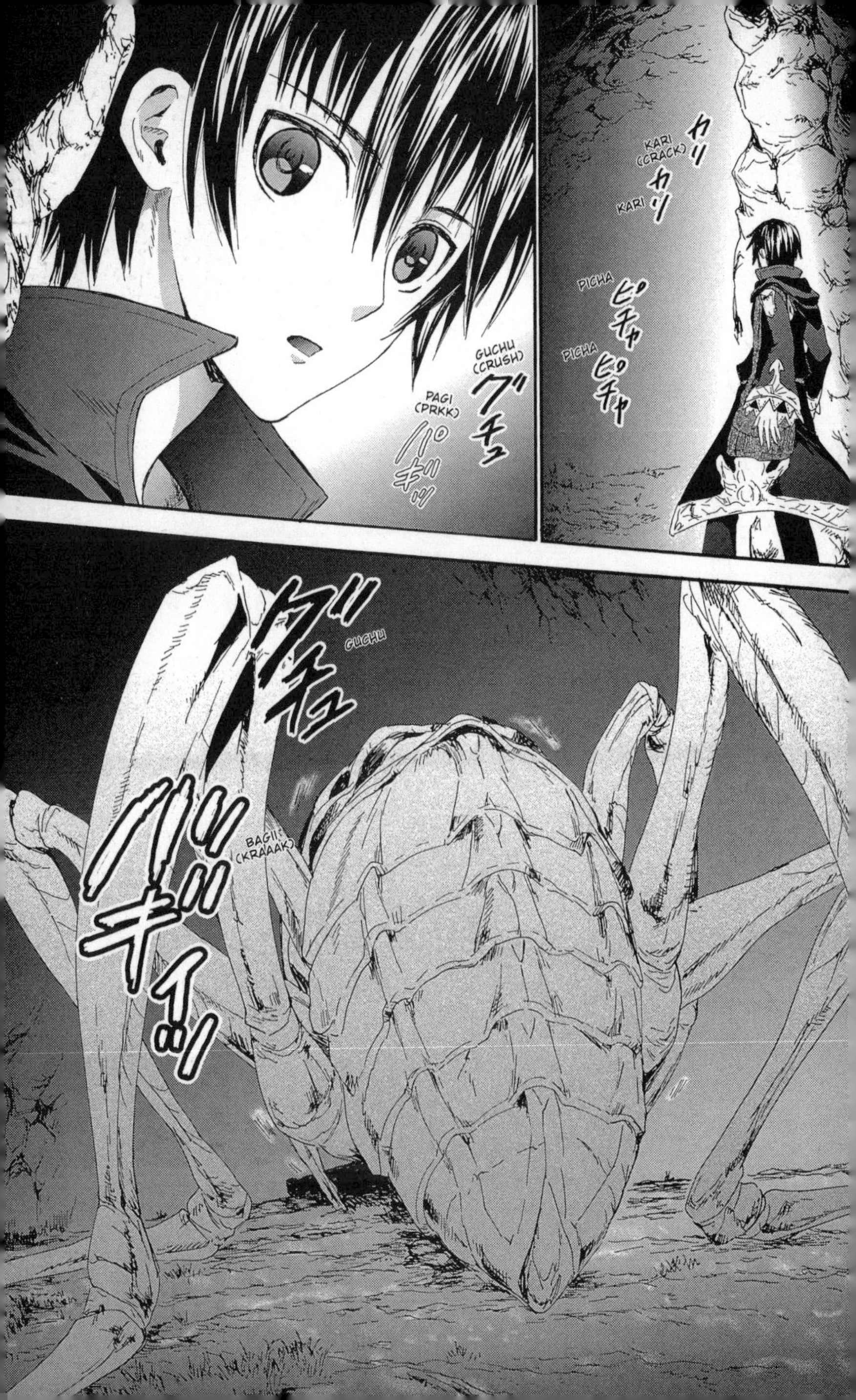
カリ
KARI (CRACK)
カリ
KARI
ピチャ
PICHA
ピチャ
PICHA
グチュ
GUCHU (CRUSH)
パギッ
PAGI (PRKK)
グチュ
GUCHU
バギィッ
BAGII (KRAAAK)

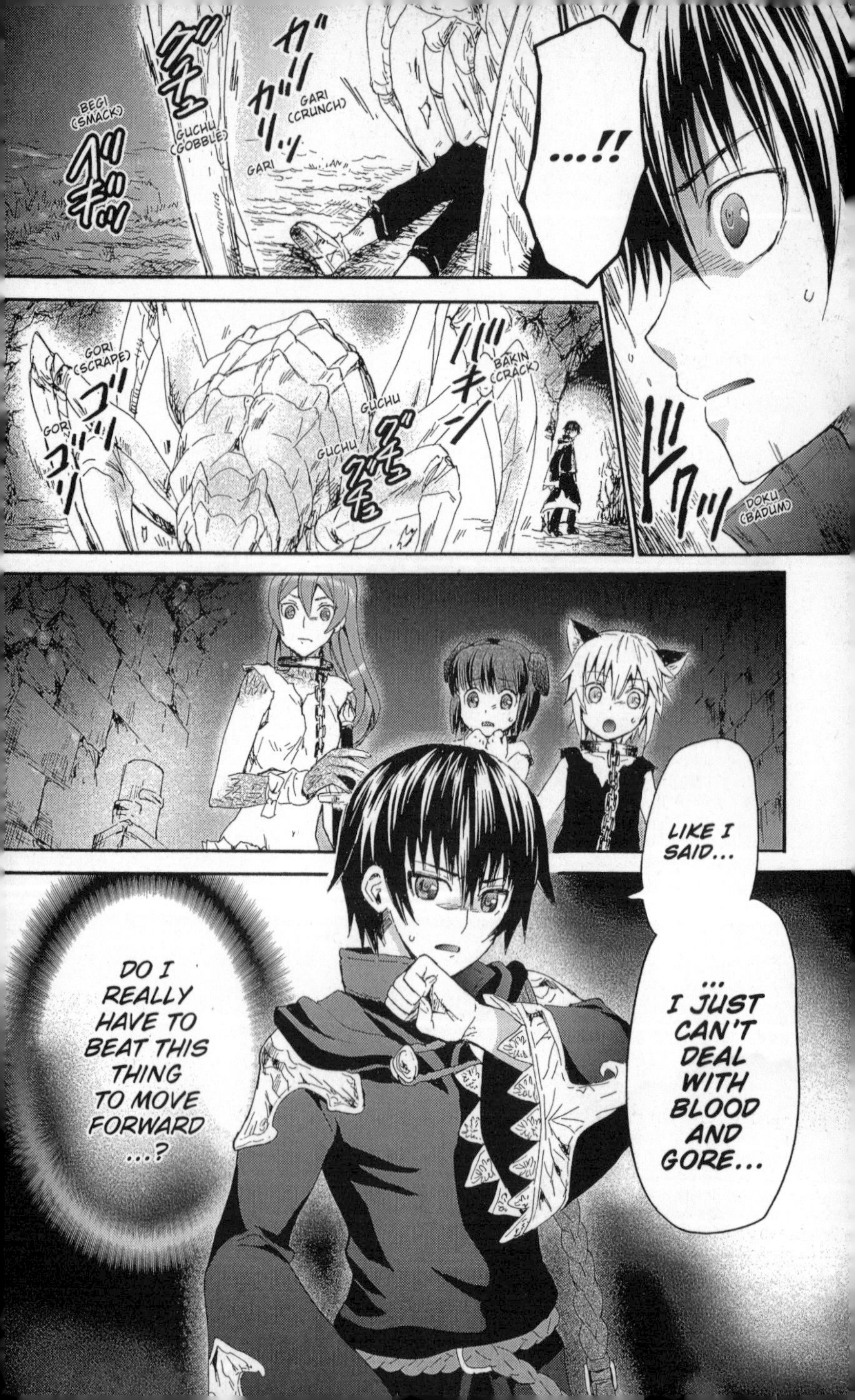

...!!
DOKU (BADUM)
GARI (CRUNCH)
GARI
GUCHU (GOBBLE)
BEGI (SMACK)
BAKIN (CRACK)
GUCHU
GUCHU
GORI (SCRAPE)
GORI
LIKE I SAID...
... I JUST CAN'T DEAL WITH BLOOD AND GORE...
DO I REALLY HAVE TO BEAT THIS THING TO MOVE FORWARD ...?

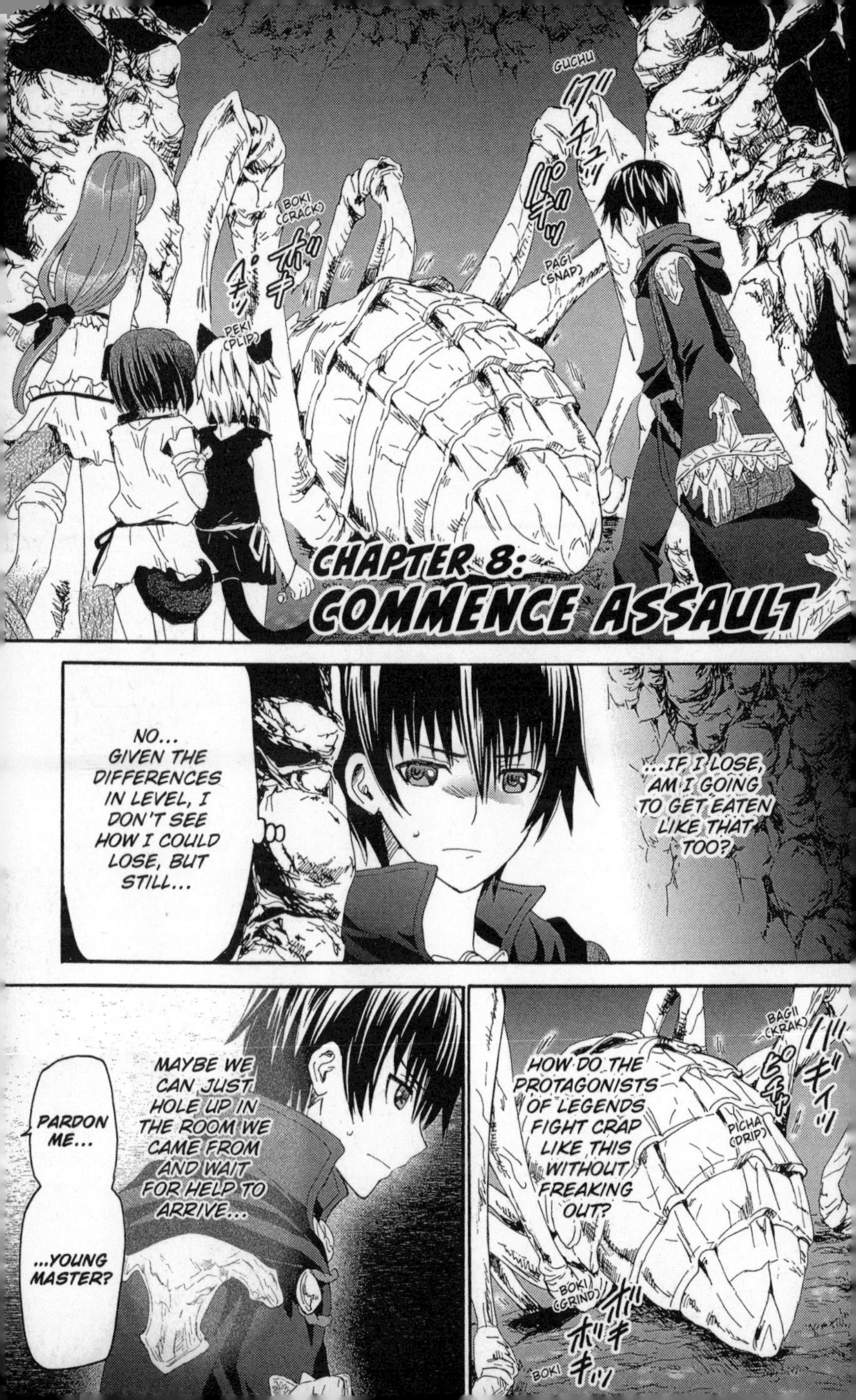
GUCHU
PAGI (SNAP)
BOKI (CRACK)
PEKI (PLIP)
CHAPTER 8: COMMENCE ASSAULT
...IF I LOSE, AM I GOING TO GET EATEN LIKE THAT TOO?
NO... GIVEN THE DIFFERENCES IN LEVEL, I DON'T SEE HOW I COULD LOSE, BUT STILL...
BAGII (KRAK)
PICHA (DRIP)
HOW DO THE PROTAGONISTS OF LEGENDS FIGHT CRAP LIKE THIS WITHOUT FREAKING OUT?
BOKI (GRIND)
BOKI
MAYBE WE CAN JUST HOLE UP IN THE ROOM WE CAME FROM AND WAIT FOR HELP TO ARRIVE...
PARDON ME...
...YOUNG MASTER?

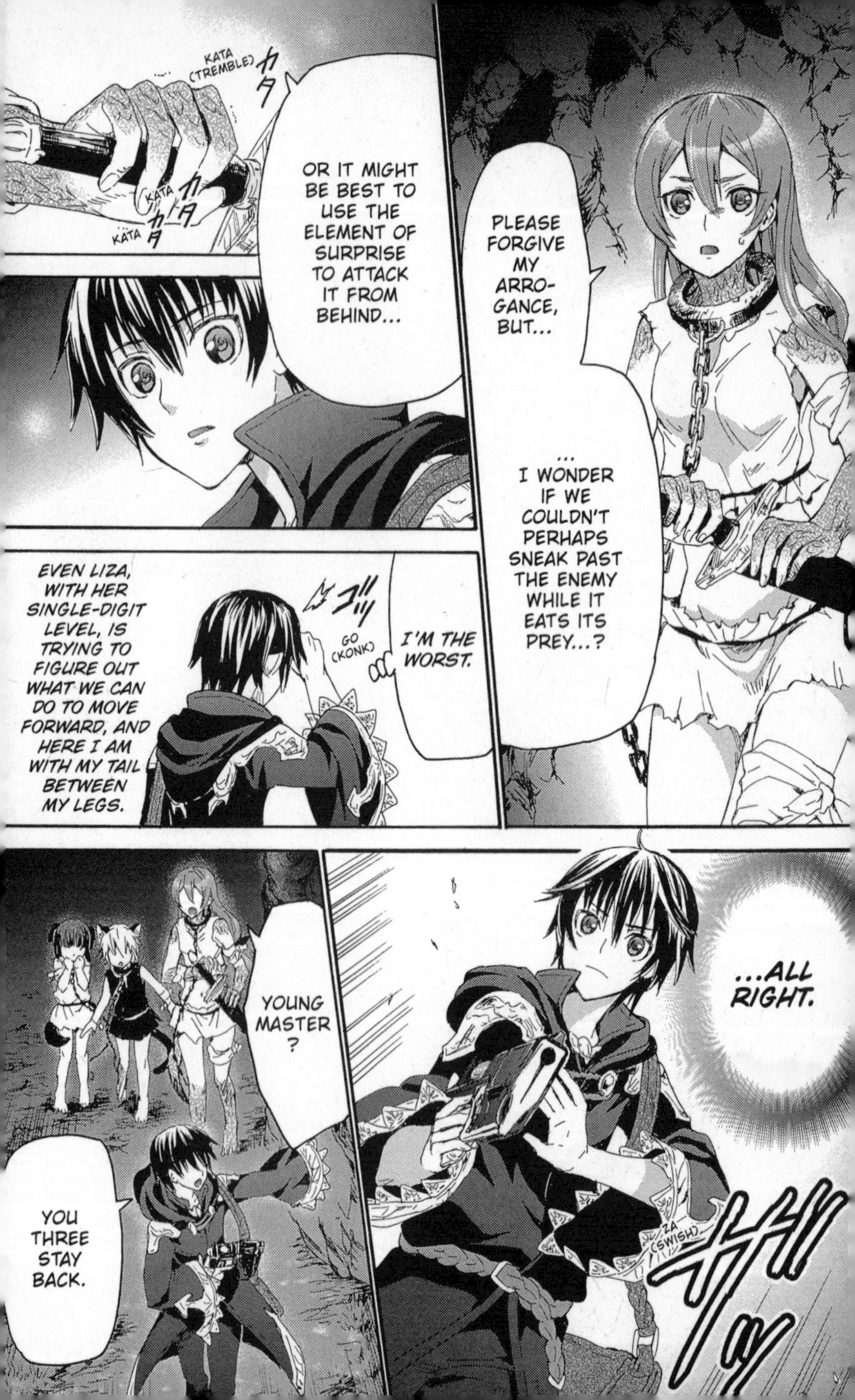
PLEASE FORGIVE MY ARROGANCE, BUT...
... I WONDER IF WE COULDN'T PERHAPS SNEAK PAST THE ENEMY WHILE IT EATS ITS PREY...?
OR IT MIGHT BE BEST TO USE THE ELEMENT OF SURPRISE TO ATTACK IT FROM BEHIND...
KATA (TREMBLE)
......
KATA
KATA
I'M THE WORST.
GO (KONK)
EVEN LIZA, WITH HER SINGLE-DIGIT LEVEL, IS TRYING TO FIGURE OUT WHAT WE CAN DO TO MOVE FORWARD, AND HERE I AM WITH MY TAIL BETWEEN MY LEGS.
...ALL RIGHT.
ZA (SWISH)
YOUNG MASTER?
YOU THREE STAY BACK.

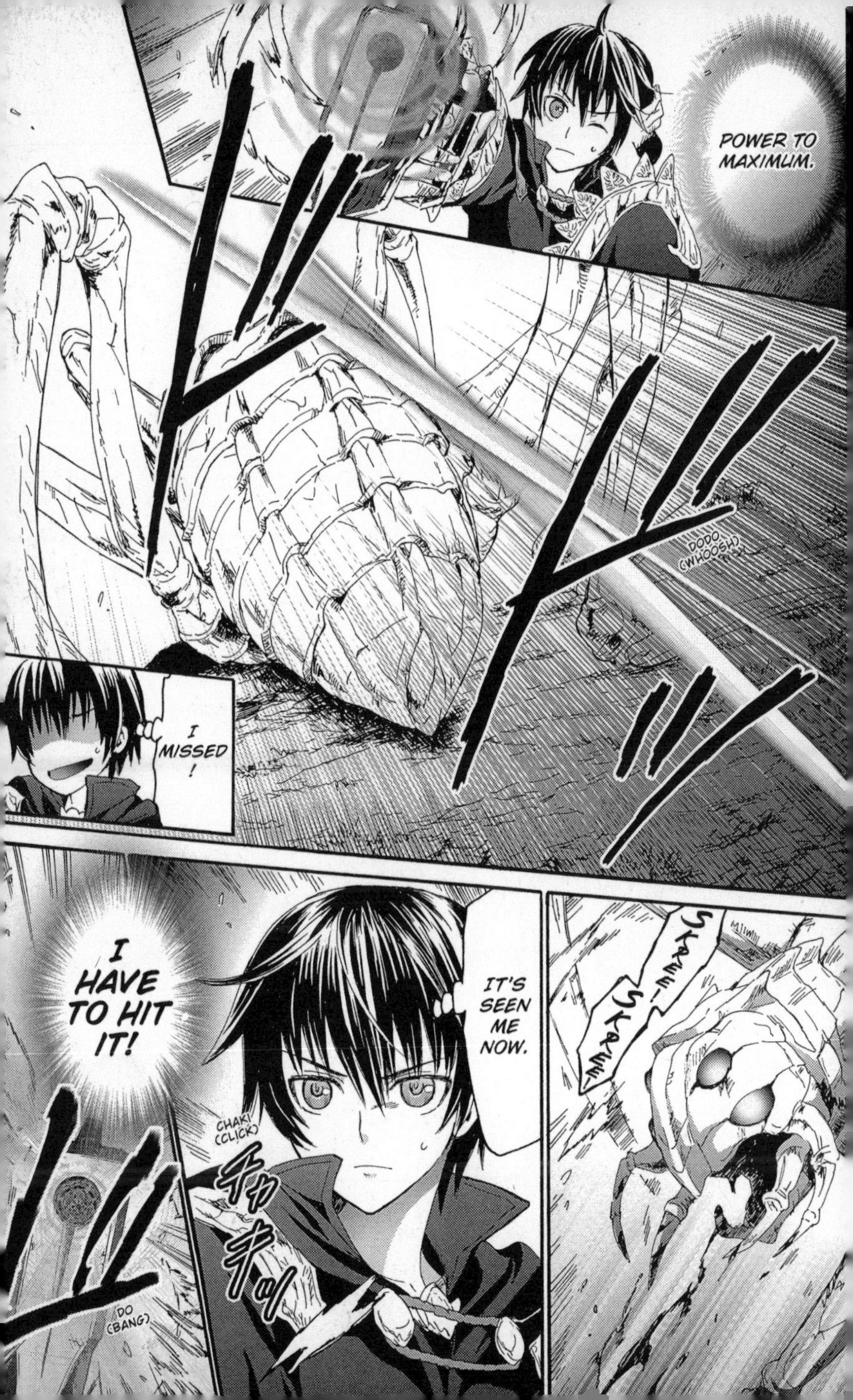
POWER TO MAXIMUM.
DODO (WHOOSH)
I MISSED!
SKREE-!
SKREE-!
SKREE-
IT'S SEEN ME NOW.
CHAKI (CLICK)
I HAVE TO HIT IT!
DO (BANG)

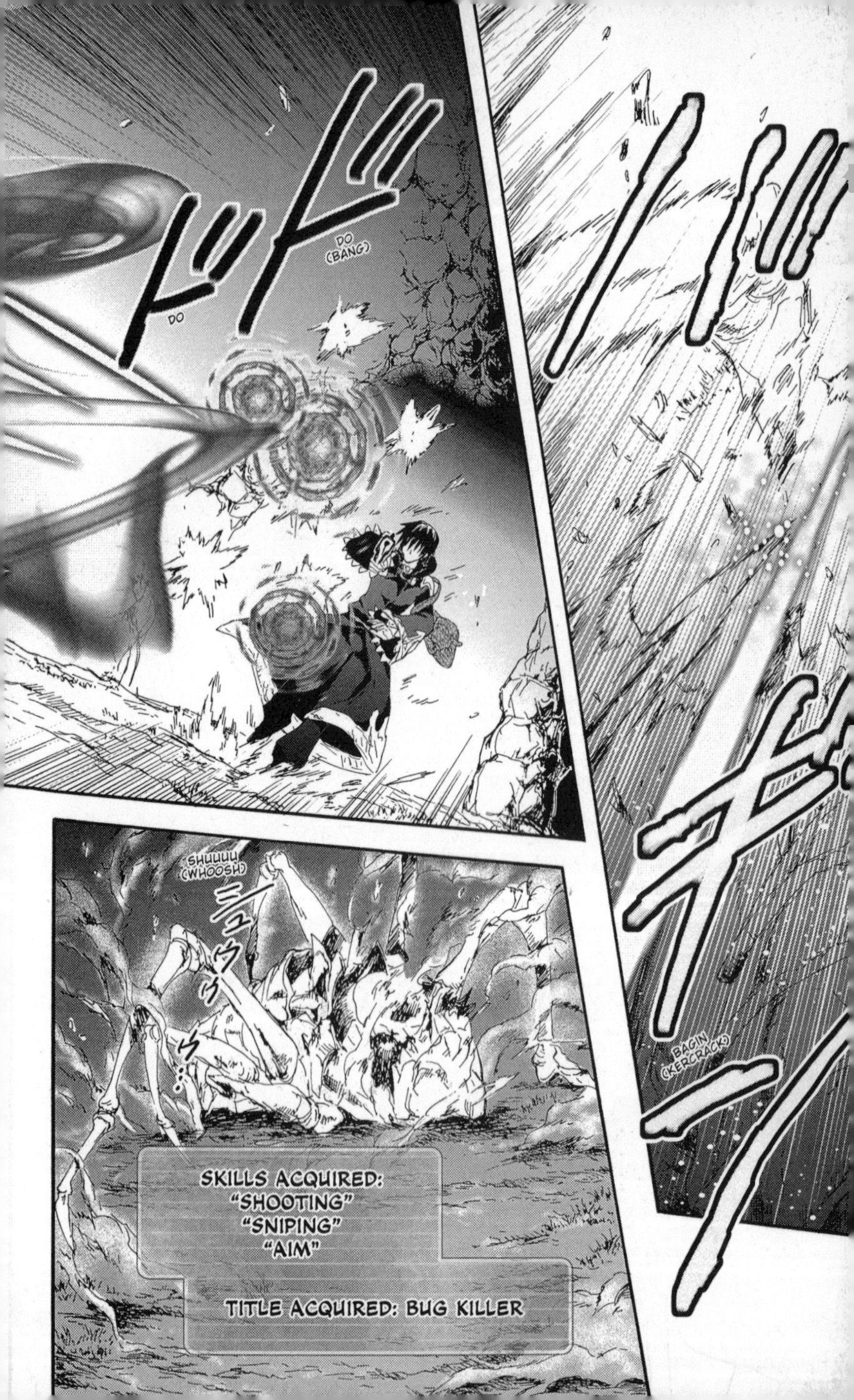
BAGIN
(KERCRACK)
DO
(BANG)
DO
SHUUUU
(WHOOSH)
SKILLS ACQUIRED:
"SHOOTING"
"SNIPING"
"AIM"
TITLE ACQUIRED: BUG KILLER

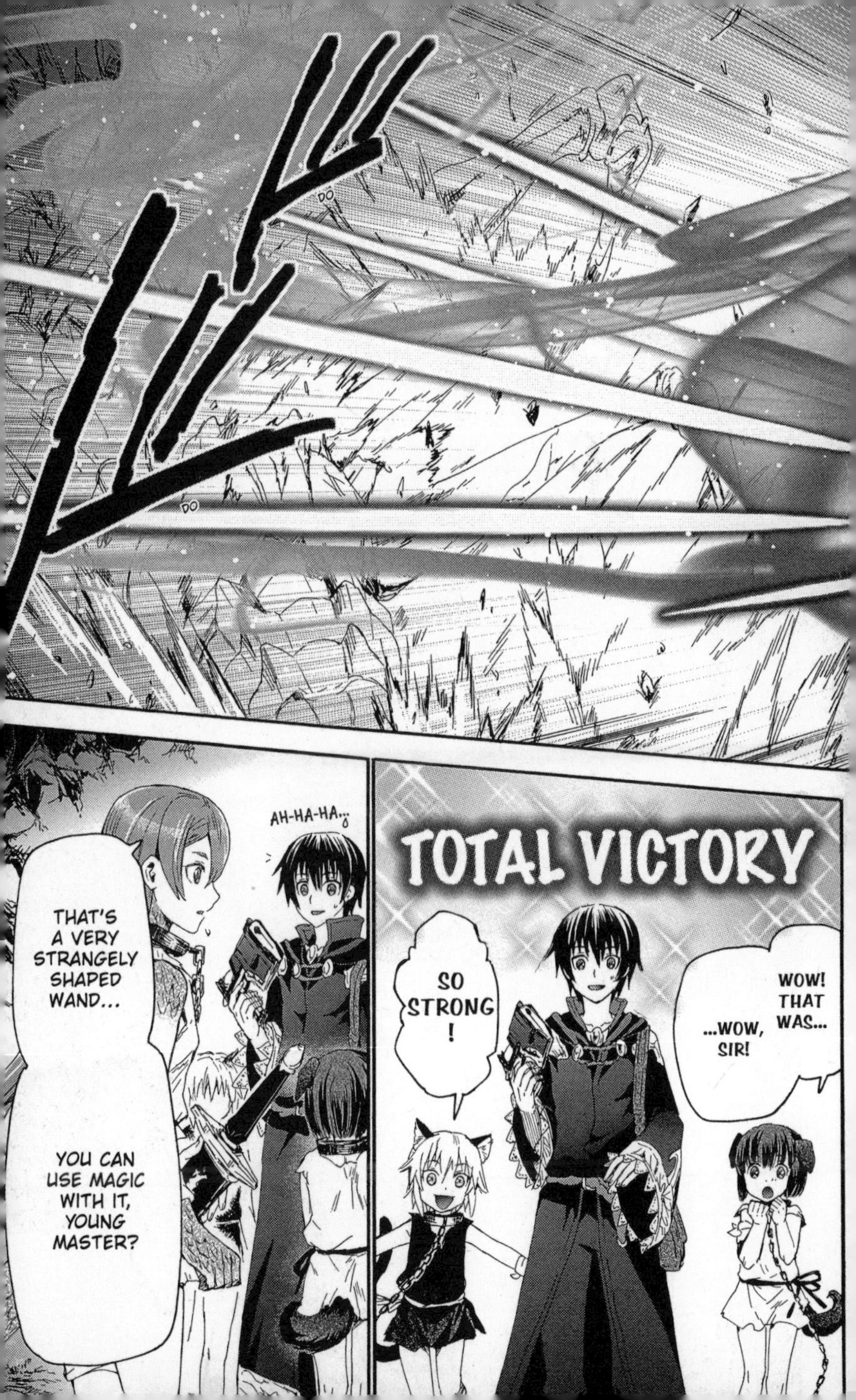
DO
DO
TOTAL VICTORY
WOW! THAT WAS... ...WOW, SIR!
SO STRONG!
AH-HA-HA...
THAT'S A VERY STRANGELY SHAPED WAND... YOU CAN USE MAGIC WITH IT, YOUNG MASTER?

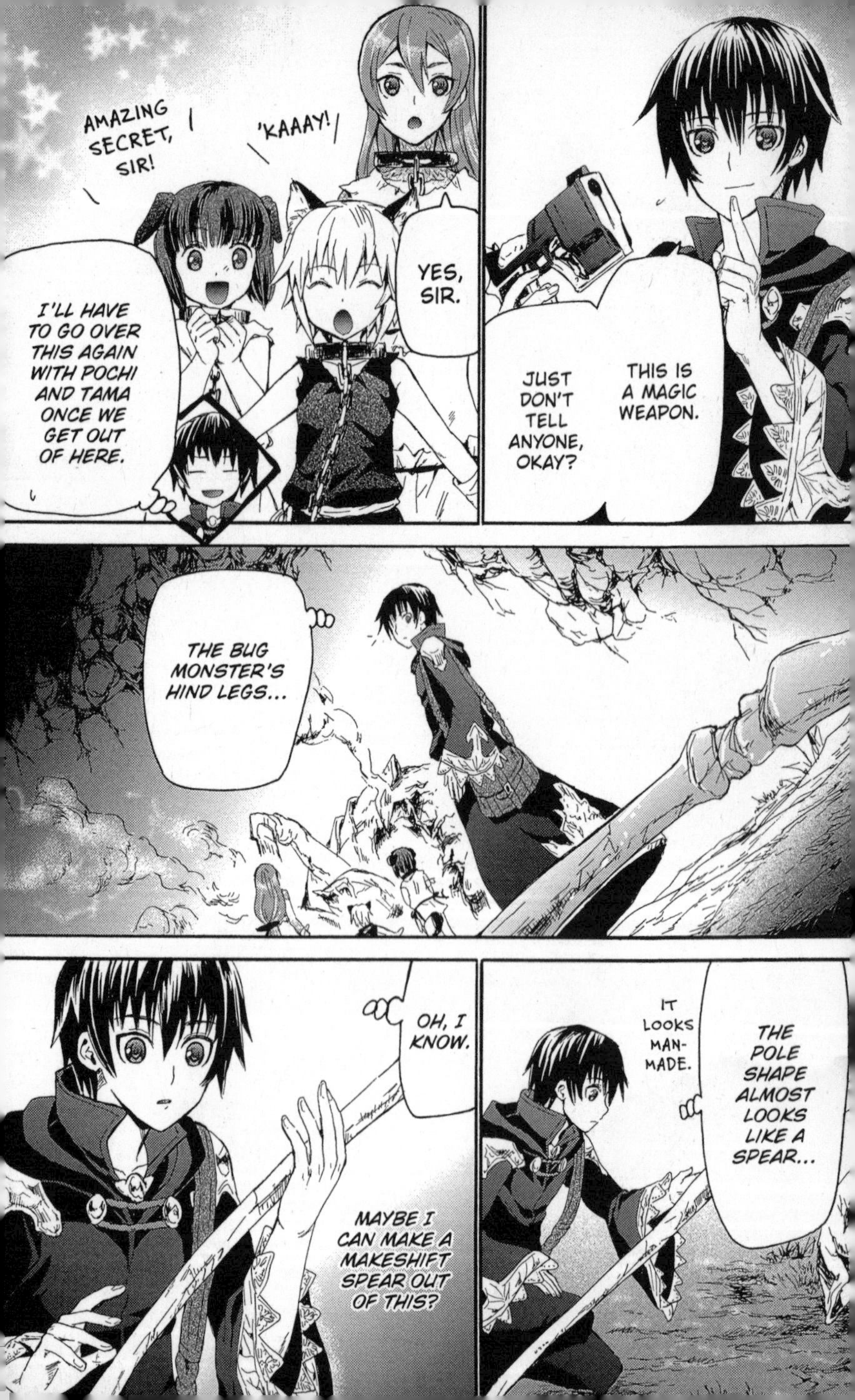
THIS IS A MAGIC WEAPON.
JUST DON'T TELL ANYONE, OKAY?
'KAAAY!
AMAZING SECRET, SIR!
YES, SIR.
I'LL HAVE TO GO OVER THIS AGAIN WITH POCHI AND TAMA ONCE WE GET OUT OF HERE.
THE BUG MONSTER'S HIND LEGS...
THE POLE SHAPE ALMOST LOOKS LIKE A SPEAR...
IT LOOKS MAN-MADE.
OH, I KNOW.
MAYBE I CAN MAKE A MAKESHIFT SPEAR OUT OF THIS?

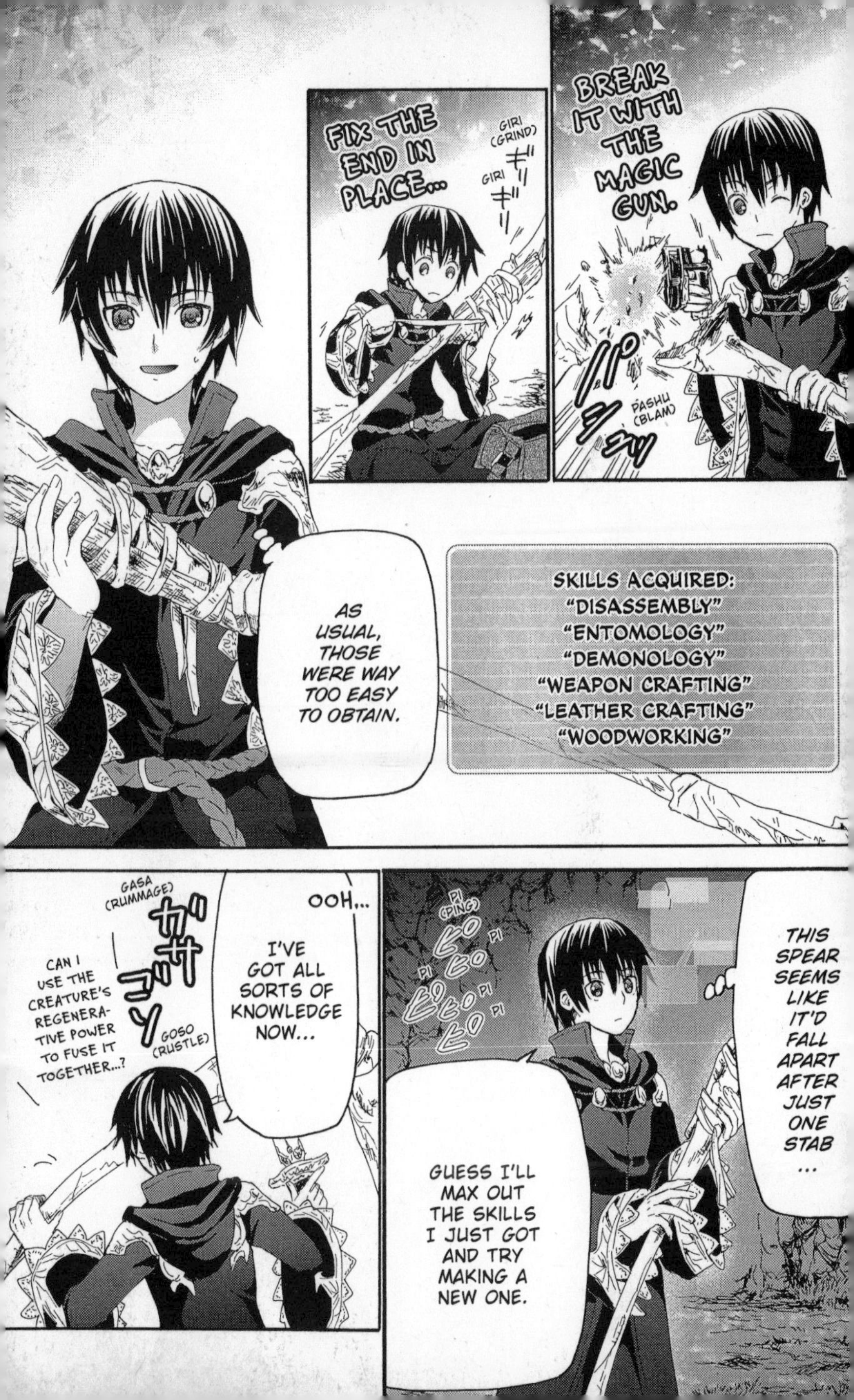
BREAK IT WITH THE MAGIC GUN.
PASHU (BLAM)
FIX THE END IN PLACE...
GIRI (GRIND)
GIRI
SKILLS ACQUIRED:
"DISASSEMBLY"
"ENTOMOLOGY"
"DEMONOLOGY"
"WEAPON CRAFTING"
"LEATHER CRAFTING"
"WOODWORKING"
AS USUAL, THOSE WERE WAY TOO EASY TO OBTAIN.
THIS SPEAR SEEMS LIKE IT'D FALL APART AFTER JUST ONE STAB...
PI (PING)
PI
PI
PI
PI
GUESS I'LL MAX OUT THE SKILLS I JUST GOT AND TRY MAKING A NEW ONE.
OOH...
I'VE GOT ALL SORTS OF KNOWLEDGE NOW...
GASA (RUMMAGE)
CAN I USE THE CREATURE'S REGENERATIVE POWER TO FUSE IT TOGETHER...?
GOSO (RUSTLE)

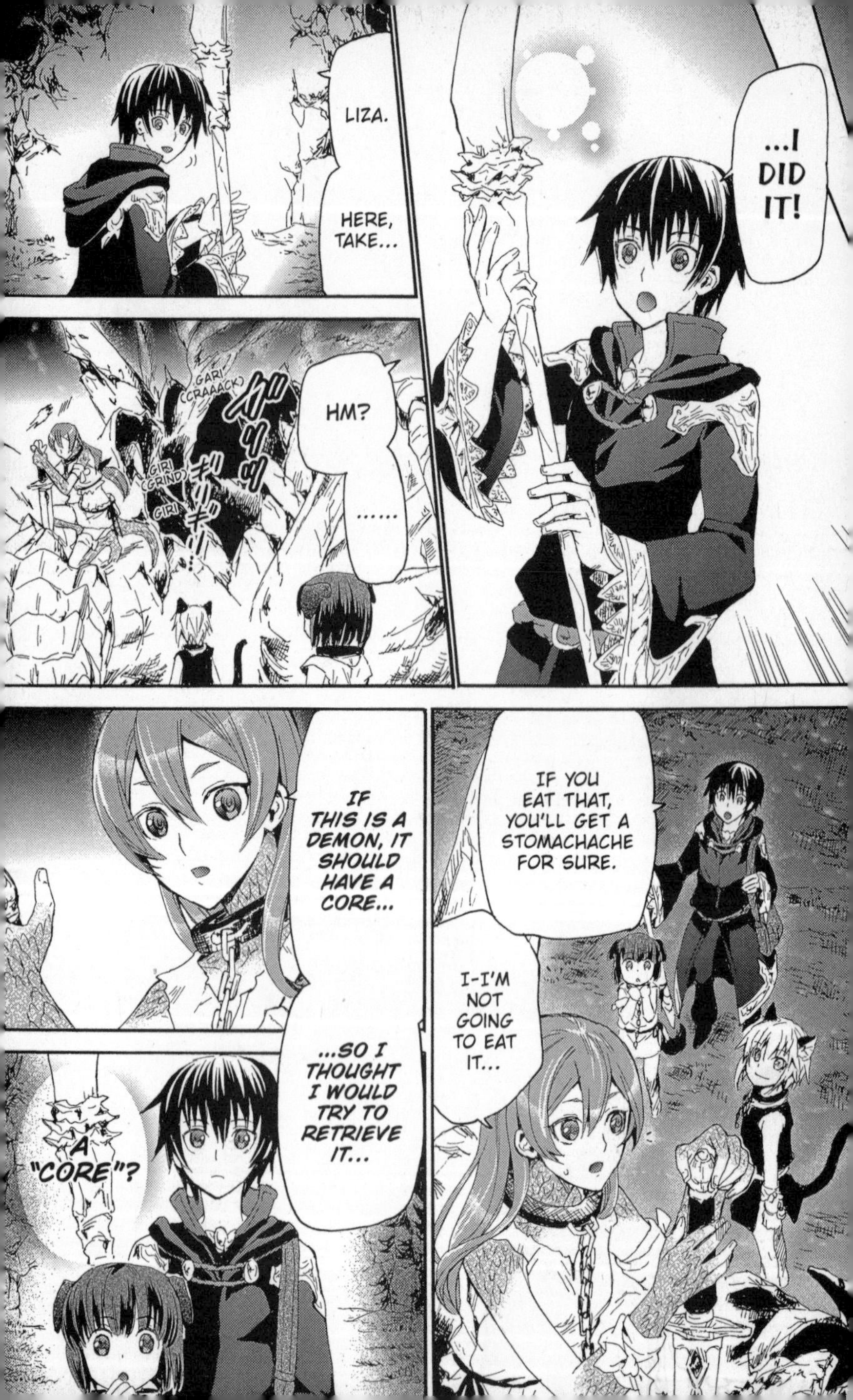
...I DID IT!
LIZA.
HERE, TAKE...
GARI (CRAAACK)
GIRI (GRIND) GIRI
HM?
......
IF YOU EAT THAT, YOU'LL GET A STOMACHACHE FOR SURE.
I-I'M NOT GOING TO EAT IT...
IF THIS IS A DEMON, IT SHOULD HAVE A CORE...
...SO I THOUGHT I WOULD TRY TO RETRIEVE IT...
A "CORE"?

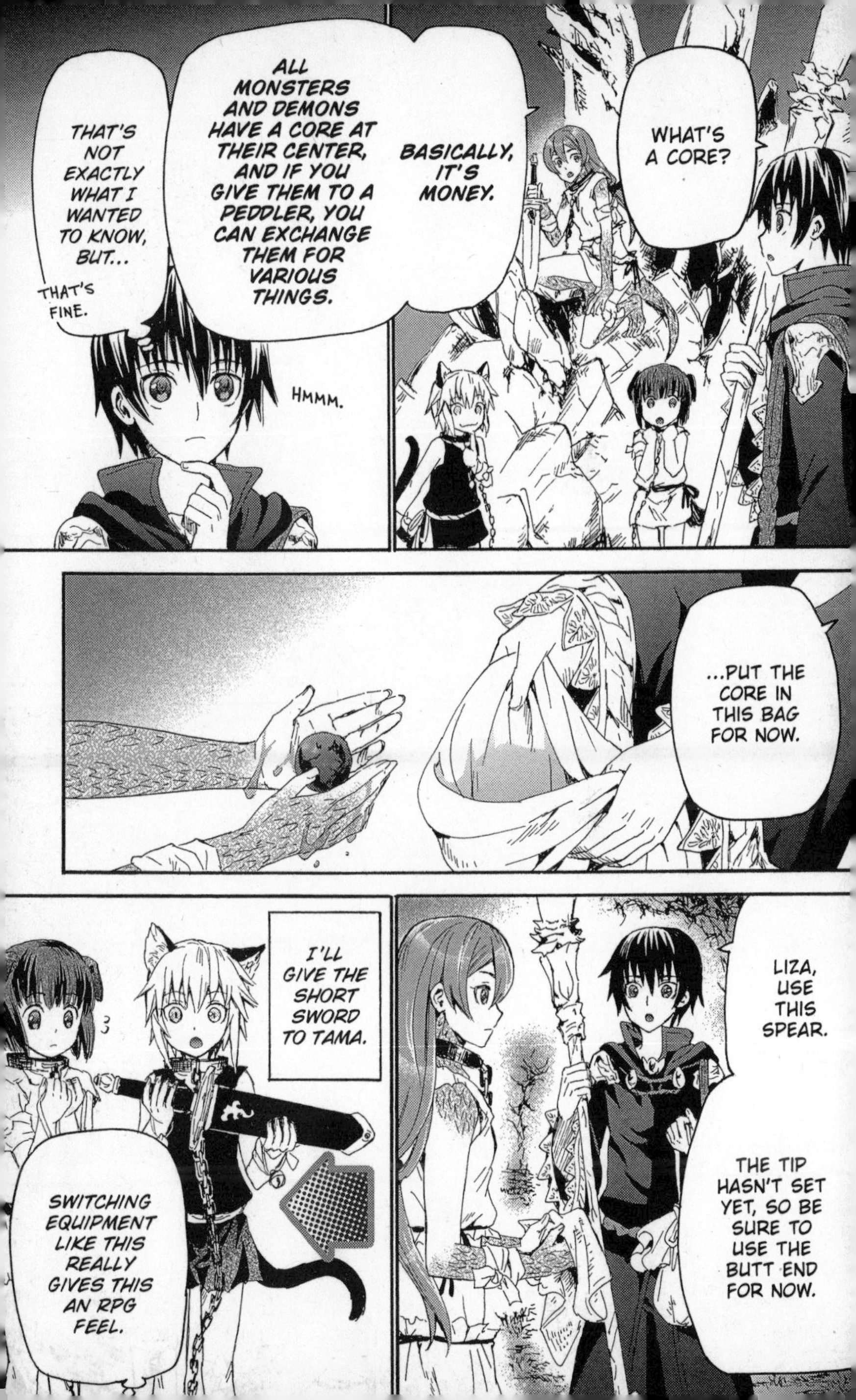
WHAT'S A CORE?
BASICALLY, IT'S MONEY.
ALL MONSTERS AND DEMONS HAVE A CORE AT THEIR CENTER, AND IF YOU GIVE THEM TO A PEDDLER, YOU CAN EXCHANGE THEM FOR VARIOUS THINGS.
THAT'S NOT EXACTLY WHAT I WANTED TO KNOW, BUT...
THAT'S FINE.
HMMM.
...PUT THE CORE IN THIS BAG FOR NOW.
LIZA, USE THIS SPEAR.
THE TIP HASN'T SET YET, SO BE SURE TO USE THE BUTT END FOR NOW.
I'LL GIVE THE SHORT SWORD TO TAMA.
SWITCHING EQUIPMENT LIKE THIS REALLY GIVES THIS AN RPG FEEL.

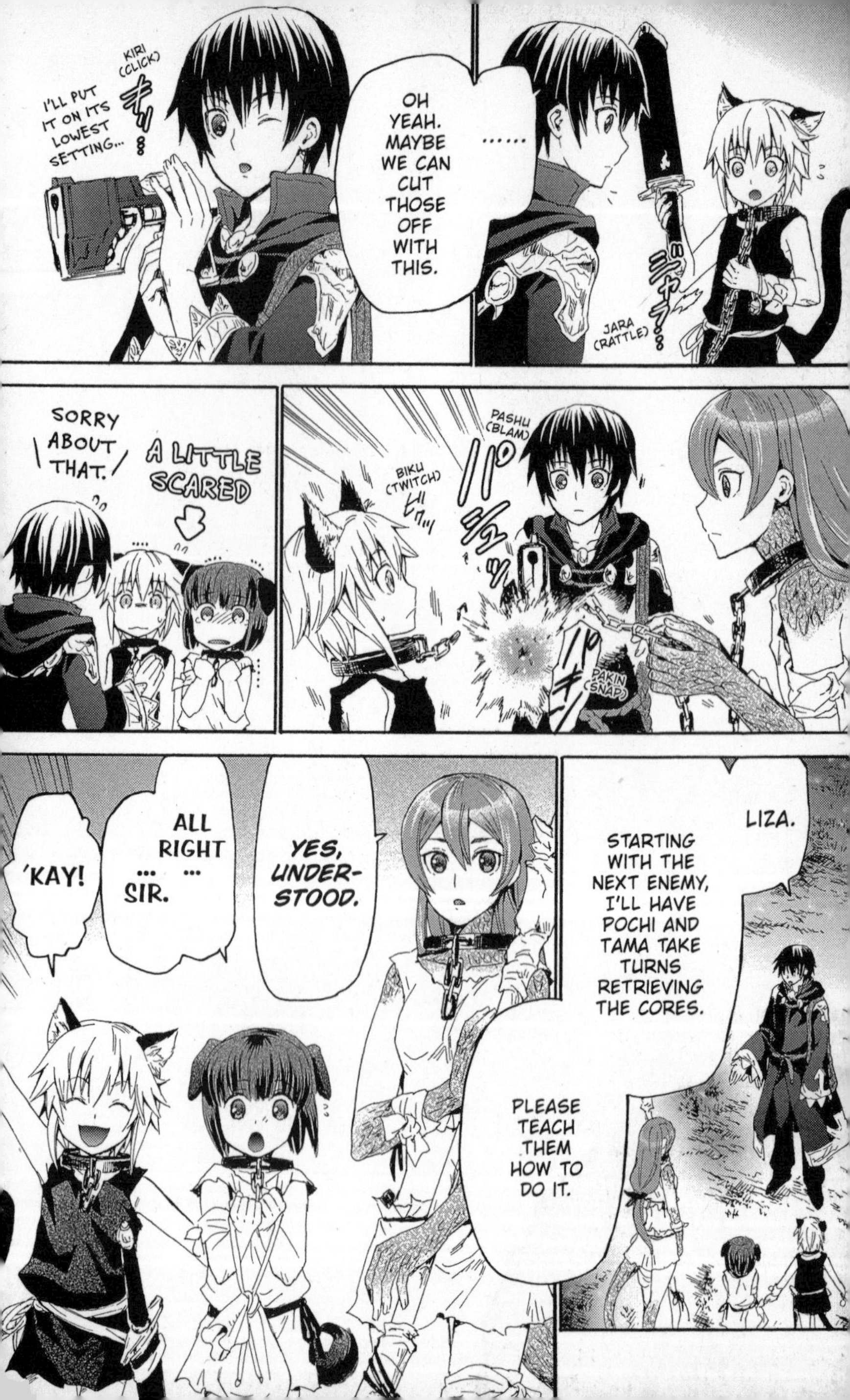

......
JARA (RATTLE)
OH YEAH. MAYBE WE CAN CUT THOSE OFF WITH THIS.
KIRI (CLICK)
I'LL PUT IT ON ITS LOWEST SETTING...
PASHU (BLAM)
BIKU (TWITCH)
PAKIN (SNAP)
SORRY ABOUT THAT.
A LITTLE SCARED
LIZA.
STARTING WITH THE NEXT ENEMY, I'LL HAVE POCHI AND TAMA TAKE TURNS RETRIEVING THE CORES.
PLEASE TEACH THEM HOW TO DO IT.
YES, UNDERSTOOD.
ALL RIGHT ... SIR.
'KAY!

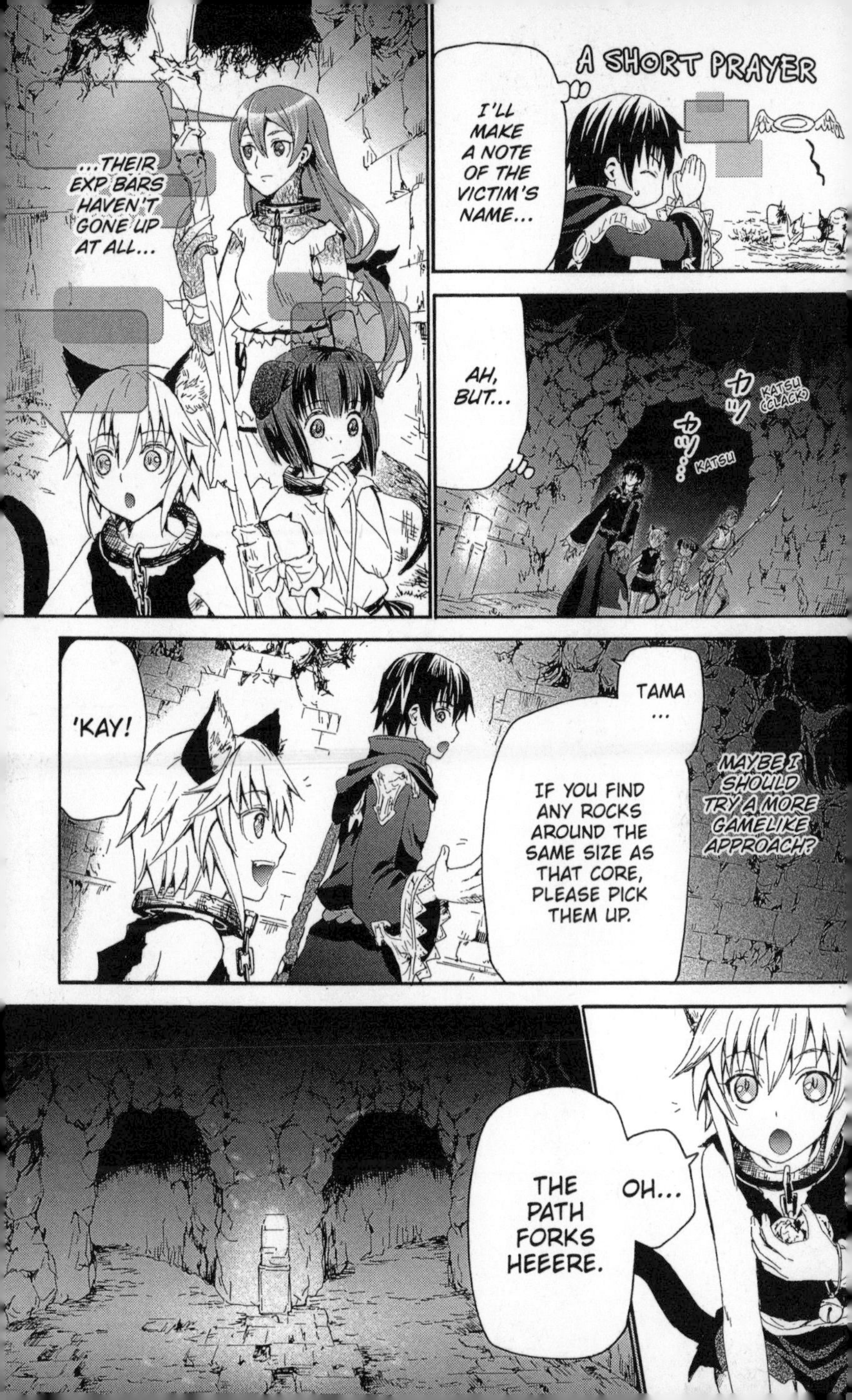
A SHORT PRAYER
I'LL MAKE A NOTE OF THE VICTIM'S NAME...
AH, BUT...
カッ KATSU (CLACK)
カツ... KATSU
...THEIR EXP BARS HAVEN'T GONE UP AT ALL...
MAYBE I SHOULD TRY A MORE GAMELIKE APPROACH?
TAMA...
IF YOU FIND ANY ROCKS AROUND THE SAME SIZE AS THAT CORE, PLEASE PICK THEM UP.
'KAY!
OH...
THE PATH FORKS HEEERE.

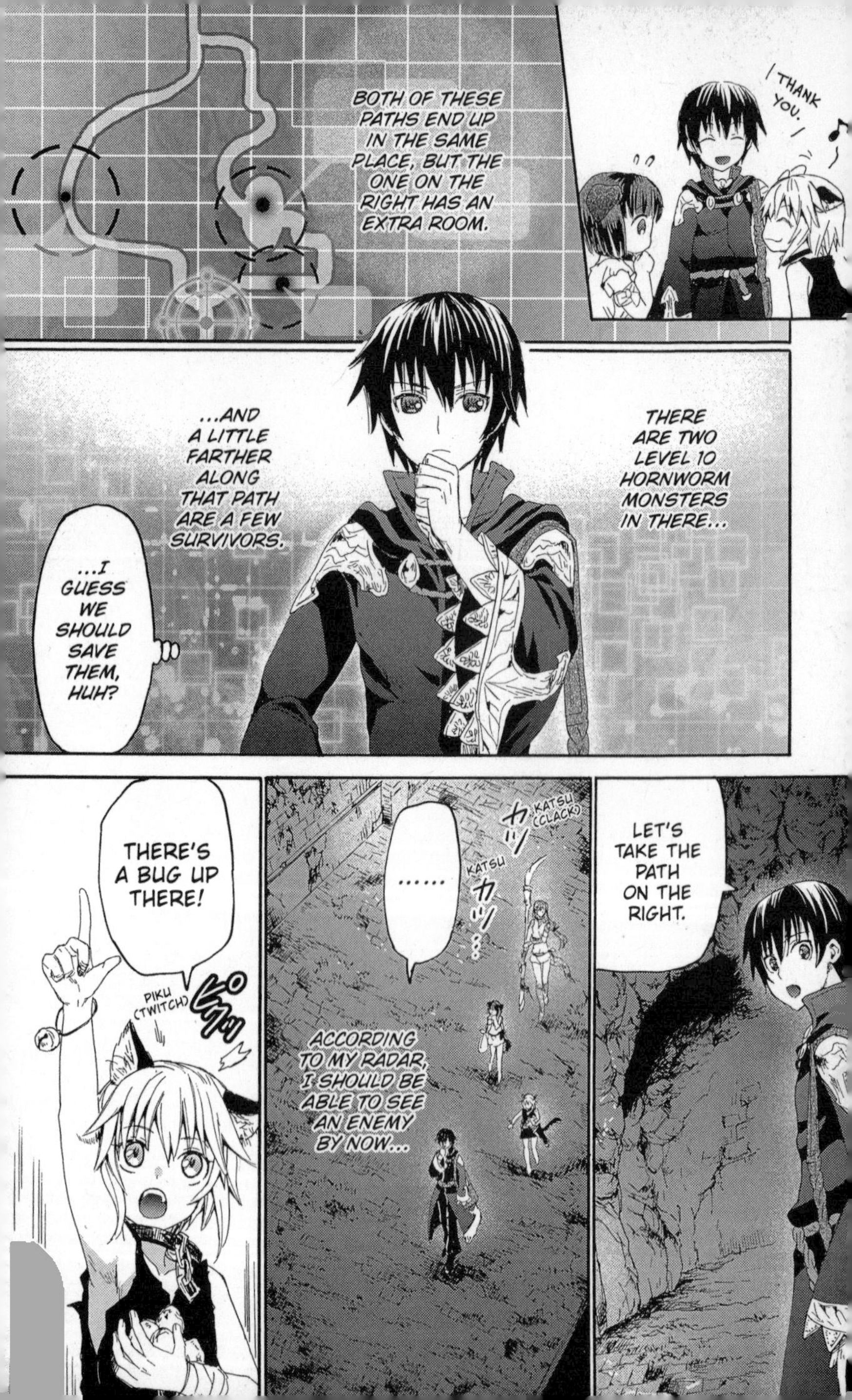
THANK YOU.
BOTH OF THESE PATHS END UP IN THE SAME PLACE, BUT THE ONE ON THE RIGHT HAS AN EXTRA ROOM.
THERE ARE TWO LEVEL 10 HORNWORM MONSTERS IN THERE...
...AND A LITTLE FARTHER ALONG THAT PATH ARE A FEW SURVIVORS.
...I GUESS WE SHOULD SAVE THEM, HUH?
LET'S TAKE THE PATH ON THE RIGHT.
KATSU (CLACK)
KATSU
......
ACCORDING TO MY RADAR, I SHOULD BE ABLE TO SEE AN ENEMY BY NOW...
THERE'S A BUG UP THERE!
PIKU (TWITCH)

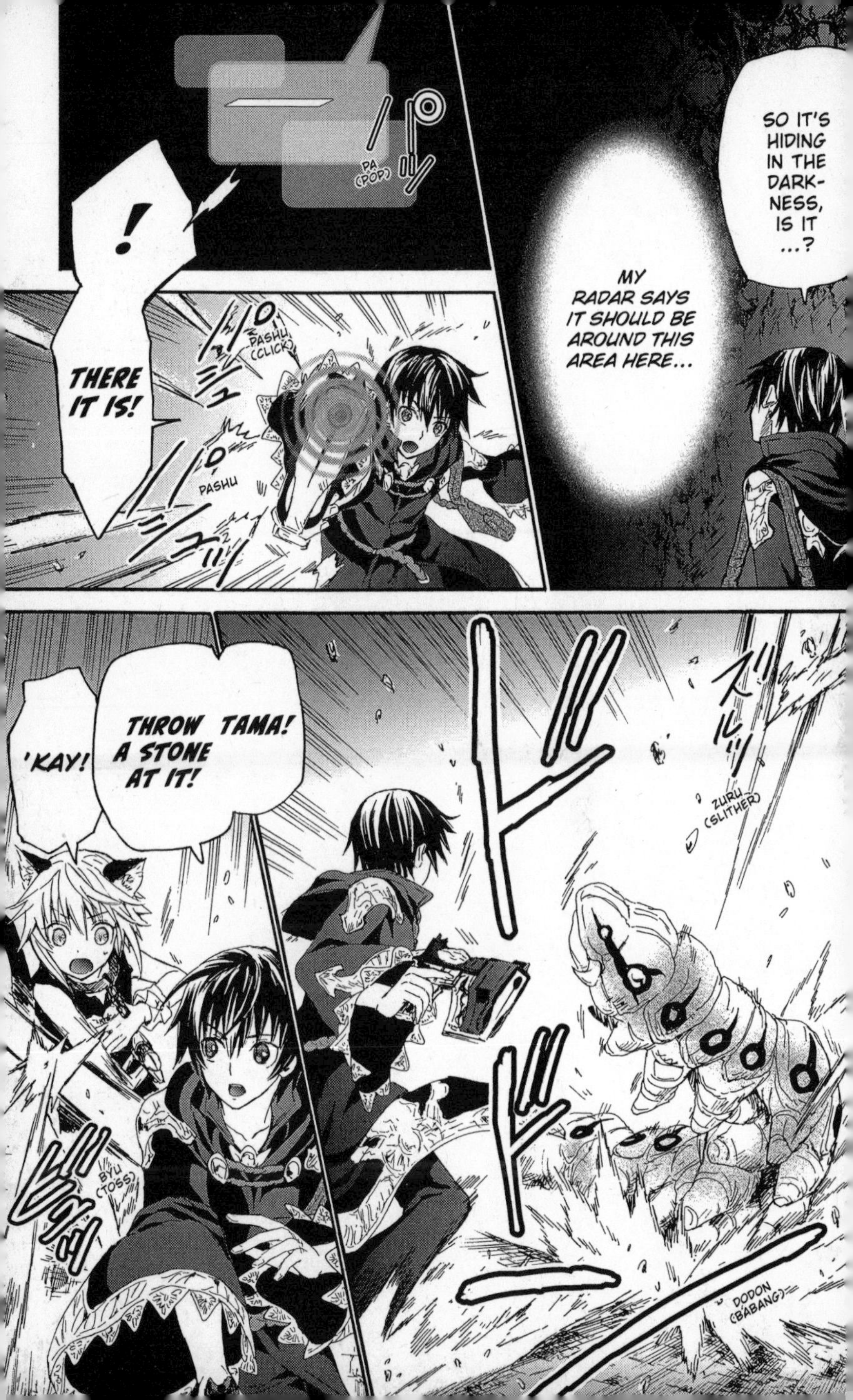
SO IT'S HIDING IN THE DARKNESS, IS IT ...?
MY RADAR SAYS IT SHOULD BE AROUND THIS AREA HERE...
PA (POP)
!
PASHU (CLICK)
THERE IT IS!
PASHU
ZURU (SLITHER)
TAMA! THROW A STONE AT IT!
'KAY!
DODON (BABANG)
BYU (TOSS)

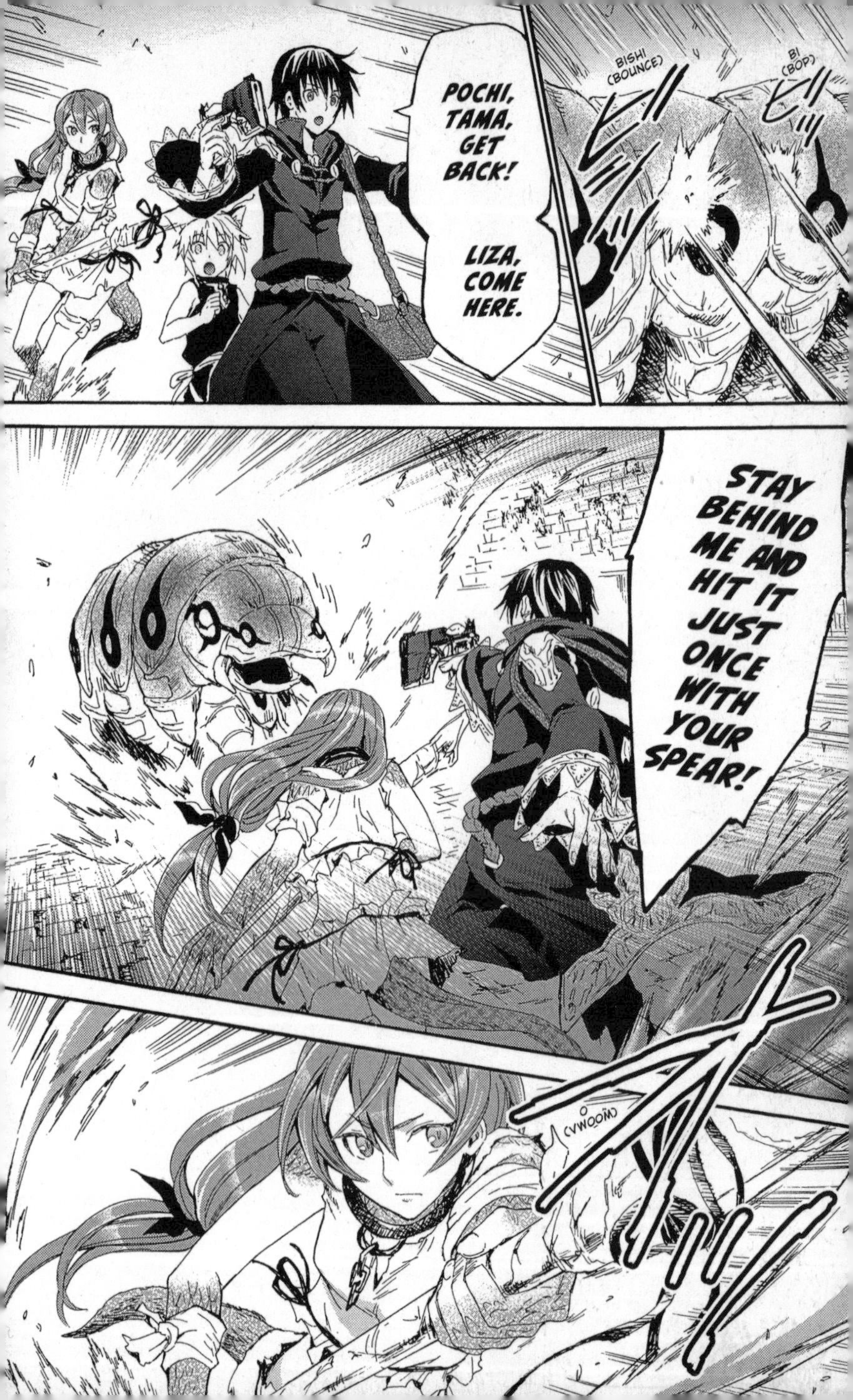
BISHI (BOUNCE)
BI (BOP)
POCHI, TAMA, GET BACK!
LIZA, COME HERE.
STAY BEHIND ME AND HIT IT JUST ONCE WITH YOUR SPEAR!
O (VWOOM)

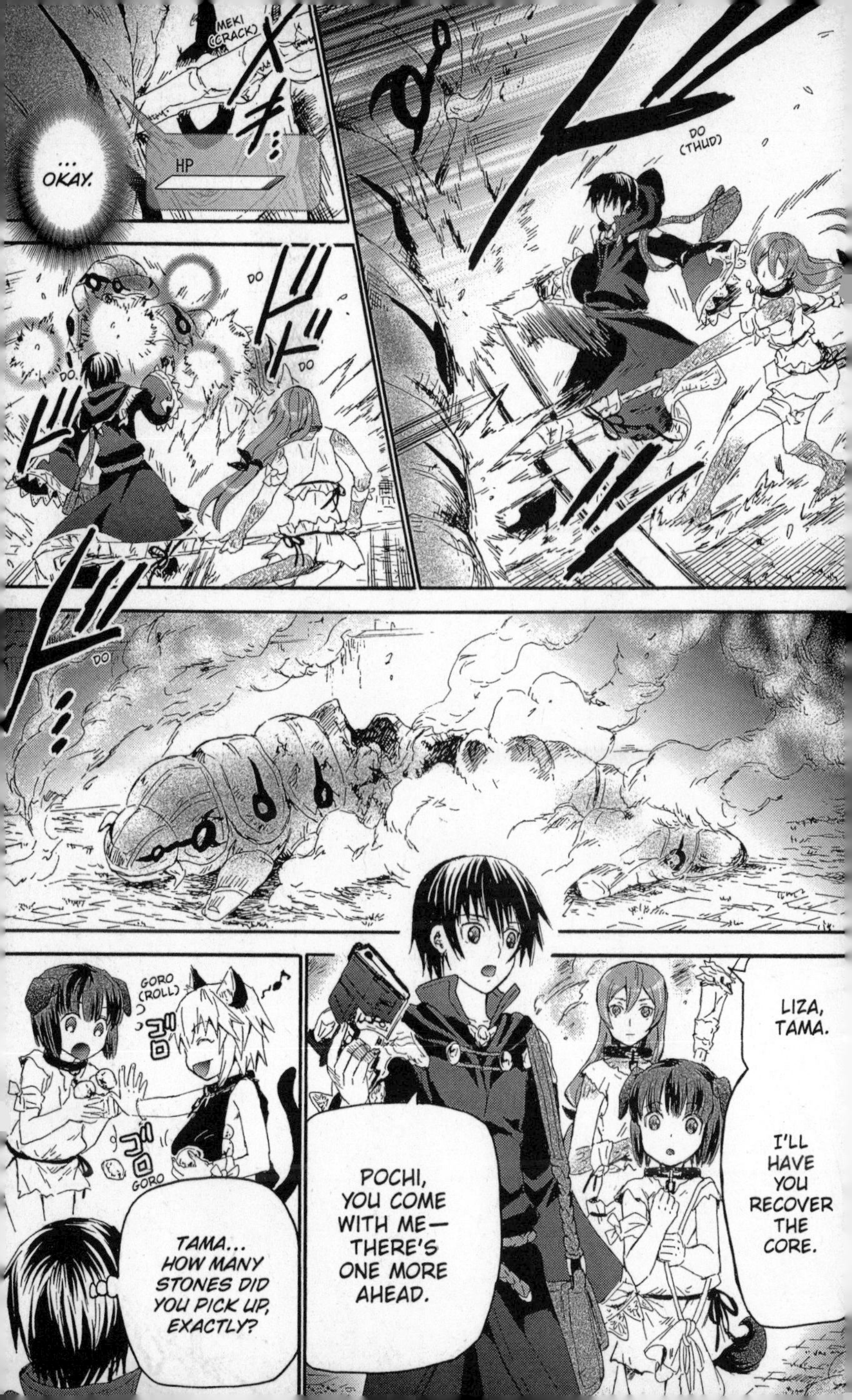
DO (THUD)
MEKI (CRACK)
... OKAY.
HP
DO
DO
DO.
DO
LIZA, TAMA.
I'LL HAVE YOU RECOVER THE CORE.
POCHI, YOU COME WITH ME— THERE'S ONE MORE AHEAD.
GORO (ROLL)
GORO
TAMA... HOW MANY STONES DID YOU PICK UP, EXACTLY?

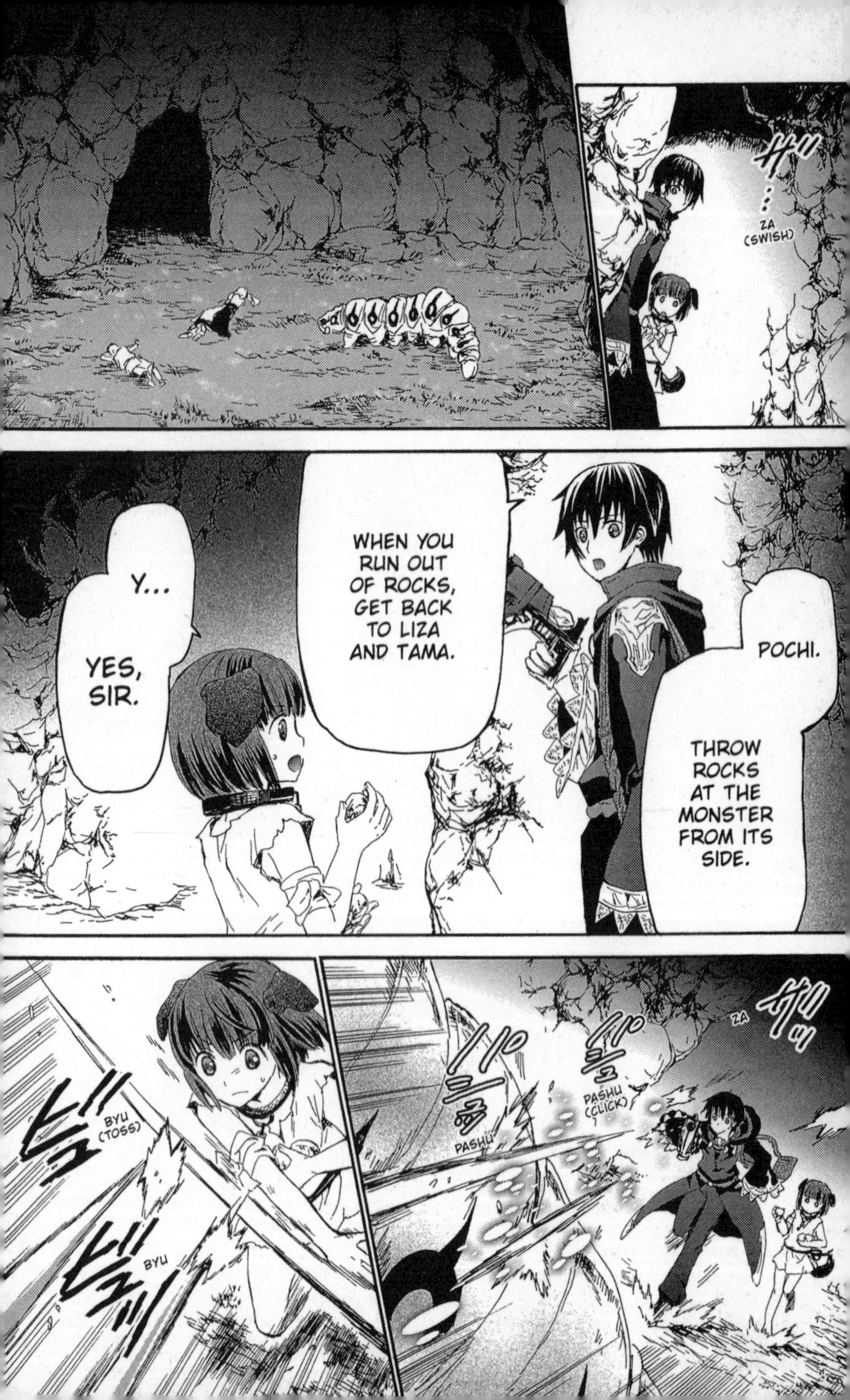
ZA (SWISH)
POCHI.
THROW ROCKS AT THE MONSTER FROM ITS SIDE.
WHEN YOU RUN OUT OF ROCKS, GET BACK TO LIZA AND TAMA.
Y...
YES, SIR.
ZA
PASHU (CLICK)
PASHU
BYU (TOSS)
BYU

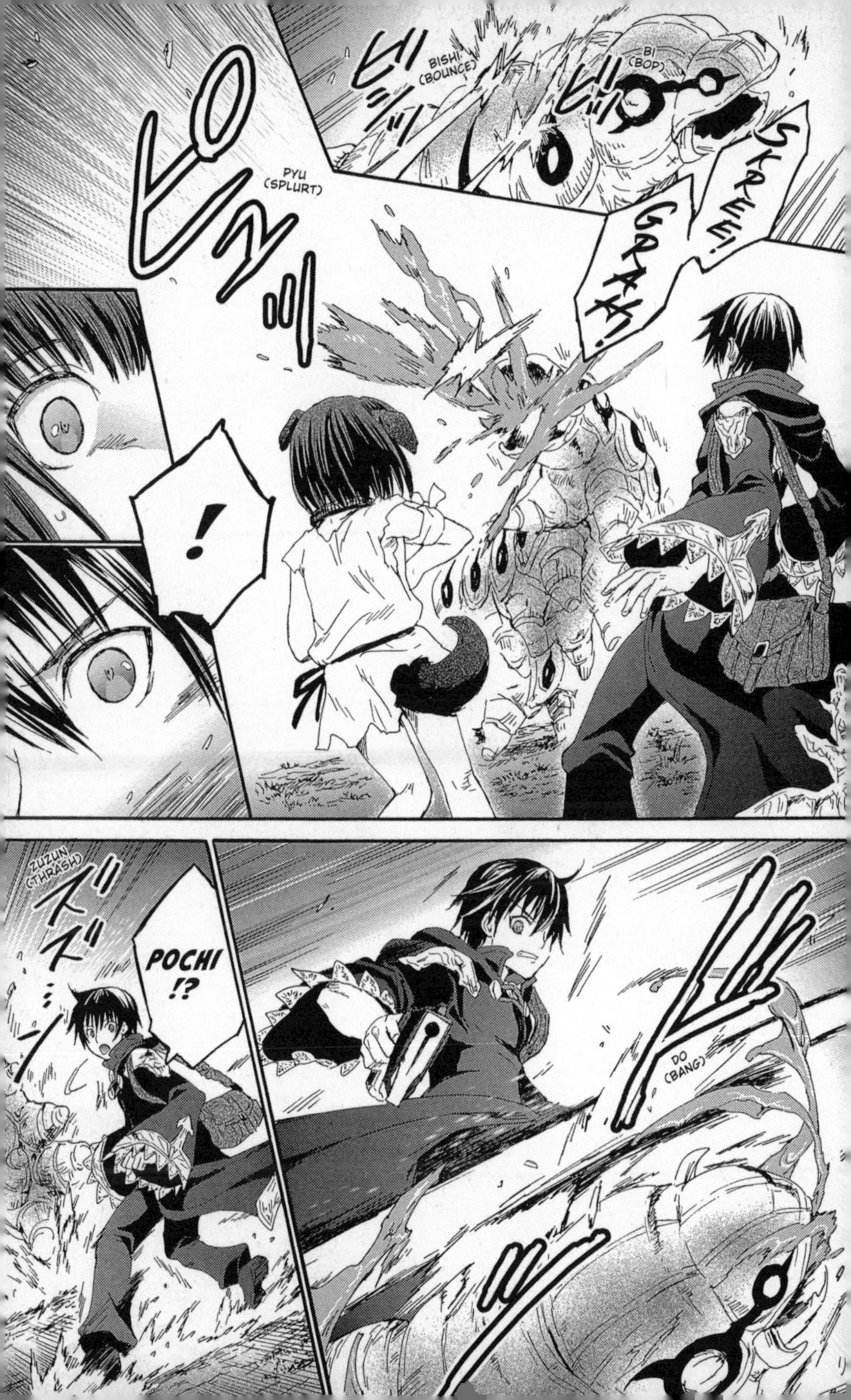
BI (BOP)
SKREE!
GRAAH!
BISHI (BOUNCE)
PYU (SPLURT)
!
DO (BANG)
POCHI !?
ZUZUN (THRASH)

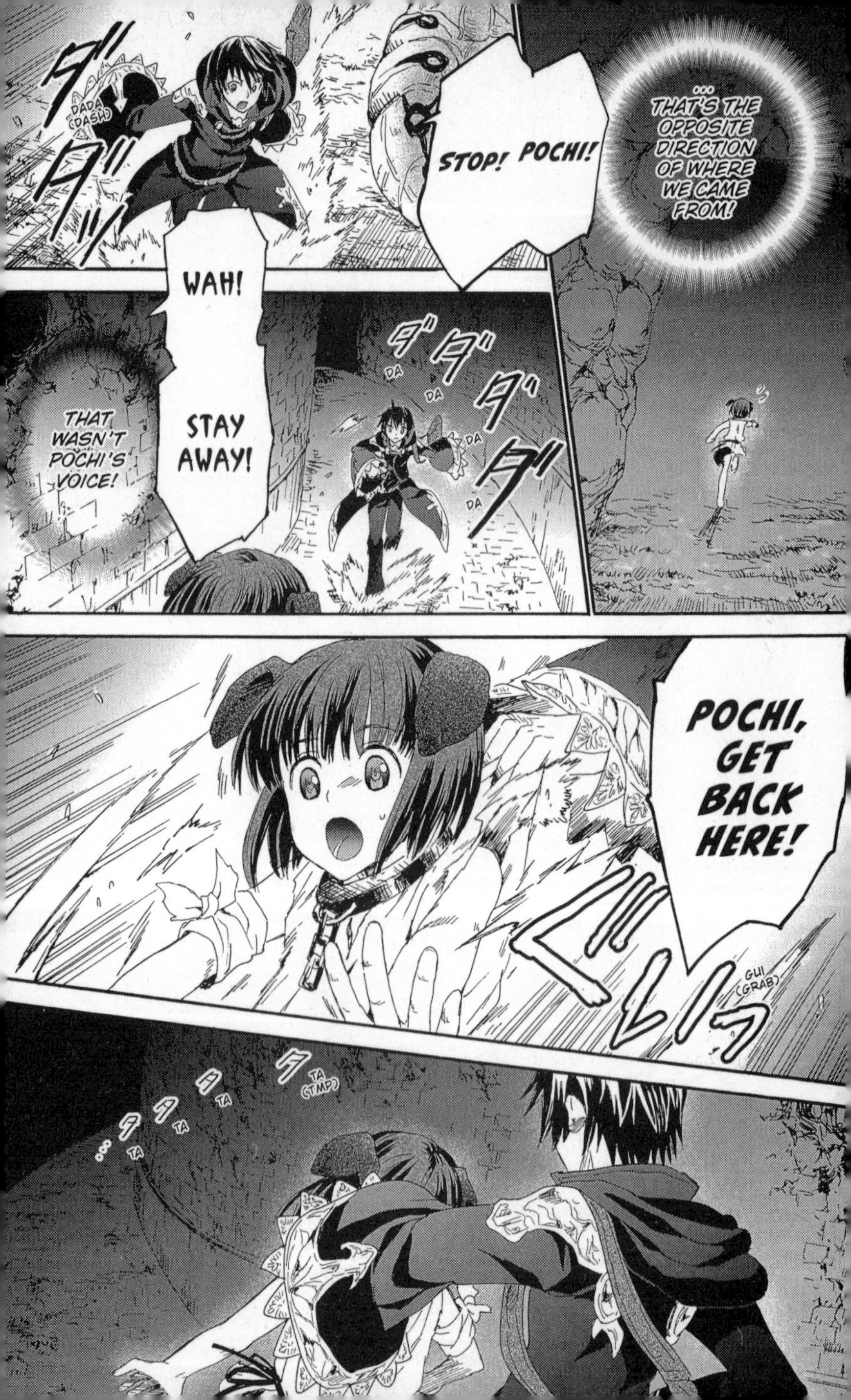
STOP! POCHI!
...THAT'S THE OPPOSITE DIRECTION OF WHERE WE CAME FROM!
DADA (DASH)
WAH!
STAY AWAY!
DA DA DA DA
THAT WASN'T POCHI'S VOICE!
POCHI, GET BACK HERE!
GUI (GRAB)
TA (TMP) TA TA TA...

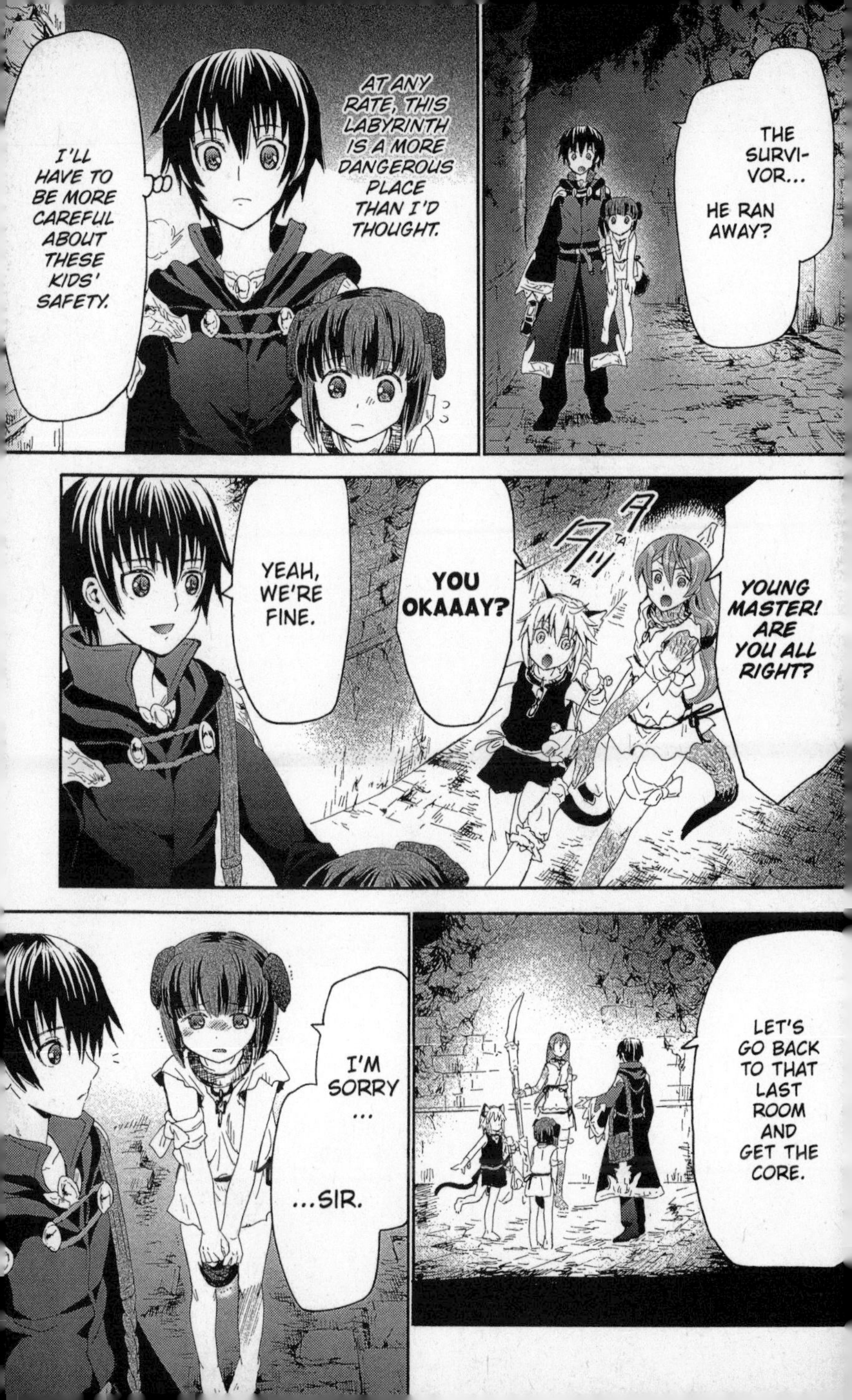
THE SURVIVOR...
HE RAN AWAY?
AT ANY RATE, THIS LABYRINTH IS A MORE DANGEROUS PLACE THAN I'D THOUGHT.
I'LL HAVE TO BE MORE CAREFUL ABOUT THESE KIDS' SAFETY.
YOUNG MASTER! ARE YOU ALL RIGHT?
TA TA
YOU OKAAAY?
YEAH, WE'RE FINE.
LET'S GO BACK TO THAT LAST ROOM AND GET THE CORE.
I'M SORRY...
...SIR.

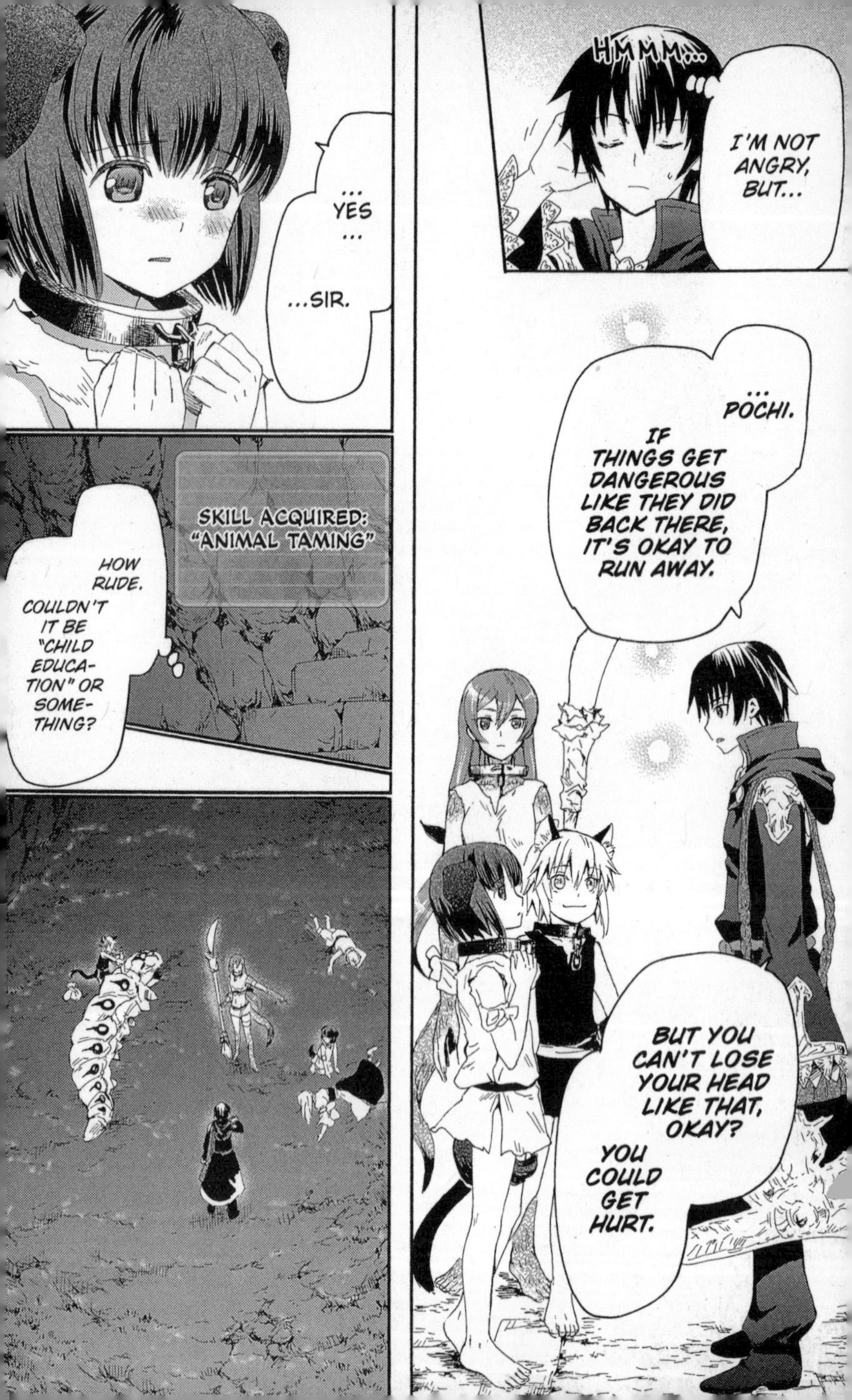
HMMM...
I'M NOT ANGRY, BUT...
... POCHI.
IF THINGS GET DANGEROUS LIKE THEY DID BACK THERE, IT'S OKAY TO RUN AWAY.
BUT YOU CAN'T LOSE YOUR HEAD LIKE THAT, OKAY?
YOU COULD GET HURT.
... YES ...
...SIR.
SKILL ACQUIRED: "ANIMAL TAMING"
HOW RUDE. COULDN'T IT BE "CHILD EDUCATION" OR SOMETHING?

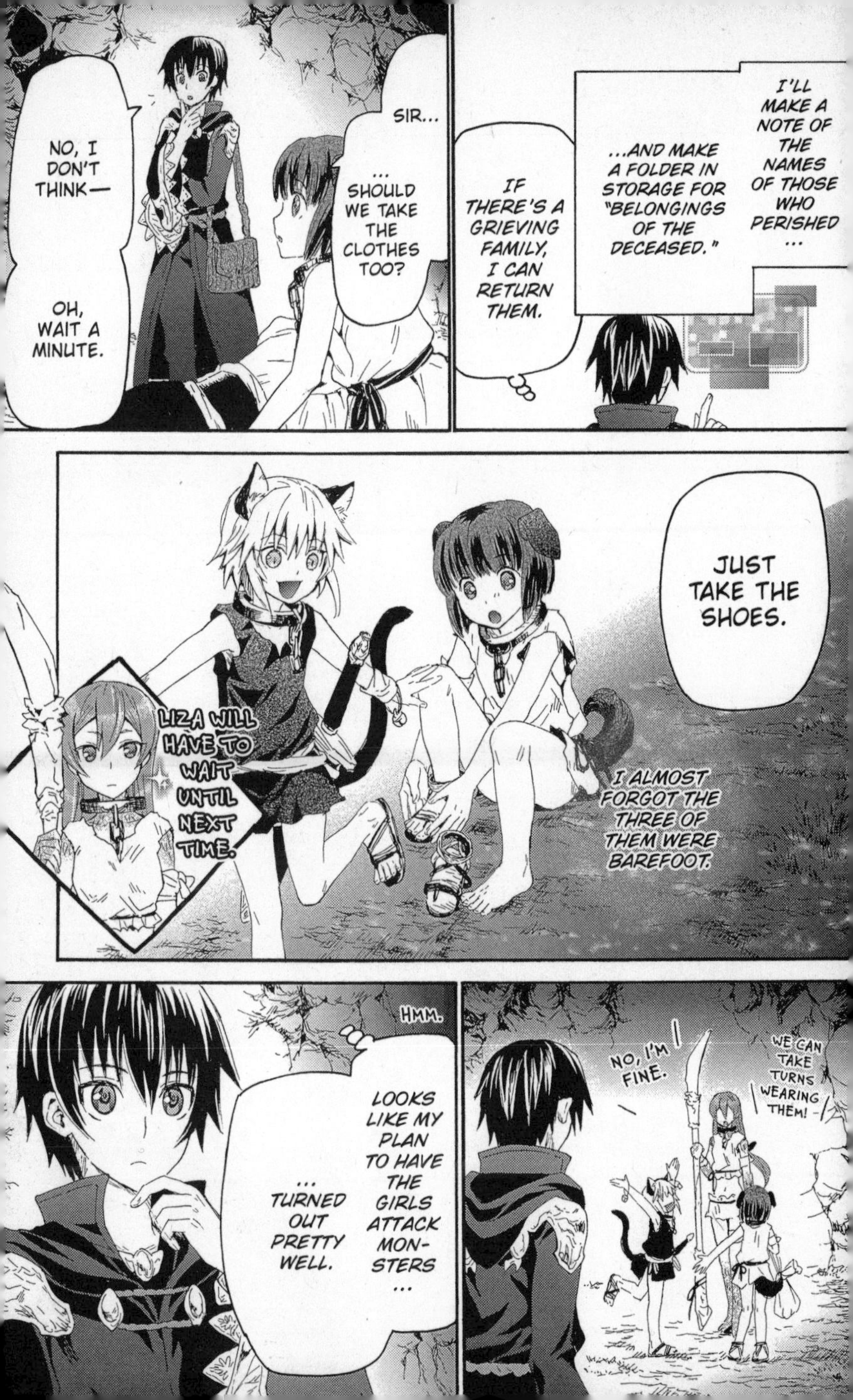
I'LL MAKE A NOTE OF THE NAMES OF THOSE WHO PERISHED ...
...AND MAKE A FOLDER IN STORAGE FOR "BELONGINGS OF THE DECEASED."
IF THERE'S A GRIEVING FAMILY, I CAN RETURN THEM.
SIR...
... SHOULD WE TAKE THE CLOTHES TOO?
NO, I DON'T THINK—
OH, WAIT A MINUTE.
JUST TAKE THE SHOES.
I ALMOST FORGOT THE THREE OF THEM WERE BAREFOOT.
LIZA WILL HAVE TO WAIT UNTIL NEXT TIME.
WE CAN TAKE TURNS WEARING THEM!
NO, I'M FINE.
HMM.
LOOKS LIKE MY PLAN TO HAVE THE GIRLS ATTACK MON-STERS ...
... TURNED OUT PRETTY WELL.

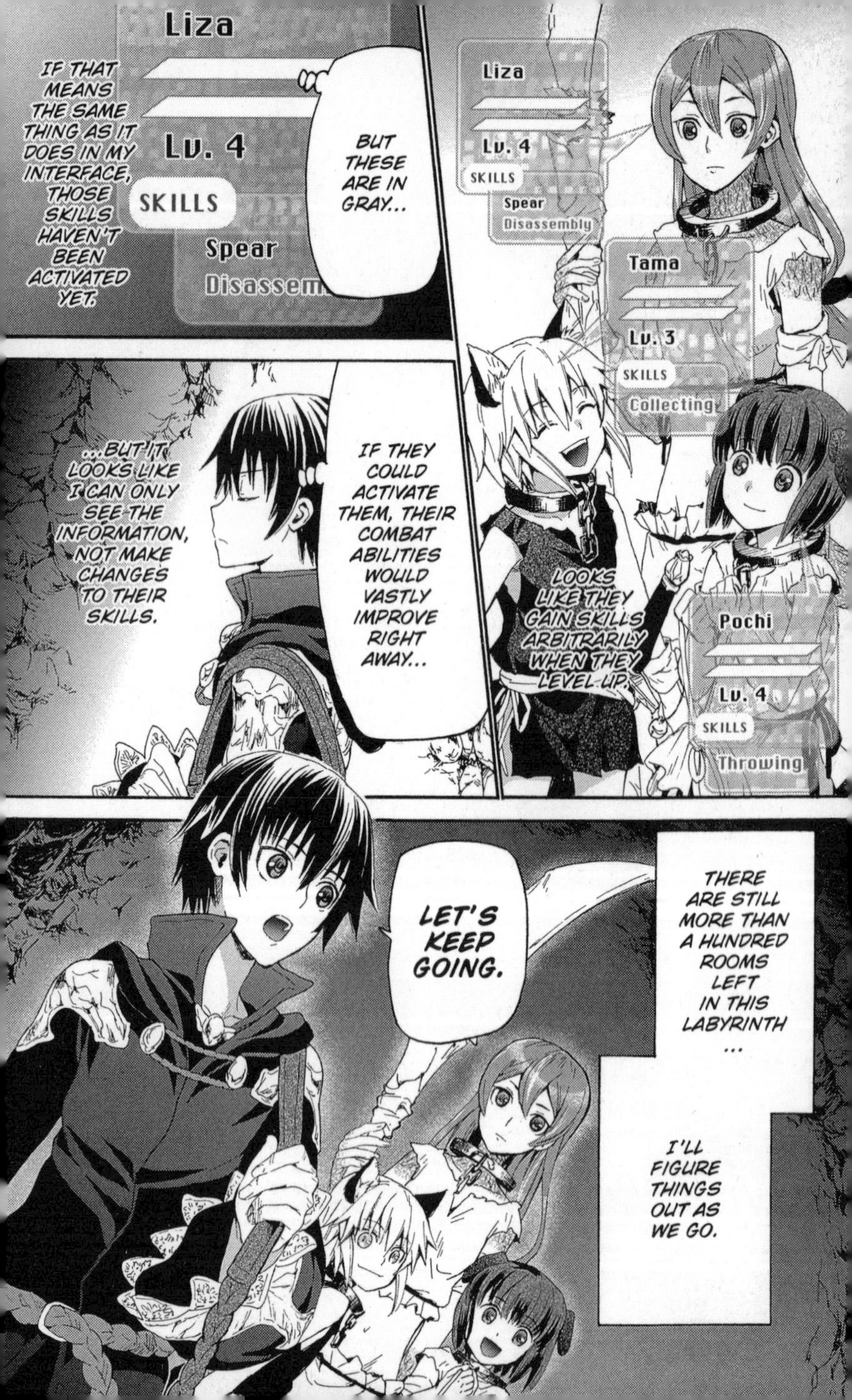
Liza
Lv. 4
SKILLS
Spear
Disassembly
Tama
Lv. 3
SKILLS
Collecting
LOOKS LIKE THEY GAIN SKILLS ARBITRARILY WHEN THEY LEVEL UP.
Pochi
Lv. 4
SKILLS
Throwing
Liza
Lv. 4
SKILLS
Spear
BUT THESE ARE IN GRAY...
IF THAT MEANS THE SAME THING AS IT DOES IN MY INTERFACE, THOSE SKILLS HAVEN'T BEEN ACTIVATED YET.
IF THEY COULD ACTIVATE THEM, THEIR COMBAT ABILITIES WOULD VASTLY IMPROVE RIGHT AWAY...
...BUT IT LOOKS LIKE I CAN ONLY SEE THE INFORMATION, NOT MAKE CHANGES TO THEIR SKILLS.
THERE ARE STILL MORE THAN A HUNDRED ROOMS LEFT IN THIS LABYRINTH...
LET'S KEEP GOING.
I'LL FIGURE THINGS OUT AS WE GO.

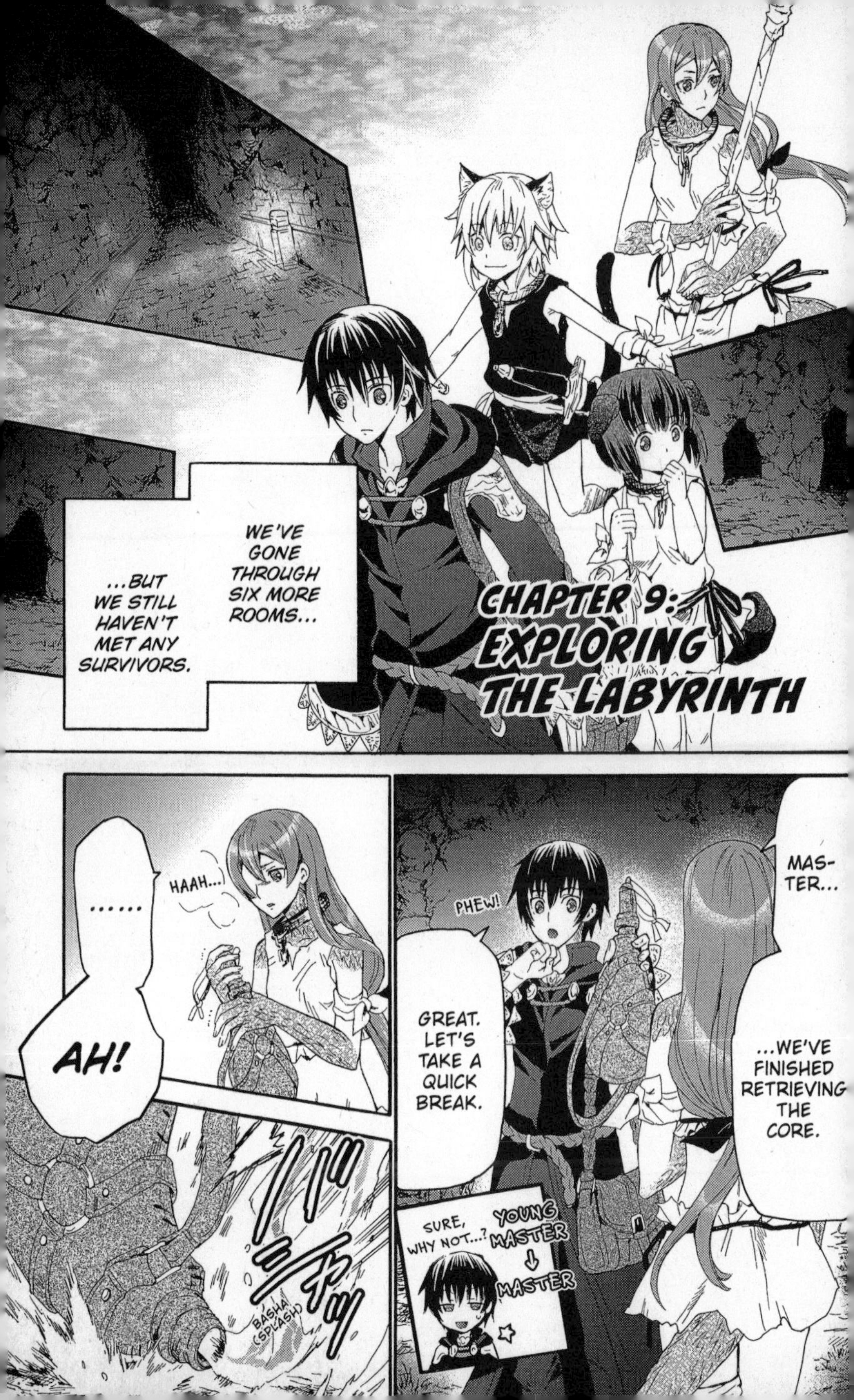

CHAPTER 9: EXPLORING THE LABYRINTH
WE'VE GONE THROUGH SIX MORE ROOMS...
...BUT WE STILL HAVEN'T MET ANY SURVIVORS.
MAS-TER...
...WE'VE FINISHED RETRIEVING THE CORE.
PHEW!
GREAT. LET'S TAKE A QUICK BREAK.
YOUNG MASTER ↓ MASTER
SURE, WHY NOT...?
HAAH...
......
AH!
BASHA (SPLASH)

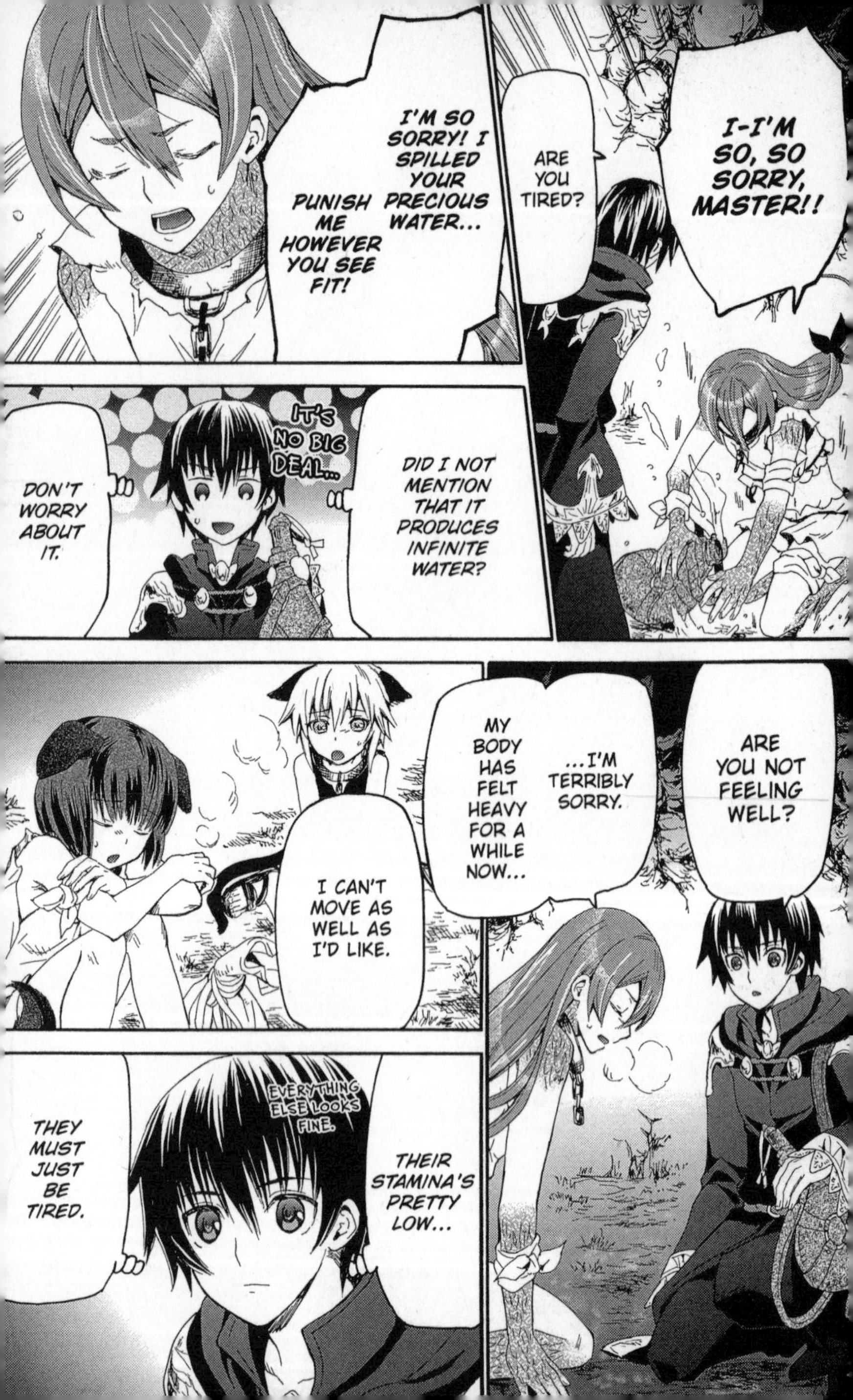
I-I'M SO, SO SORRY, MASTER!!
ARE YOU TIRED?
I'M SO SORRY! I SPILLED YOUR PRECIOUS WATER...
PUNISH ME HOWEVER YOU SEE FIT!
DID I NOT MENTION THAT IT PRODUCES INFINITE WATER?
IT'S NO BIG DEAL...
DON'T WORRY ABOUT IT.
ARE YOU NOT FEELING WELL?
...I'M TERRIBLY SORRY.
MY BODY HAS FELT HEAVY FOR A WHILE NOW...
I CAN'T MOVE AS WELL AS I'D LIKE.
THEIR STAMINA'S PRETTY LOW...
EVERYTHING ELSE LOOKS FINE.
THEY MUST JUST BE TIRED.

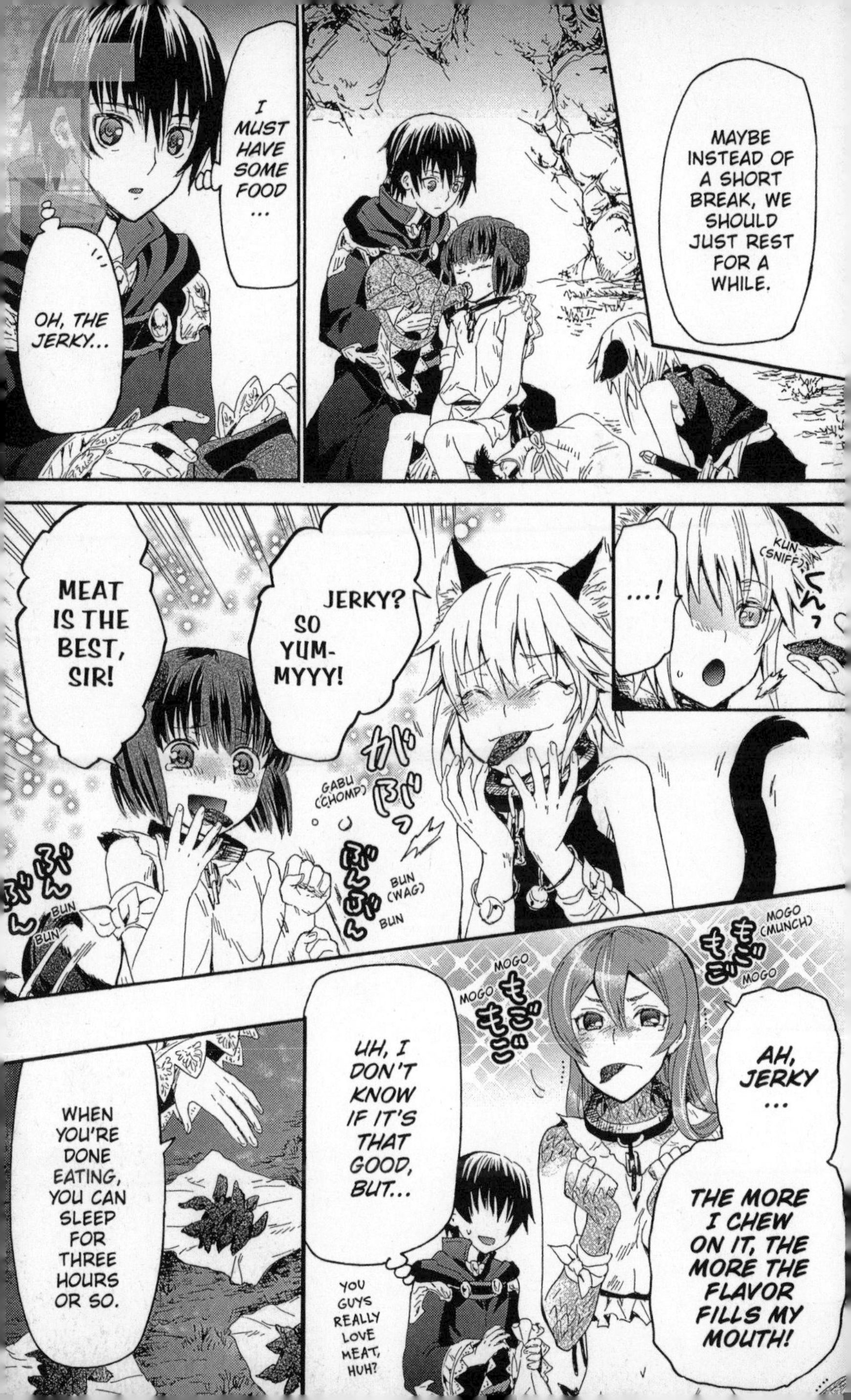
MAYBE INSTEAD OF A SHORT BREAK, WE SHOULD JUST REST FOR A WHILE.
I MUST HAVE SOME FOOD...
OH, THE JERKY...
KUN (SNIFF)
...!
JERKY? SO YUM-MYYY!
GABU (CHOMP)
BUN (WAG) BUN
MEAT IS THE BEST, SIR!
BUN BUN
MOGO (MUNCH) MOGO
AH, JERKY...
THE MORE I CHEW ON IT, THE MORE THE FLAVOR FILLS MY MOUTH!
MOGO MOGO
UH, I DON'T KNOW IF IT'S THAT GOOD, BUT...
YOU GUYS REALLY LOVE MEAT, HUH?
WHEN YOU'RE DONE EATING, YOU CAN SLEEP FOR THREE HOURS OR SO.

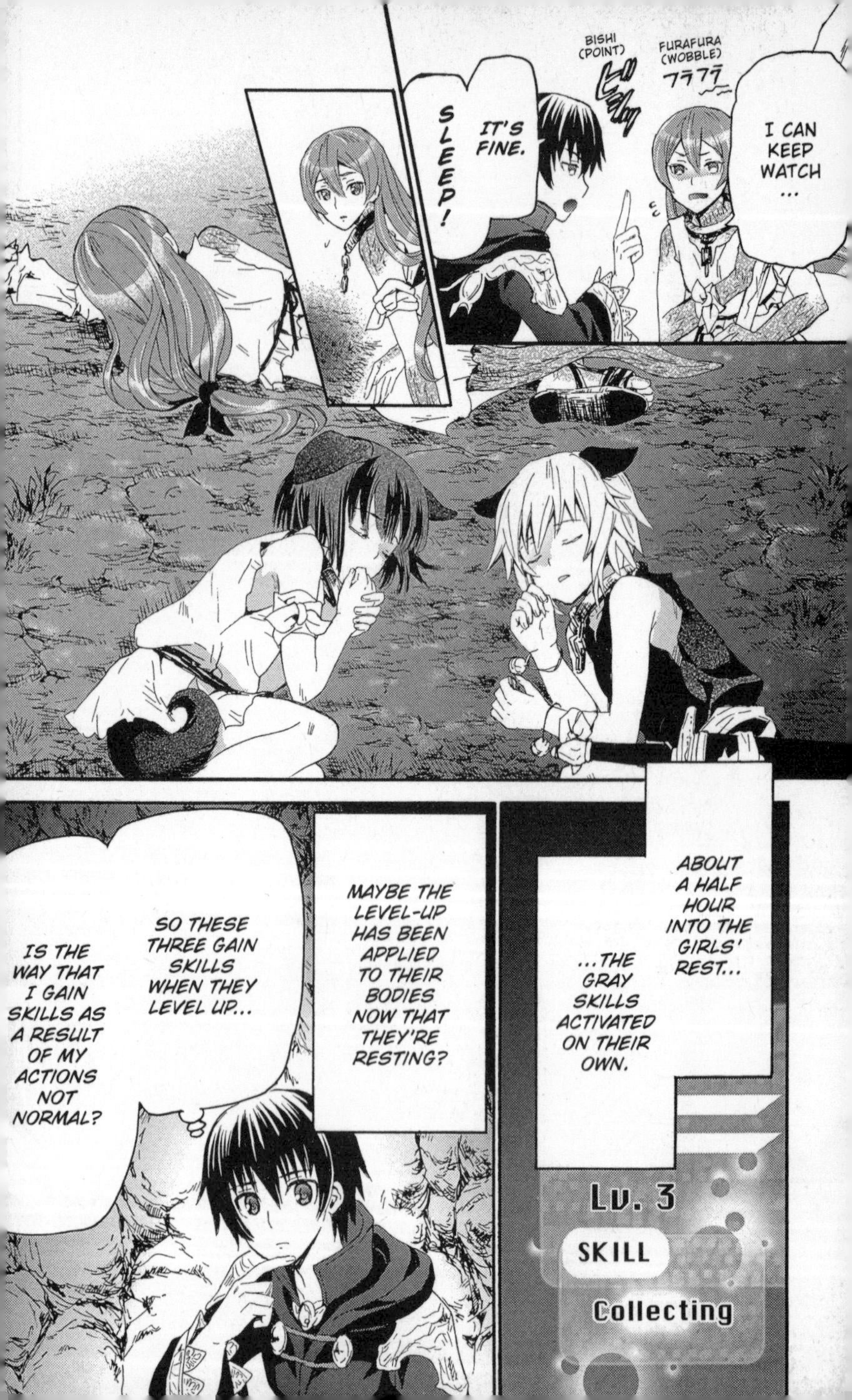
I CAN KEEP WATCH ...
FURAFURA (WOBBLE)
フラフラ
BISHI (POINT)
IT'S FINE.
SLEEP!
ABOUT A HALF HOUR INTO THE GIRLS' REST...
...THE GRAY SKILLS ACTIVATED ON THEIR OWN.
Lv. 3
SKILL
Collecting
MAYBE THE LEVEL-UP HAS BEEN APPLIED TO THEIR BODIES NOW THAT THEY'RE RESTING?
SO THESE THREE GAIN SKILLS WHEN THEY LEVEL UP...
IS THE WAY THAT I GAIN SKILLS AS A RESULT OF MY ACTIONS NOT NORMAL?

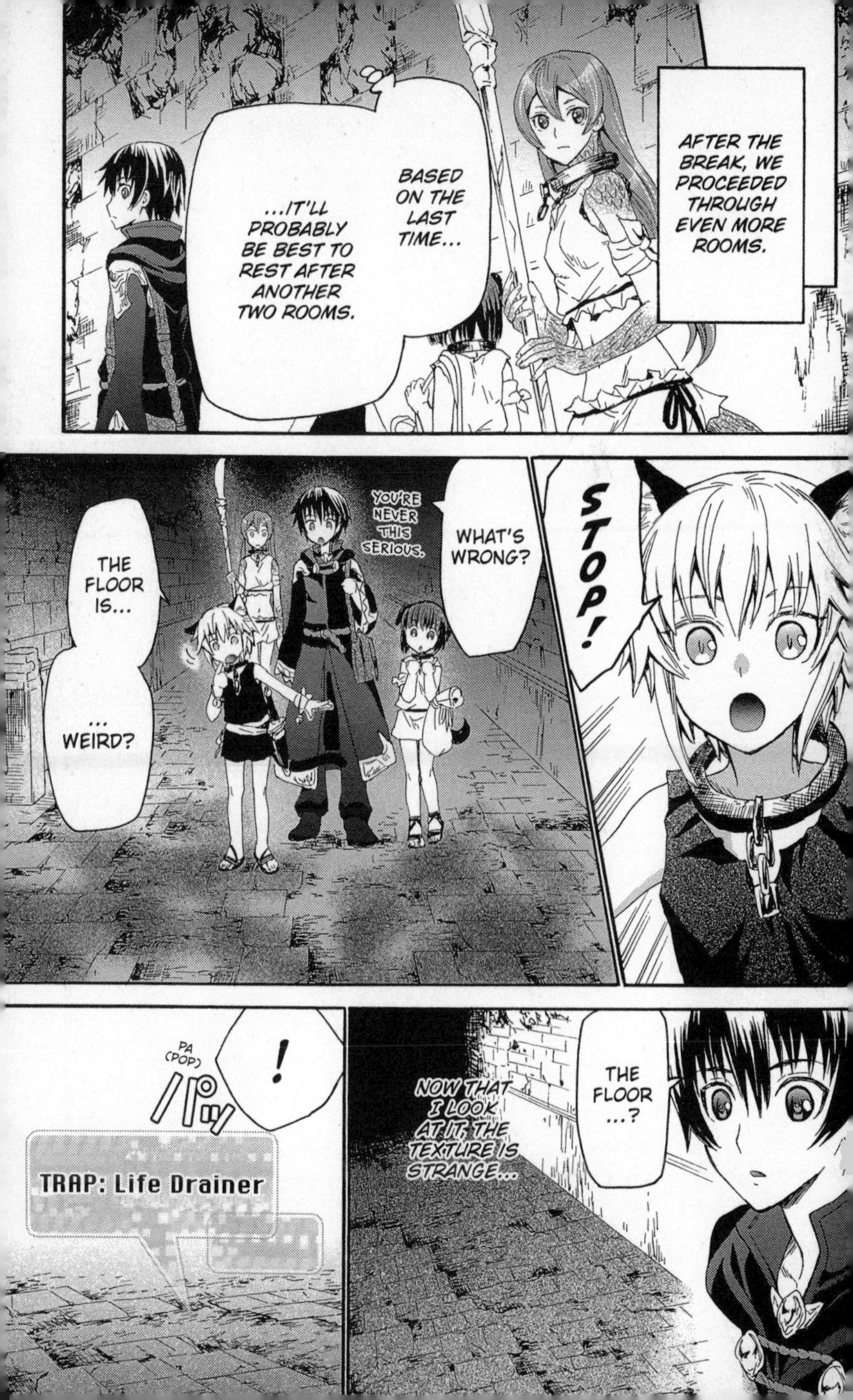
AFTER THE BREAK, WE PROCEEDED THROUGH EVEN MORE ROOMS.
BASED ON THE LAST TIME...
...IT'LL PROBABLY BE BEST TO REST AFTER ANOTHER TWO ROOMS.
STOP!
WHAT'S WRONG?
YOU'RE NEVER THIS SERIOUS.
THE FLOOR IS...
...WEIRD?
THE FLOOR ...?
NOW THAT I LOOK AT IT, THE TEXTURE IS STRANGE...
!
PA (POP)
パッ
TRAP: Life Drainer

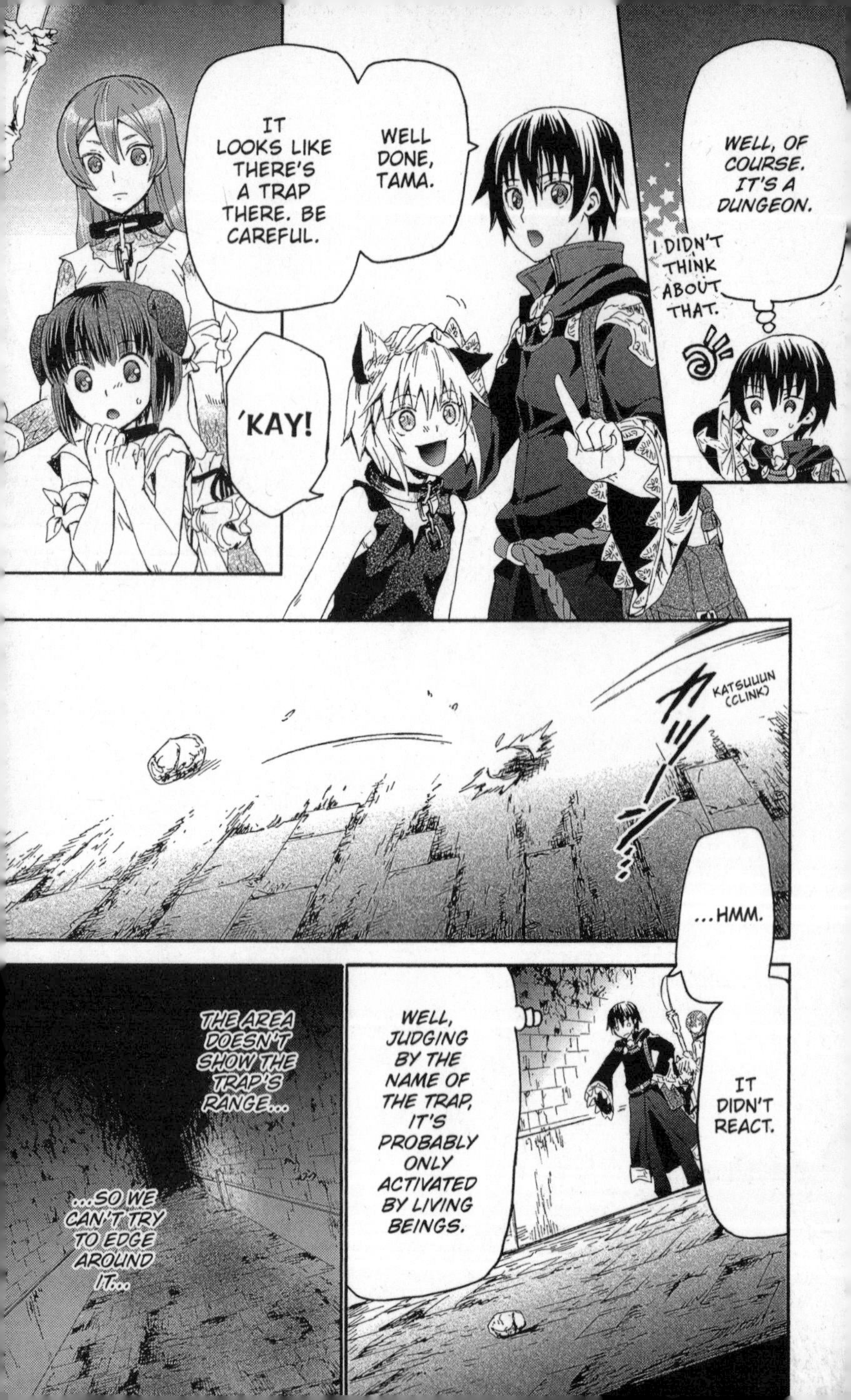
WELL, OF COURSE. IT'S A DUNGEON.
I DIDN'T THINK ABOUT THAT.
WELL DONE, TAMA.
IT LOOKS LIKE THERE'S A TRAP THERE. BE CAREFUL.
'KAY!
KATSUUUN (CLINK)
...HMM.
IT DIDN'T REACT.
WELL, JUDGING BY THE NAME OF THE TRAP, IT'S PROBABLY ONLY ACTIVATED BY LIVING BEINGS.
THE AREA DOESN'T SHOW THE TRAP'S RANGE...
...SO WE CAN'T TRY TO EDGE AROUND IT...

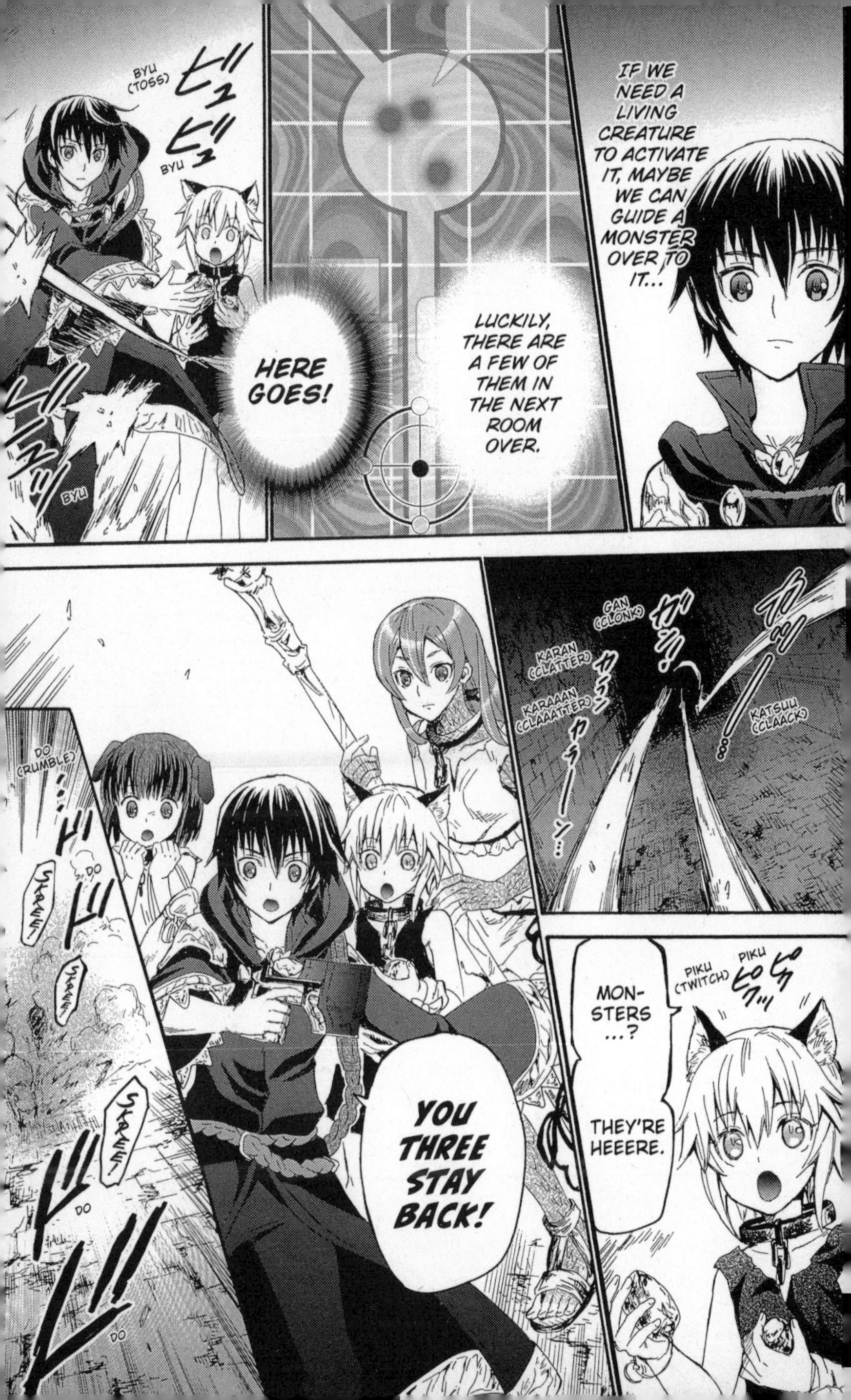
IF WE NEED A LIVING CREATURE TO ACTIVATE IT, MAYBE WE CAN GUIDE A MONSTER OVER TO IT...
LUCKILY, THERE ARE A FEW OF THEM IN THE NEXT ROOM OVER.
HERE GOES!
BYU (TOSS)
BYU
BYU
GAN (CLONK)
KARAN (CLATTER)
KARAAAN (CLAAATTER)
KATSUU (CLAACK)
PIKU (TWITCH) PIKU
MON-STERS ...?
THEY'RE HEEERE.
DO (RUMBLE)
DO
SKREE!
SKREE!
SKREE!
DO
DO
YOU THREE STAY BACK!

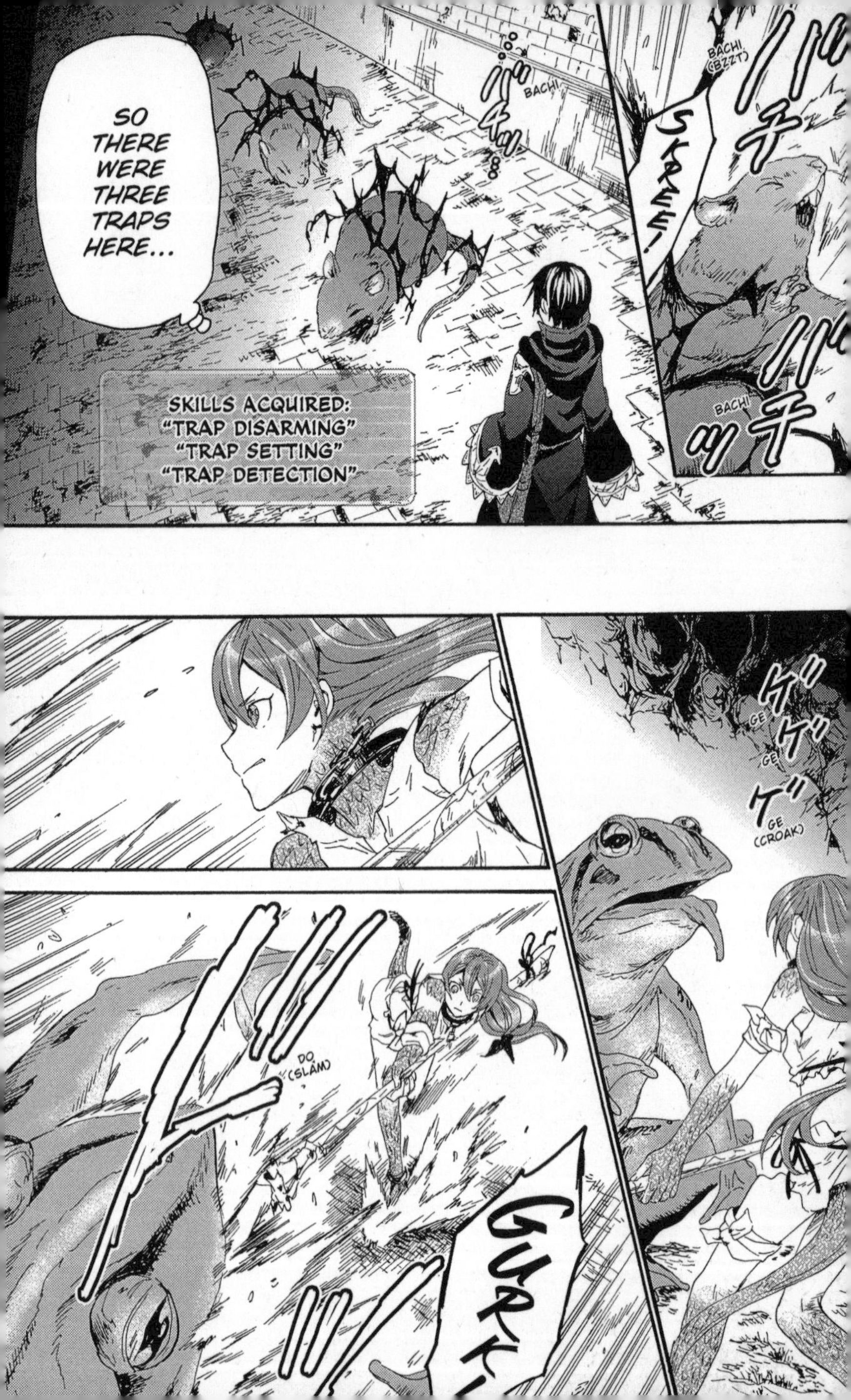
BACHI (BZZT)
SKREE!
BACHI
BACHI
SO THERE WERE THREE TRAPS HERE...
SKILLS ACQUIRED:
"TRAP DISARMING"
"TRAP SETTING"
"TRAP DETECTION"
GE
GE
GE (CROAK)
DO (SLAM)
GURK!

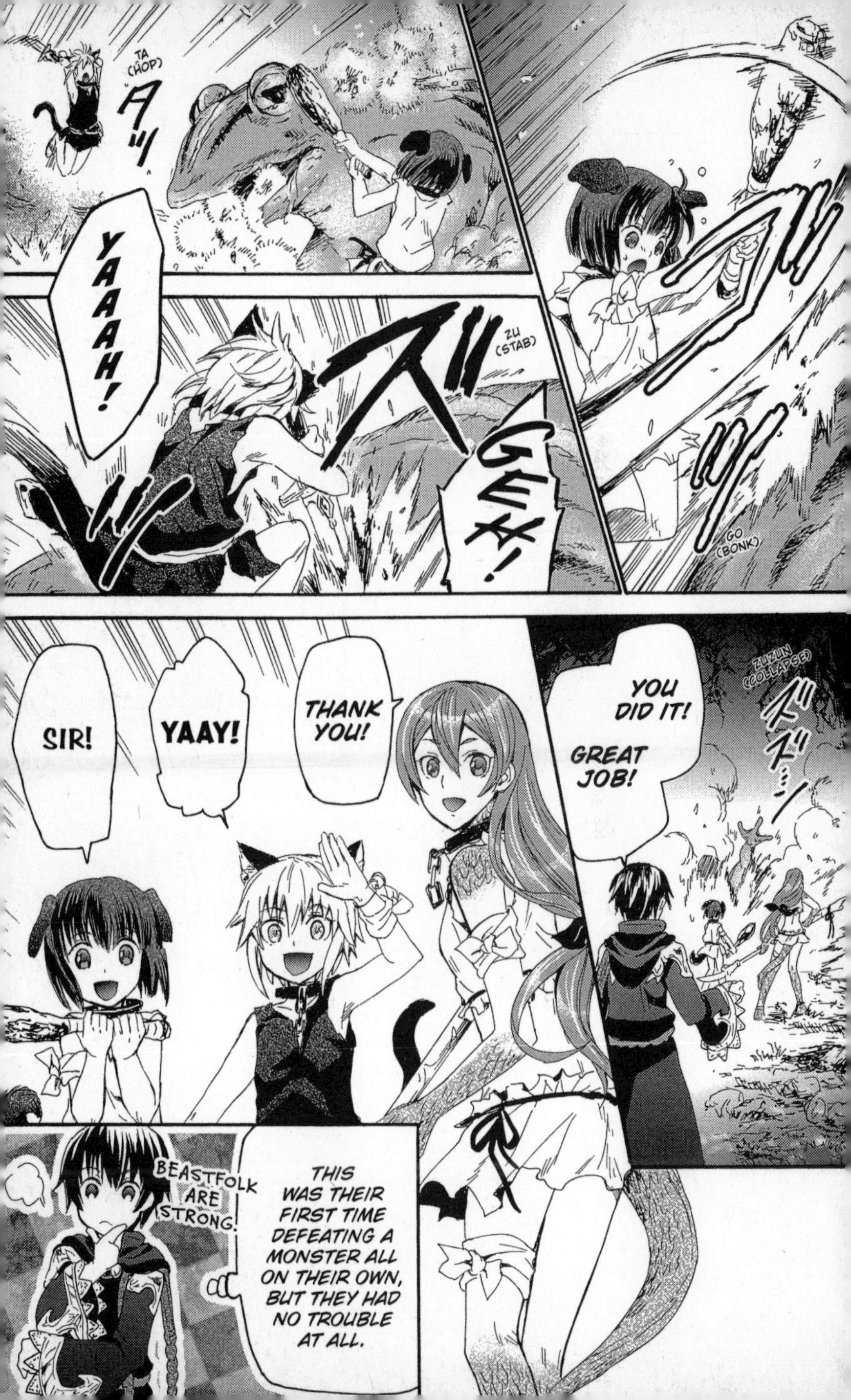
GO (BONK)
TA (HOP)
ZU (STAB)
GEH!
YAAAAH!
ZUZUN (COLLAPSE)
YOU DID IT!
GREAT JOB!
THANK YOU!
YAAY!
SIR!
THIS WAS THEIR FIRST TIME DEFEATING A MONSTER ALL ON THEIR OWN, BUT THEY HAD NO TROUBLE AT ALL.
BEASTFOLK ARE STRONG.

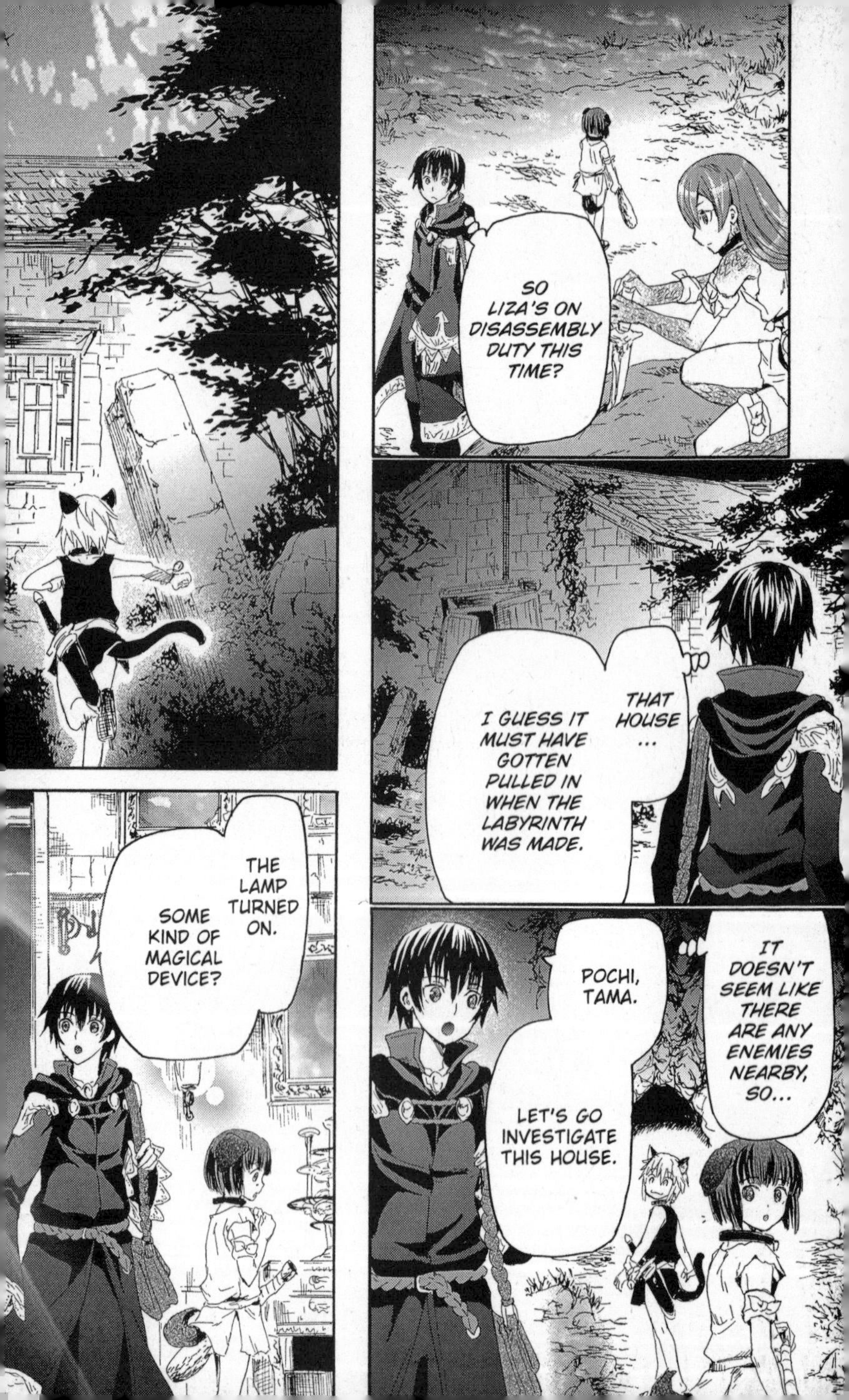
SO LIZA'S ON DISASSEMBLY DUTY THIS TIME?
THAT HOUSE...
I GUESS IT MUST HAVE GOTTEN PULLED IN WHEN THE LABYRINTH WAS MADE.
IT DOESN'T SEEM LIKE THERE ARE ANY ENEMIES NEARBY, SO...
POCHI, TAMA.
LET'S GO INVESTIGATE THIS HOUSE.
THE LAMP TURNED ON.
SOME KIND OF MAGICAL DEVICE?

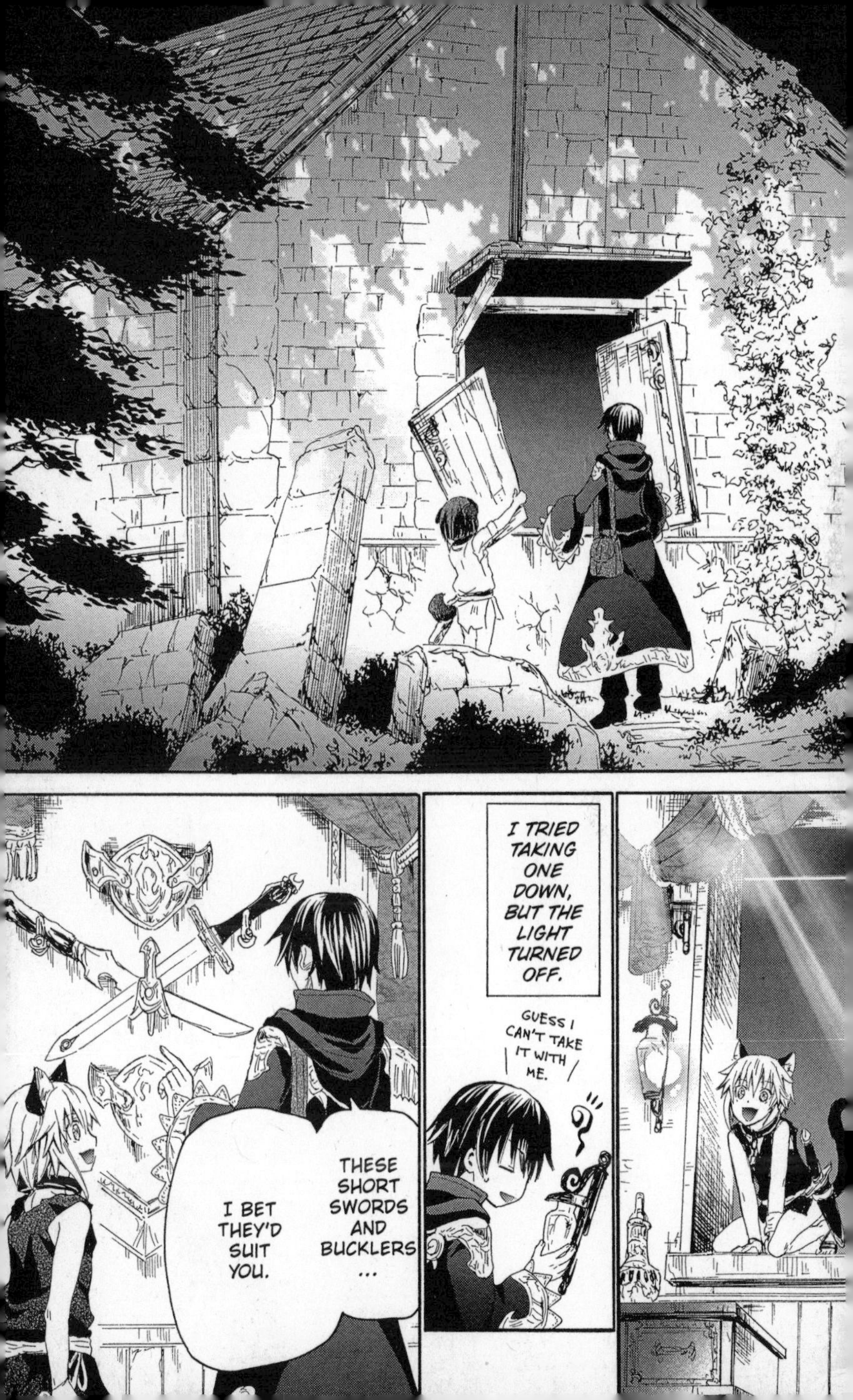
I TRIED TAKING ONE DOWN, BUT THE LIGHT TURNED OFF.
GUESS I CAN'T TAKE IT WITH ME.
?
THESE SHORT SWORDS AND BUCKLERS...
I BET THEY'D SUIT YOU.

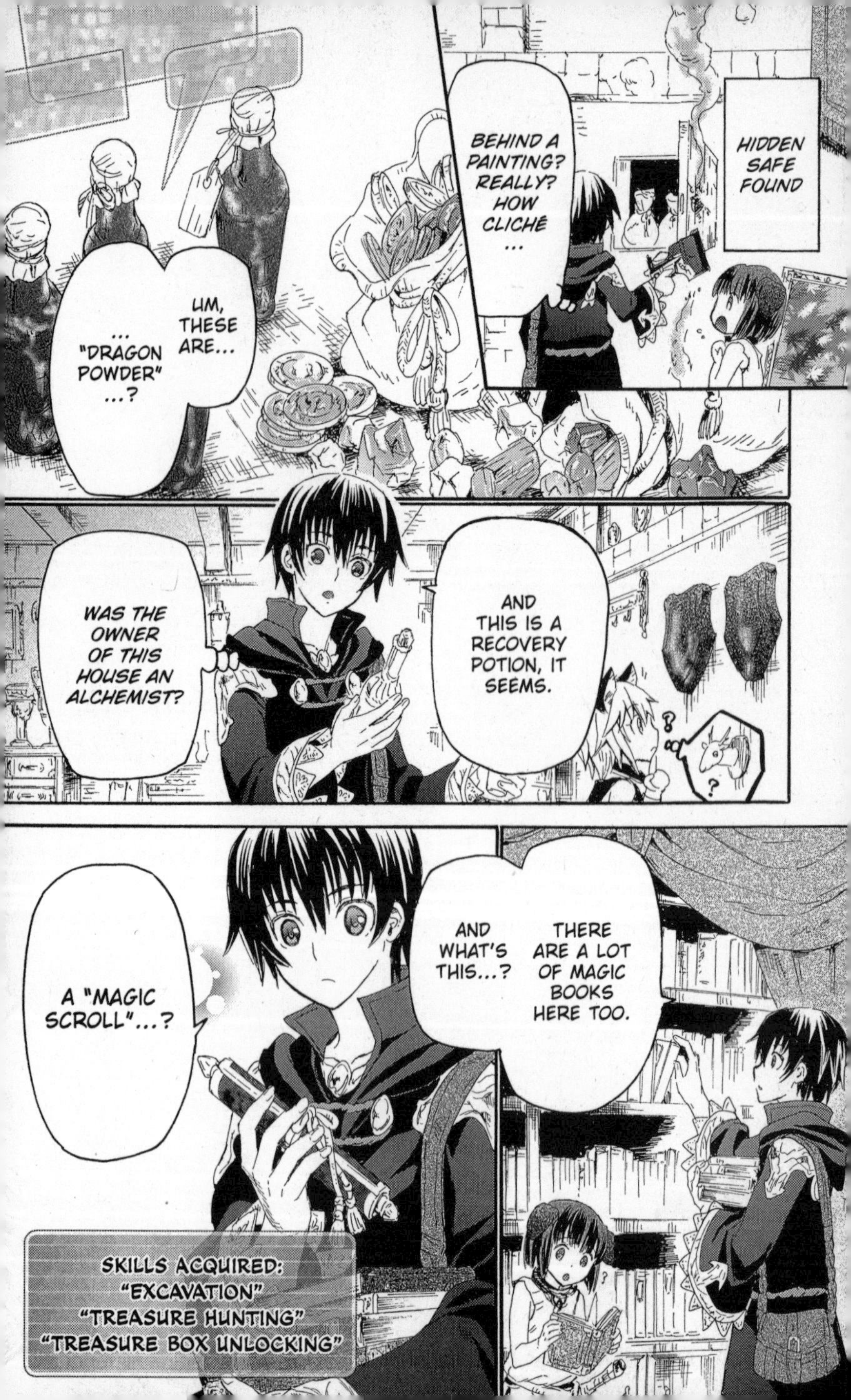
HIDDEN SAFE FOUND
BEHIND A PAINTING? REALLY? HOW CLICHÉ ...
UM, THESE ARE...
... "DRAGON POWDER" ...?
AND THIS IS A RECOVERY POTION, IT SEEMS.
WAS THE OWNER OF THIS HOUSE AN ALCHEMIST?
THERE ARE A LOT OF MAGIC BOOKS HERE TOO.
AND WHAT'S THIS...?
A "MAGIC SCROLL"...?
SKILLS ACQUIRED: "EXCAVATION" "TREASURE HUNTING" "TREASURE BOX UNLOCKING"

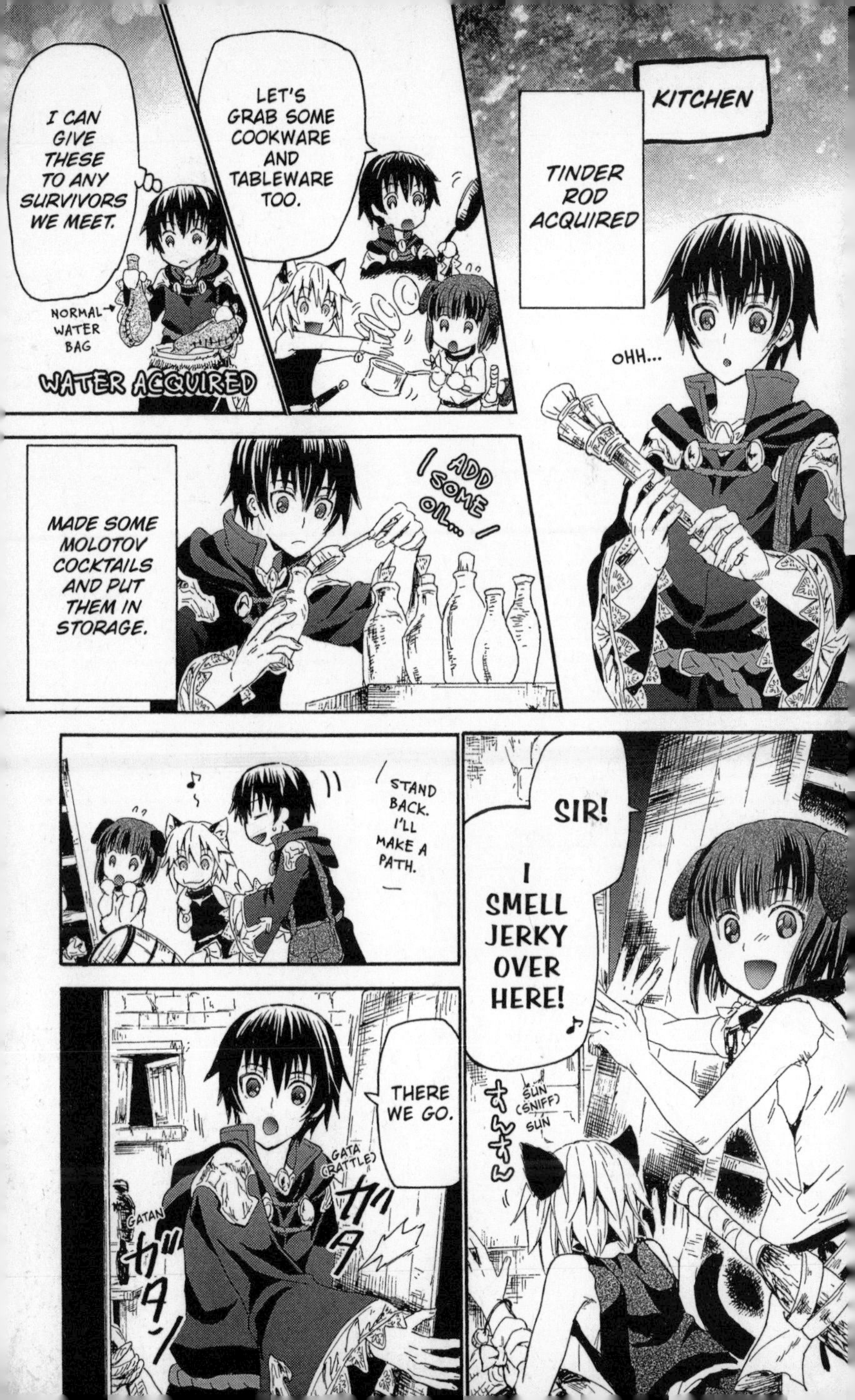
KITCHEN
TINDER ROD ACQUIRED
OHH...
LET'S GRAB SOME COOKWARE AND TABLEWARE TOO.
I CAN GIVE THESE TO ANY SURVIVORS WE MEET.
NORMAL WATER BAG
WATER ACQUIRED
I ADD SOME OIL...
MADE SOME MOLOTOV COCKTAILS AND PUT THEM IN STORAGE.
SIR!
I SMELL JERKY OVER HERE!
SUN (SNIFF) SUN
すんすん
STAND BACK. I'LL MAKE A PATH.
THERE WE GO.
GATA (RATTLE)
ガタ
GATAN
ガタン

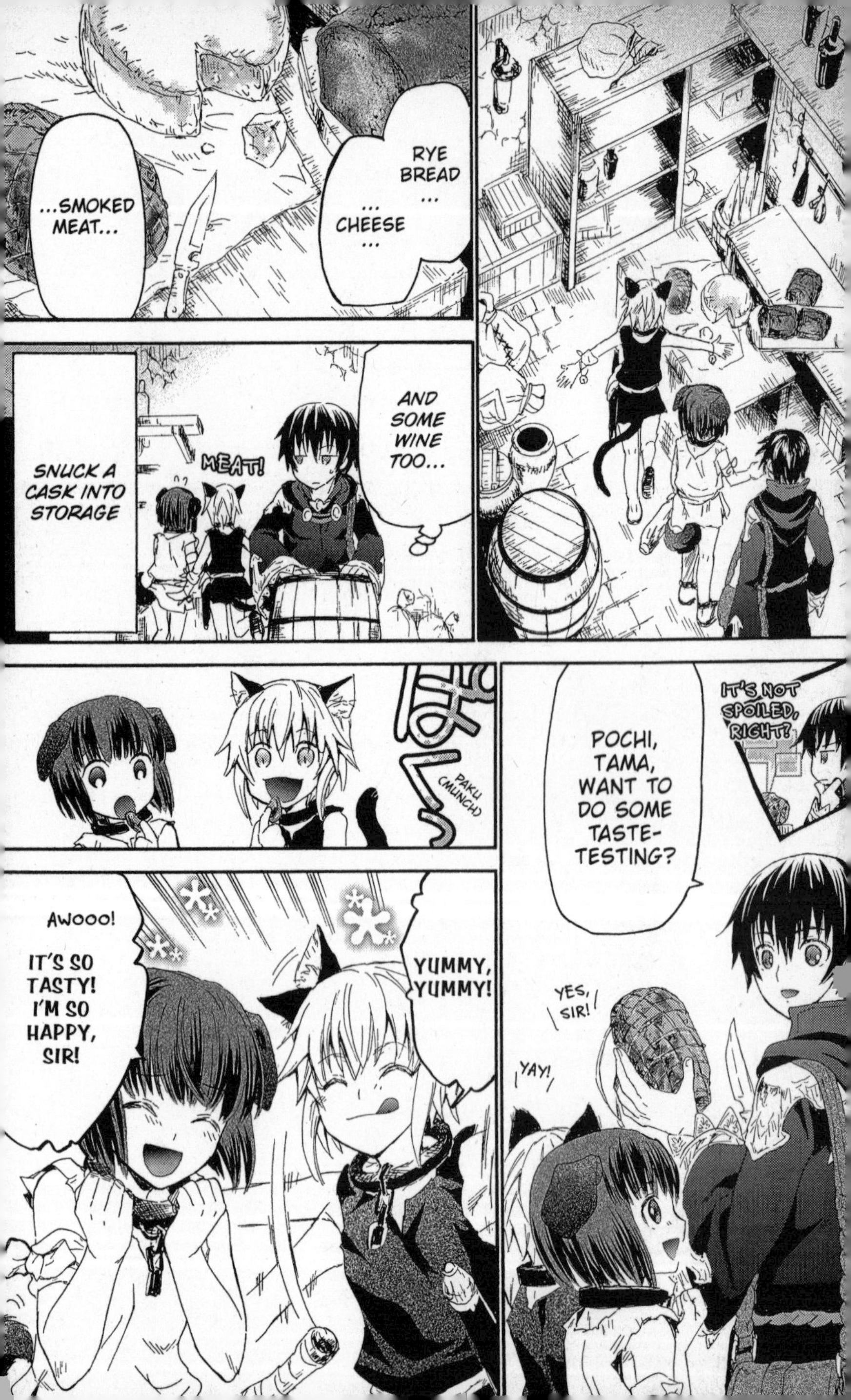
RYE BREAD ... CHEESE ...
...SMOKED MEAT...
AND SOME WINE TOO...
MEAT!
SNUCK A CASK INTO STORAGE
IT'S NOT SPOILED, RIGHT?
POCHI, TAMA, WANT TO DO SOME TASTE-TESTING?
YES, SIR!
YAY!
PAKU (MUNCH)
YUMMY, YUMMY!
AWOOO!
IT'S SO TASTY! I'M SO HAPPY, SIR!

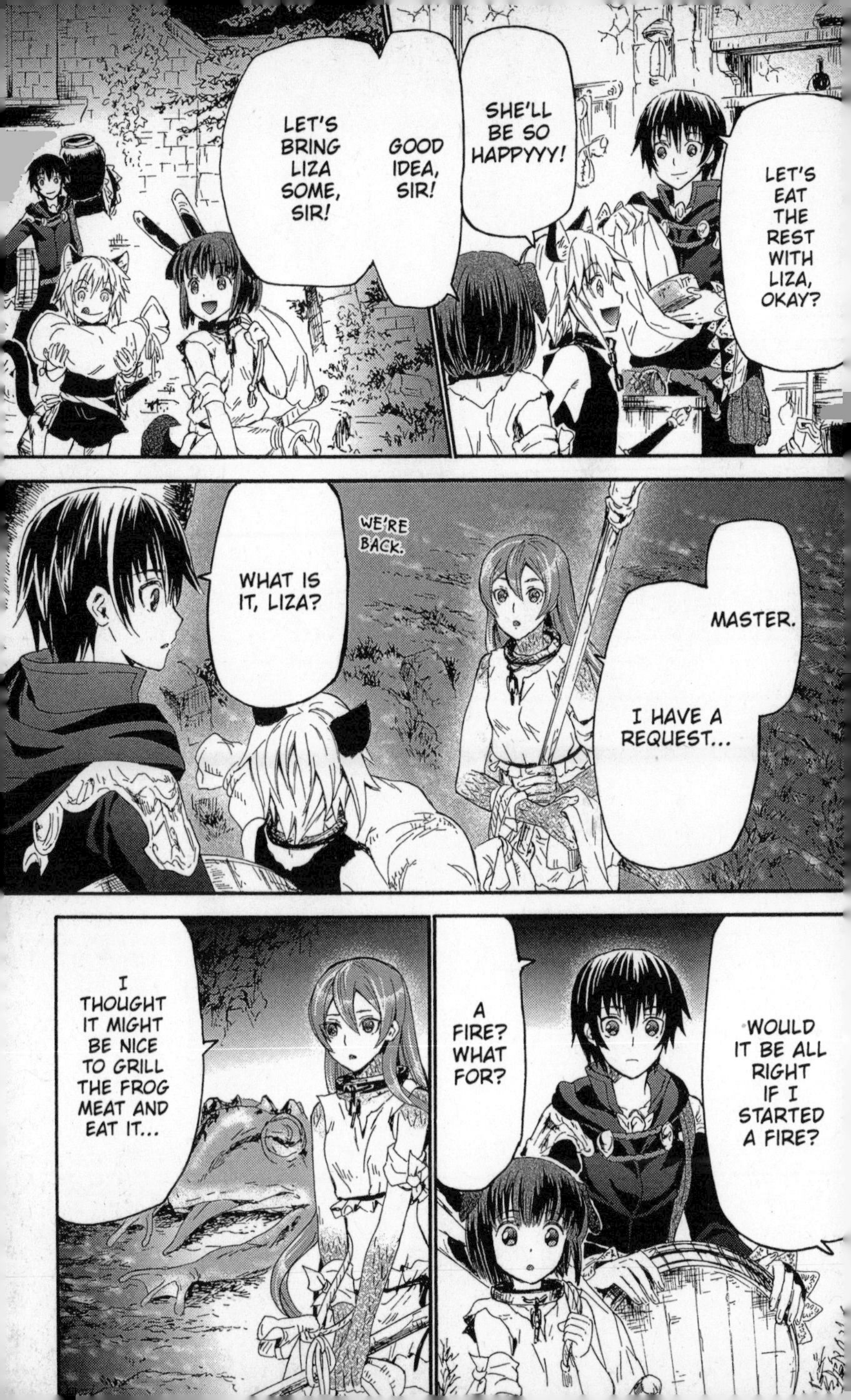
LET'S EAT THE REST WITH LIZA, OKAY?
SHE'LL BE SO HAPPYYY!
GOOD IDEA, SIR!
LET'S BRING LIZA SOME, SIR!
WE'RE BACK.
MASTER.
I HAVE A REQUEST...
WHAT IS IT, LIZA?
WOULD IT BE ALL RIGHT IF I STARTED A FIRE?
A FIRE? WHAT FOR?
I THOUGHT IT MIGHT BE NICE TO GRILL THE FROG MEAT AND EAT IT...

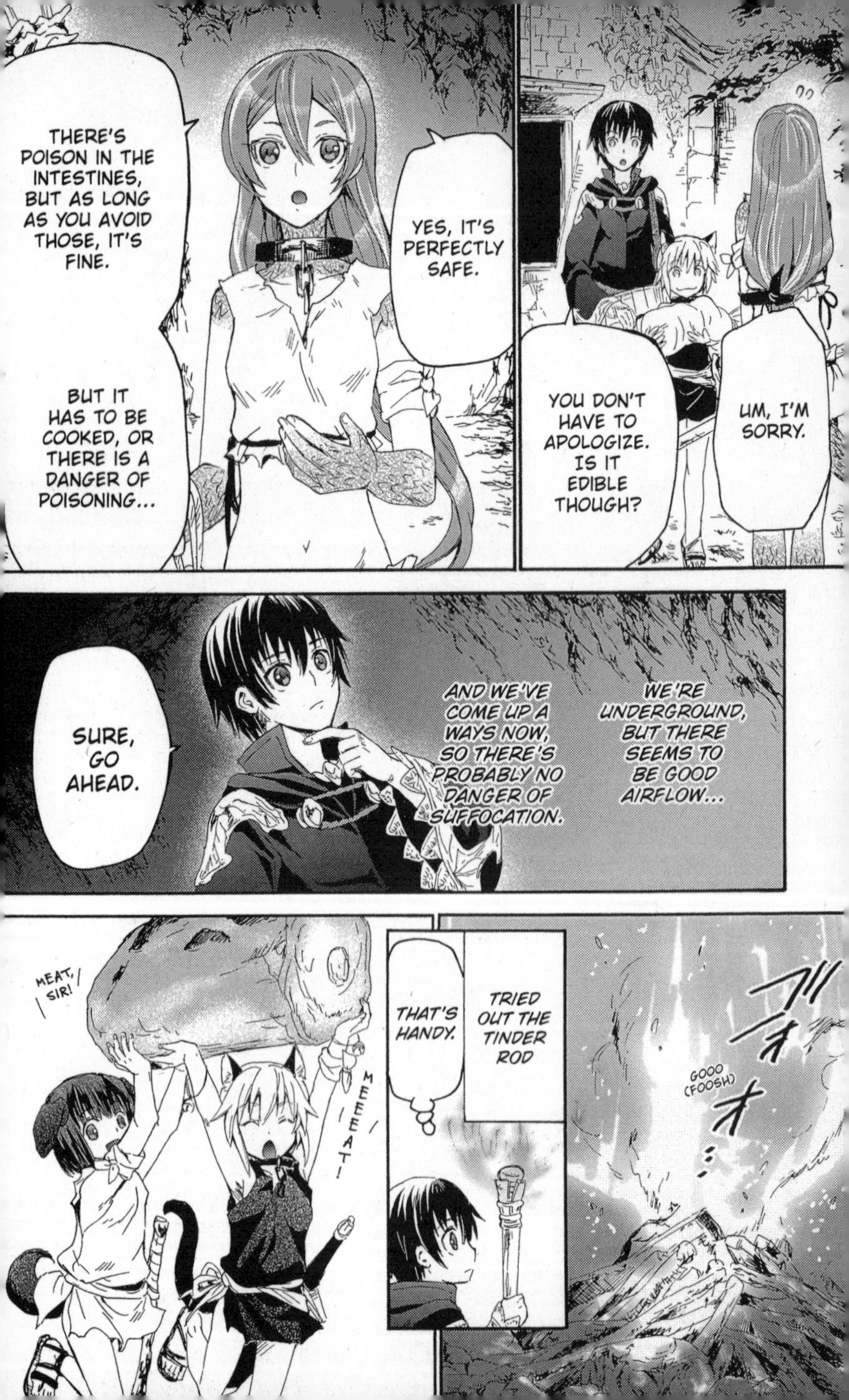
UM, I'M SORRY.
YOU DON'T HAVE TO APOLOGIZE. IS IT EDIBLE THOUGH?
YES, IT'S PERFECTLY SAFE.
THERE'S POISON IN THE INTESTINES, BUT AS LONG AS YOU AVOID THOSE, IT'S FINE.
BUT IT HAS TO BE COOKED, OR THERE IS A DANGER OF POISONING...
WE'RE UNDERGROUND, BUT THERE SEEMS TO BE GOOD AIRFLOW...
AND WE'VE COME UP A WAYS NOW, SO THERE'S PROBABLY NO DANGER OF SUFFOCATION.
SURE, GO AHEAD.
GOOO (FOOSH)
TRIED OUT THE TINDER ROD
THAT'S HANDY.
MEEEAT!
MEAT, SIR!

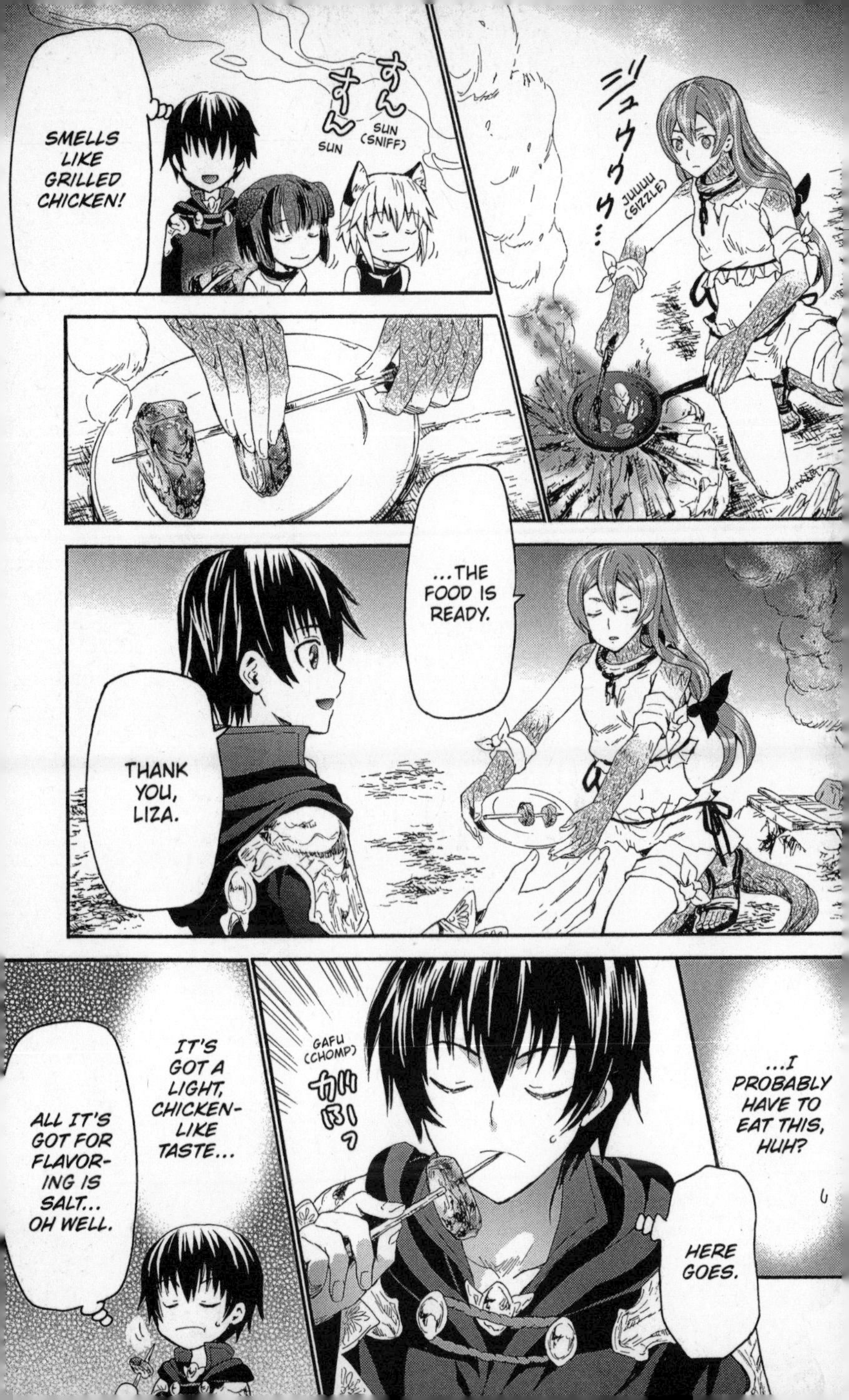
ジュウウウ…
JUUUU (SIZZLE)
すん すん
SUN SUN (SNIFF)
SMELLS LIKE GRILLED CHICKEN!
...THE FOOD IS READY.
THANK YOU, LIZA.
...I PROBABLY HAVE TO EAT THIS, HUH?
HERE GOES.
GAFU (CHOMP)
IT'S GOT A LIGHT, CHICKEN-LIKE TASTE...
ALL IT'S GOT FOR FLAVOR-ING IS SALT... OH WELL.

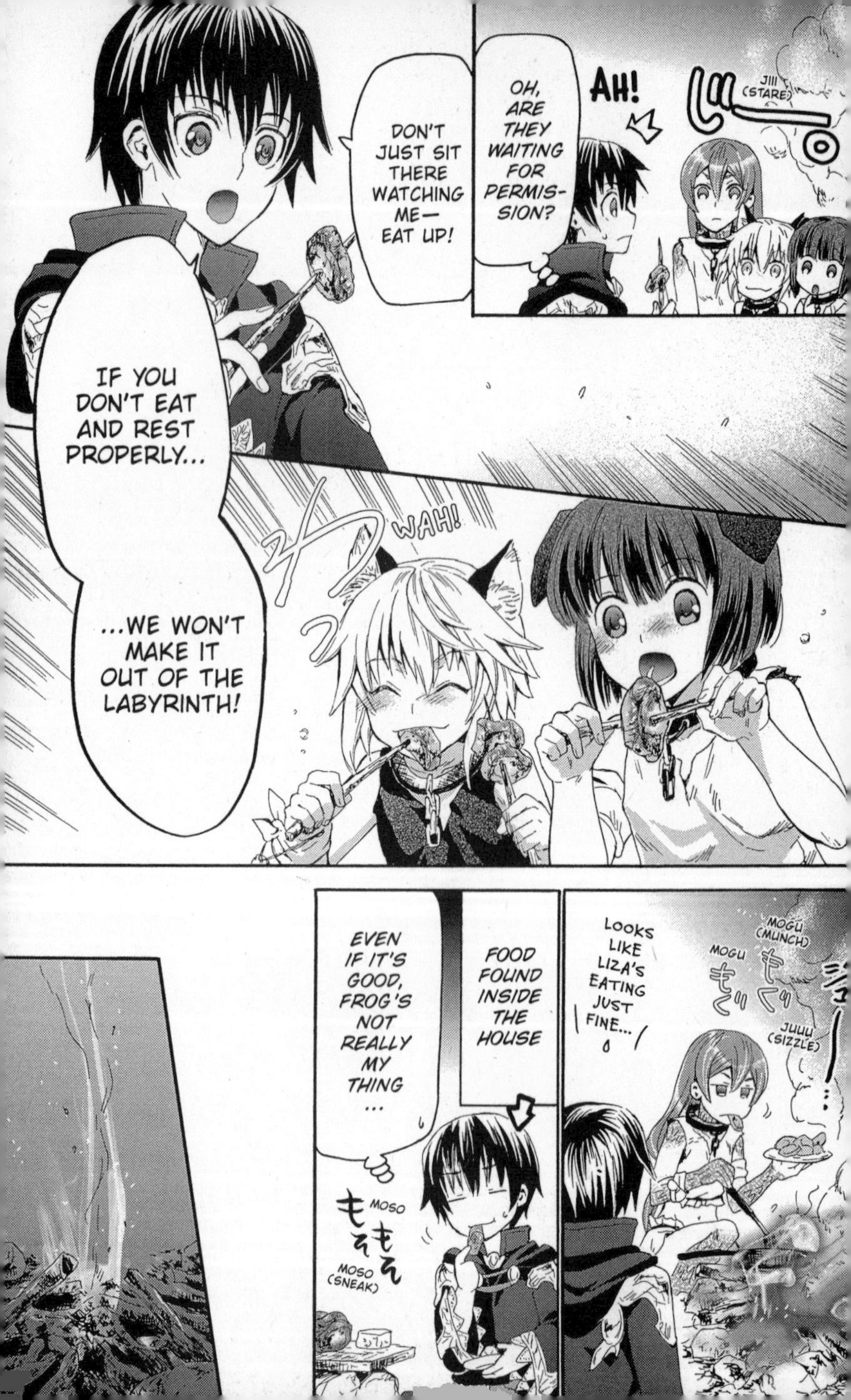
JIII (STARE)
AH!
OH, ARE THEY WAITING FOR PERMISSION?
DON'T JUST SIT THERE WATCHING ME—EAT UP!
IF YOU DON'T EAT AND REST PROPERLY...
WAH!
...WE WON'T MAKE IT OUT OF THE LABYRINTH!
MOGU (MUNCH) MOGU
JUUU (SIZZLE)
LOOKS LIKE LIZA'S EATING JUST FINE...
FOOD FOUND INSIDE THE HOUSE
EVEN IF IT'S GOOD, FROG'S NOT REALLY MY THING...
MOSO MOSO (SNEAK)

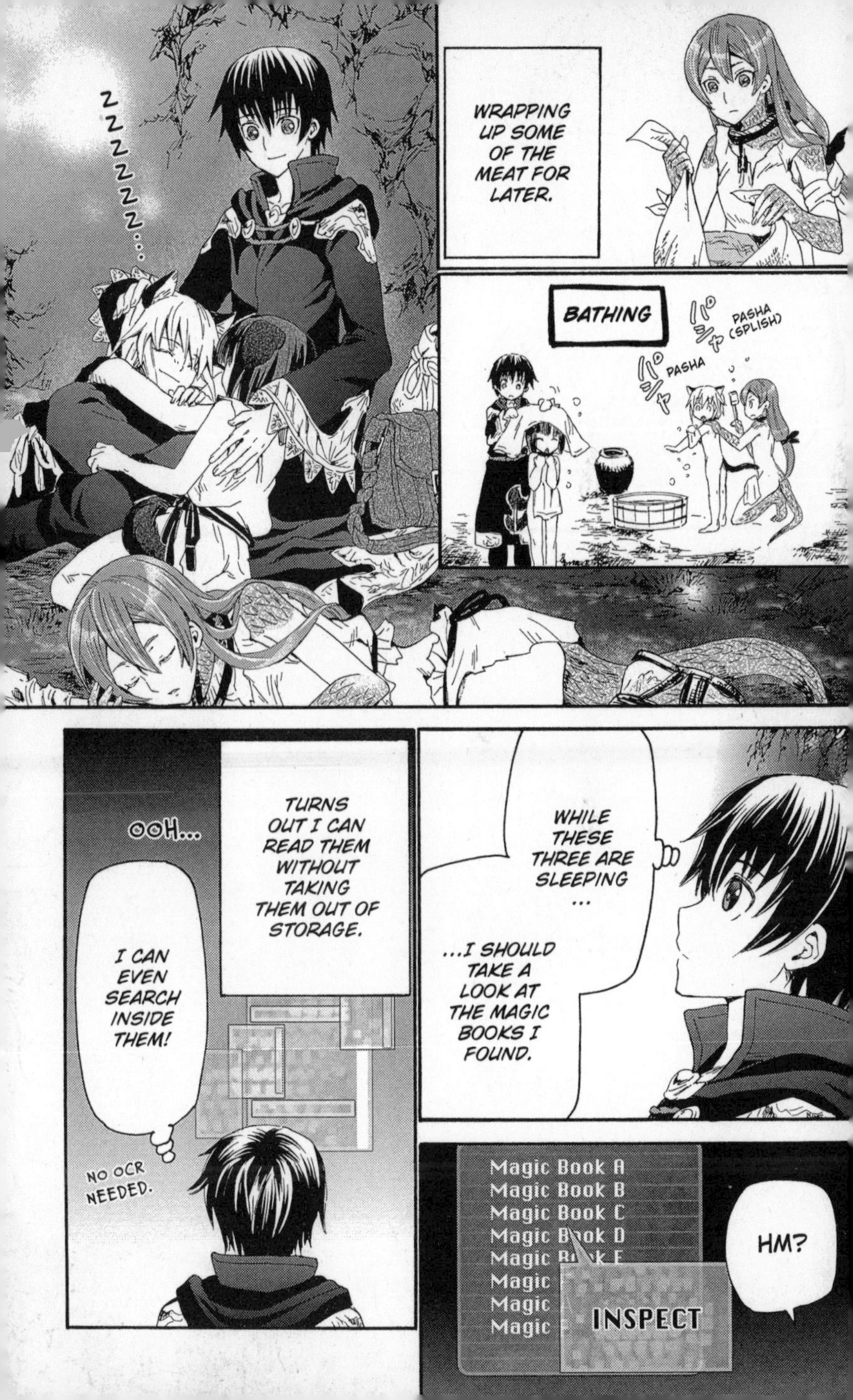
WRAPPING UP SOME OF THE MEAT FOR LATER.
BATHING
パシャ
PASHA (SPLISH)
パシャ
PASHA
ZZZZZZZ...
WHILE THESE THREE ARE SLEEPING...
...I SHOULD TAKE A LOOK AT THE MAGIC BOOKS I FOUND.
Magic Book A
Magic Book B
Magic Book C
Magic Book D
Magic Book E
Magic
Magic
Magic
INSPECT
HM?
OOH...
TURNS OUT I CAN READ THEM WITHOUT TAKING THEM OUT OF STORAGE.
I CAN EVEN SEARCH INSIDE THEM!
NO OCR NEEDED.

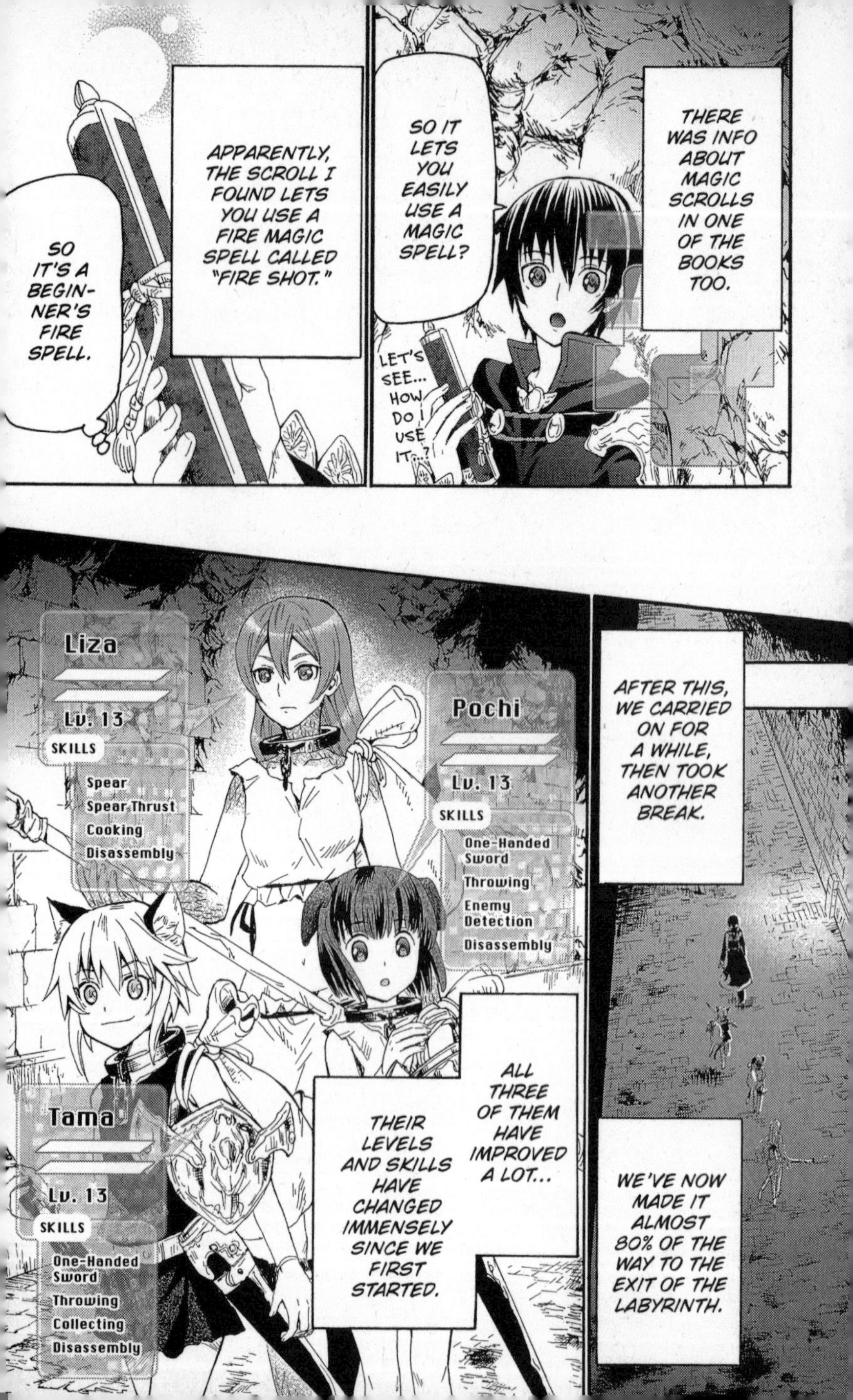
THERE WAS INFO ABOUT MAGIC SCROLLS IN ONE OF THE BOOKS TOO.
SO IT LETS YOU EASILY USE A MAGIC SPELL?
LET'S SEE... HOW DO I USE IT...?
APPARENTLY, THE SCROLL I FOUND LETS YOU USE A FIRE MAGIC SPELL CALLED "FIRE SHOT."
SO IT'S A BEGINNER'S FIRE SPELL.
AFTER THIS, WE CARRIED ON FOR A WHILE, THEN TOOK ANOTHER BREAK.
WE'VE NOW MADE IT ALMOST 80% OF THE WAY TO THE EXIT OF THE LABYRINTH.
Liza
Lv. 13
SKILLS
Spear
Spear Thrust
Cooking
Disassembly
Pochi
Lv. 13
SKILLS
One-Handed Sword
Throwing
Enemy Detection
Disassembly
ALL THREE OF THEM HAVE IMPROVED A LOT...
THEIR LEVELS AND SKILLS HAVE CHANGED IMMENSELY SINCE WE FIRST STARTED.
Tama
Lv. 13
SKILLS
One-Handed Sword
Throwing
Collecting
Disassembly

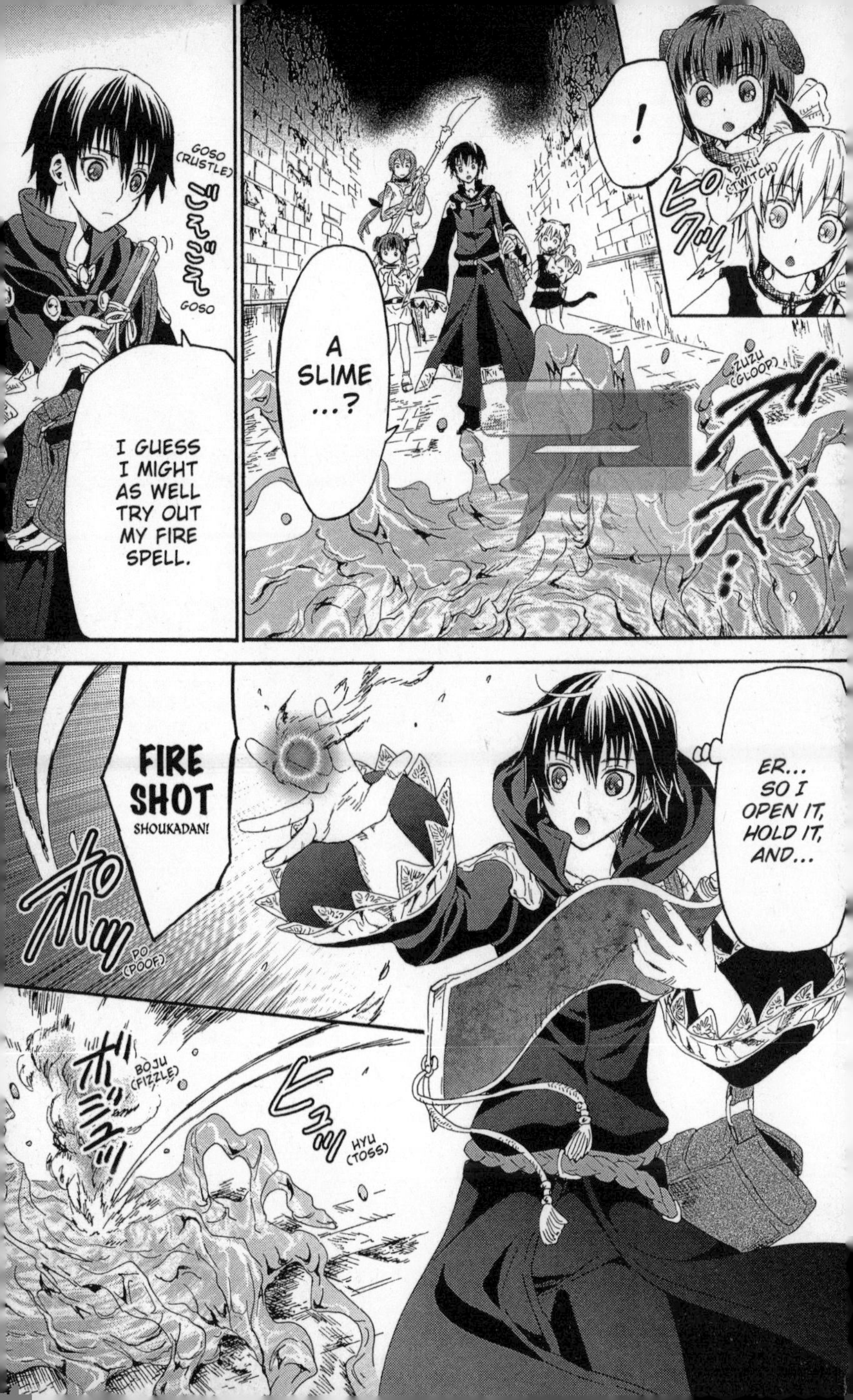
!
PIKU (TWITCH)
A SLIME ...?
ZUZU (GLOOP)
GOSO (RUSTLE)
GOSO
I GUESS I MIGHT AS WELL TRY OUT MY FIRE SPELL.
ER... SO I OPEN IT, HOLD IT, AND...
FIRE SHOT
SHOUKADAN!
PO (POOF)
HYU (TOSS)
BOJU (FIZZLE)

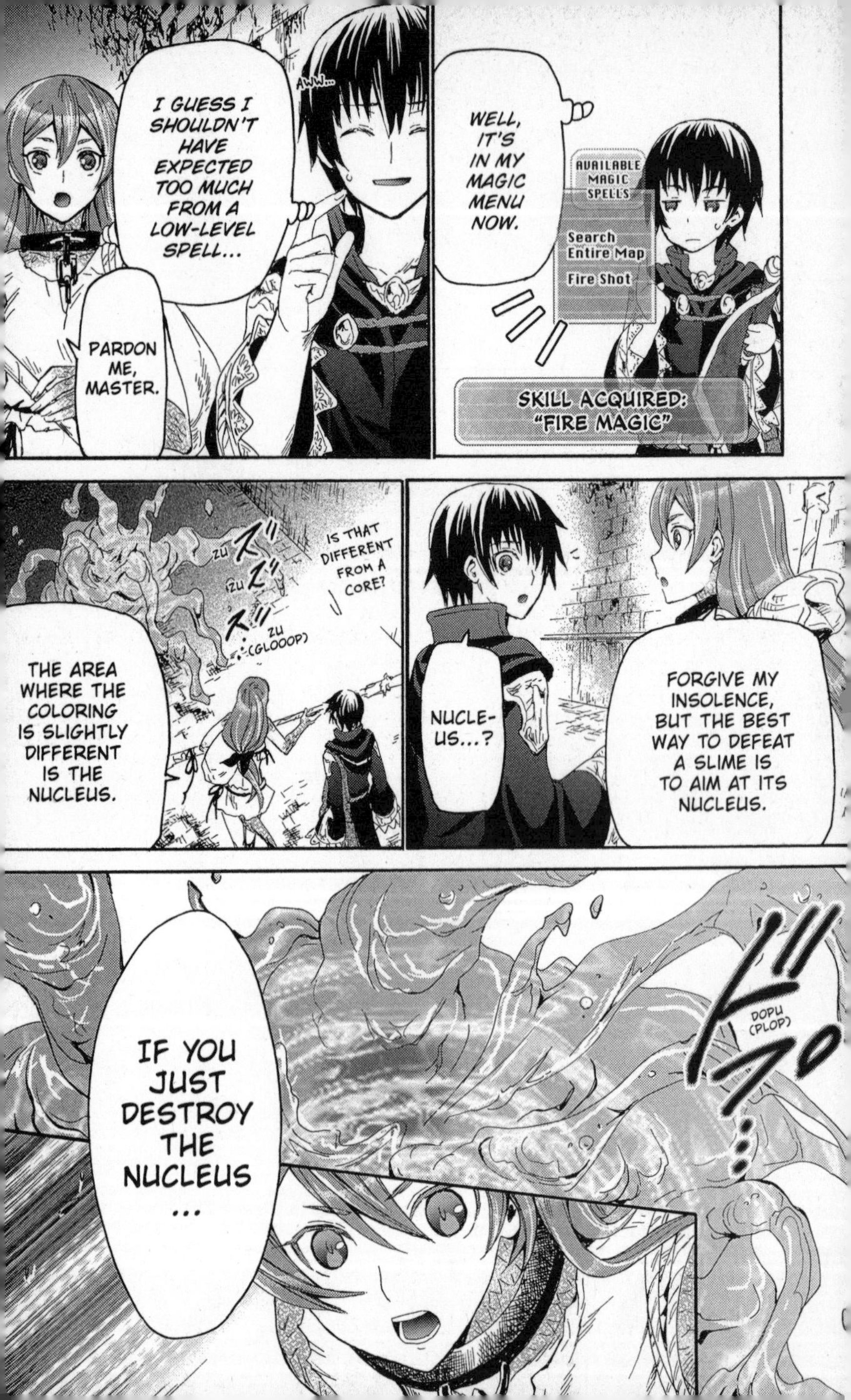
SKILL ACQUIRED: "FIRE MAGIC"
AVAILABLE MAGIC SPELLS
Search Entire Map
Fire Shot
WELL, IT'S IN MY MAGIC MENU NOW.
AWW...
I GUESS I SHOULDN'T HAVE EXPECTED TOO MUCH FROM A LOW-LEVEL SPELL...
PARDON ME, MASTER.
FORGIVE MY INSOLENCE, BUT THE BEST WAY TO DEFEAT A SLIME IS TO AIM AT ITS NUCLEUS.
NUCLE-US...?
IS THAT DIFFERENT FROM A CORE?
ZU ZU ZU (GLOOOP)
THE AREA WHERE THE COLORING IS SLIGHTLY DIFFERENT IS THE NUCLEUS.
DOPU (PLOP)
IF YOU JUST DESTROY THE NUCLEUS ...

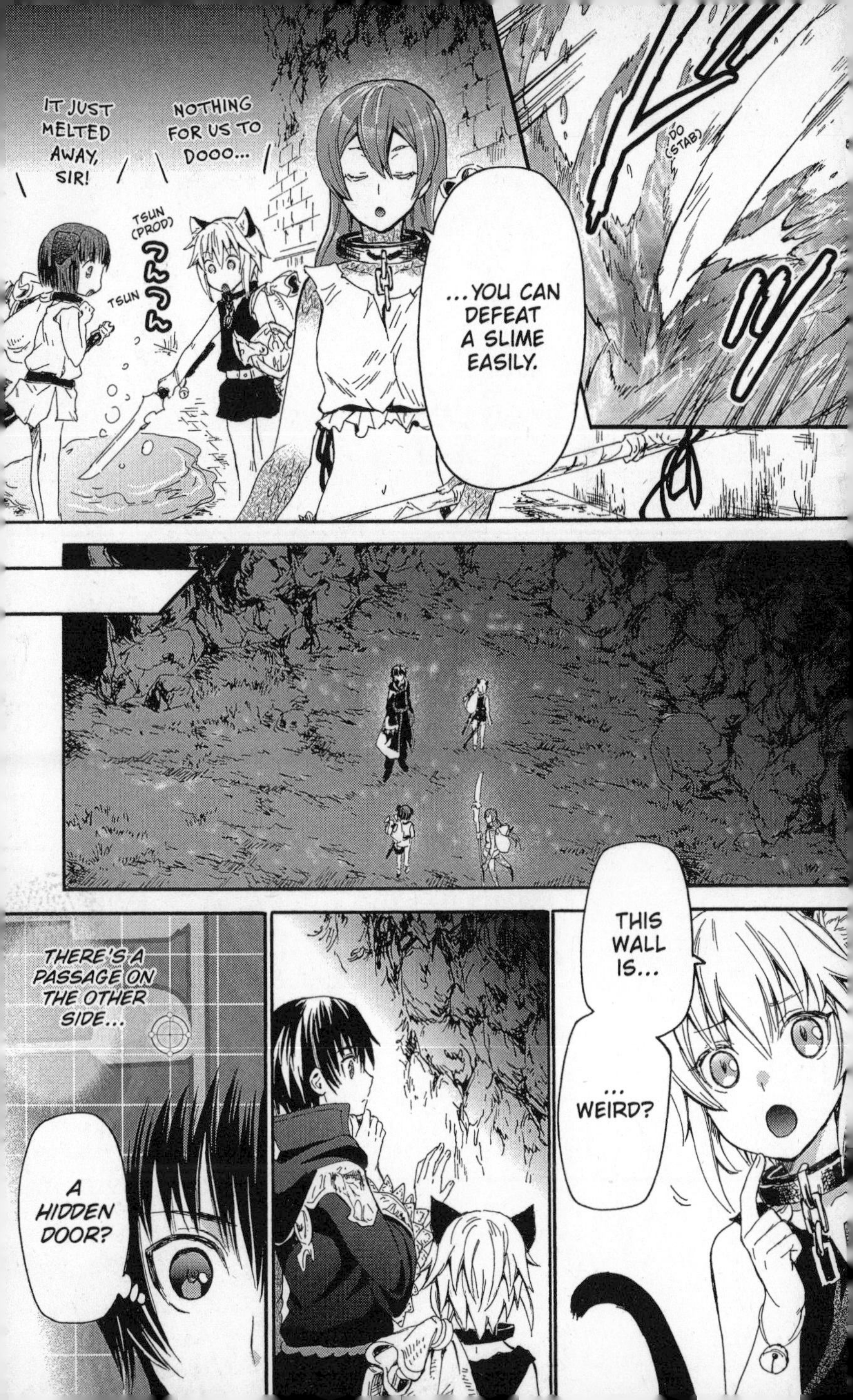
DO (STAB)
...YOU CAN DEFEAT A SLIME EASILY.
NOTHING FOR US TO DOOO...
IT JUST MELTED AWAY, SIR!
TSUN (PROD)
つんつん
TSUN
THIS WALL IS...
...WEIRD?
THERE'S A PASSAGE ON THE OTHER SIDE...
A HIDDEN DOOR?

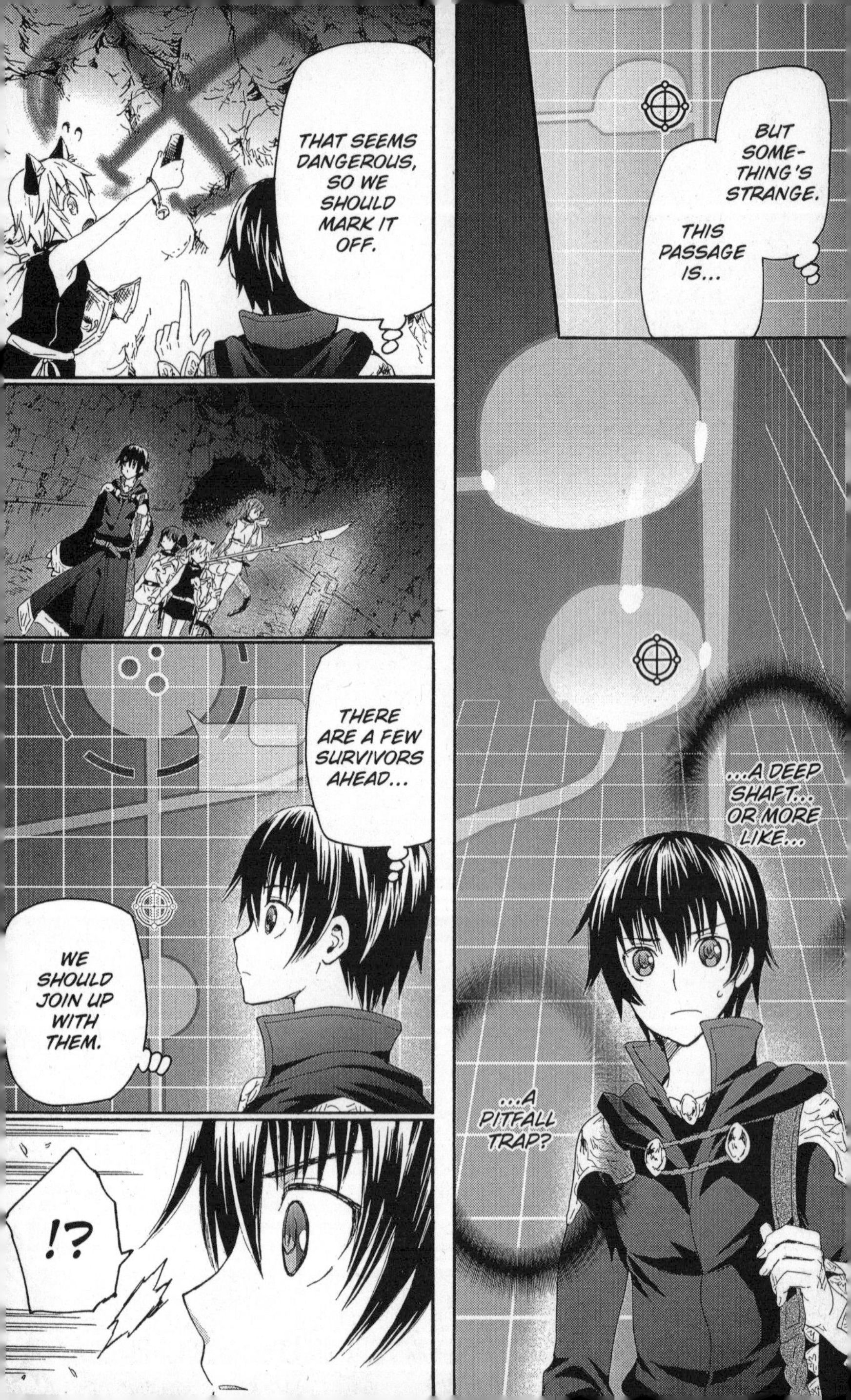
THAT SEEMS DANGEROUS, SO WE SHOULD MARK IT OFF.
THERE ARE A FEW SURVIVORS AHEAD...
WE SHOULD JOIN UP WITH THEM.
!?
BUT SOME-THING'S STRANGE.
THIS PASSAGE IS...
...A DEEP SHAFT... OR MORE LIKE...
...A PITFALL TRAP?

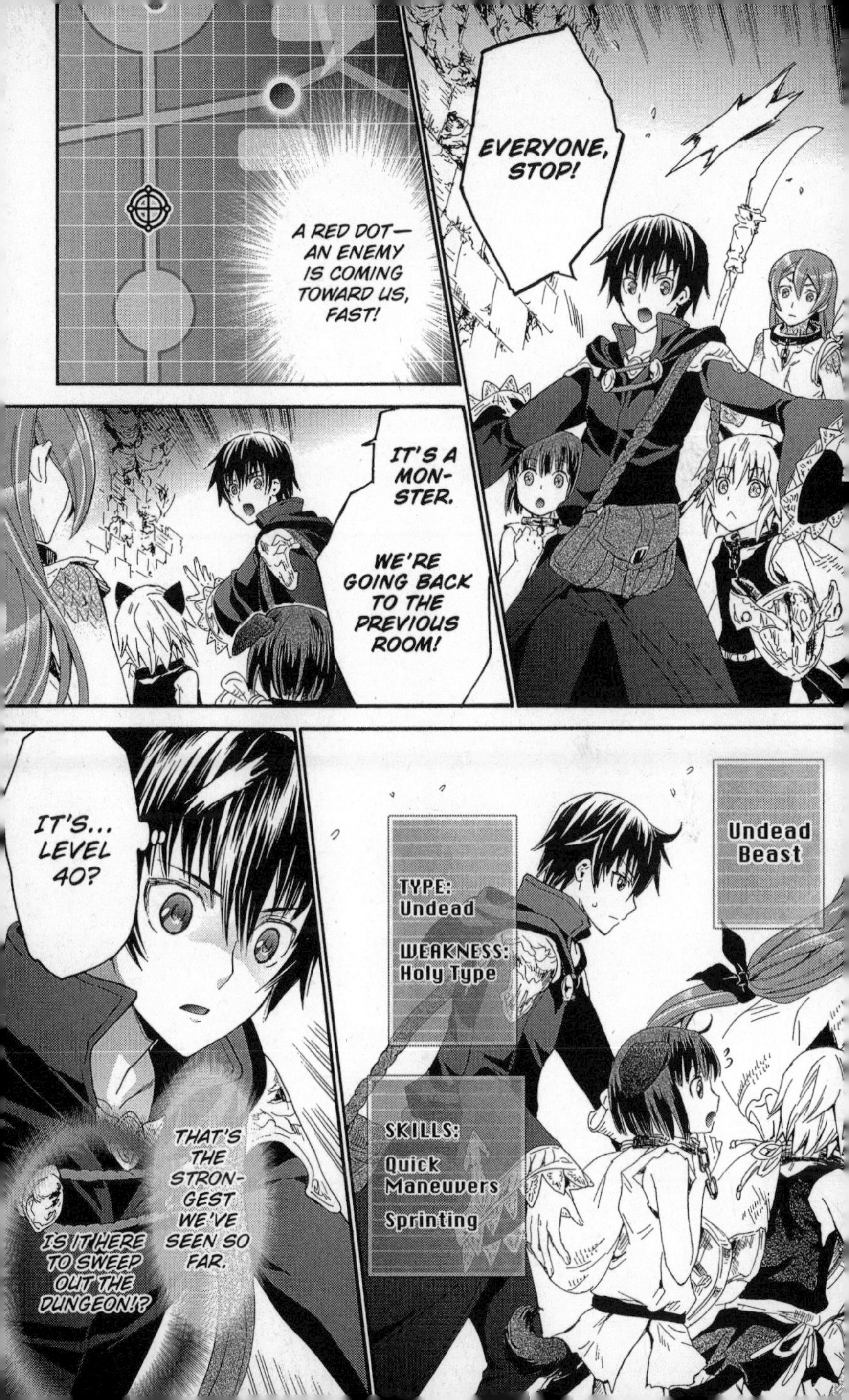
EVERYONE, STOP!
A RED DOT—AN ENEMY IS COMING TOWARD US, FAST!
IT'S A MON-STER.
WE'RE GOING BACK TO THE PREVIOUS ROOM!
Undead Beast
TYPE: Undead
WEAKNESS: Holy Type
SKILLS:
Quick Maneuvers
Sprinting
IT'S... LEVEL 40?
THAT'S THE STRON-GEST WE'VE SEEN SO FAR.
IS IT HERE TO SWEEP OUT THE DUNGEON!?

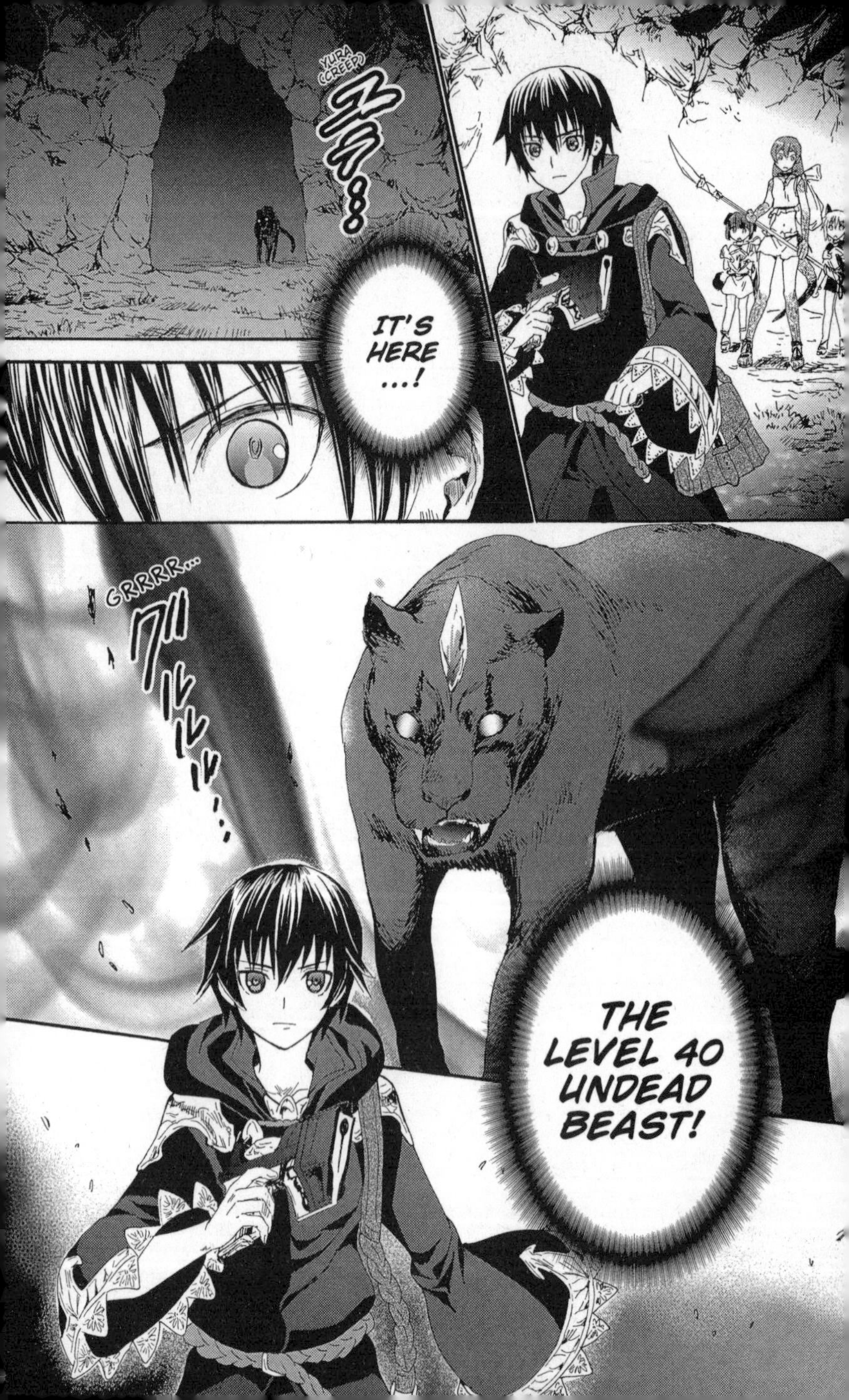
YURA (CREEP)
IT'S HERE ...!
GRRRR...
THE LEVEL 40 UNDEAD BEAST!

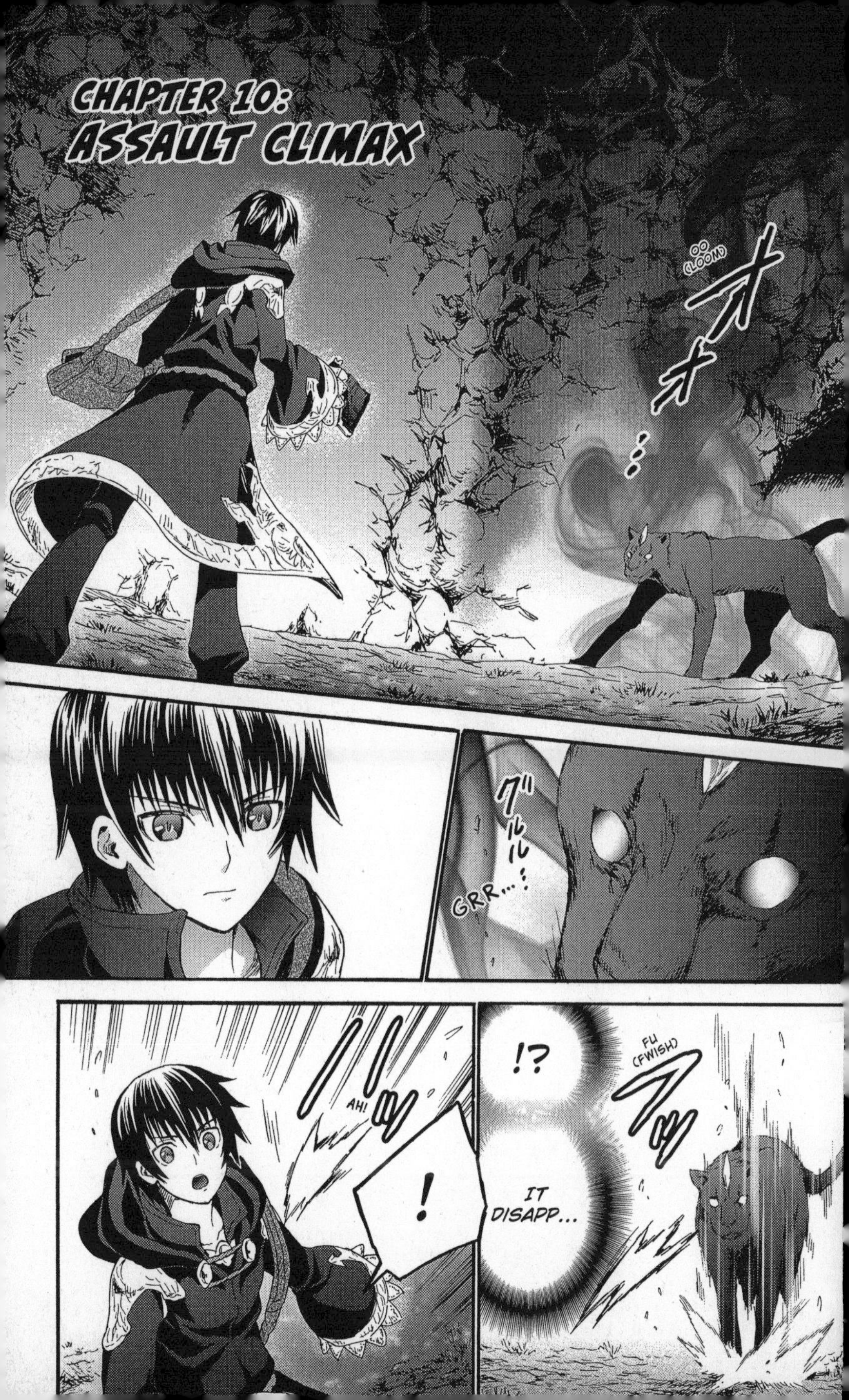
CHAPTER 10:
ASSAULT CLIMAX
OO (LOOM)
オォォ…
グルル…!
GRR...!
!?
FU (FWISH)
IT DISAPP...
AH!
!

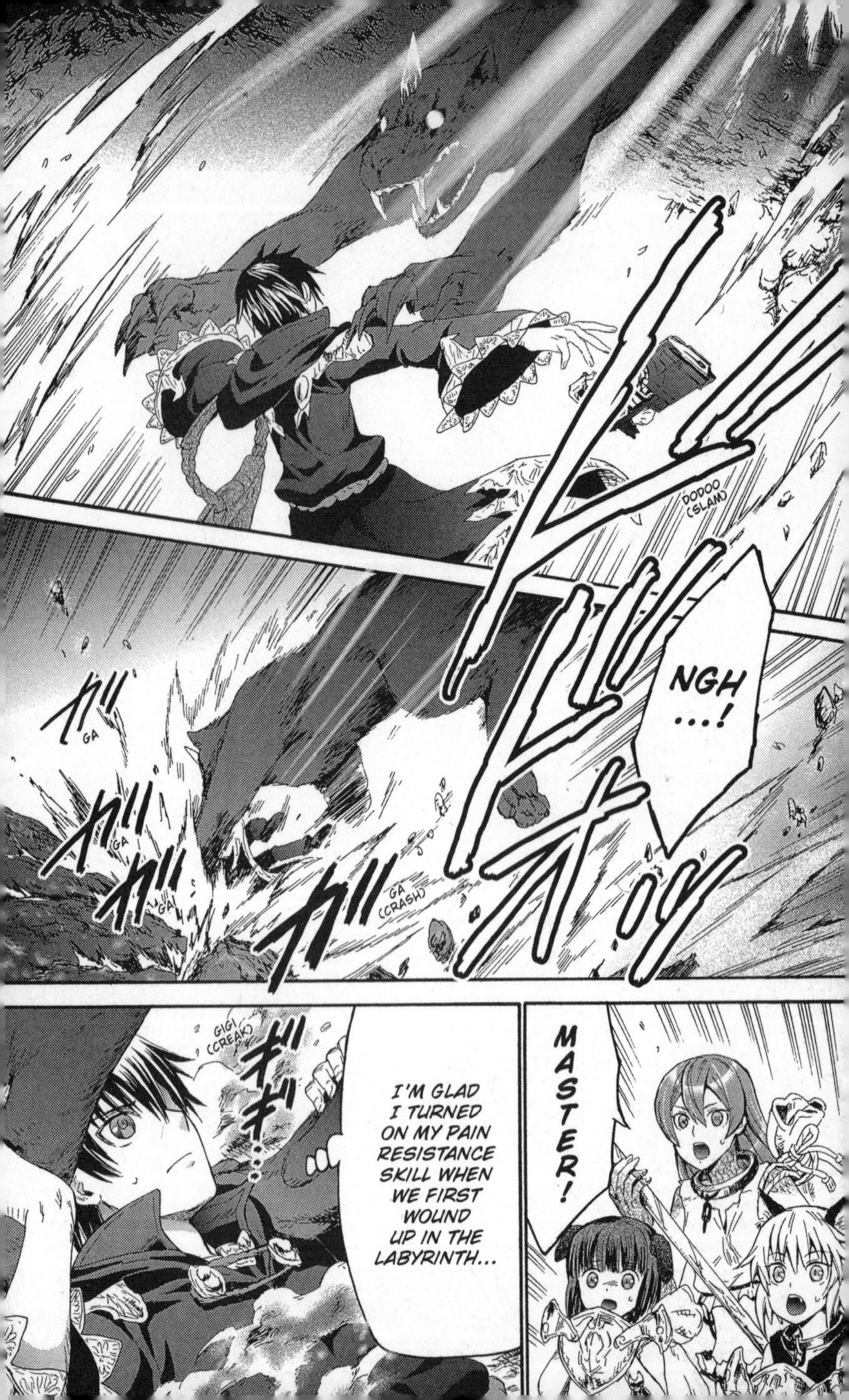
DODOO (SLAM)
NGH...!
GA (CRASH)
GA
GA
GA
MASTER!
GIGI (CREAK)
I'M GLAD I TURNED ON MY PAIN RESISTANCE SKILL WHEN WE FIRST WOUND UP IN THE LABYRINTH...

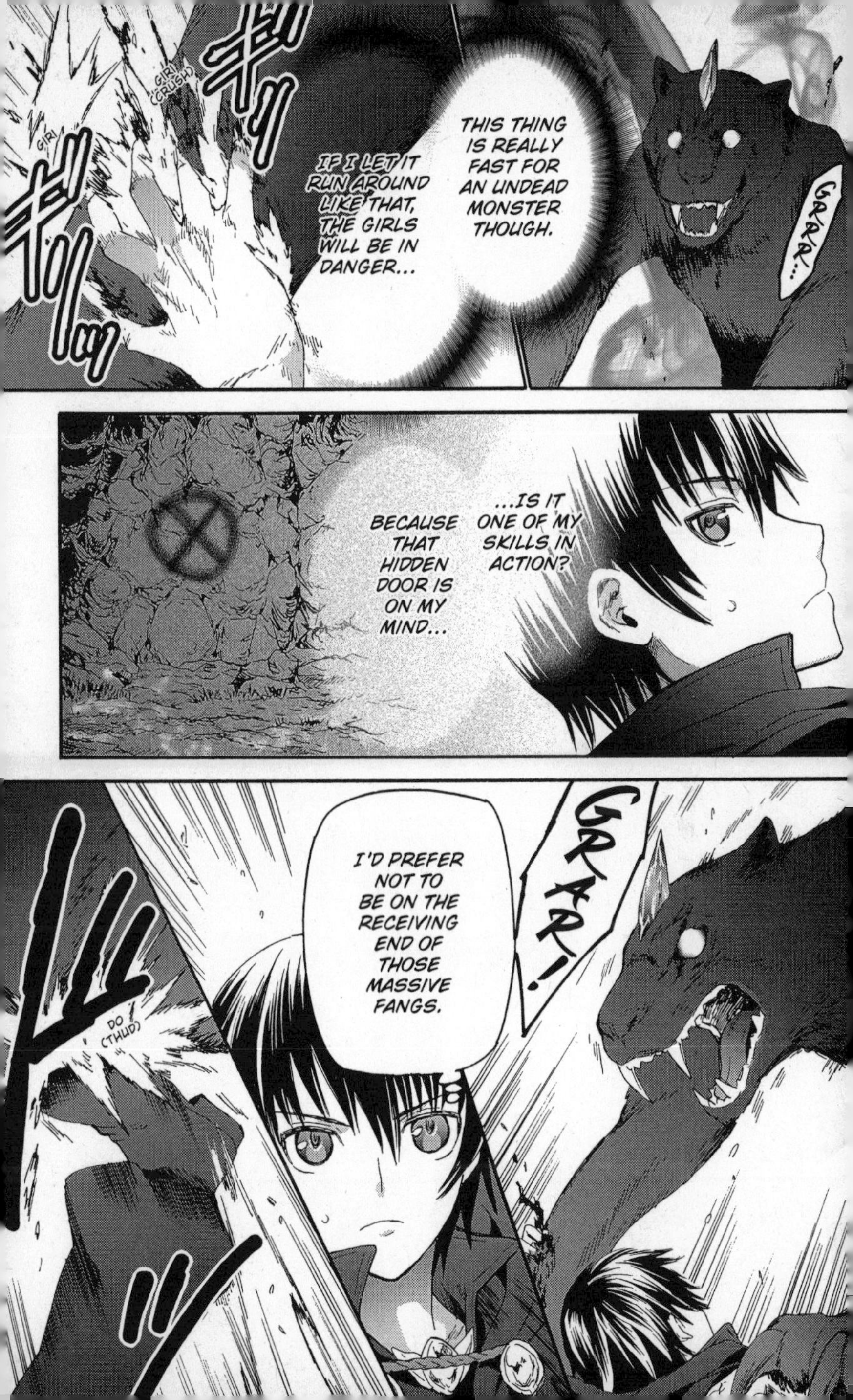

GRRRR...
THIS THING IS REALLY FAST FOR AN UNDEAD MONSTER THOUGH.
IF I LET IT RUN AROUND LIKE THAT, THE GIRLS WILL BE IN DANGER...
GIRI (CRUSH)
GIRI
...IS IT ONE OF MY SKILLS IN ACTION?
BECAUSE THAT HIDDEN DOOR IS ON MY MIND...
GRAR!
I'D PREFER NOT TO BE ON THE RECEIVING END OF THOSE MASSIVE FANGS.
DO (THUD)

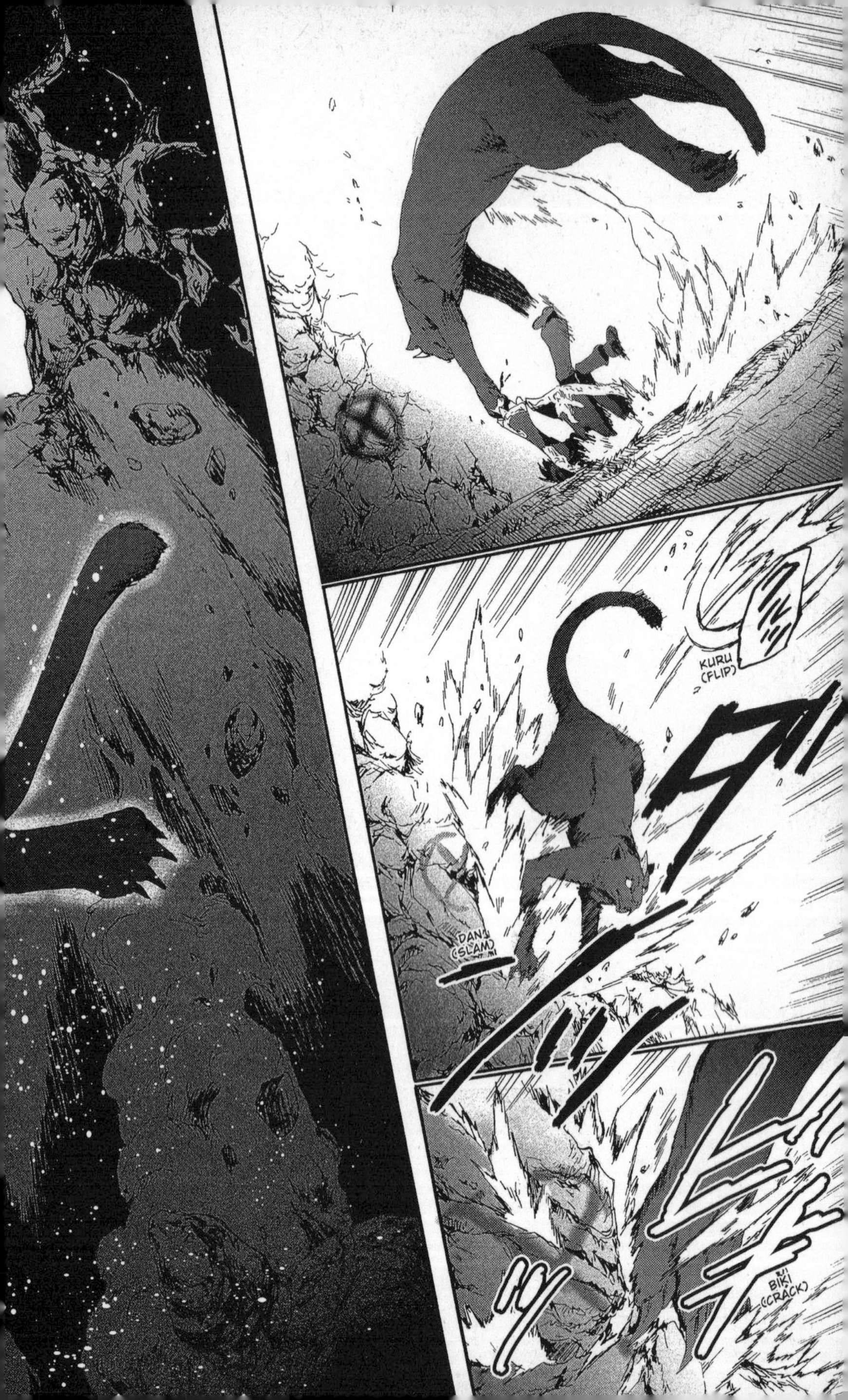
KURU (FLIP)
DAN (SLAM)
BIKI (CRACK)

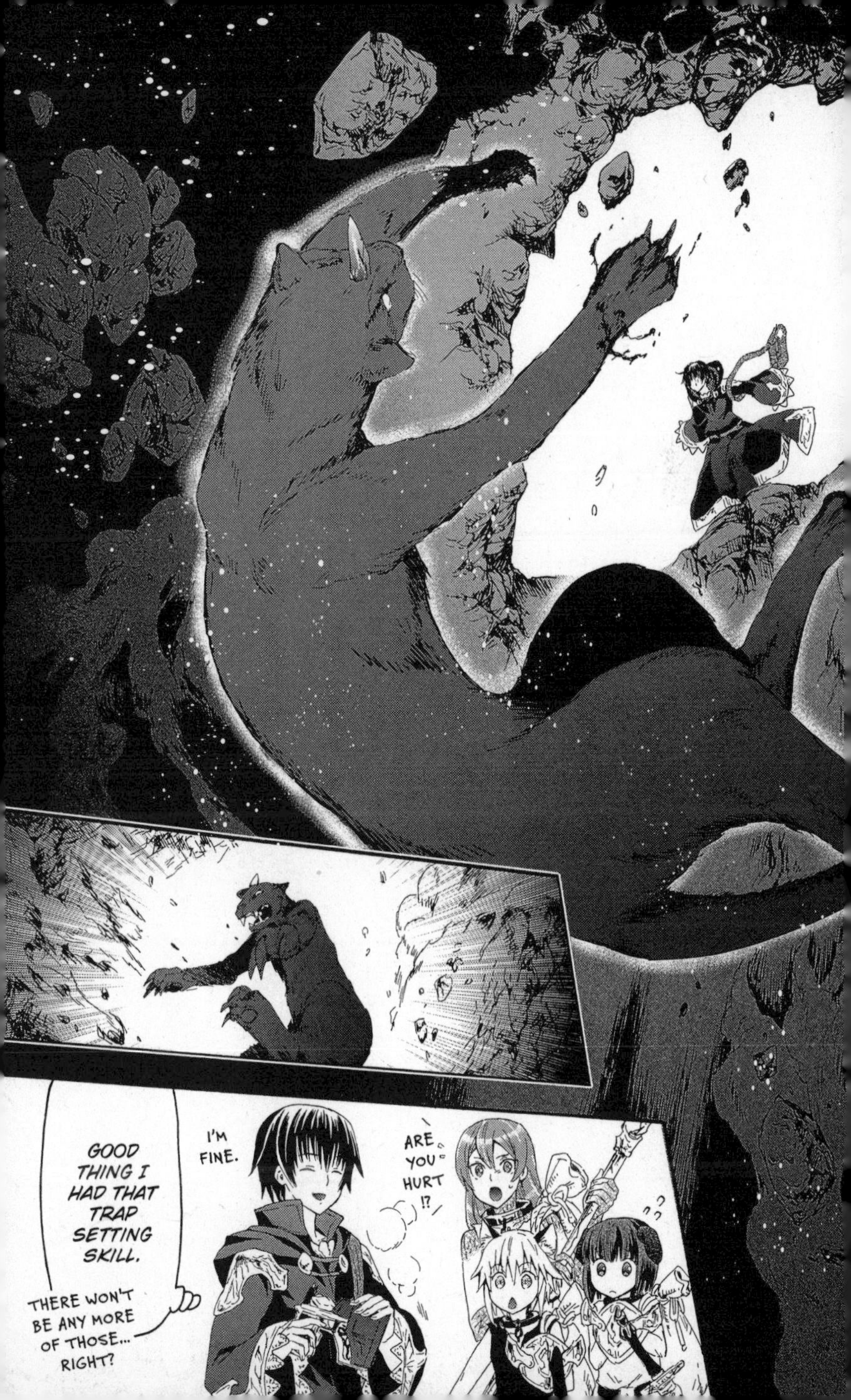
ARE YOU HURT!?
I'M FINE.
GOOD THING I HAD THAT TRAP SETTING SKILL.
THERE WON'T BE ANY MORE OF THOSE... RIGHT?

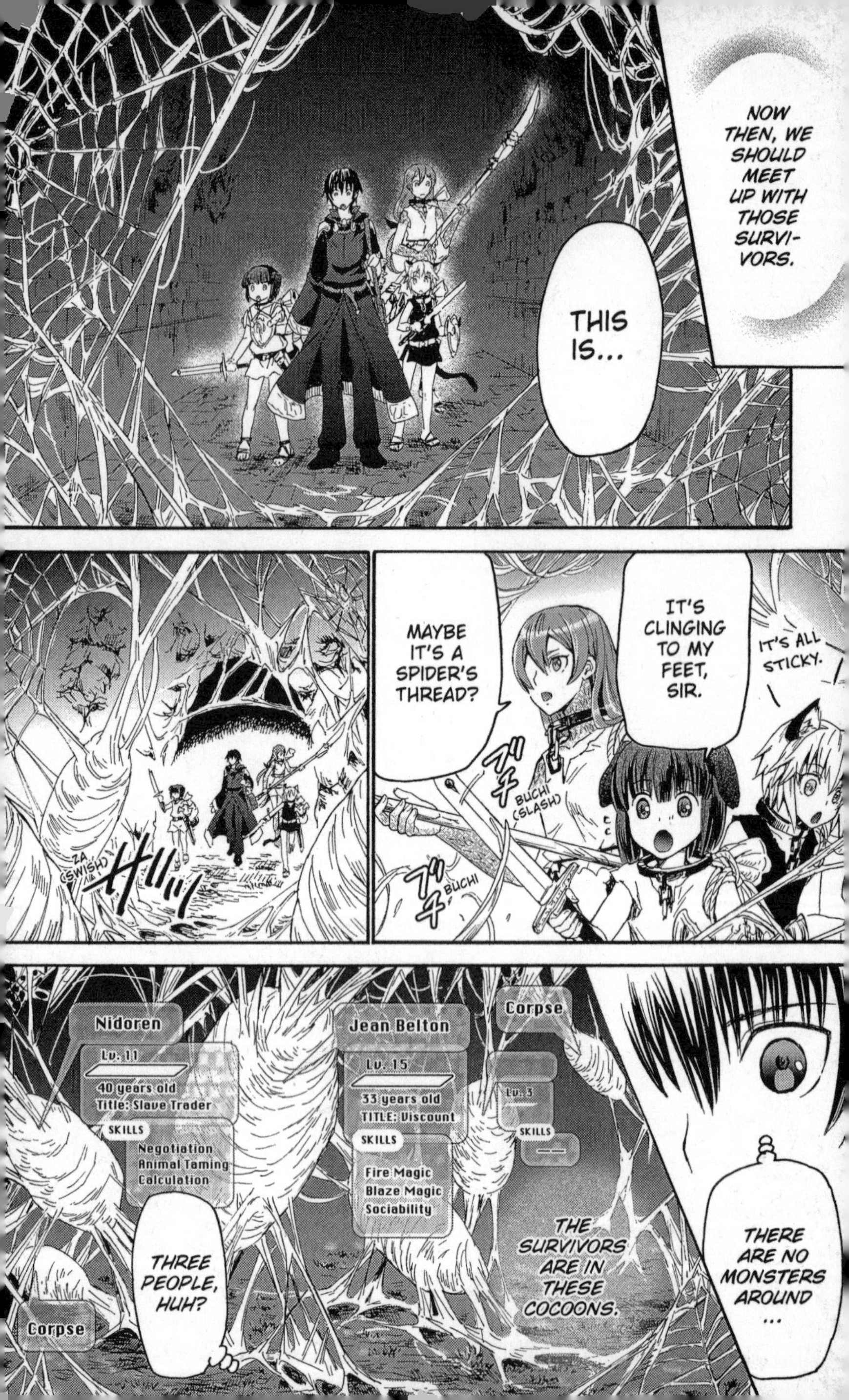
NOW THEN, WE SHOULD MEET UP WITH THOSE SURVIVORS.
THIS IS...
IT'S ALL STICKY.
IT'S CLINGING TO MY FEET, SIR.
MAYBE IT'S A SPIDER'S THREAD?
BUCHI (SLASH)
BUCHI
ZA (SWISH)
THERE ARE NO MONSTERS AROUND ...
THE SURVIVORS ARE IN THESE COCOONS.
Corpse
Lv. 3
SKILLS
——
Jean Belton
Lv. 15
33 years old
TITLE: Viscount
SKILLS
Fire Magic
Blaze Magic
Sociability
Nidoren
Lv. 11
40 years old
Title: Slave Trader
SKILLS
Negotiation
Animal Taming
Calculation
THREE PEOPLE, HUH?
Corpse

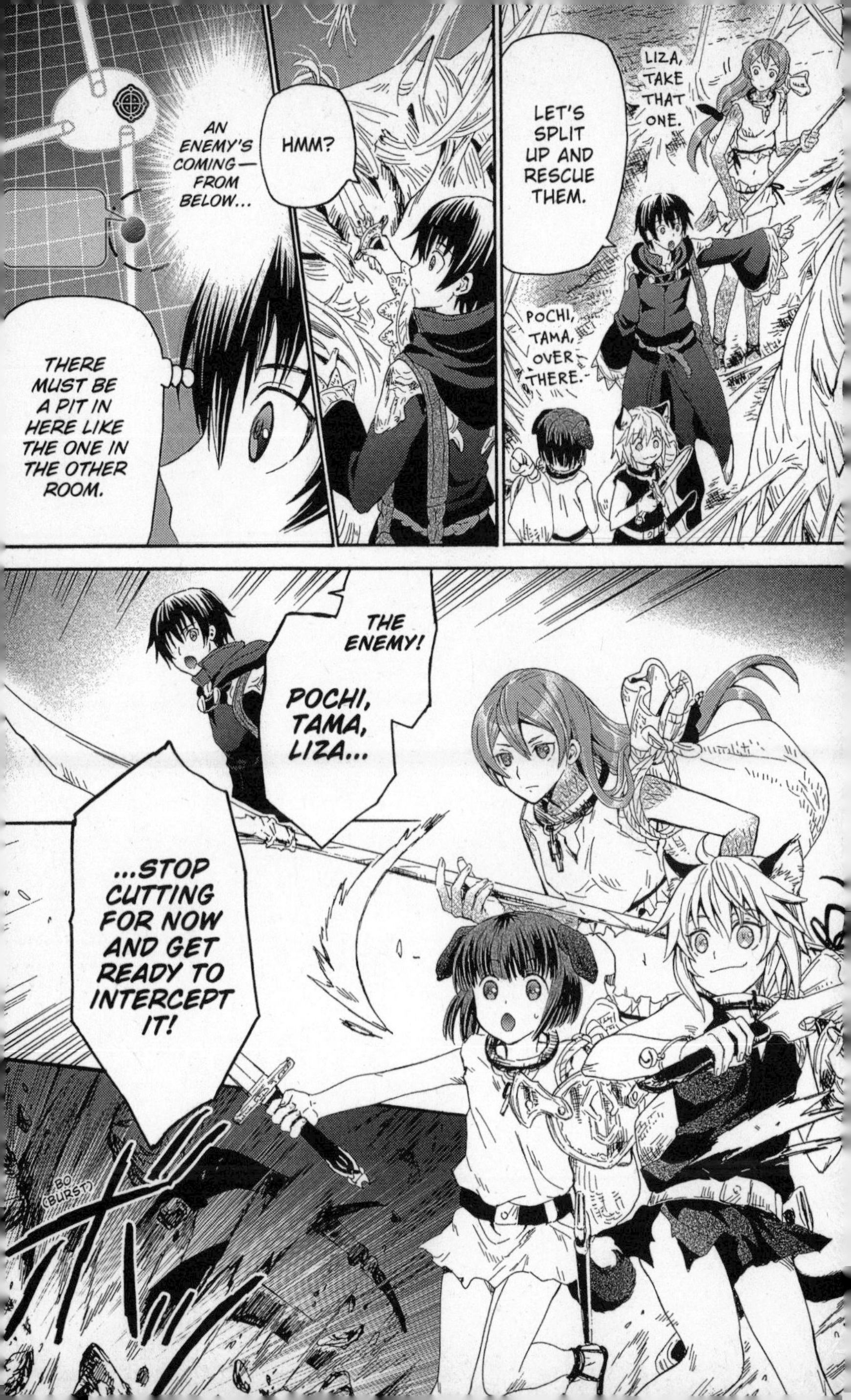
LET'S SPLIT UP AND RESCUE THEM.
LIZA, TAKE THAT ONE.
POCHI, TAMA, OVER THERE.
HMM?
AN ENEMY'S COMING— FROM BELOW...
THERE MUST BE A PIT IN HERE LIKE THE ONE IN THE OTHER ROOM.
THE ENEMY!
POCHI, TAMA, LIZA...
...STOP CUTTING FOR NOW AND GET READY TO INTERCEPT IT!
BO (BURST)

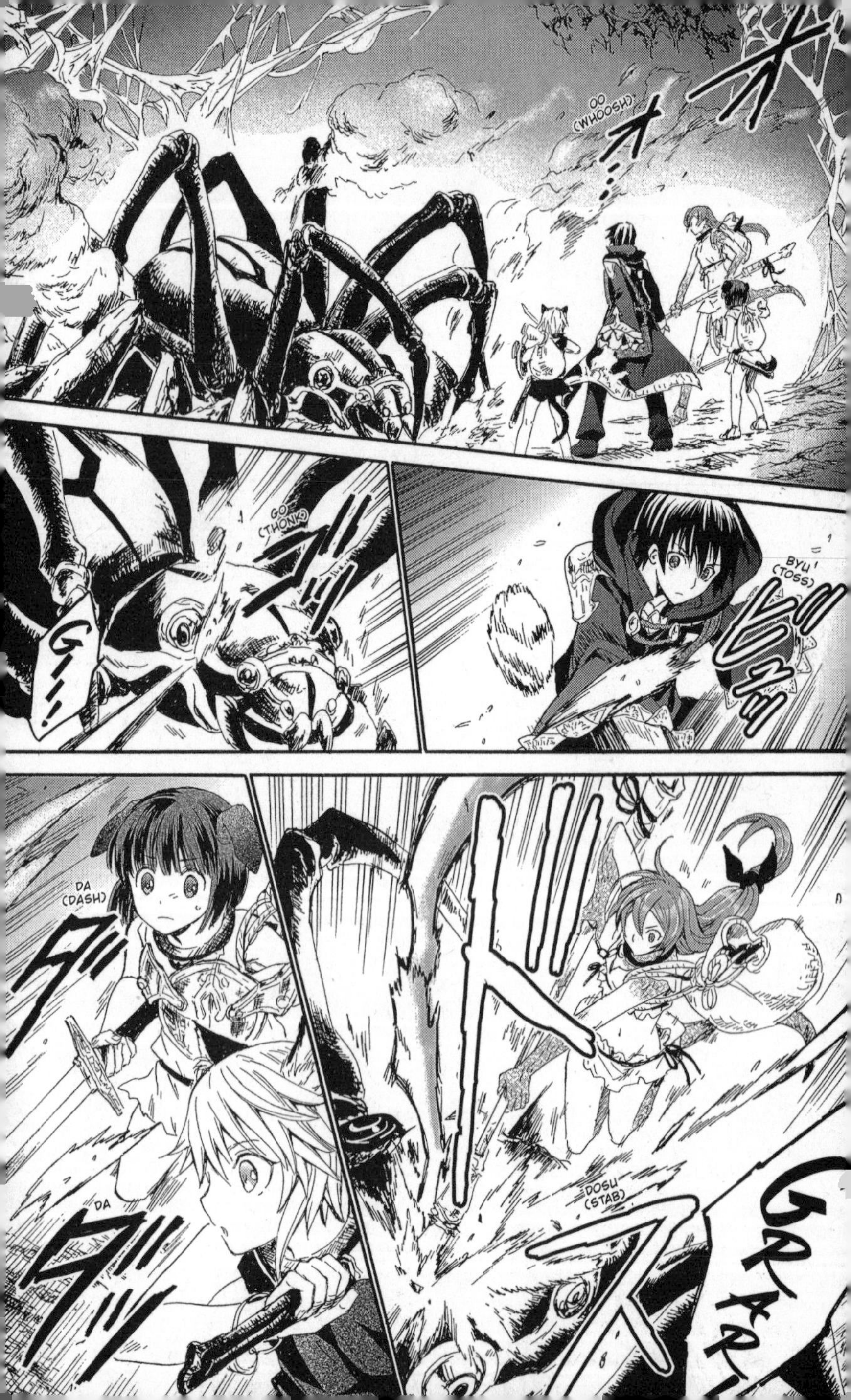

OO (WHOOSH)
BYU (TOSS)
GO (THONK)
G--!
DOSU (STAB)
GRARI!
DA (DASH)
DA

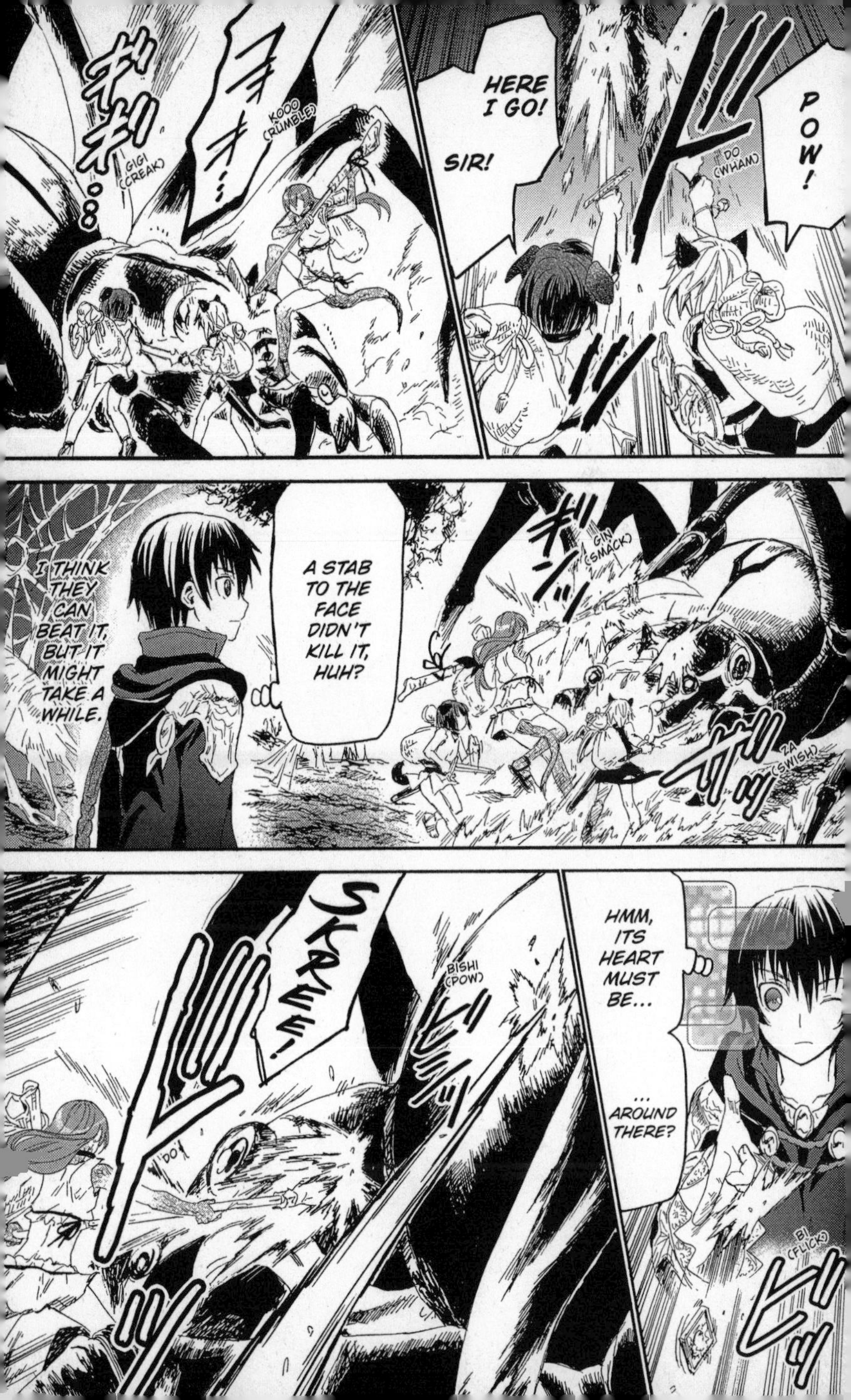

HERE I GO!
SIR!
POW!
DO (WHAM)
KOOO (RUMBLE)
GIGI (CREAK)
GIN (SMACK)
ZA (SWISH)
A STAB TO THE FACE DIDN'T KILL IT, HUH?
I THINK THEY CAN BEAT IT, BUT IT MIGHT TAKE A WHILE.
HMM, ITS HEART MUST BE...
...AROUND THERE?
BI (FLICK)
SKREE!
BISHI (POW)
DO

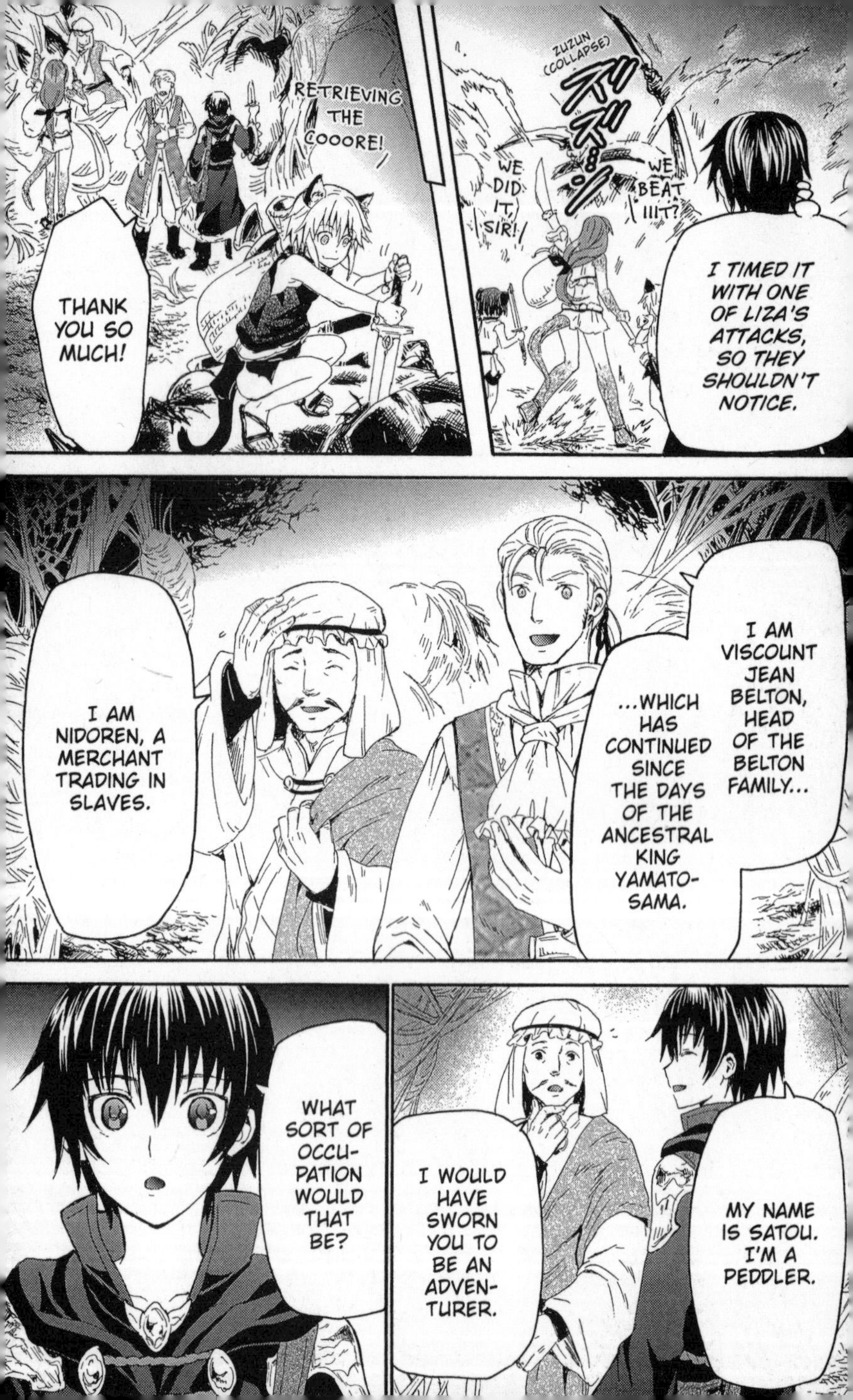
ZUZUN (COLLAPSE)
I TIMED IT WITH ONE OF LIZA'S ATTACKS, SO THEY SHOULDN'T NOTICE.
WE BEAT IIIT?
WE DID IT, SIR!
RETRIEVING THE COOORE!
THANK YOU SO MUCH!
I AM VISCOUNT JEAN BELTON, HEAD OF THE BELTON FAMILY...
...WHICH HAS CONTINUED SINCE THE DAYS OF THE ANCESTRAL KING YAMATO-SAMA.
I AM NIDOREN, A MERCHANT TRADING IN SLAVES.
MY NAME IS SATOU. I'M A PEDDLER.
I WOULD HAVE SWORN YOU TO BE AN ADVEN-TURER.
WHAT SORT OF OCCU-PATION WOULD THAT BE?

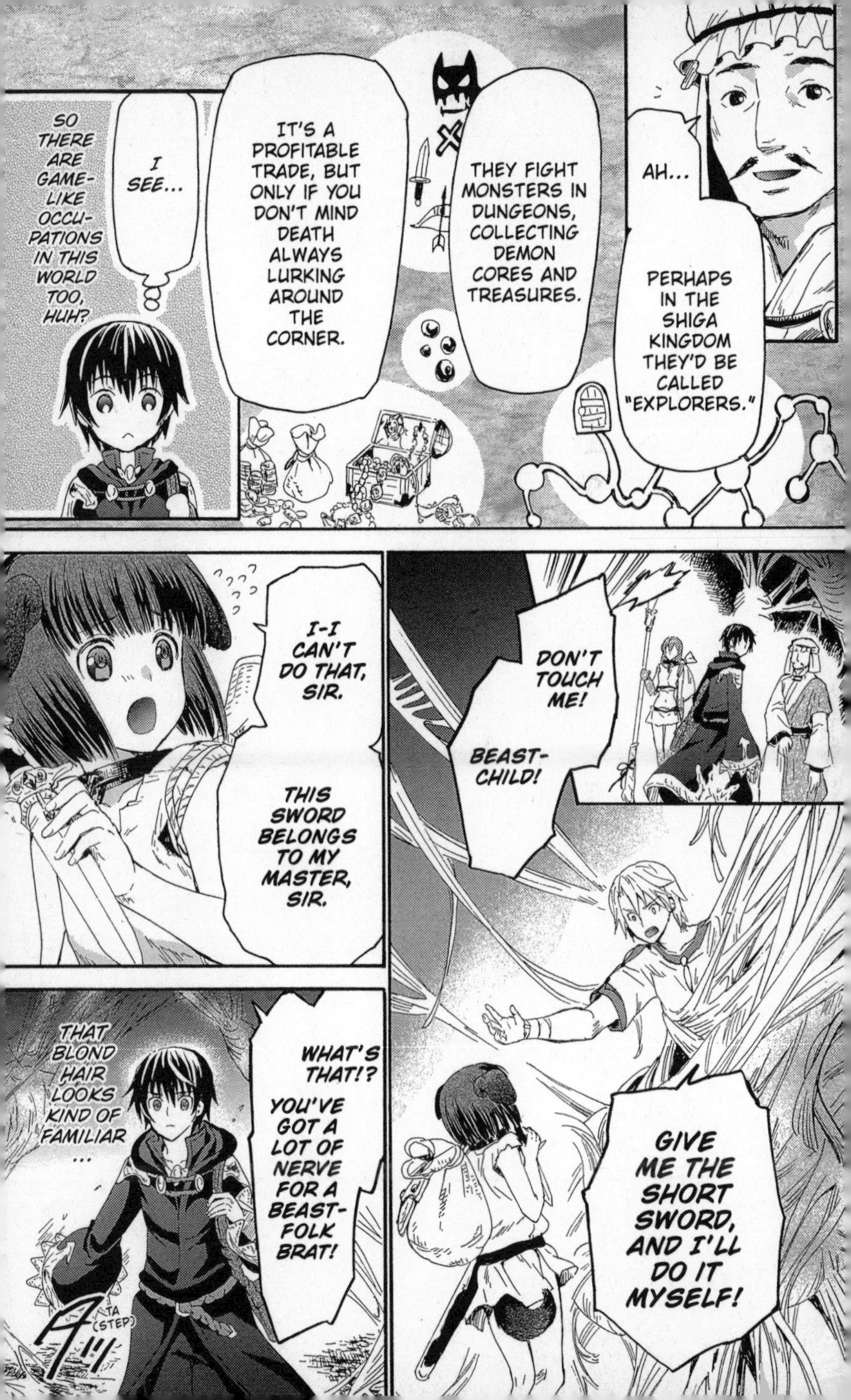
AH…
PERHAPS IN THE SHIGA KINGDOM THEY'D BE CALLED "EXPLORERS."
THEY FIGHT MONSTERS IN DUNGEONS, COLLECTING DEMON CORES AND TREASURES.
IT'S A PROFITABLE TRADE, BUT ONLY IF YOU DON'T MIND DEATH ALWAYS LURKING AROUND THE CORNER.
I SEE…
SO THERE ARE GAME-LIKE OCCU-PATIONS IN THIS WORLD TOO, HUH?
DON'T TOUCH ME!
BEAST-CHILD!
GIVE ME THE SHORT SWORD, AND I'LL DO IT MYSELF!
I-I CAN'T DO THAT, SIR.
THIS SWORD BELONGS TO MY MASTER, SIR.
WHAT'S THAT!?
YOU'VE GOT A LOT OF NERVE FOR A BEAST-FOLK BRAT!
THAT BLOND HAIR LOOKS KIND OF FAMILIAR …
TA (STEP)

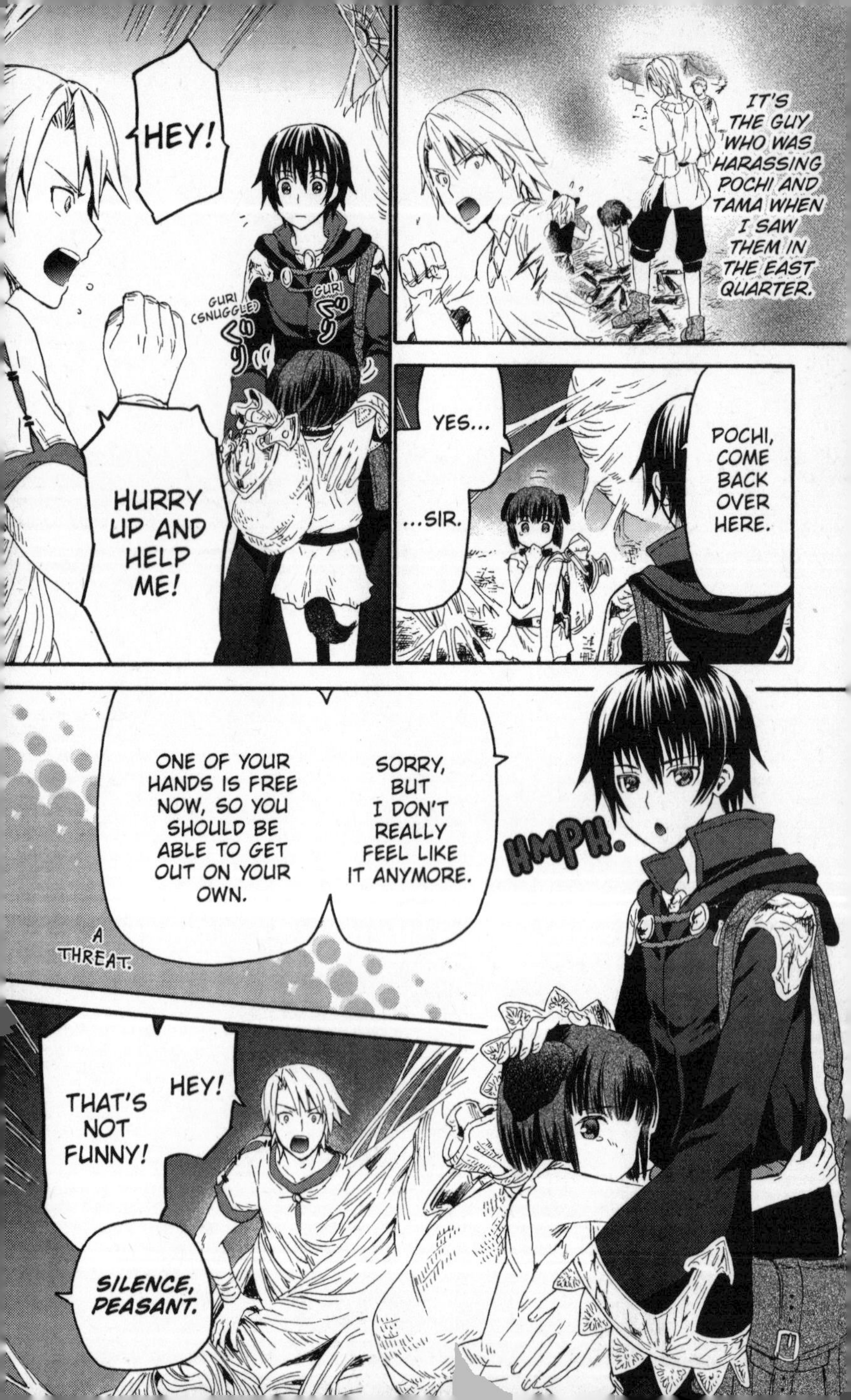
IT'S THE GUY WHO WAS HARASSING POCHI AND TAMA WHEN I SAW THEM IN THE EAST QUARTER.
POCHI, COME BACK OVER HERE.
YES...
...SIR.
HEY!
GURI
GURI (SNUGGLE)
HURRY UP AND HELP ME!
HMPH.
SORRY, BUT I DON'T REALLY FEEL LIKE IT ANYMORE.
ONE OF YOUR HANDS IS FREE NOW, SO YOU SHOULD BE ABLE TO GET OUT ON YOUR OWN.
A THREAT.
HEY!
THAT'S NOT FUNNY!
SILENCE, PEASANT.

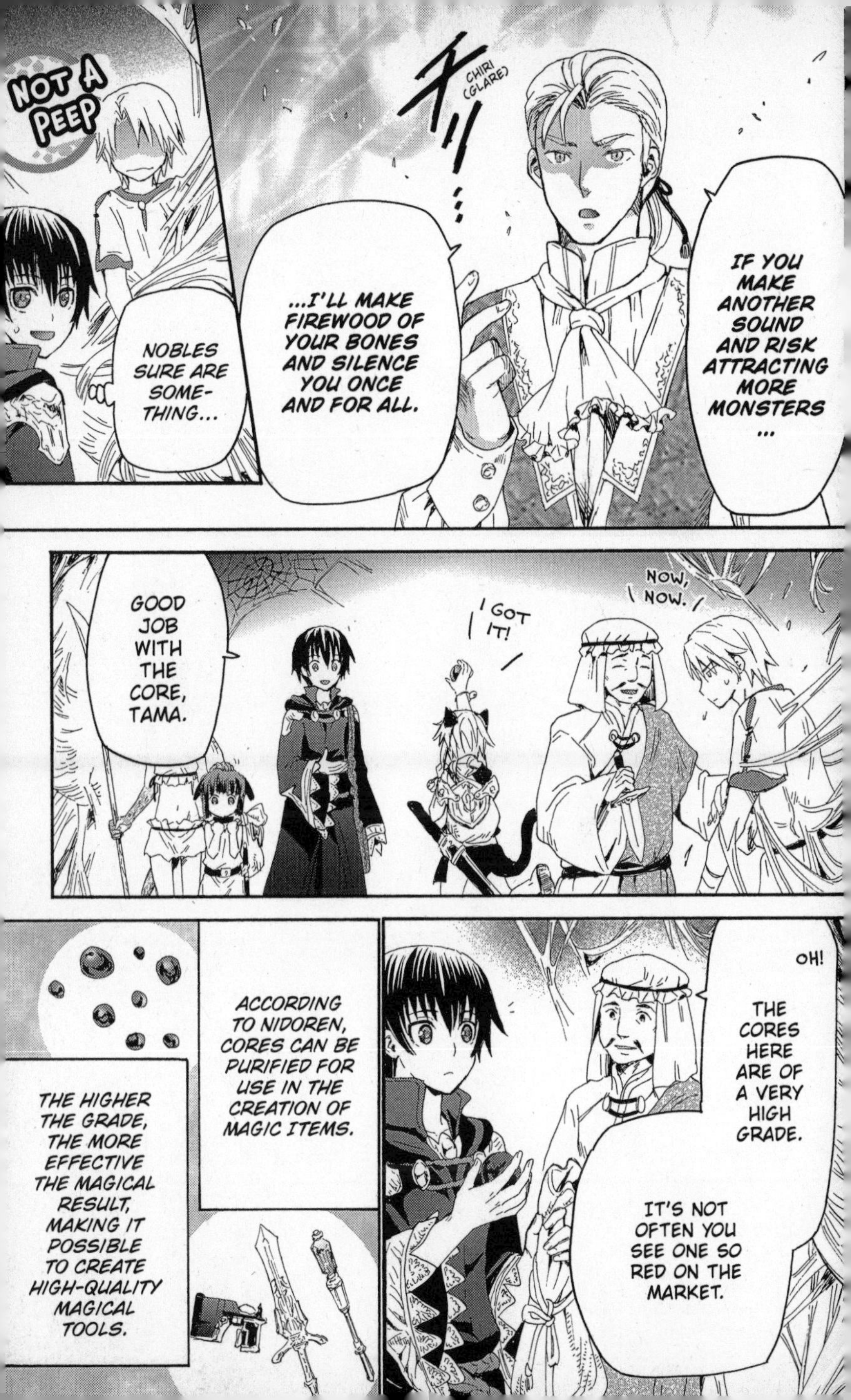
IF YOU MAKE ANOTHER SOUND AND RISK ATTRACTING MORE MONSTERS...
...I'LL MAKE FIREWOOD OF YOUR BONES AND SILENCE YOU ONCE AND FOR ALL.
CHIRI (GLARE)
NOT A PEEP
NOBLES SURE ARE SOME-THING...
NOW, NOW.
I GOT IT!
GOOD JOB WITH THE CORE, TAMA.
OH!
THE CORES HERE ARE OF A VERY HIGH GRADE.
IT'S NOT OFTEN YOU SEE ONE SO RED ON THE MARKET.
ACCORDING TO NIDOREN, CORES CAN BE PURIFIED FOR USE IN THE CREATION OF MAGIC ITEMS.
THE HIGHER THE GRADE, THE MORE EFFECTIVE THE MAGICAL RESULT, MAKING IT POSSIBLE TO CREATE HIGH-QUALITY MAGICAL TOOLS.

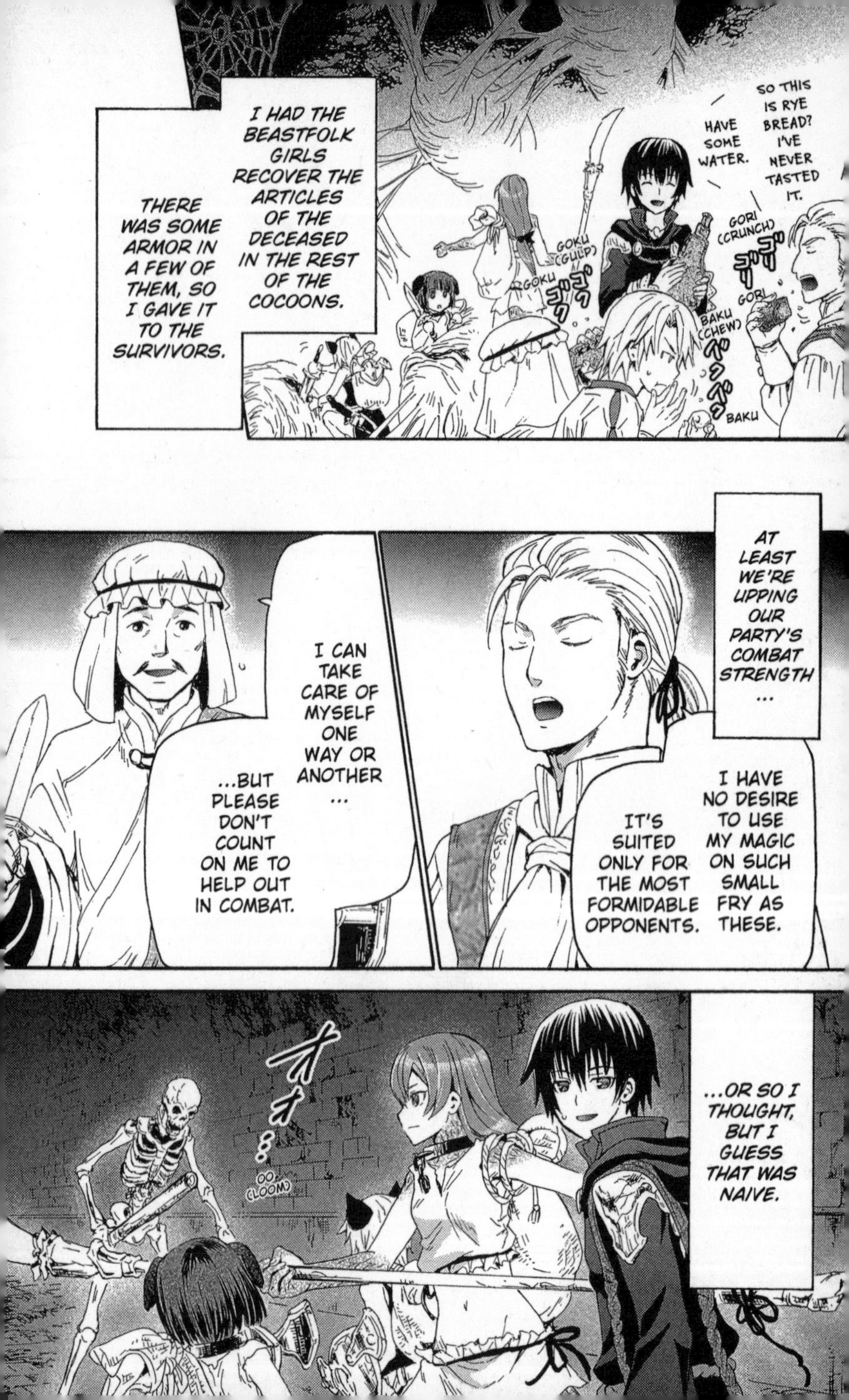
SO THIS IS RYE BREAD? I'VE NEVER TASTED IT.
HAVE SOME WATER.
GORI (CRUNCH)
GORI
GOKU (GULP)
GOKU
BAKU (CHEW)
BAKU
I HAD THE BEASTFOLK GIRLS RECOVER THE ARTICLES OF THE DECEASED IN THE REST OF THE COCOONS.
THERE WAS SOME ARMOR IN A FEW OF THEM, SO I GAVE IT TO THE SURVIVORS.
AT LEAST WE'RE UPPING OUR PARTY'S COMBAT STRENGTH...
I HAVE NO DESIRE TO USE MY MAGIC ON SUCH SMALL FRY AS THESE.
IT'S SUITED ONLY FOR THE MOST FORMIDABLE OPPONENTS.
I CAN TAKE CARE OF MYSELF ONE WAY OR ANOTHER...
...BUT PLEASE DON'T COUNT ON ME TO HELP OUT IN COMBAT.
...OR SO I THOUGHT, BUT I GUESS THAT WAS NAIVE.
OO (LOOM)

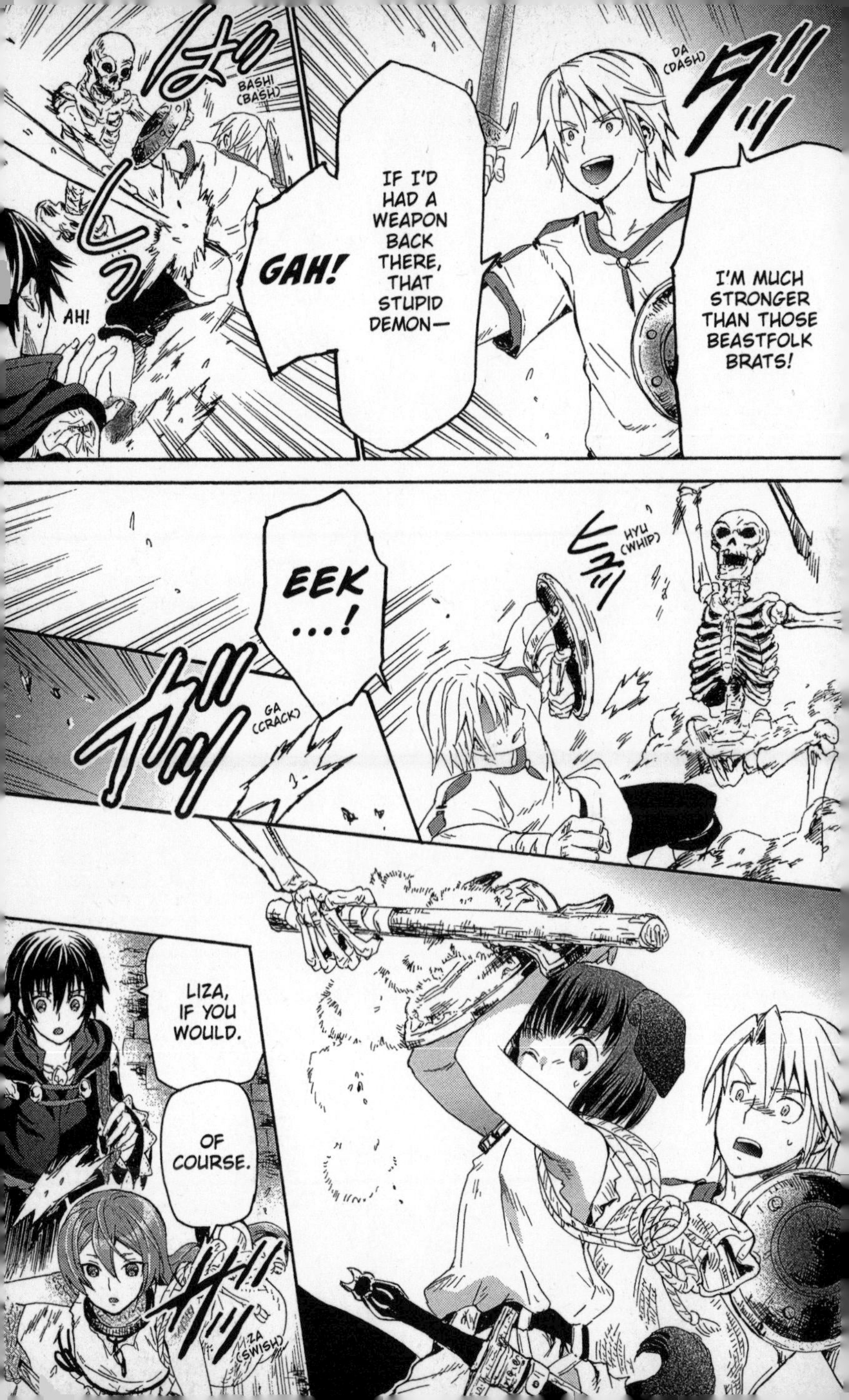
DA (DASH)
I'M MUCH STRONGER THAN THOSE BEASTFOLK BRATS!
IF I'D HAD A WEAPON BACK THERE, THAT STUPID DEMON—
BASHI (BASH)
GAH!
AH!
HYU (WHIP)
EEK ...!
GA (CRACK)
LIZA, IF YOU WOULD.
OF COURSE.
ZA (SWISH)

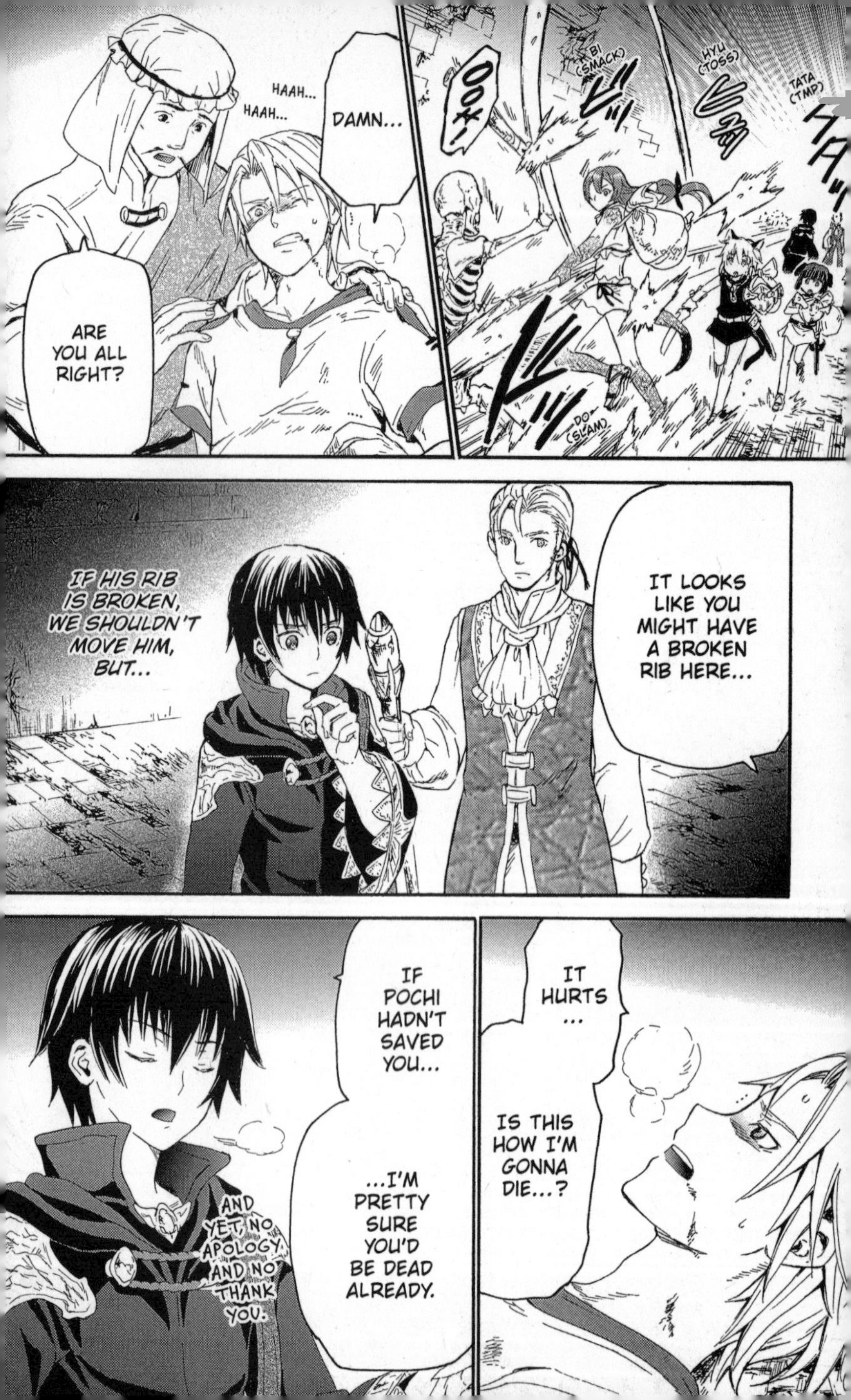
TATA (TMP)
HYU (TOSS)
BI (SMACK)
DO (SLAM)
DAMN...
HAAH... HAAH...
...
ARE YOU ALL RIGHT?
IT LOOKS LIKE YOU MIGHT HAVE A BROKEN RIB HERE...
IF HIS RIB IS BROKEN, WE SHOULDN'T MOVE HIM, BUT...
IT HURTS...
IS THIS HOW I'M GONNA DIE...?
IF POCHI HADN'T SAVED YOU...
...I'M PRETTY SURE YOU'D BE DEAD ALREADY.
AND YET, NO APOLOGY AND NO THANK YOU.

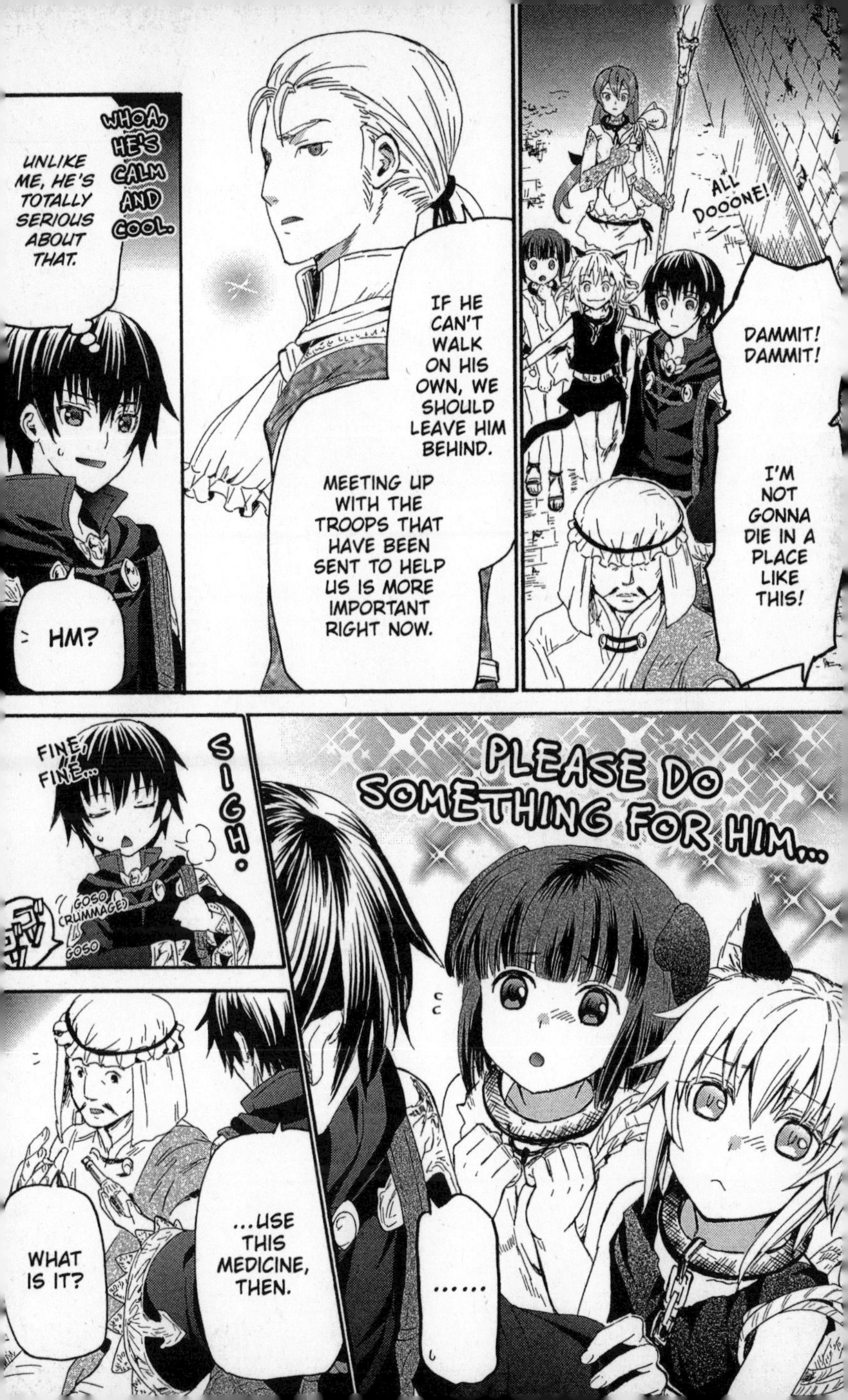
ALL DOOONE!
DAMMIT! DAMMIT!
I'M NOT GONNA DIE IN A PLACE LIKE THIS!
IF HE CAN'T WALK ON HIS OWN, WE SHOULD LEAVE HIM BEHIND.
MEETING UP WITH THE TROOPS THAT HAVE BEEN SENT TO HELP US IS MORE IMPORTANT RIGHT NOW.
WHOA, HE'S CALM AND COOL.
UNLIKE ME, HE'S TOTALLY SERIOUS ABOUT THAT.
HM?
PLEASE DO SOMETHING FOR HIM...
......
SIGH.
FINE, FINE...
GOSO (RUMMAGE) GOSO
...USE THIS MEDICINE, THEN.
WHAT IS IT?

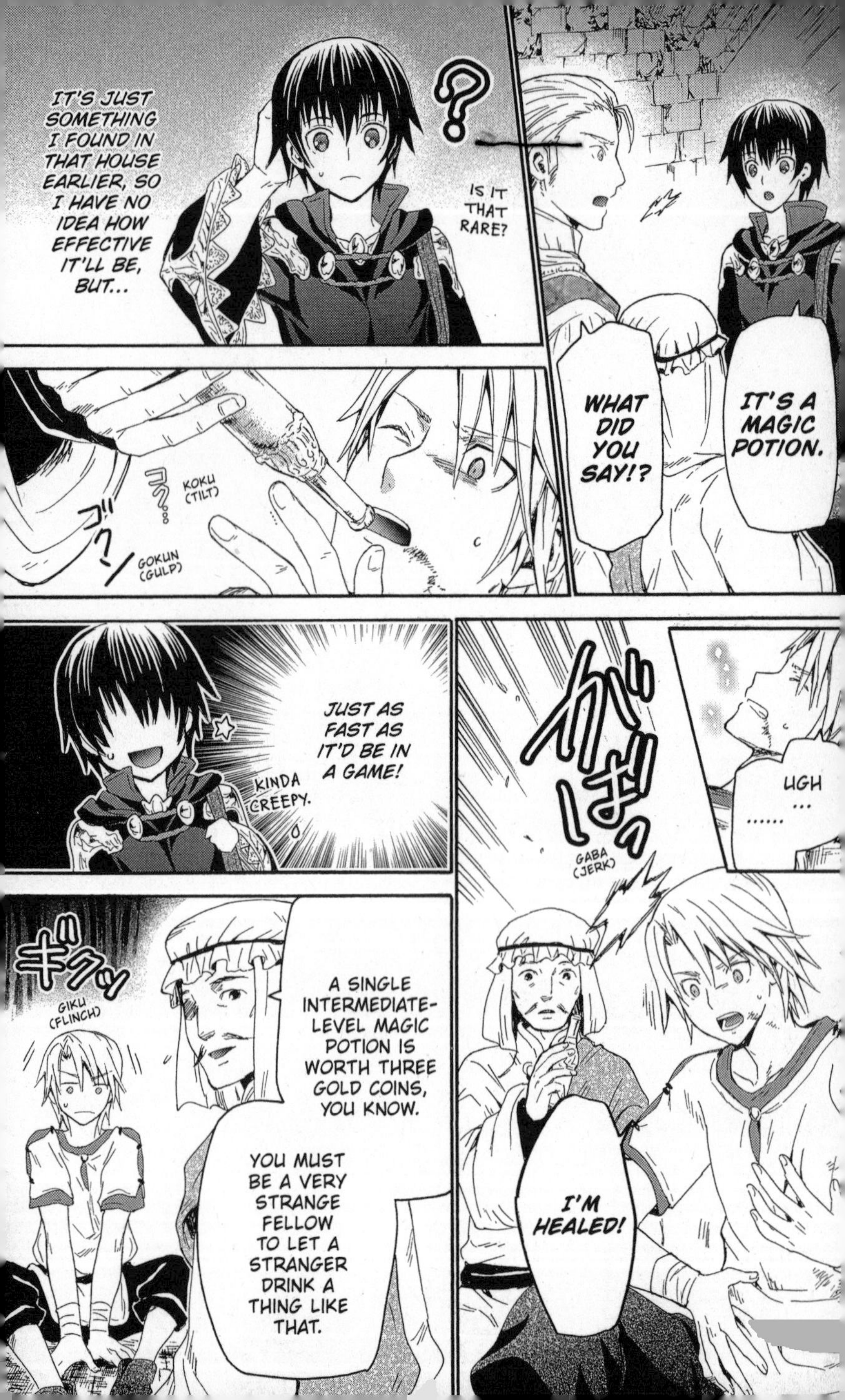
IT'S A MAGIC POTION.
WHAT DID YOU SAY!?
IS IT THAT RARE?
IT'S JUST SOMETHING I FOUND IN THAT HOUSE EARLIER, SO I HAVE NO IDEA HOW EFFECTIVE IT'LL BE, BUT...
KOKU (TILT)
GOKUN (GULP)
UGH ... .
JUST AS FAST AS IT'D BE IN A GAME!
KINDA CREEPY.
GABA (JERK)
I'M HEALED!
A SINGLE INTERMEDIATE-LEVEL MAGIC POTION IS WORTH THREE GOLD COINS, YOU KNOW.
YOU MUST BE A VERY STRANGE FELLOW TO LET A STRANGER DRINK A THING LIKE THAT.
GIKU (FLINCH)

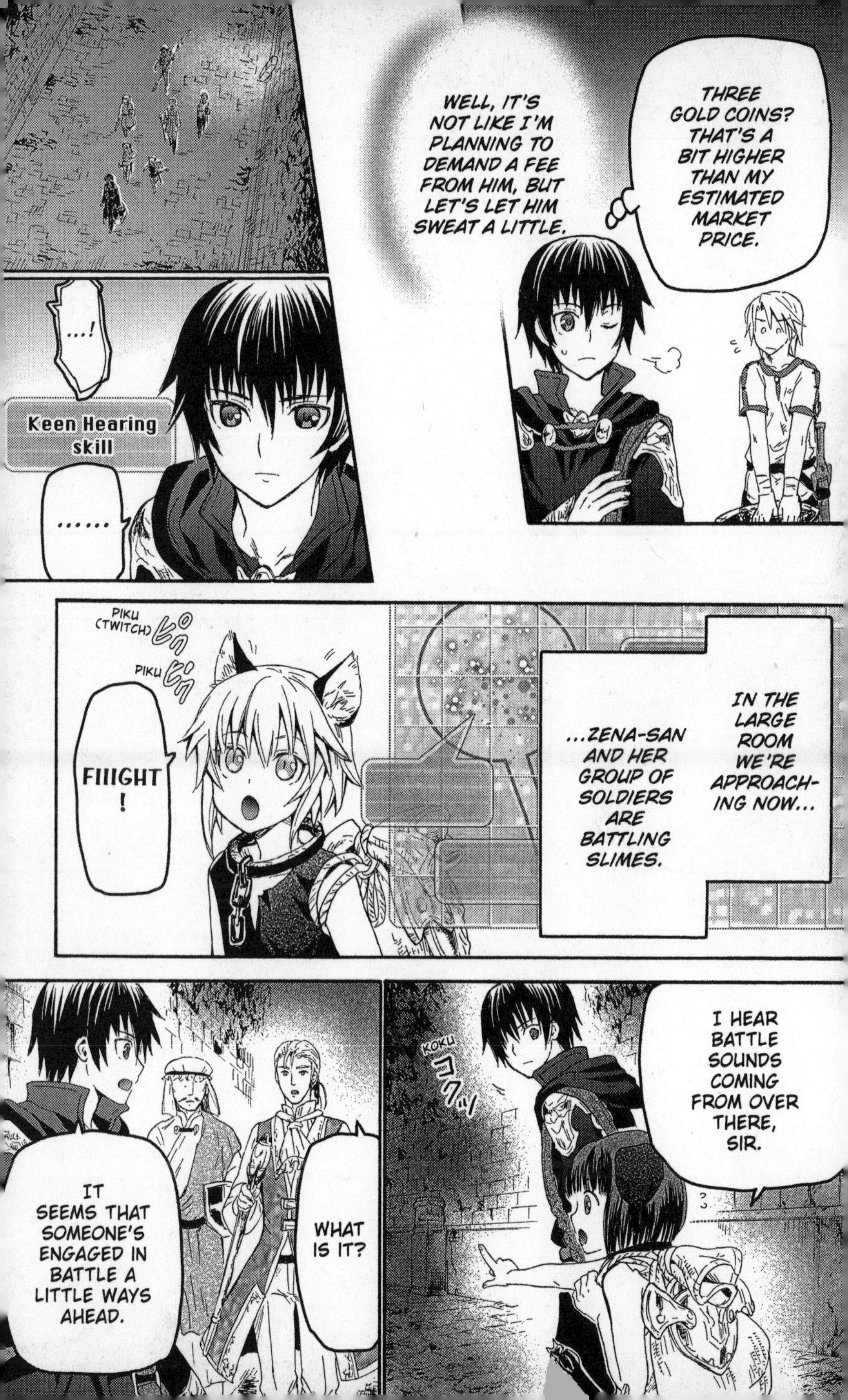

THREE GOLD COINS? THAT'S A BIT HIGHER THAN MY ESTIMATED MARKET PRICE.
WELL, IT'S NOT LIKE I'M PLANNING TO DEMAND A FEE FROM HIM, BUT LET'S LET HIM SWEAT A LITTLE.
...!
Keen Hearing skill
......
IN THE LARGE ROOM WE'RE APPROACHING NOW...
...ZENA-SAN AND HER GROUP OF SOLDIERS ARE BATTLING SLIMES.
PIKU (TWITCH)
PIKU
FIIIGHT!
I HEAR BATTLE SOUNDS COMING FROM OVER THERE, SIR.
KOKU
WHAT IS IT?
IT SEEMS THAT SOMEONE'S ENGAGED IN BATTLE A LITTLE WAYS AHEAD.

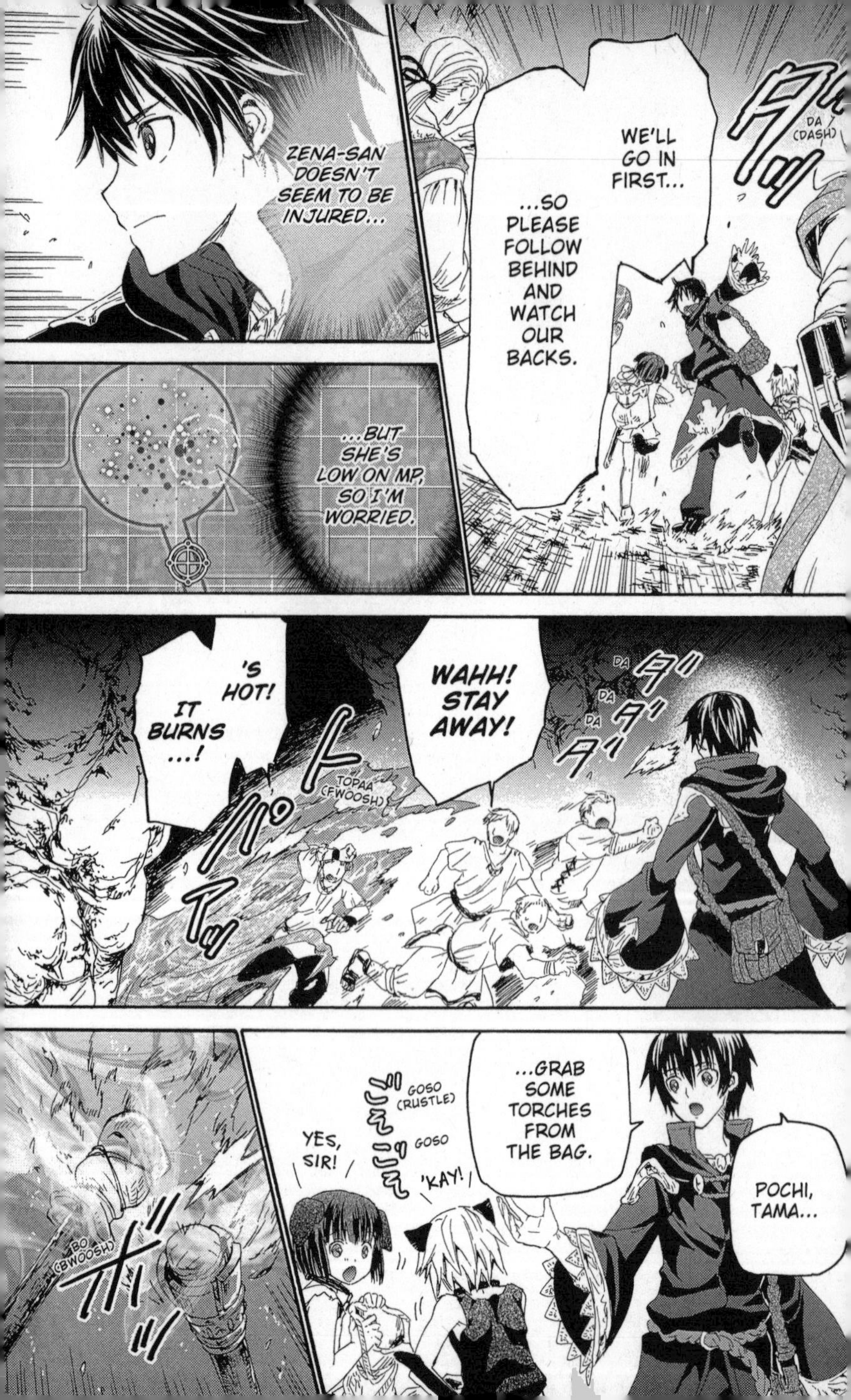
DA (DASH)
WE'LL GO IN FIRST...
...SO PLEASE FOLLOW BEHIND AND WATCH OUR BACKS.
ZENA-SAN DOESN'T SEEM TO BE INJURED...
...BUT SHE'S LOW ON MP, SO I'M WORRIED.
DA DA DA
WAHH! STAY AWAY!
TOPAA (FWOOSH)
'S HOT!
IT BURNS ...!
POCHI, TAMA...
...GRAB SOME TORCHES FROM THE BAG.
'KAY!
GOSO (RUSTLE)
GOSO
YES, SIR!
BO (BWOOSH)

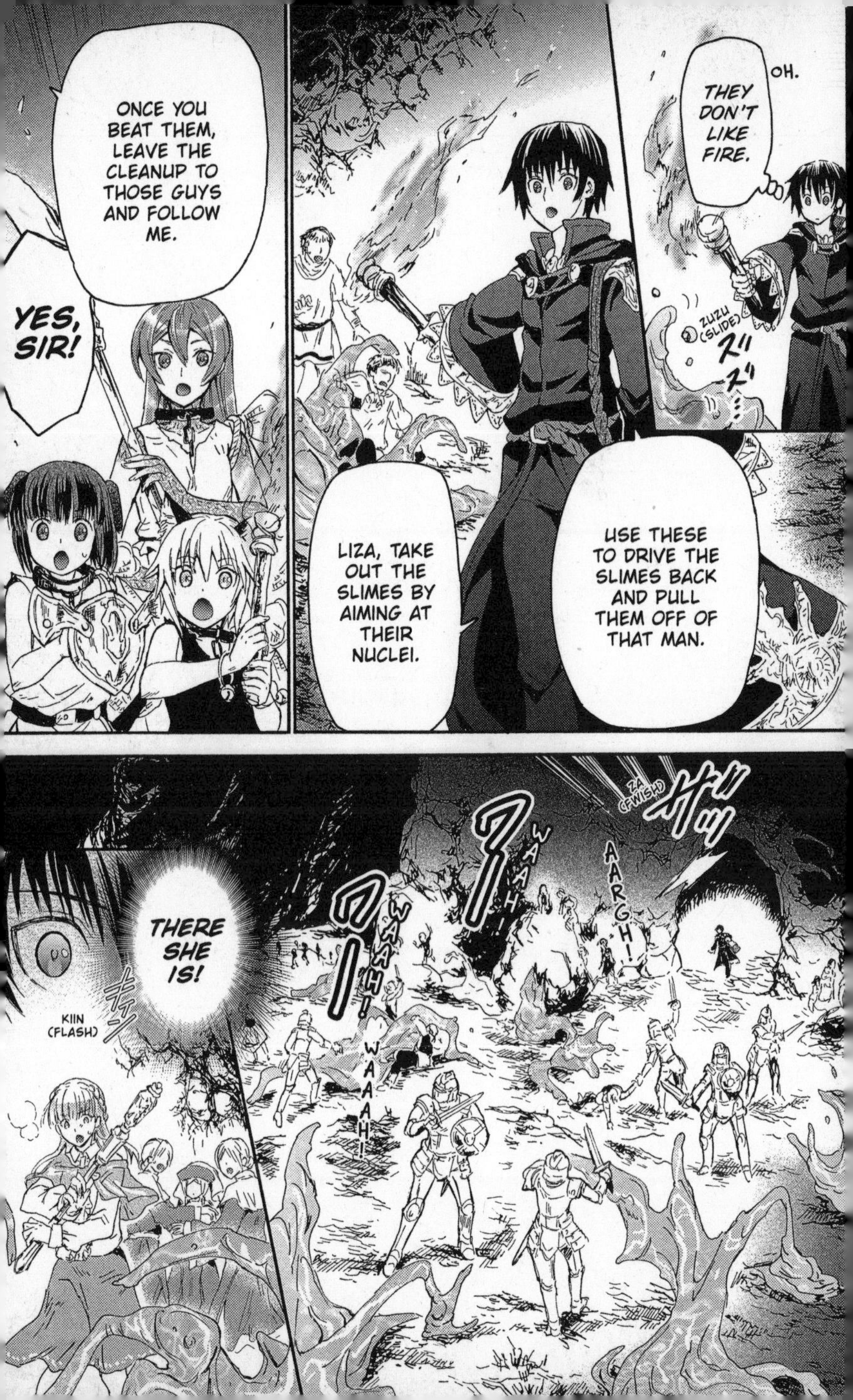
OH.
THEY DON'T LIKE FIRE.
ZUZU (SLIDE)
USE THESE TO DRIVE THE SLIMES BACK AND PULL THEM OFF OF THAT MAN.
LIZA, TAKE OUT THE SLIMES BY AIMING AT THEIR NUCLEI.
ONCE YOU BEAT THEM, LEAVE THE CLEANUP TO THOSE GUYS AND FOLLOW ME.
YES, SIR!
ZA (FWISH)
AARGH!
WAAAH!
WAAAH!
WAAAAH!
THERE SHE IS!
KIIN (FLASH)

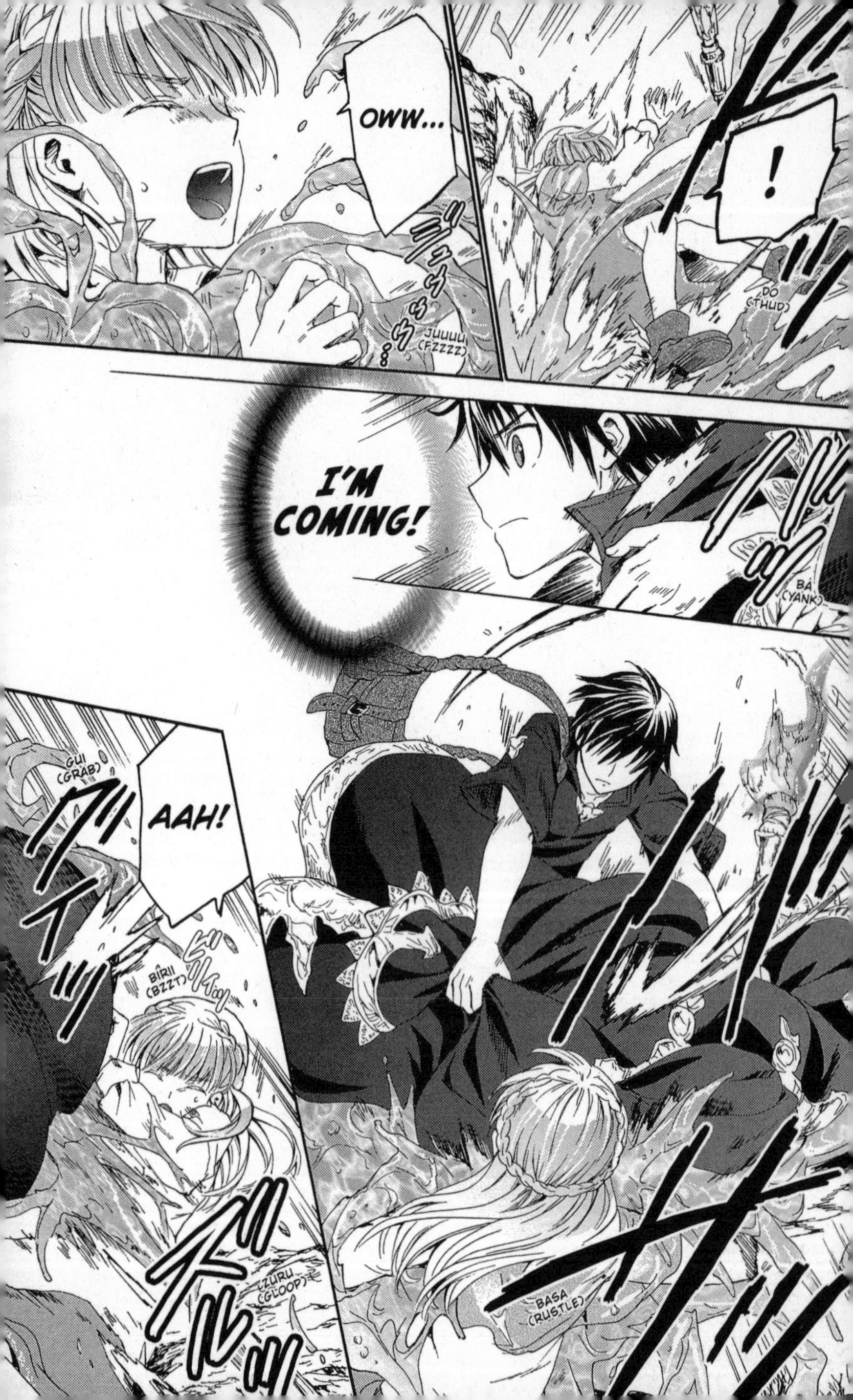
!
DO (THUD)
OWW...
JUUUU (FZZZZ)
I'M COMING!
BA (YANK)
BASA (RUSTLE)
GUI (GRAB)
AAH!
BIRII (BZZT)
ZURU (GLOOP)

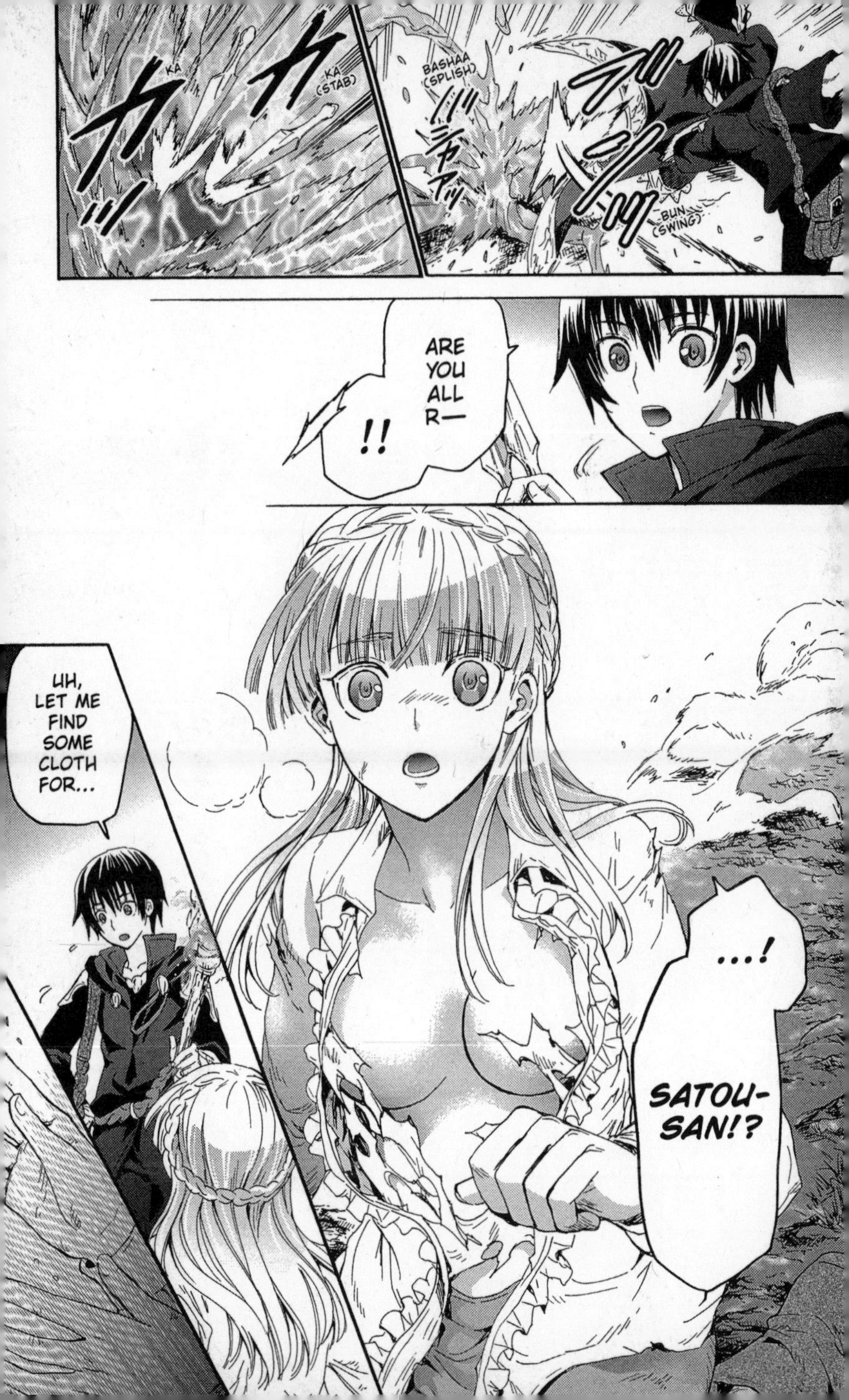
BASHAA (SPLISH)
BUN (SWING)
KA (STAB)
KA
ARE YOU ALL R—
!!
...!
SATOU-SAN!?
UH, LET ME FIND SOME CLOTH FOR...

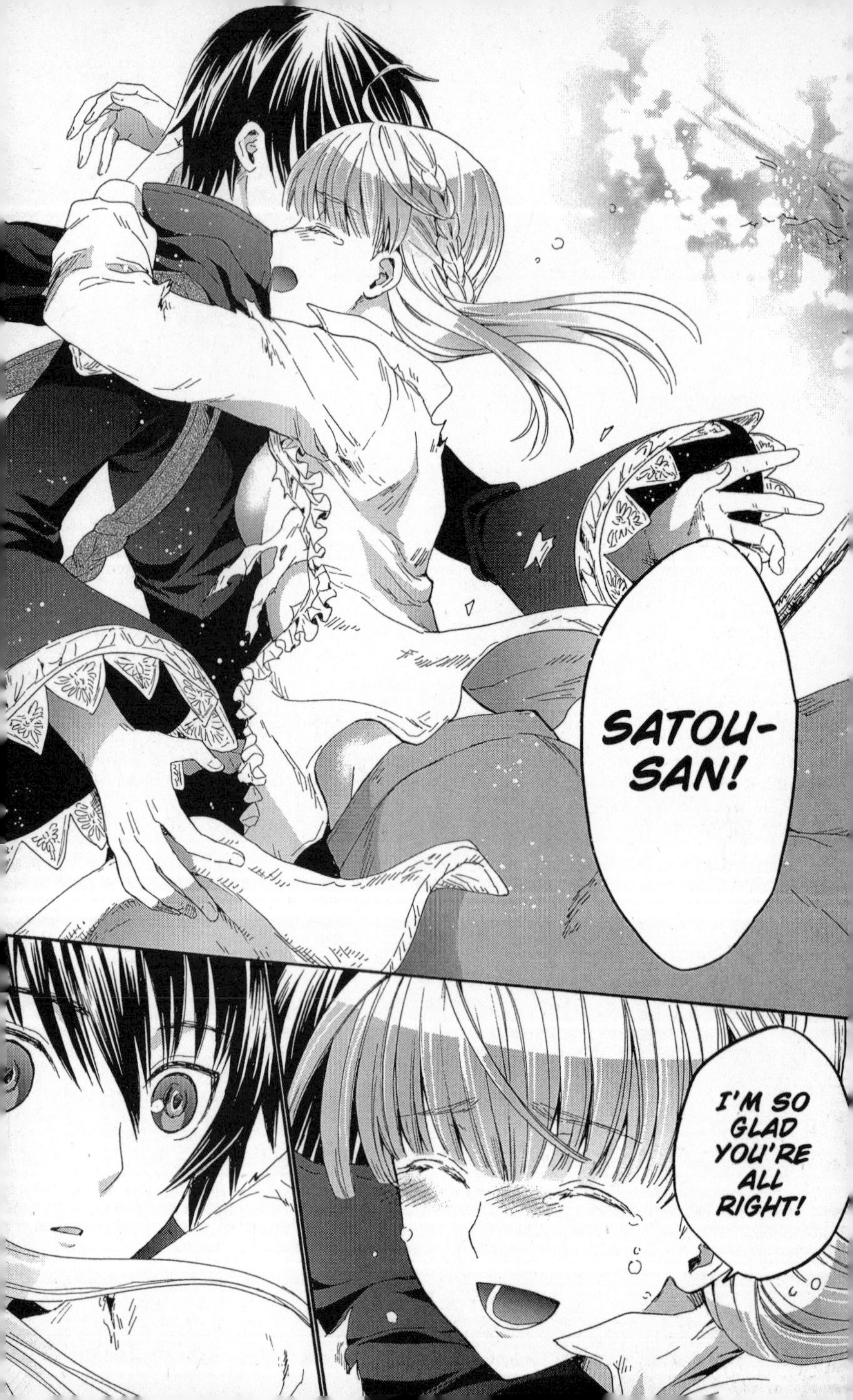
SATOU-SAN!
I'M SO GLAD YOU'RE ALL RIGHT!

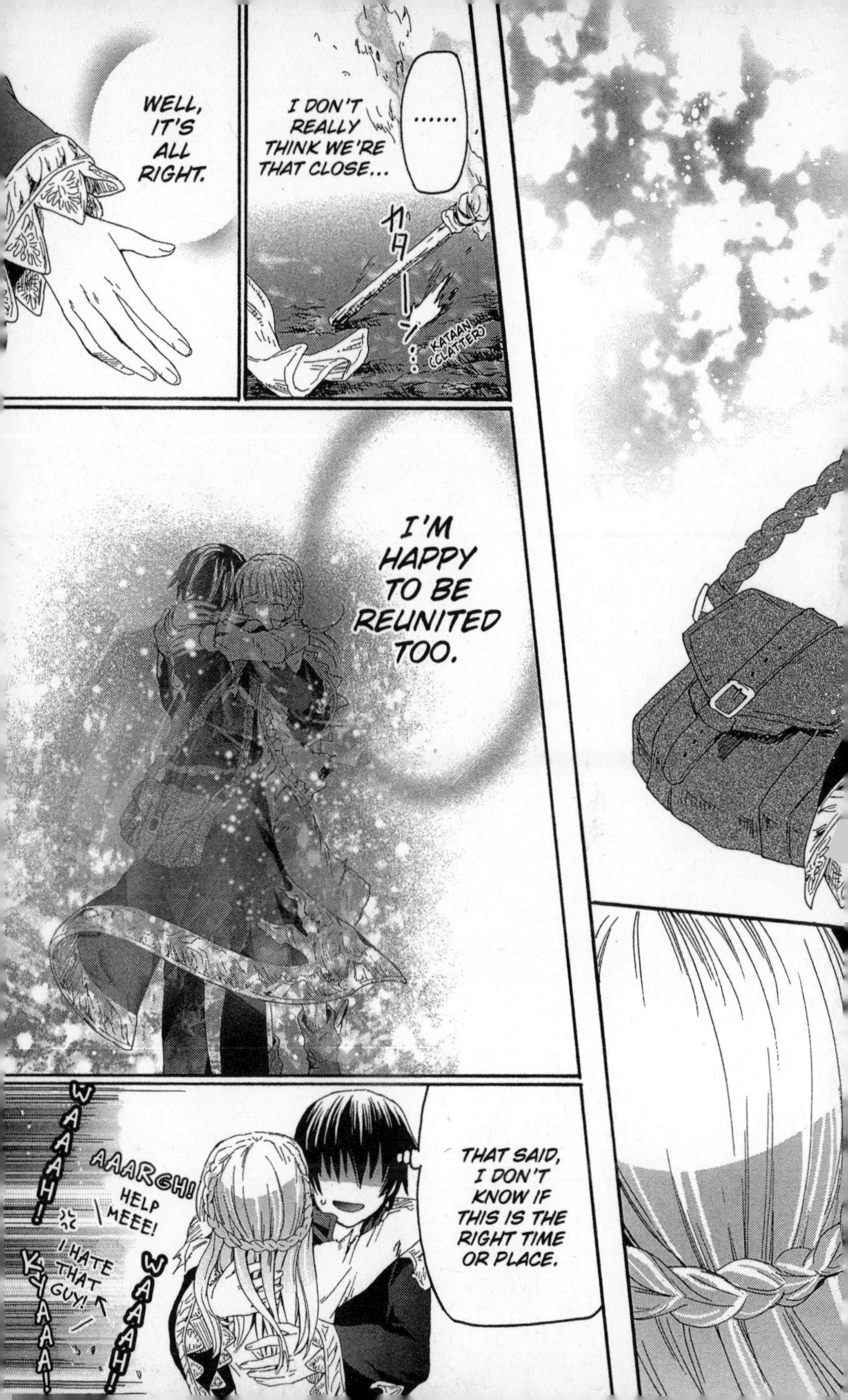
......
I DON'T REALLY THINK WE'RE THAT CLOSE...
KATAAN (CLATTER)
WELL, IT'S ALL RIGHT.
I'M HAPPY TO BE REUNITED TOO.
THAT SAID, I DON'T KNOW IF THIS IS THE RIGHT TIME OR PLACE.
WAAAAH!
I HATE THAT GUY!
AAARGH! HELP MEEE!
WAAAAH!
KYAAAA!

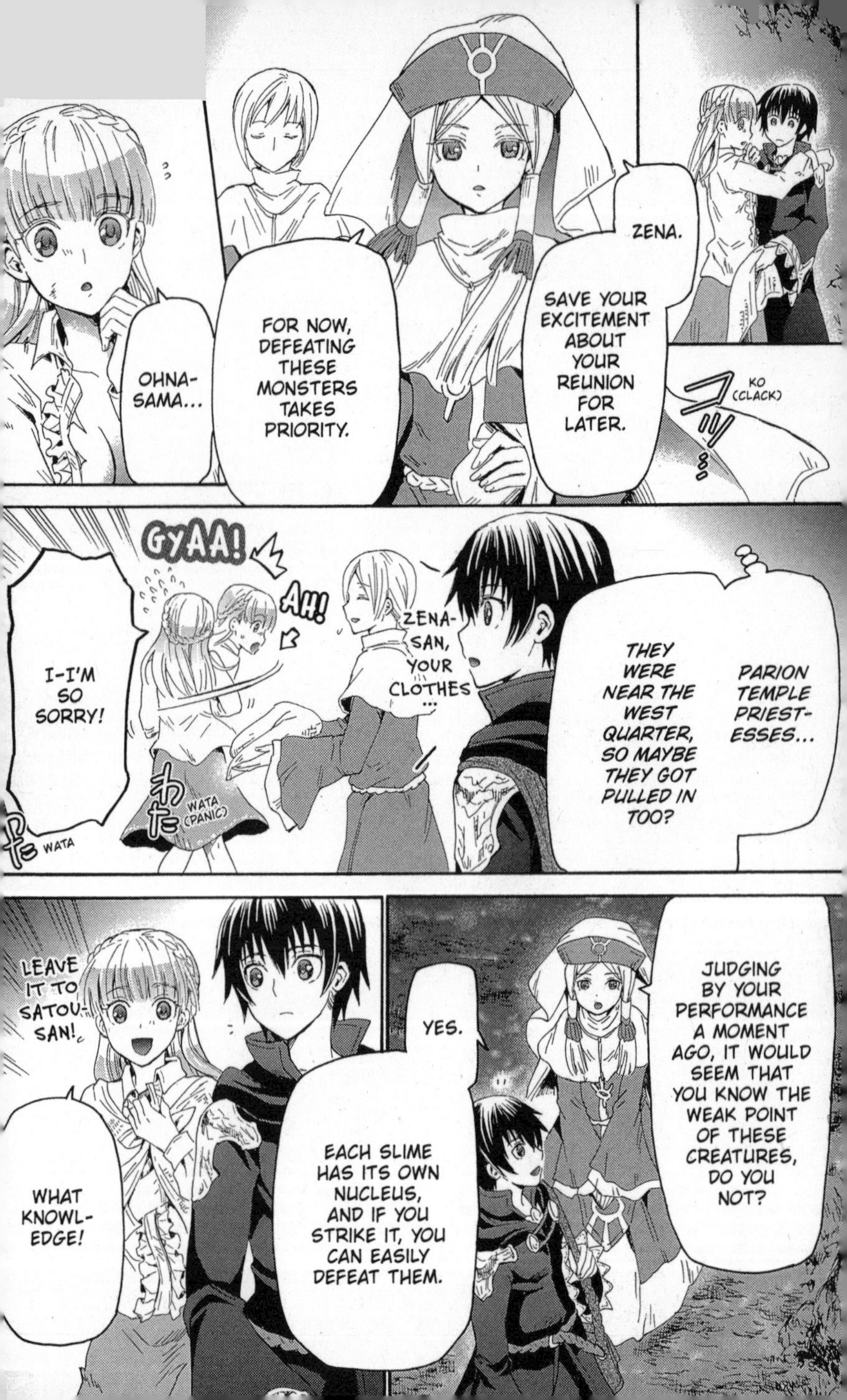
KO (CLACK)
ZENA.
SAVE YOUR EXCITEMENT ABOUT YOUR REUNION FOR LATER.
FOR NOW, DEFEATING THESE MONSTERS TAKES PRIORITY.
OHNA-SAMA...
PARION TEMPLE PRIEST-ESSES...
THEY WERE NEAR THE WEST QUARTER, SO MAYBE THEY GOT PULLED IN TOO?
ZENA-SAN, YOUR CLOTHES...
AH!
GyAA!
I-I'M SO SORRY!
WATA (PANIC)
WATA
JUDGING BY YOUR PERFORMANCE A MOMENT AGO, IT WOULD SEEM THAT YOU KNOW THE WEAK POINT OF THESE CREATURES, DO YOU NOT?
YES.
EACH SLIME HAS ITS OWN NUCLEUS, AND IF YOU STRIKE IT, YOU CAN EASILY DEFEAT THEM.
LEAVE IT TO SATOU-SAN!
WHAT KNOWL-EDGE!

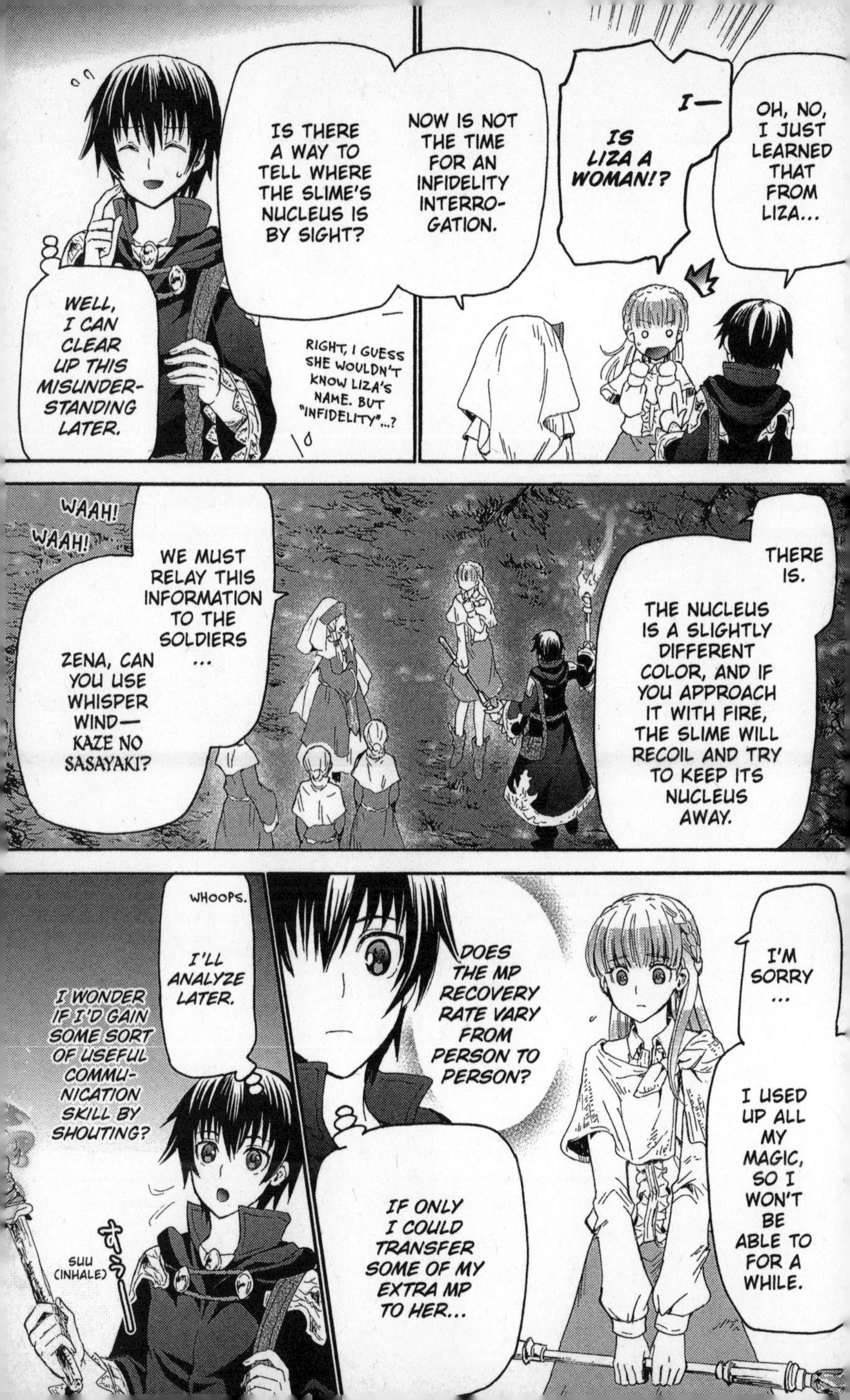
OH, NO, I JUST LEARNED THAT FROM LIZA...
I—
IS LIZA A WOMAN!?
NOW IS NOT THE TIME FOR AN INFIDELITY INTERROGATION.
IS THERE A WAY TO TELL WHERE THE SLIME'S NUCLEUS IS BY SIGHT?
RIGHT, I GUESS SHE WOULDN'T KNOW LIZA'S NAME. BUT "INFIDELITY"...?
WELL, I CAN CLEAR UP THIS MISUNDERSTANDING LATER.
THERE IS.
THE NUCLEUS IS A SLIGHTLY DIFFERENT COLOR, AND IF YOU APPROACH IT WITH FIRE, THE SLIME WILL RECOIL AND TRY TO KEEP ITS NUCLEUS AWAY.
WE MUST RELAY THIS INFORMATION TO THE SOLDIERS...
WAAH!
WAAH!
ZENA, CAN YOU USE WHISPER WIND—KAZE NO SASAYAKI?
I'M SORRY...
I USED UP ALL MY MAGIC, SO I WON'T BE ABLE TO FOR A WHILE.
DOES THE MP RECOVERY RATE VARY FROM PERSON TO PERSON?
IF ONLY I COULD TRANSFER SOME OF MY EXTRA MP TO HER...
WHOOPS.
I'LL ANALYZE LATER.
I WONDER IF I'D GAIN SOME SORT OF USEFUL COMMUNICATION SKILL BY SHOUTING?
SUU (INHALE)

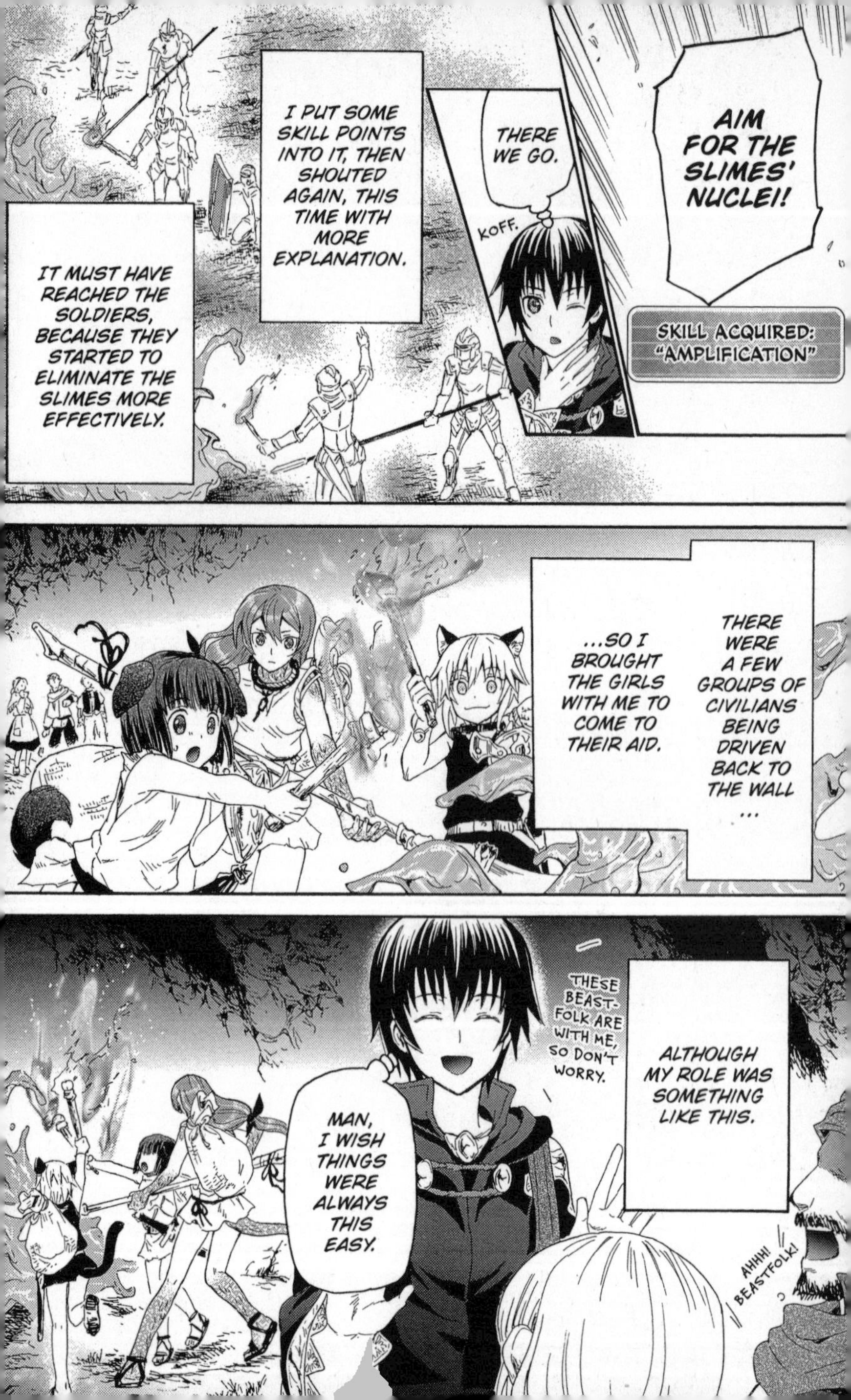
AIM FOR THE SLIMES' NUCLEI!
SKILL ACQUIRED: "AMPLIFICATION"
THERE WE GO.
KOFF.
I PUT SOME SKILL POINTS INTO IT, THEN SHOUTED AGAIN, THIS TIME WITH MORE EXPLANATION.
IT MUST HAVE REACHED THE SOLDIERS, BECAUSE THEY STARTED TO ELIMINATE THE SLIMES MORE EFFECTIVELY.
THERE WERE A FEW GROUPS OF CIVILIANS BEING DRIVEN BACK TO THE WALL...
...SO I BROUGHT THE GIRLS WITH ME TO COME TO THEIR AID.
AHHH! BEASTFOLK!
ALTHOUGH MY ROLE WAS SOMETHING LIKE THIS.
THESE BEAST-FOLK ARE WITH ME, SO DON'T WORRY.
MAN, I WISH THINGS WERE ALWAYS THIS EASY.

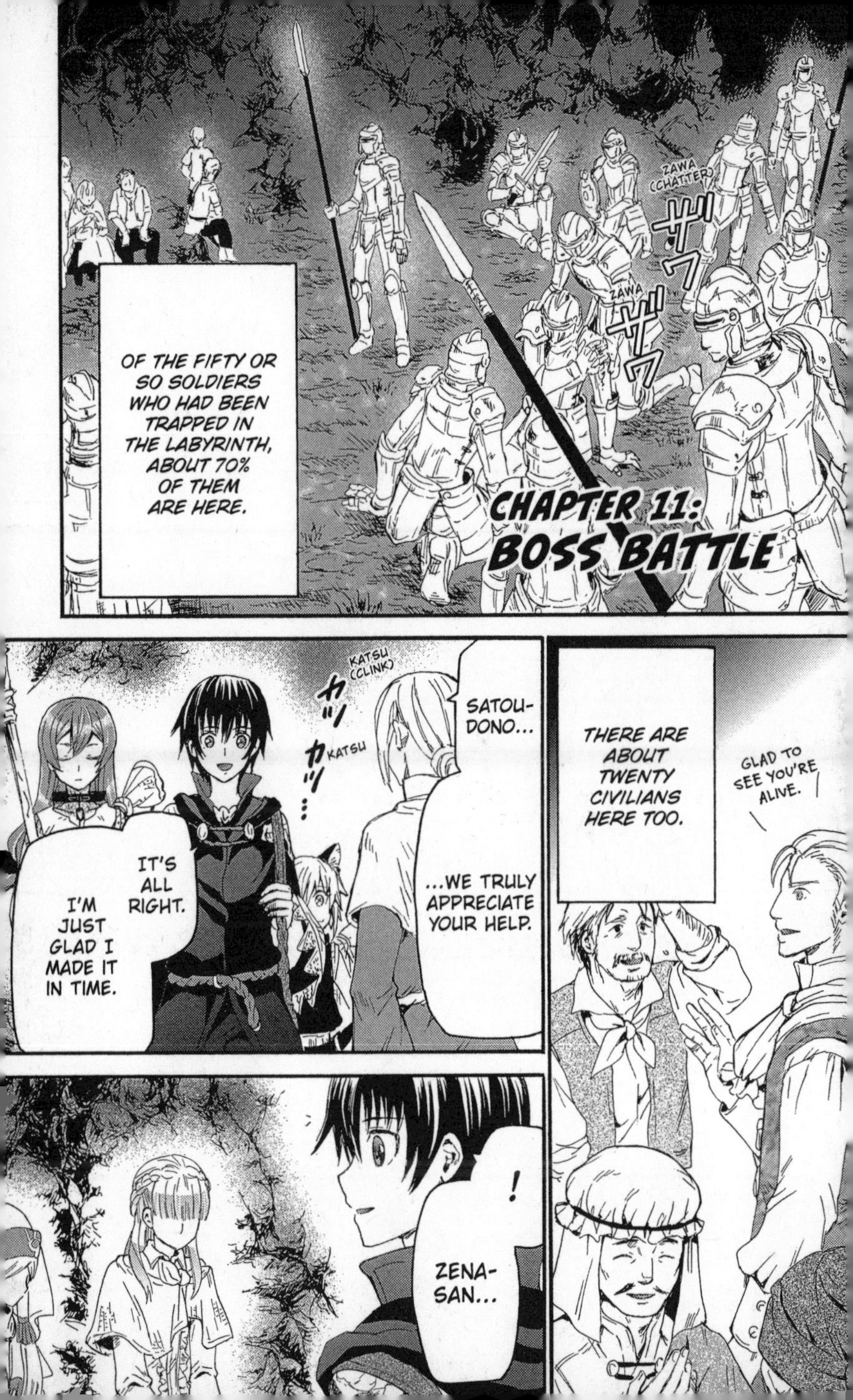
ZAWA (CHATTER)
ザワ
ZAWA
ザワ
CHAPTER 11: BOSS BATTLE
OF THE FIFTY OR SO SOLDIERS WHO HAD BEEN TRAPPED IN THE LABYRINTH, ABOUT 70% OF THEM ARE HERE.
THERE ARE ABOUT TWENTY CIVILIANS HERE TOO.
GLAD TO SEE YOU'RE ALIVE.
SATOU-DONO...
KATSU (CLINK)
カッ
KATSU
カッ...
...WE TRULY APPRECIATE YOUR HELP.
IT'S ALL RIGHT.
I'M JUST GLAD I MADE IT IN TIME.
!
ZENA-SAN...

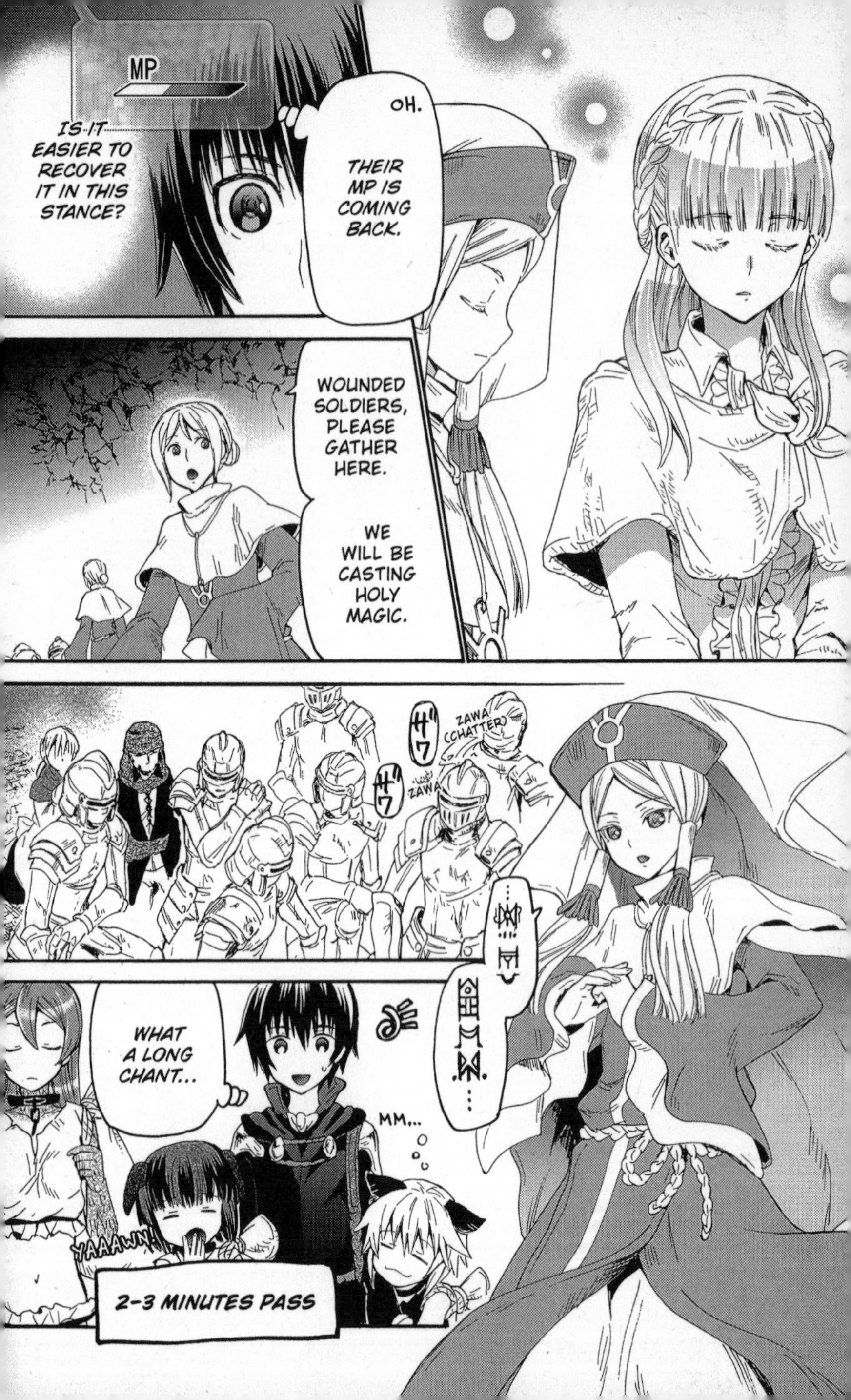

MP
OH.
THEIR MP IS COMING BACK.
IS IT EASIER TO RECOVER IT IN THIS STANCE?
WOUNDED SOLDIERS, PLEASE GATHER HERE.
WE WILL BE CASTING HOLY MAGIC.
ザワ
ZAWA (CHATTER)
ザワ
ZAWA
WHAT A LONG CHANT...
MM...
YAAAAWN
2-3 MINUTES PASS

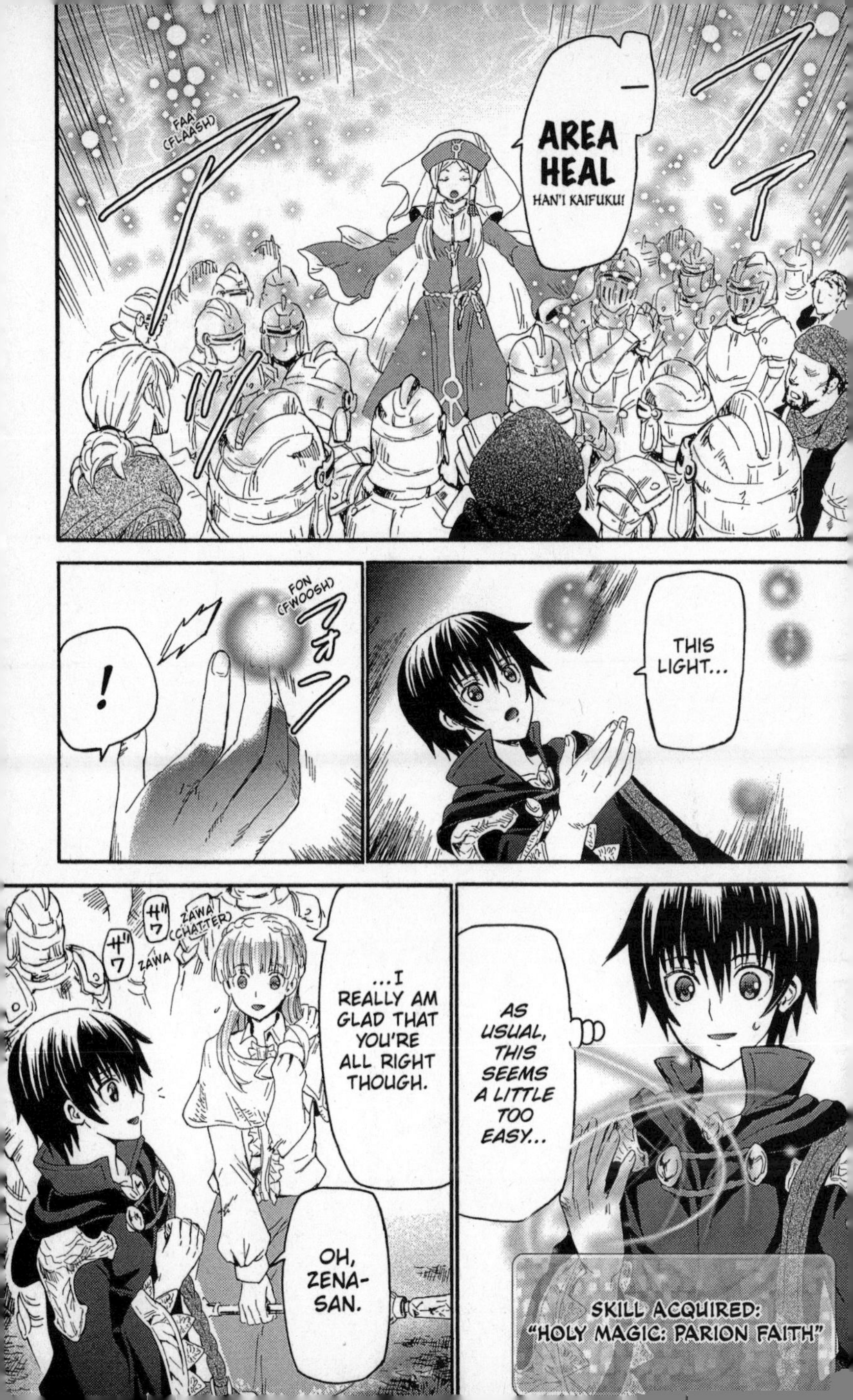
—
AREA HEAL
HAN'I KAIFUKU!
FAA (FLAASH)
THIS LIGHT...
FON (FWOOSH)
!
AS USUAL, THIS SEEMS A LITTLE TOO EASY...
SKILL ACQUIRED: "HOLY MAGIC: PARION FAITH"
...I REALLY AM GLAD THAT YOU'RE ALL RIGHT THOUGH.
ZAWA (CHATTER) ZAWA
OH, ZENA-SAN.

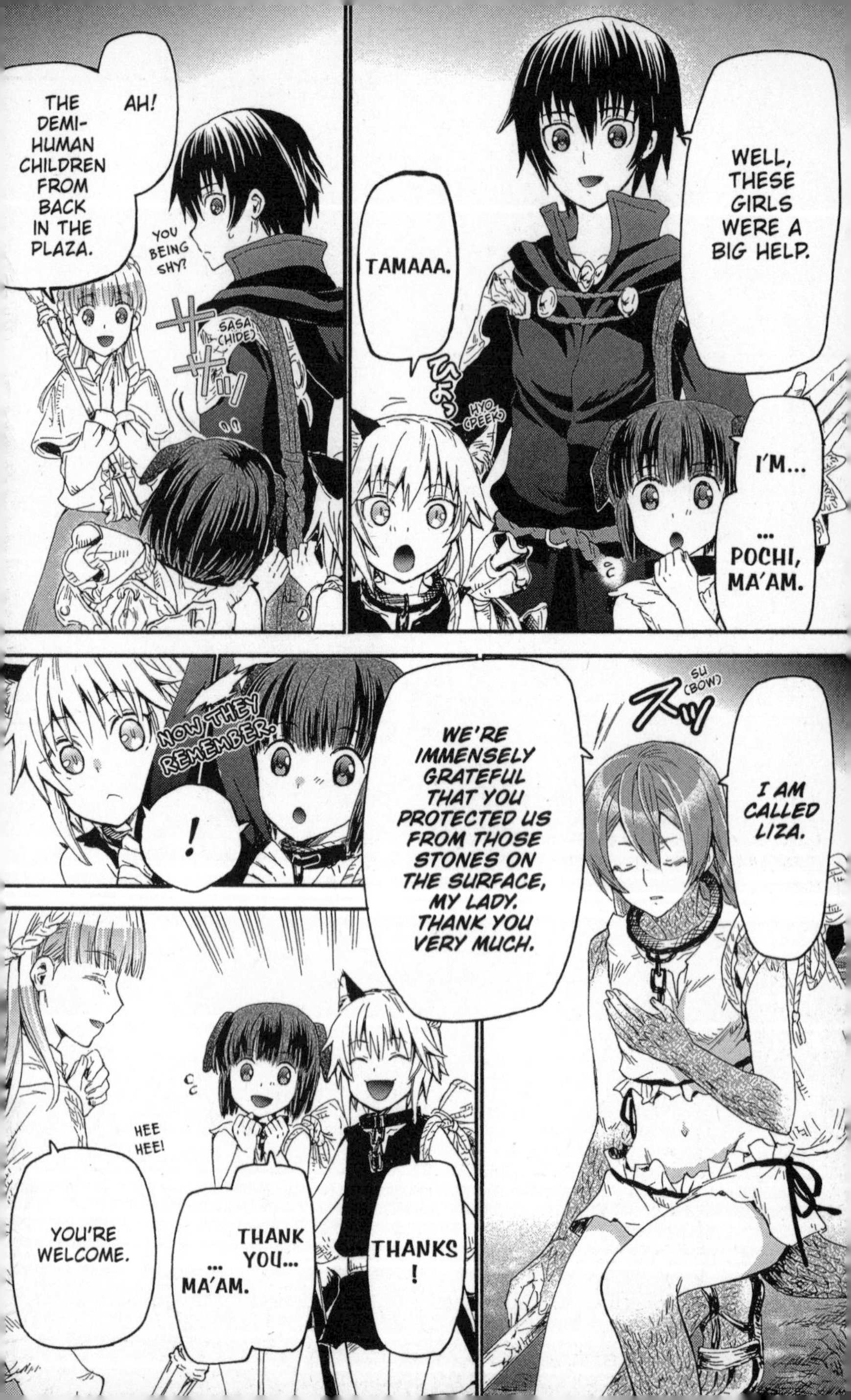
WELL, THESE GIRLS WERE A BIG HELP.
TAMAAA.
HYO (PEEK)
I'M...
...POCHI, MA'AM.
AH!
THE DEMI-HUMAN CHILDREN FROM BACK IN THE PLAZA.
YOU BEING SHY?
SASA (HIDE)
SU (BOW)
I AM CALLED LIZA.
WE'RE IMMENSELY GRATEFUL THAT YOU PROTECTED US FROM THOSE STONES ON THE SURFACE, MY LADY. THANK YOU VERY MUCH.
NOW THEY REMEMBER.
!
THANKS!
THANK YOU... ...MA'AM.
HEE HEE!
YOU'RE WELCOME.

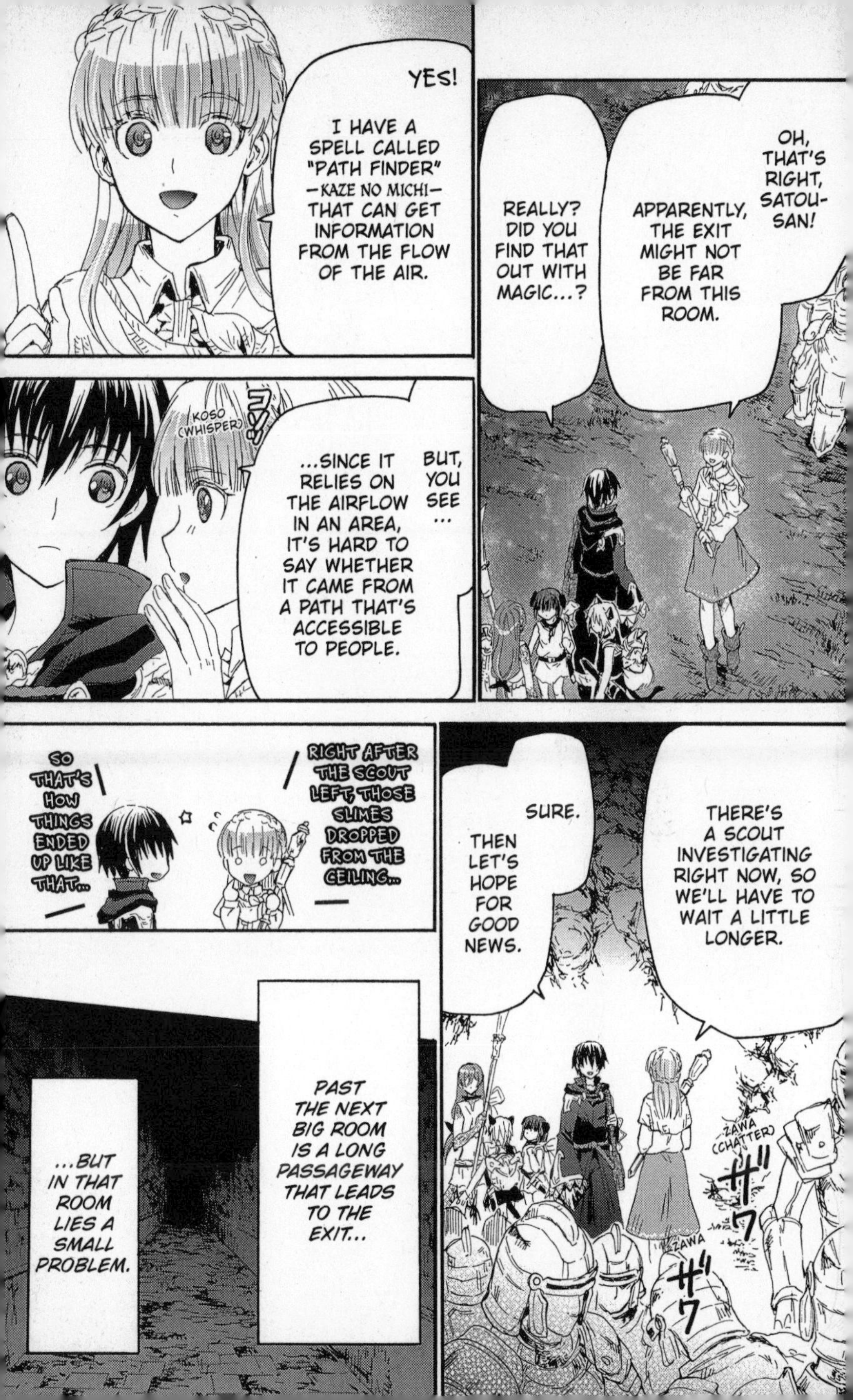
OH, THAT'S RIGHT, SATOU-SAN!
APPARENTLY, THE EXIT MIGHT NOT BE FAR FROM THIS ROOM.
REALLY? DID YOU FIND THAT OUT WITH MAGIC...?
YES!
I HAVE A SPELL CALLED "PATH FINDER" —KAZE NO MICHI— THAT CAN GET INFORMATION FROM THE FLOW OF THE AIR.
KOSO (WHISPER)
BUT, YOU SEE...
...SINCE IT RELIES ON THE AIRFLOW IN AN AREA, IT'S HARD TO SAY WHETHER IT CAME FROM A PATH THAT'S ACCESSIBLE TO PEOPLE.
THERE'S A SCOUT INVESTIGATING RIGHT NOW, SO WE'LL HAVE TO WAIT A LITTLE LONGER.
SURE.
THEN LET'S HOPE FOR GOOD NEWS.
ZAWA (CHATTER)
ZAWA
RIGHT AFTER THE SCOUT LEFT, THOSE SLIMES DROPPED FROM THE CEILING...
SO THAT'S HOW THINGS ENDED UP LIKE THAT...
PAST THE NEXT BIG ROOM IS A LONG PASSAGEWAY THAT LEADS TO THE EXIT...
...BUT IN THAT ROOM LIES A SMALL PROBLEM.

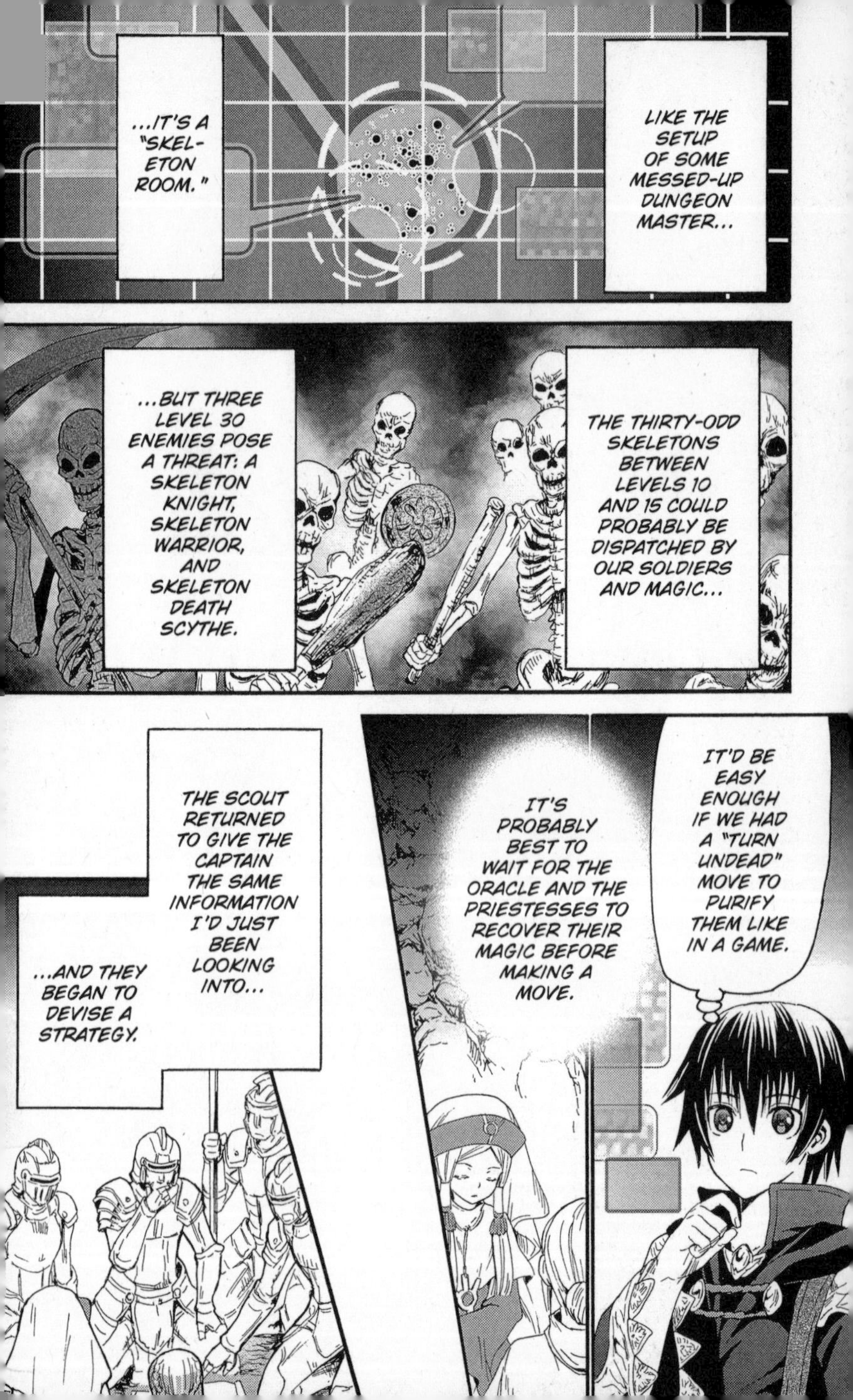
LIKE THE SETUP OF SOME MESSED-UP DUNGEON MASTER...
...IT'S A "SKEL-ETON ROOM."
THE THIRTY-ODD SKELETONS BETWEEN LEVELS 10 AND 15 COULD PROBABLY BE DISPATCHED BY OUR SOLDIERS AND MAGIC...
...BUT THREE LEVEL 30 ENEMIES POSE A THREAT: A SKELETON KNIGHT, SKELETON WARRIOR, AND SKELETON DEATH SCYTHE.
IT'D BE EASY ENOUGH IF WE HAD A "TURN UNDEAD" MOVE TO PURIFY THEM LIKE IN A GAME.
IT'S PROBABLY BEST TO WAIT FOR THE ORACLE AND THE PRIESTESSES TO RECOVER THEIR MAGIC BEFORE MAKING A MOVE.
THE SCOUT RETURNED TO GIVE THE CAPTAIN THE SAME INFORMATION I'D JUST BEEN LOOKING INTO...
...AND THEY BEGAN TO DEVISE A STRATEGY.

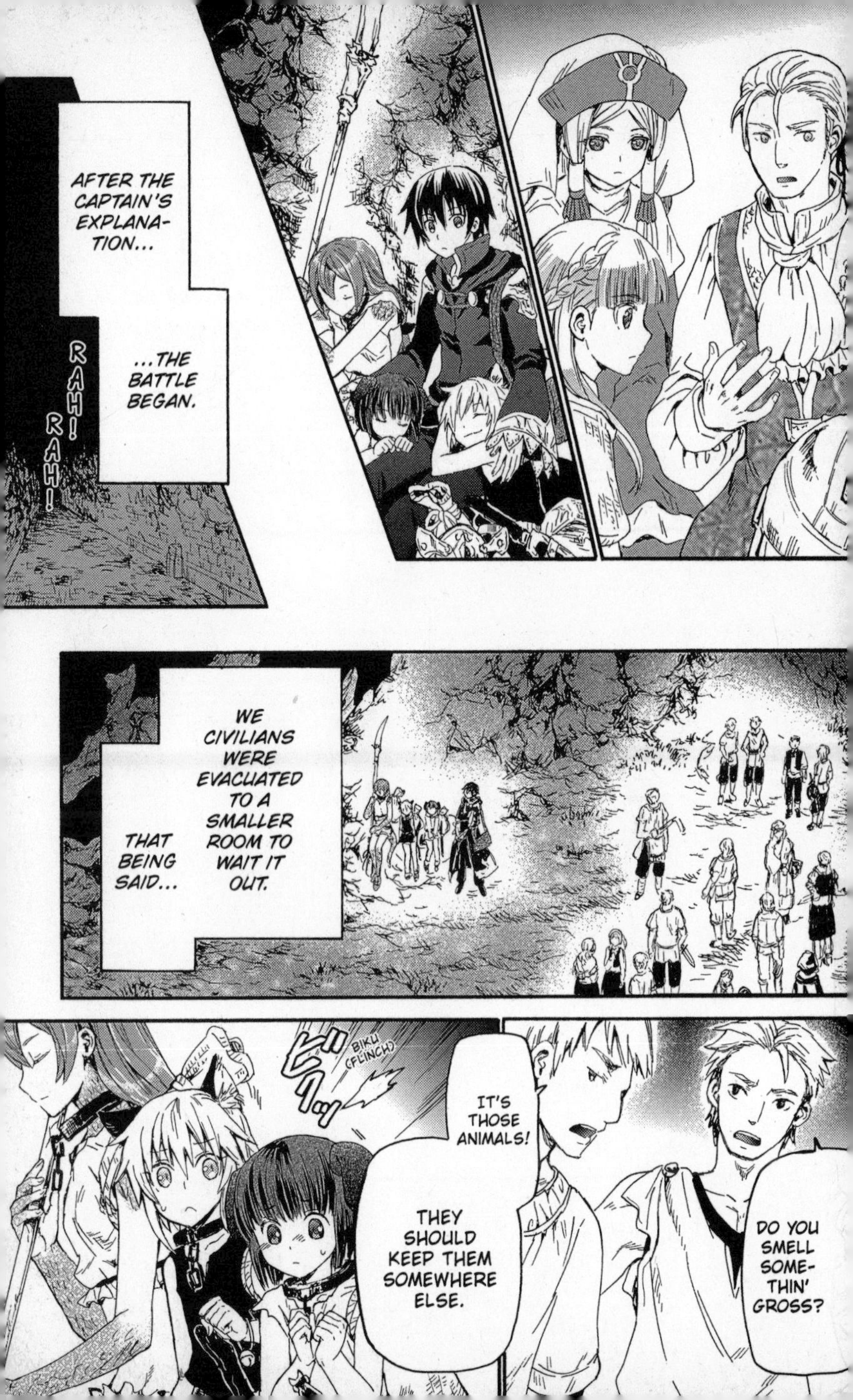
AFTER THE CAPTAIN'S EXPLANATION...
...THE BATTLE BEGAN.
RAH! RAH!
WE CIVILIANS WERE EVACUATED TO A SMALLER ROOM TO WAIT IT OUT.
THAT BEING SAID...
DO YOU SMELL SOMETHIN' GROSS?
IT'S THOSE ANIMALS!
THEY SHOULD KEEP THEM SOMEWHERE ELSE.
BIKU (FLINCH)

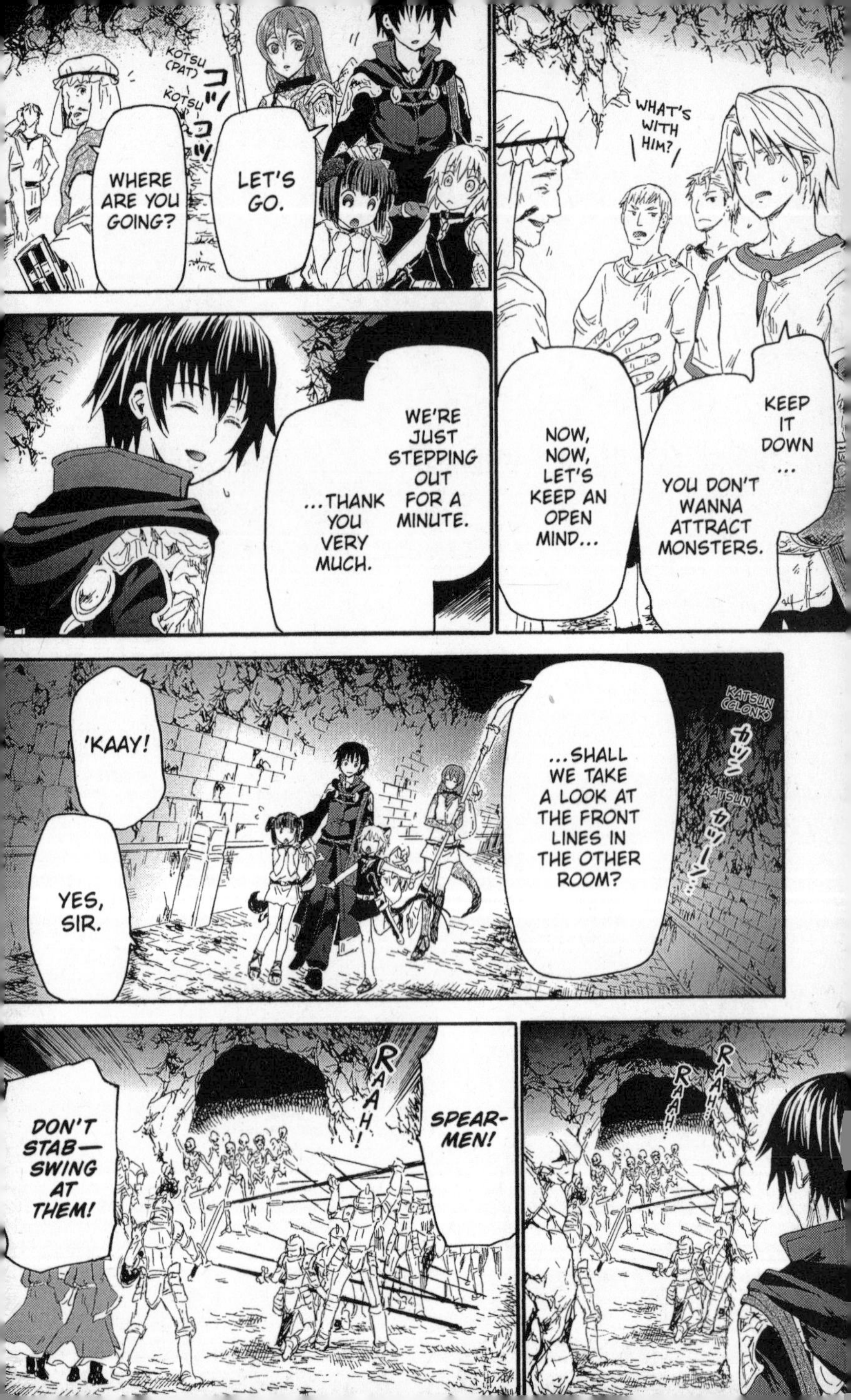
WHAT'S WITH HIM?
KEEP IT DOWN...
YOU DON'T WANNA ATTRACT MONSTERS.
NOW, NOW, LET'S KEEP AN OPEN MIND...
KOTSU (PAT)
KOTSU
LET'S GO.
WHERE ARE YOU GOING?
WE'RE JUST STEPPING OUT FOR A MINUTE.
...THANK YOU VERY MUCH.
KATSUN (CLONK)
KATSUN
...SHALL WE TAKE A LOOK AT THE FRONT LINES IN THE OTHER ROOM?
'KAAY!
YES, SIR.
RAAH...
RAAH...
RAAAH!
SPEAR-MEN!
DON'T STAB—SWING AT THEM!

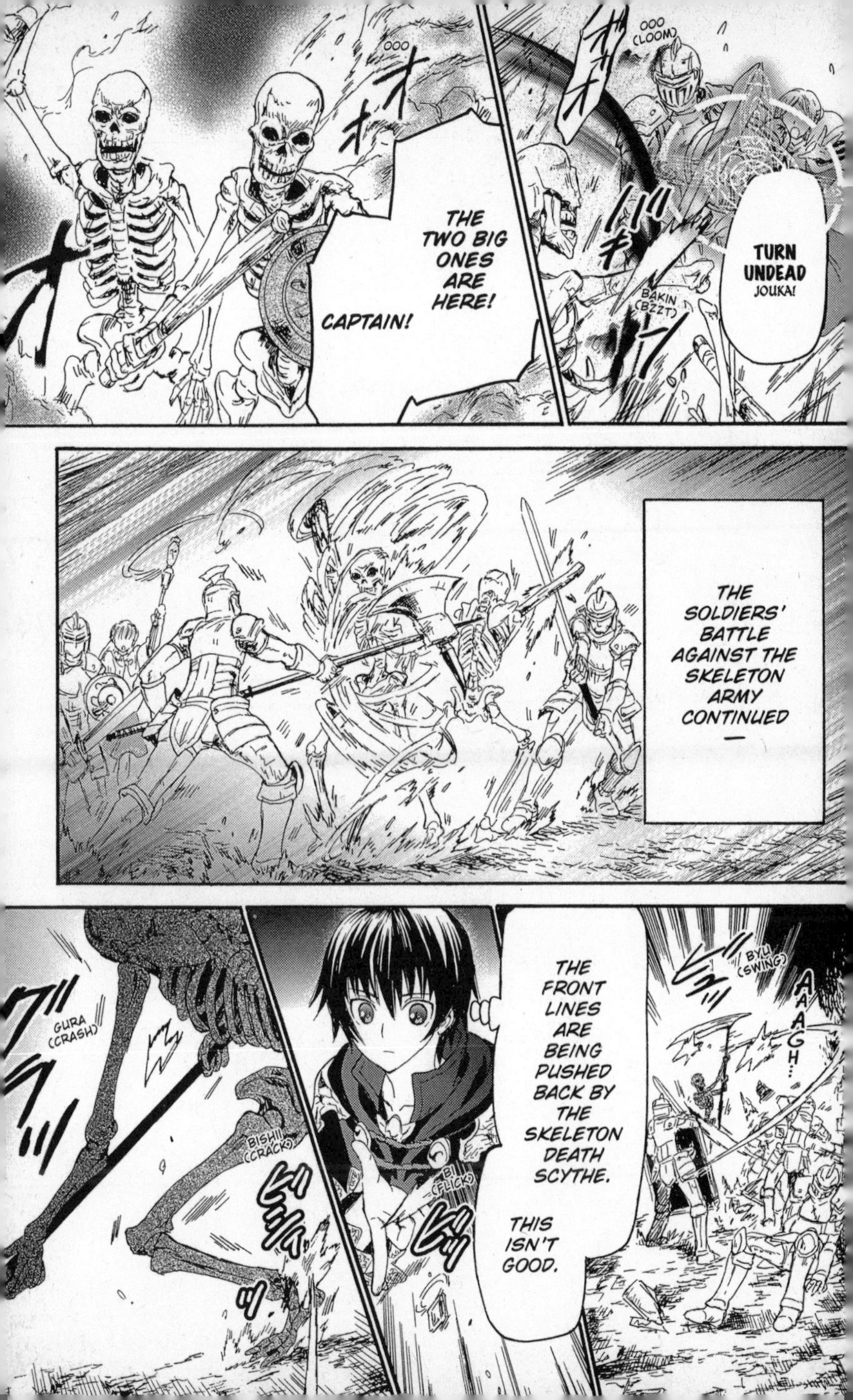
OOO (LOOM)
TURN UNDEAD JOUKA!
BAKIN (BZZT)
OOO
THE TWO BIG ONES ARE HERE!
CAPTAIN!
THE SOLDIERS' BATTLE AGAINST THE SKELETON ARMY CONTINUED —
BYU (SWING)
AAAGH...
THE FRONT LINES ARE BEING PUSHED BACK BY THE SKELETON DEATH SCYTHE.
THIS ISN'T GOOD.
BI (FLICK)
BISHI (CRACK)
GURA (CRASH)

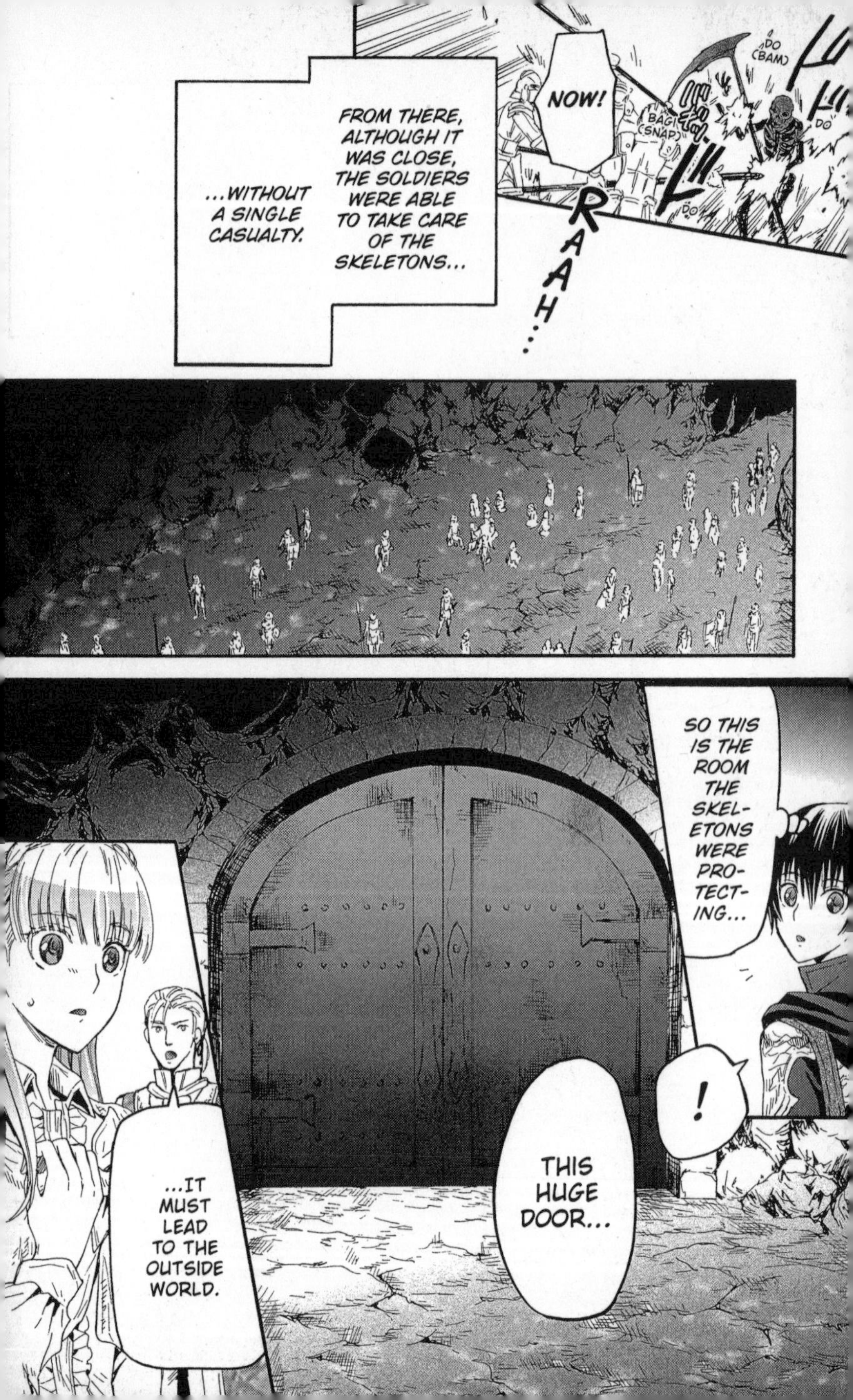
DO (BAM)
NOW!
BAGI (SNAP)
DO
DO
RAAH...
FROM THERE, ALTHOUGH IT WAS CLOSE, THE SOLDIERS WERE ABLE TO TAKE CARE OF THE SKELETONS...
...WITHOUT A SINGLE CASUALTY.
SO THIS IS THE ROOM THE SKEL-ETONS WERE PRO-TECT-ING...
!
THIS HUGE DOOR...
...IT MUST LEAD TO THE OUTSIDE WORLD.

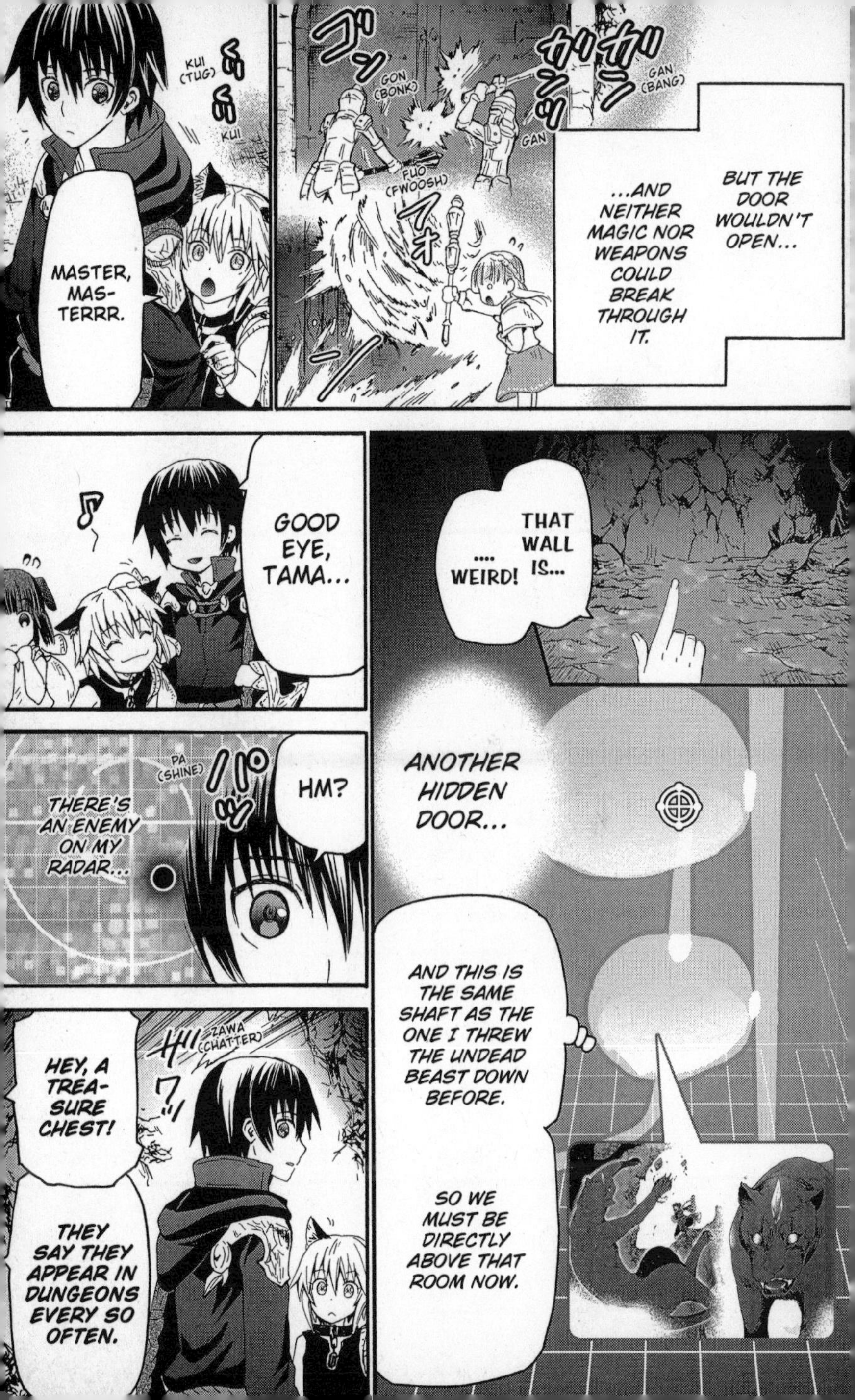
BUT THE DOOR WOULDN'T OPEN...
...AND NEITHER MAGIC NOR WEAPONS COULD BREAK THROUGH IT.
GAN (BANG)
GAN
GON (BONK)
FUO (FWOOSH)
KUI (TUG)
KUI
MASTER, MAS-TERRR.
THAT WALL IS...
....WEIRD!
ANOTHER HIDDEN DOOR...
AND THIS IS THE SAME SHAFT AS THE ONE I THREW THE UNDEAD BEAST DOWN BEFORE.
SO WE MUST BE DIRECTLY ABOVE THAT ROOM NOW.
GOOD EYE, TAMA...
HM?
PA (SHINE)
THERE'S AN ENEMY ON MY RADAR...
ZAWA (CHATTER)
HEY, A TREA-SURE CHEST!
THEY SAY THEY APPEAR IN DUNGEONS EVERY SO OFTEN.

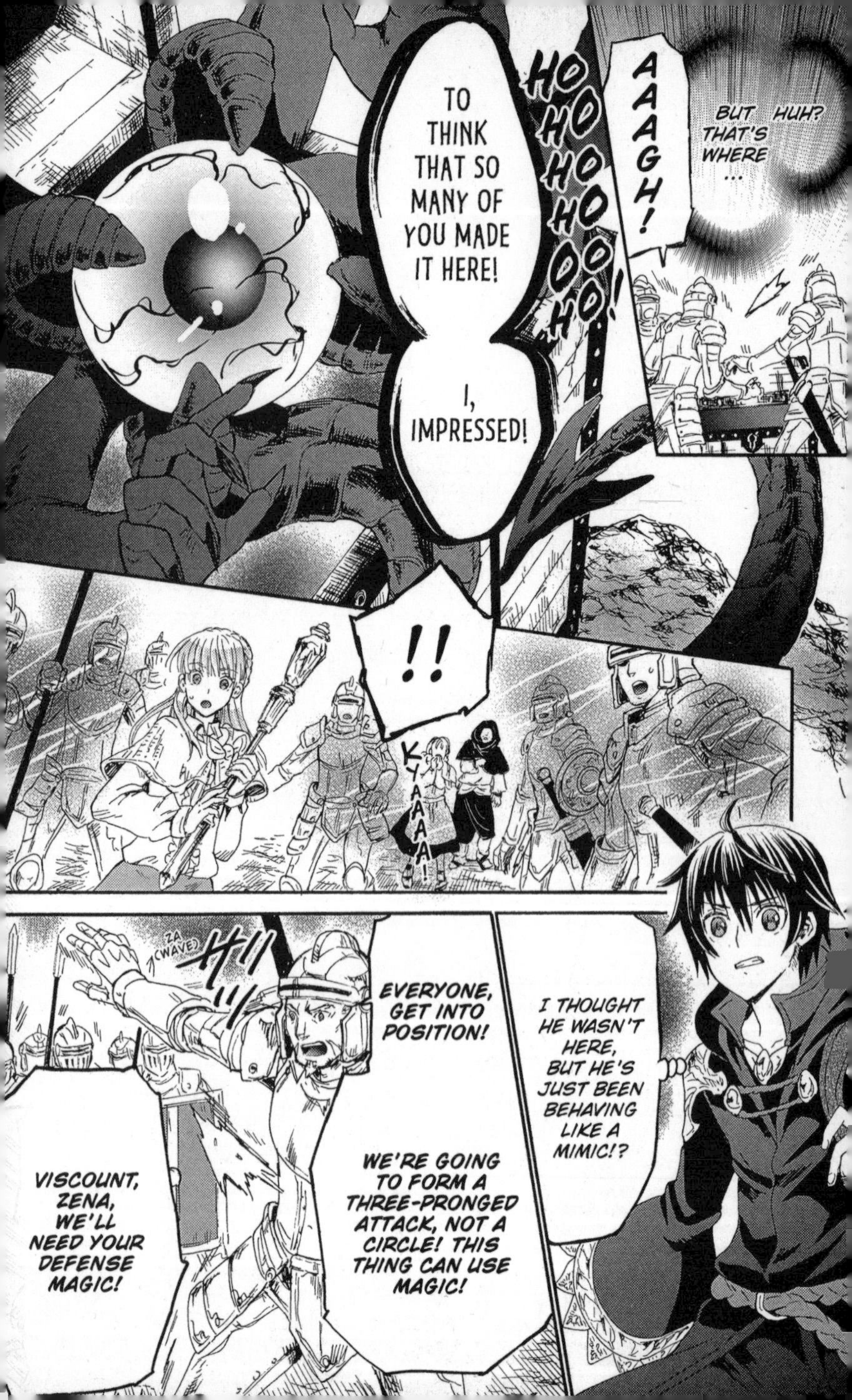
HUH?
BUT THAT'S WHERE ...
AAAAGH!
HOHOHOHOHOHOHO!
TO THINK THAT SO MANY OF YOU MADE IT HERE!
I, IMPRESSED!
!!
KYAAAAA!
I THOUGHT HE WASN'T HERE, BUT HE'S JUST BEEN BEHAVING LIKE A MIMIC!?
ZA (WAVE)
EVERYONE, GET INTO POSITION!
WE'RE GOING TO FORM A THREE-PRONGED ATTACK, NOT A CIRCLE! THIS THING CAN USE MAGIC!
VISCOUNT, ZENA, WE'LL NEED YOUR DEFENSE MAGIC!

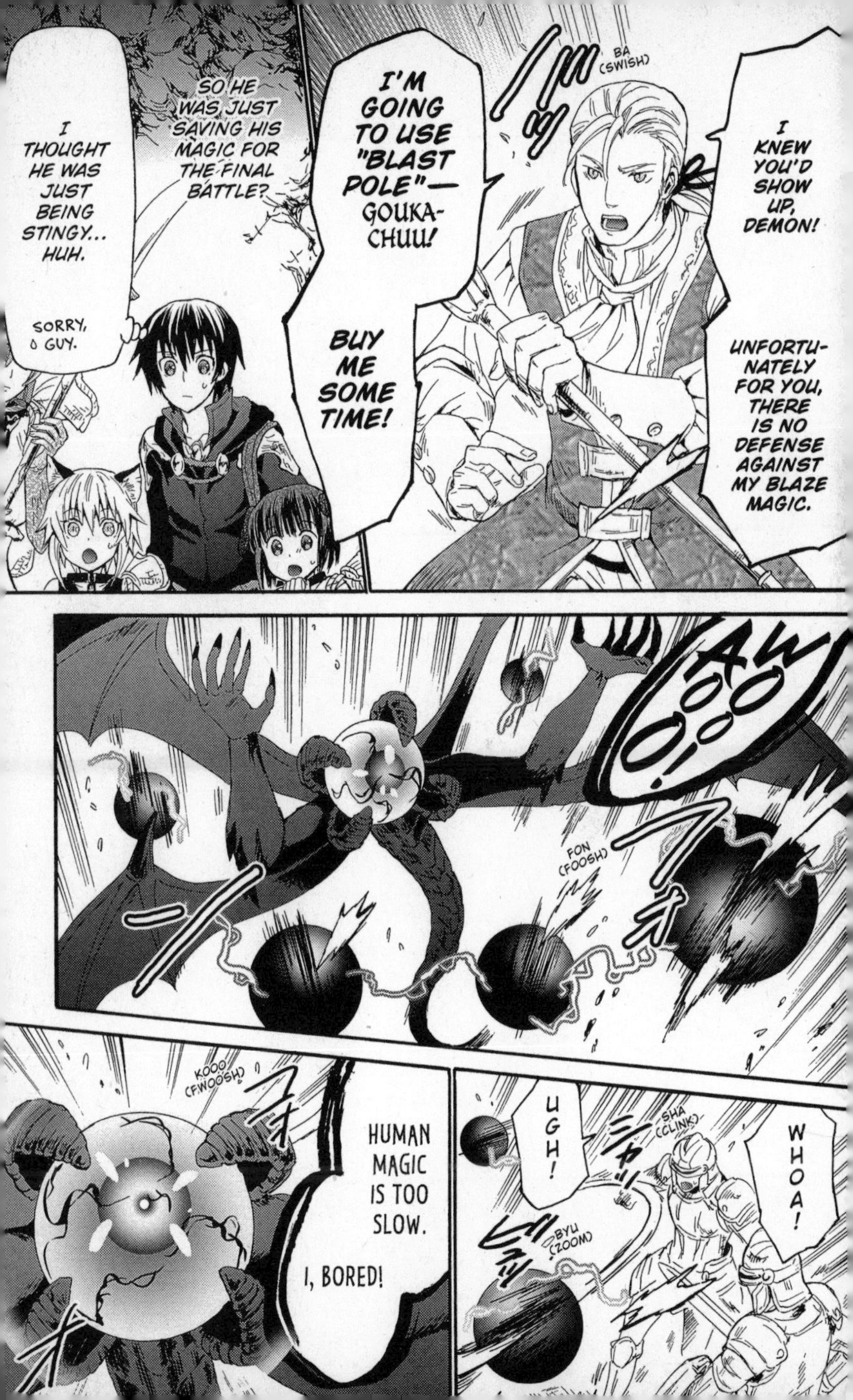
BA (SWISH)
I KNEW YOU'D SHOW UP, DEMON!
UNFORTUNATELY FOR YOU, THERE IS NO DEFENSE AGAINST MY BLAZE MAGIC.
I'M GOING TO USE "BLAST POLE"— GOUKA-CHUU!
BUY ME SOME TIME!
SO HE WAS JUST SAVING HIS MAGIC FOR THE FINAL BATTLE?
I THOUGHT HE WAS JUST BEING STINGY... HUH.
SORRY, O GUY.
AWOOOO!
FON (FOOSH)
WHOA!
SHA (CLINK)
UGH!
BYU (ZOOM)
KOOO (F.WOOSH)
HUMAN MAGIC IS TOO SLOW.
I, BORED!

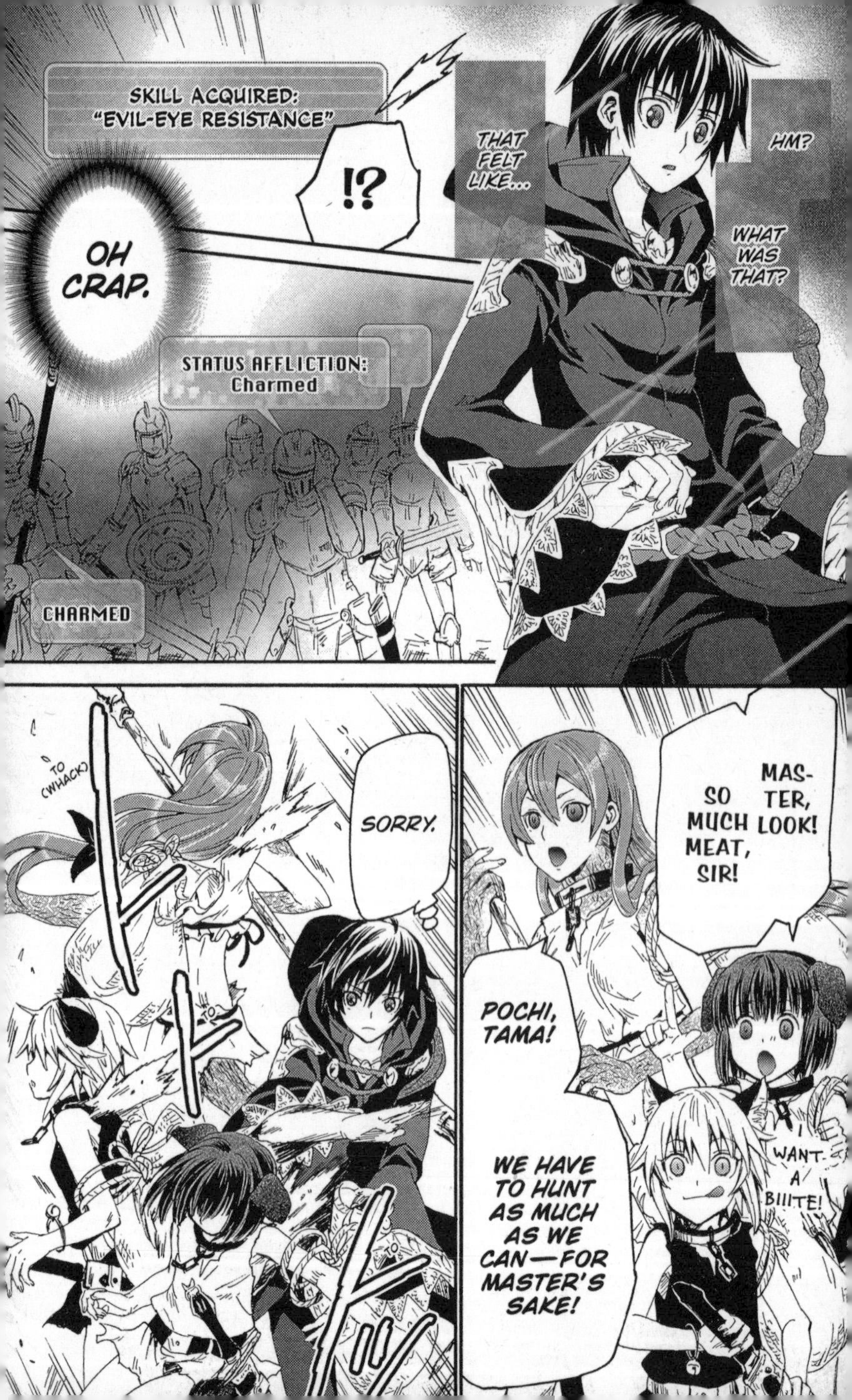
HM?
WHAT WAS THAT?
THAT FELT LIKE...
SKILL ACQUIRED: "EVIL-EYE RESISTANCE"
!?
OH CRAP.
STATUS AFFLICTION: Charmed
CHARMED
MASTER, LOOK! SO MUCH MEAT, SIR!
I WANT A BIIITE!
POCHI, TAMA!
WE HAVE TO HUNT AS MUCH AS WE CAN—FOR MASTER'S SAKE!
SORRY.
TO (WHACK)
TO
TO

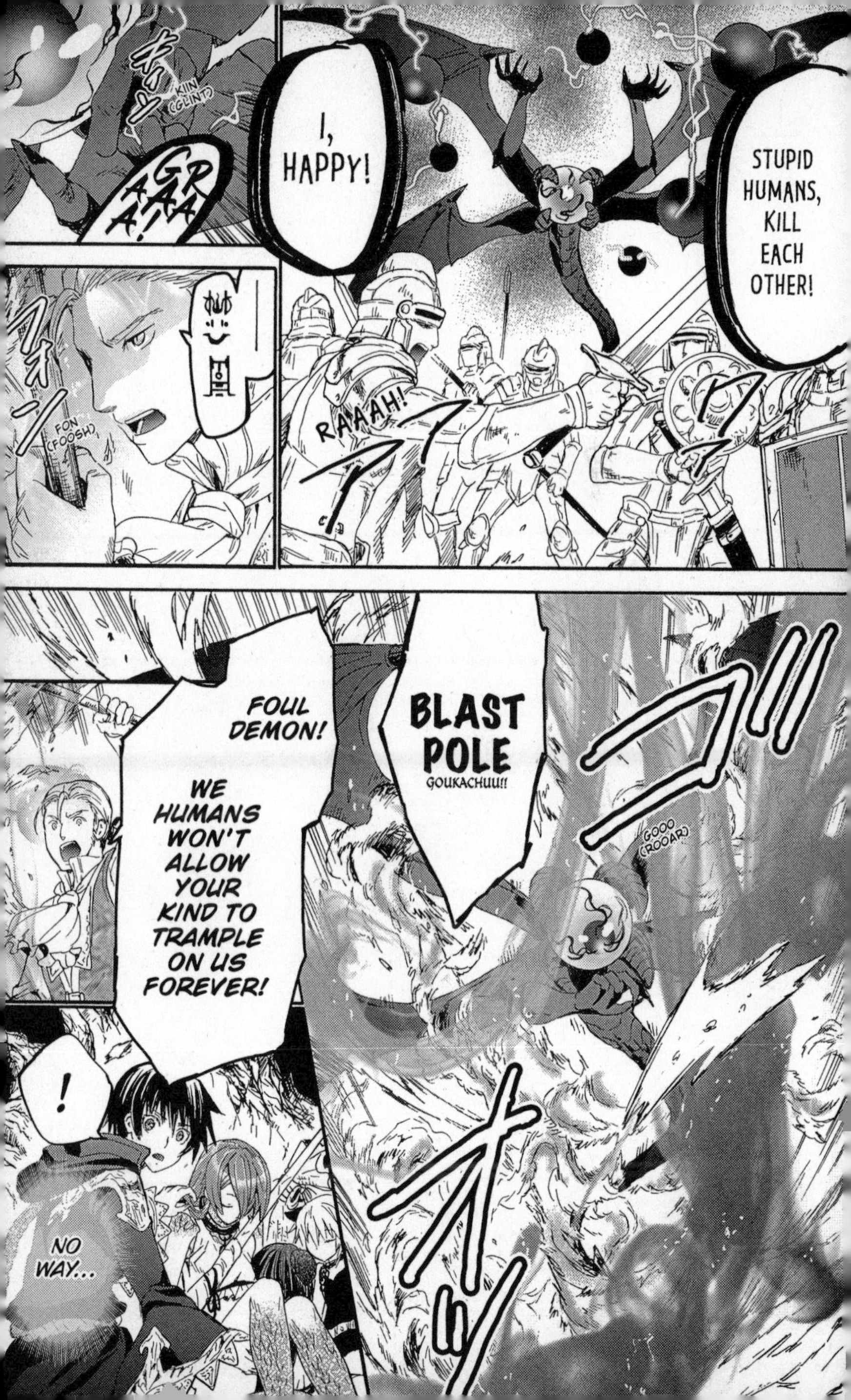
STUPID HUMANS, KILL EACH OTHER!
I, HAPPY!
RAAAH!
KIIN (GLINT)
GRAAAA!
FON (FOOSH)
BLAST POLE
GOUKACHUU!!
GOOO (ROOAR)
FOUL DEMON!
WE HUMANS WON'T ALLOW YOUR KIND TO TRAMPLE ON US FOREVER!
!
NO WAY...

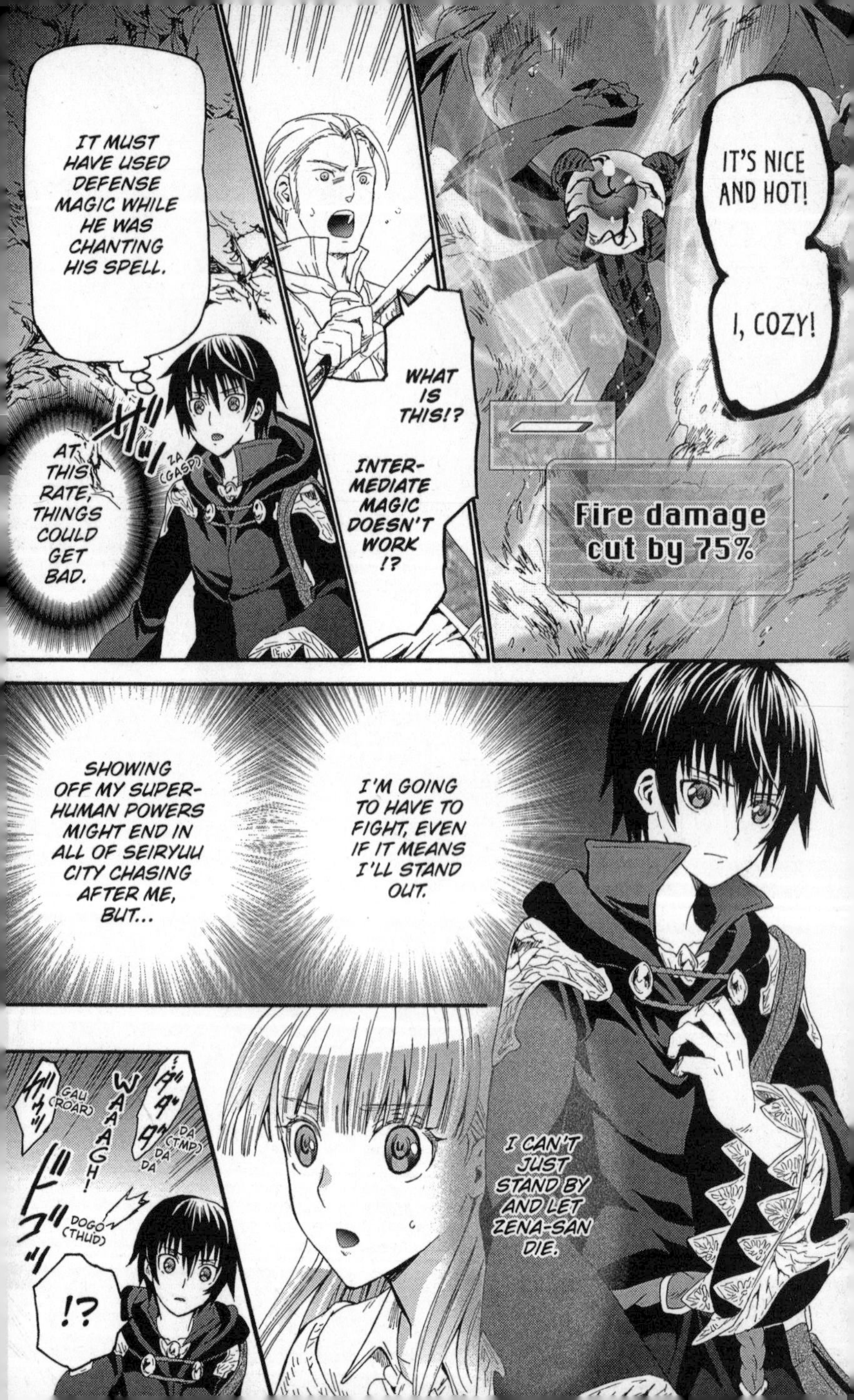
IT'S NICE AND HOT!
I, COZY!
Fire damage cut by 75%
WHAT IS THIS!?
INTER-MEDIATE MAGIC DOESN'T WORK!?
IT MUST HAVE USED DEFENSE MAGIC WHILE HE WAS CHANTING HIS SPELL.
ZA (GASP)
AT THIS RATE, THINGS COULD GET BAD.
SHOWING OFF MY SUPER-HUMAN POWERS MIGHT END IN ALL OF SEIRYUU CITY CHASING AFTER ME, BUT...
I'M GOING TO HAVE TO FIGHT, EVEN IF IT MEANS I'LL STAND OUT.
I CAN'T JUST STAND BY AND LET ZENA-SAN DIE.
GAU (ROAR)
WAAAAGH!
DA (TMP) DA DA
DOGO (THUD)
!?

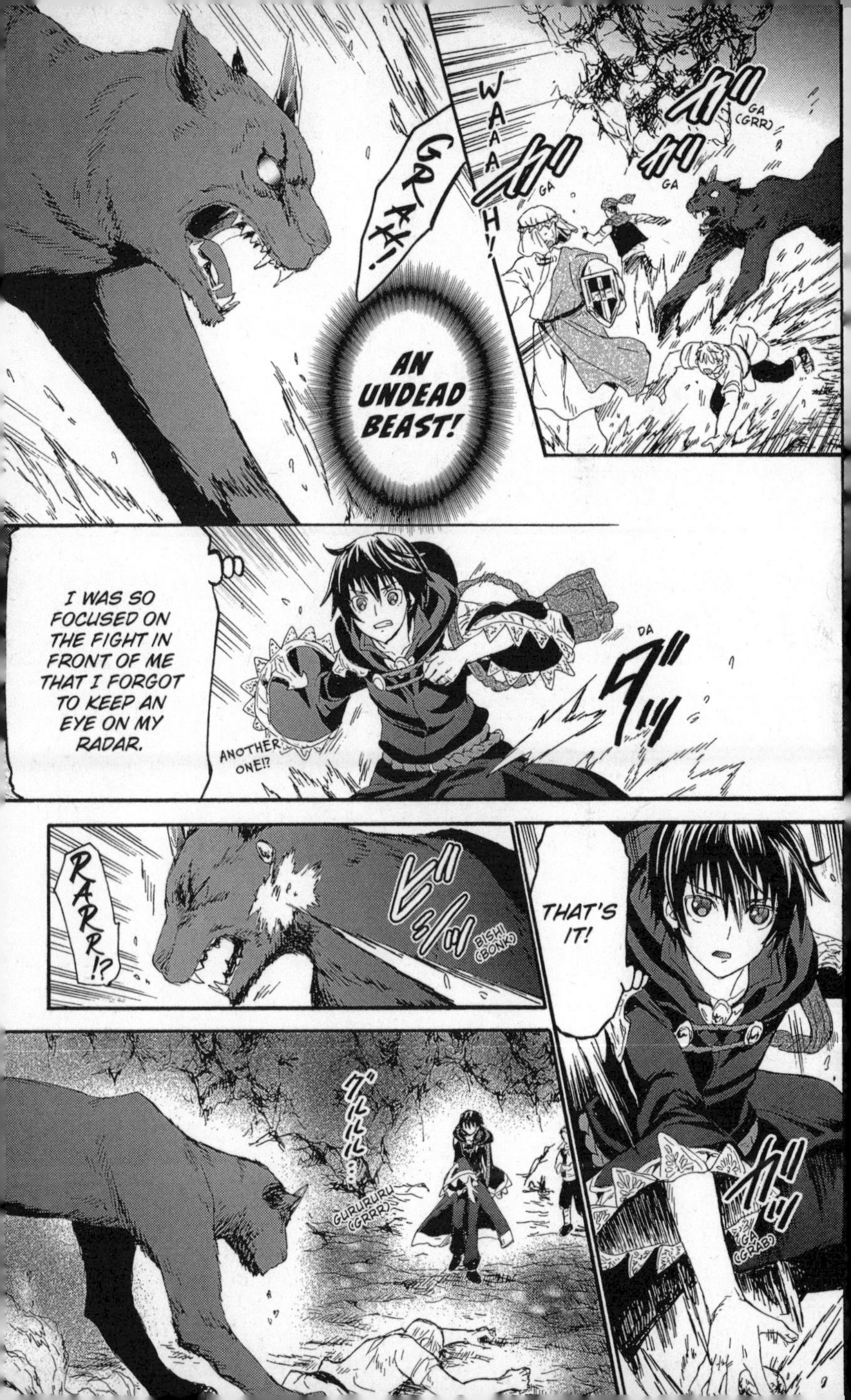
WAAAAH!
GA (GRR)
GA
GA
GRAAH!
AN UNDEAD BEAST!
DA
I WAS SO FOCUSED ON THE FIGHT IN FRONT OF ME THAT I FORGOT TO KEEP AN EYE ON MY RADAR.
ANOTHER ONE!?
THAT'S IT!
GA (GRAB)
BISHI (BONK)
RARR!?
GURURURU (GRRR)

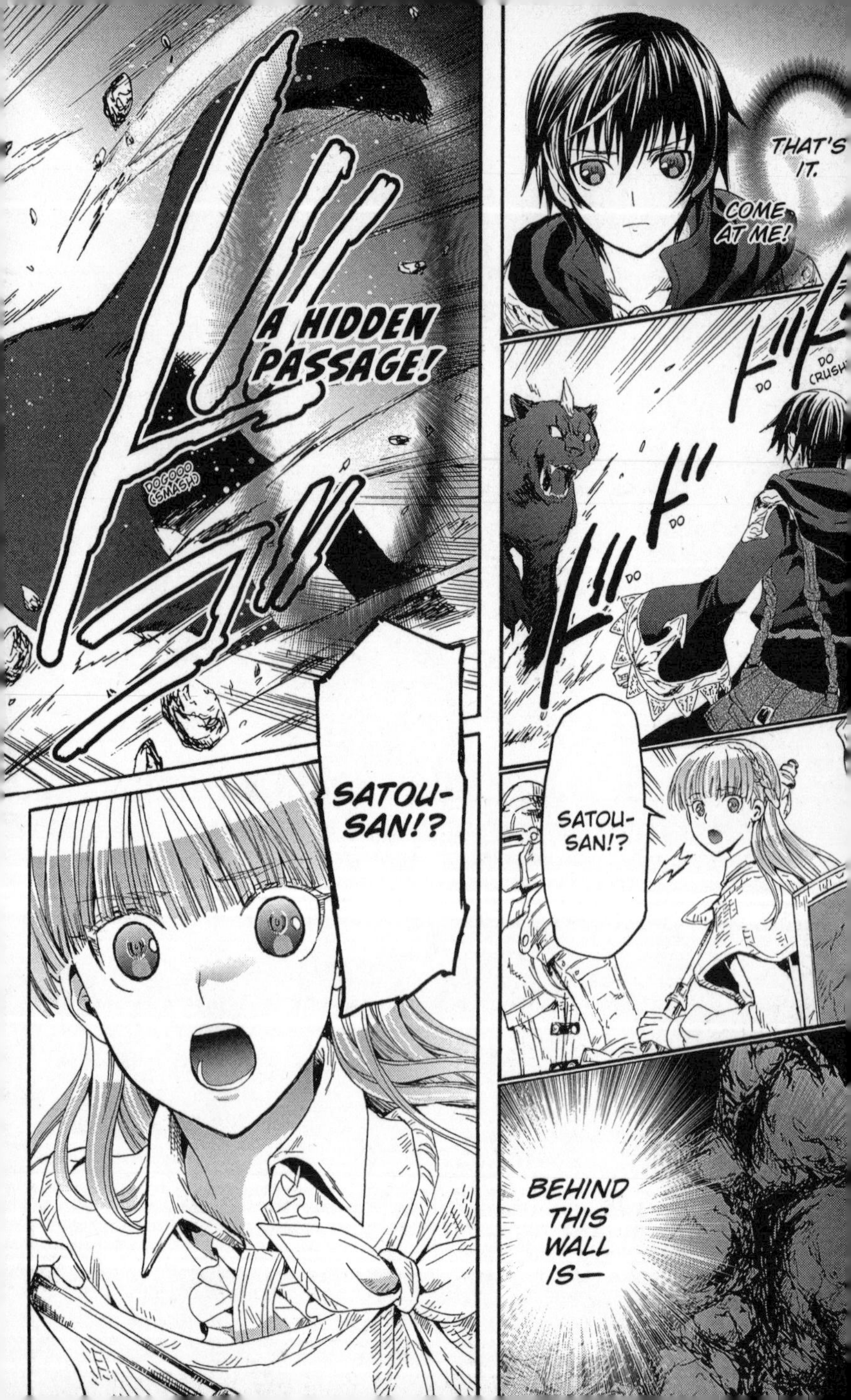

THAT'S IT.
COME AT ME!
DO DO (CRUSH)
DO
DO
A HIDDEN PASSAGE!
DOGOOO (SMASH)
SATOU-SAN!?
BEHIND THIS WALL IS—
SATOU-SAN!?

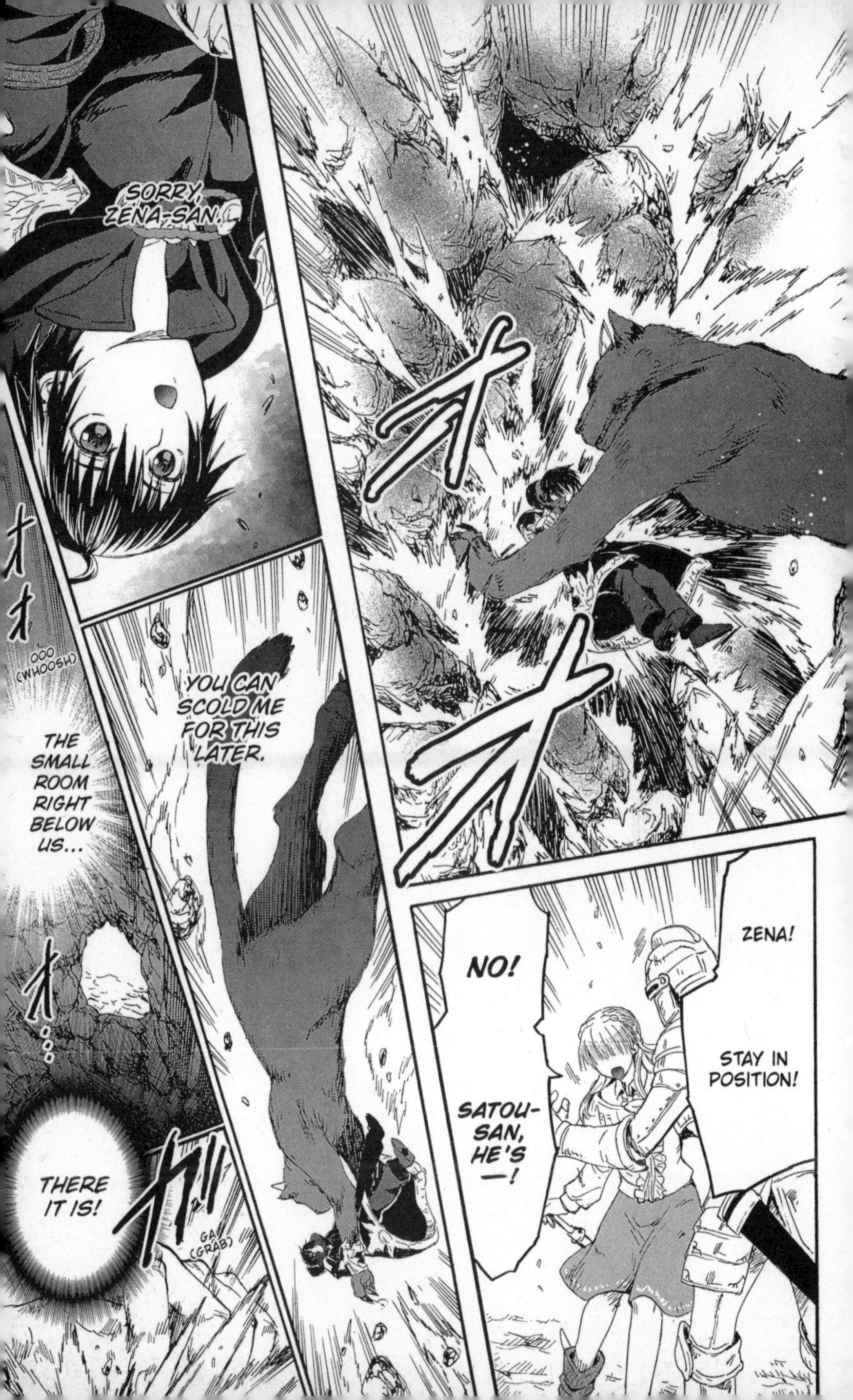

SORRY, ZENA-SAN.
OOO (WHOOSH)
YOU CAN SCOLD ME FOR THIS LATER.
THE SMALL ROOM RIGHT BELOW US...
THERE IT IS!
GA (GRAB)
ZENA!
STAY IN POSITION!
NO!
SATOU-SAN, HE'S —!

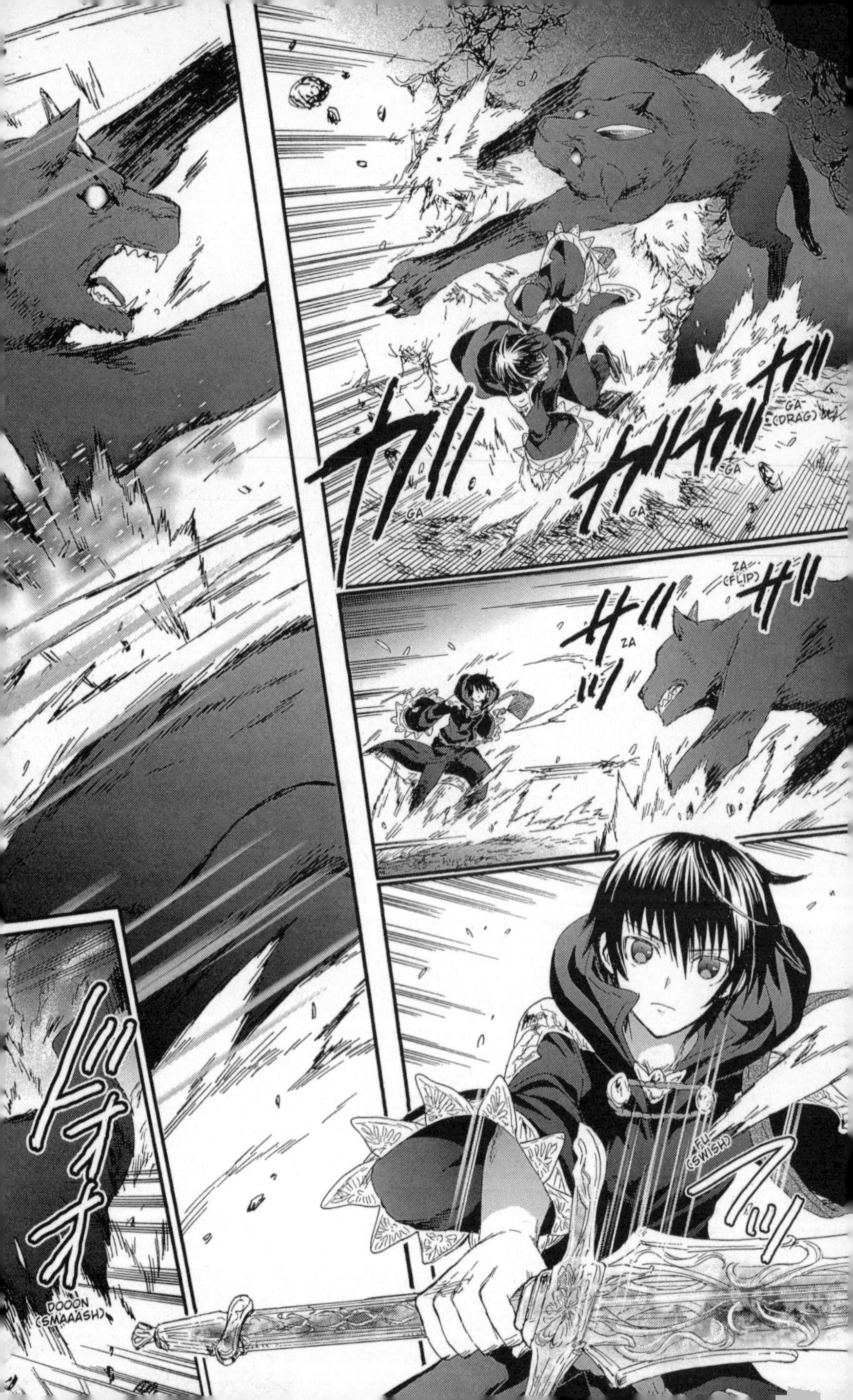
GA (DRAG)
GA
GA
GA
ZA (FLIP)
ZA
FU (SWISH)
DOOON (SMAAASH)

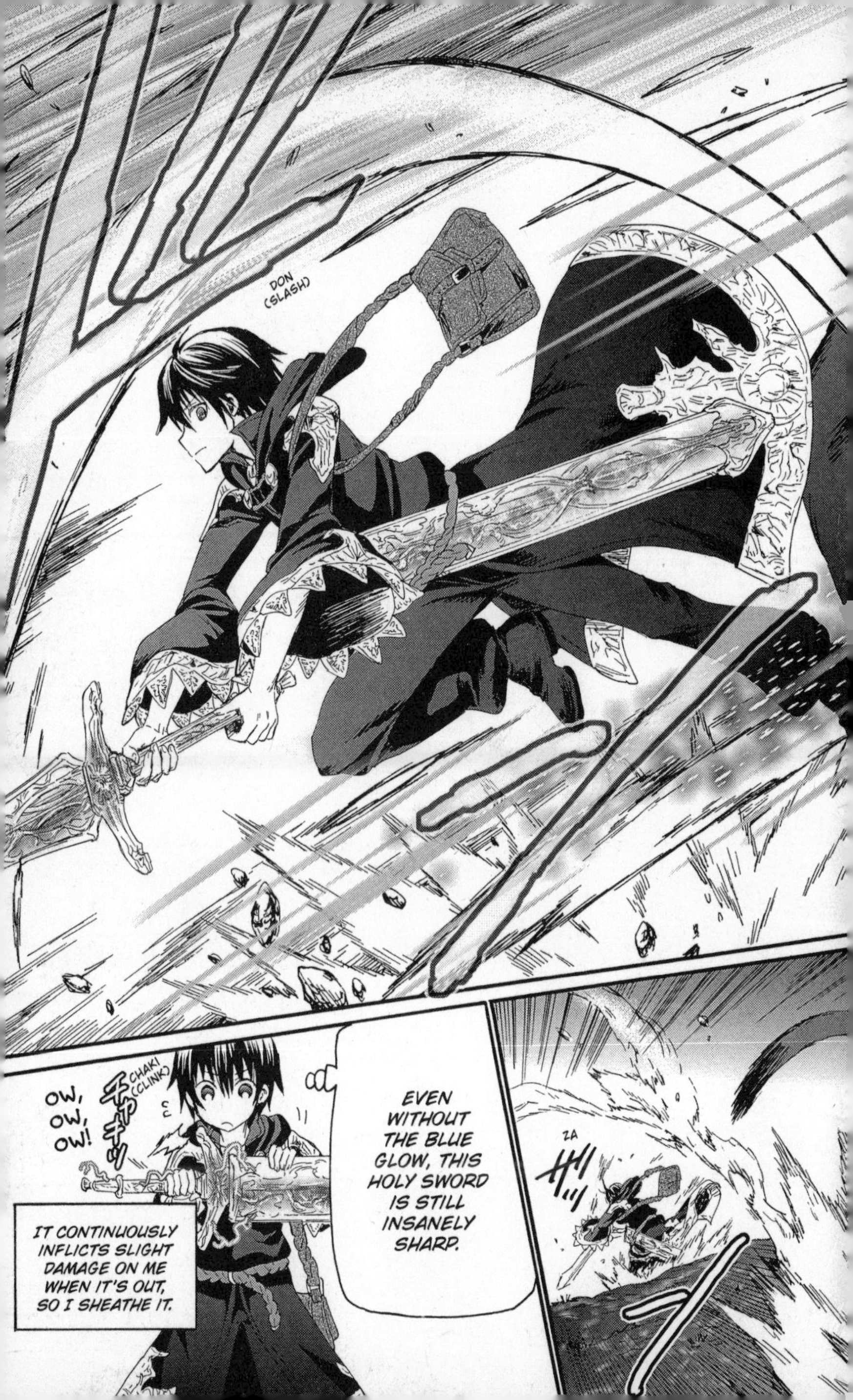
DON (SLASH)
ZA
EVEN WITHOUT THE BLUE GLOW, THIS HOLY SWORD IS STILL INSANELY SHARP.
CHAKI (CLINK)
OW, OW, OW!
IT CONTINUOUSLY INFLICTS SLIGHT DAMAGE ON ME WHEN IT'S OUT, SO I SHEATHE IT.

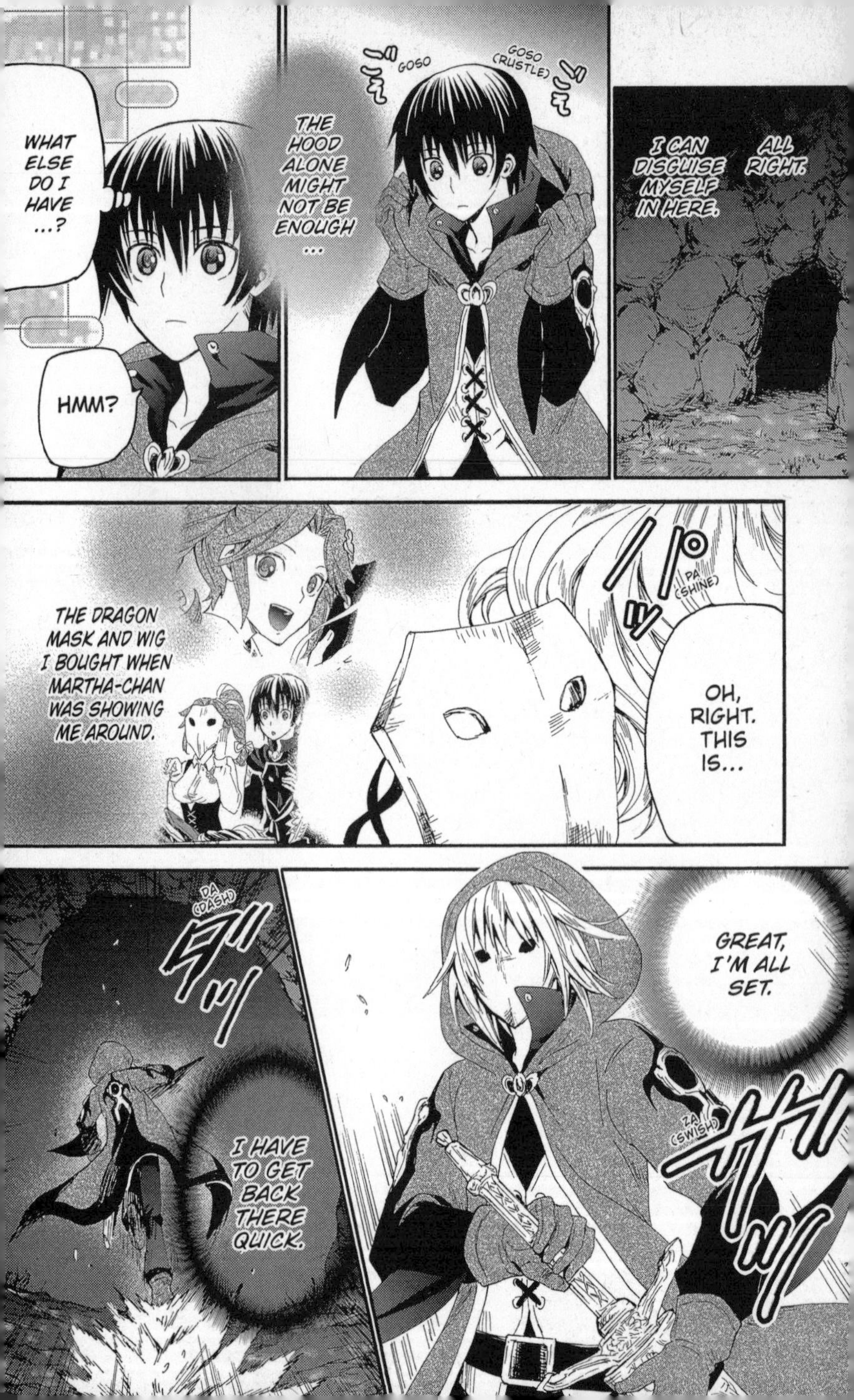

ALL RIGHT.
I CAN DISGUISE MYSELF IN HERE.
GOSO (RUSTLE)
GOSO
THE HOOD ALONE MIGHT NOT BE ENOUGH...
WHAT ELSE DO I HAVE...?
HMM?
PA (SHINE)
OH, RIGHT. THIS IS...
THE DRAGON MASK AND WIG I BOUGHT WHEN MARTHA-CHAN WAS SHOWING ME AROUND.
GREAT, I'M ALL SET.
ZA (SWISH)
DA (DASH)
I HAVE TO GET BACK THERE QUICK.

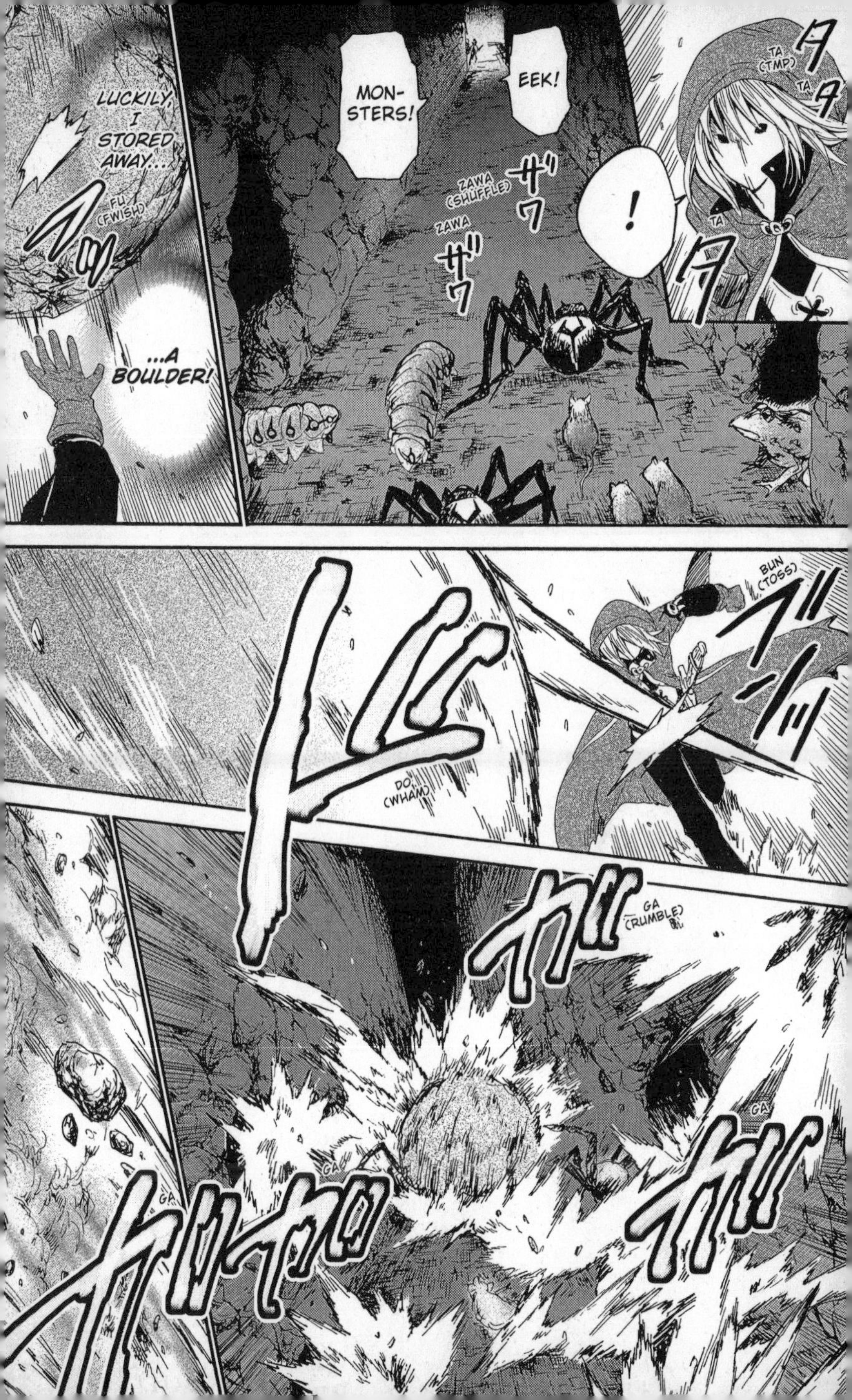
TA (TMP)
TA
TA
!
EEK!
MON-
STERS!
ZAWA (SHUFFLE)
ZAWA
LUCKILY, I STORED AWAY...
FU (FWISH)
...A BOULDER!
BUN (TOSS)
DO (WHAM)
GA (RUMBLE)
GA
GA
GA

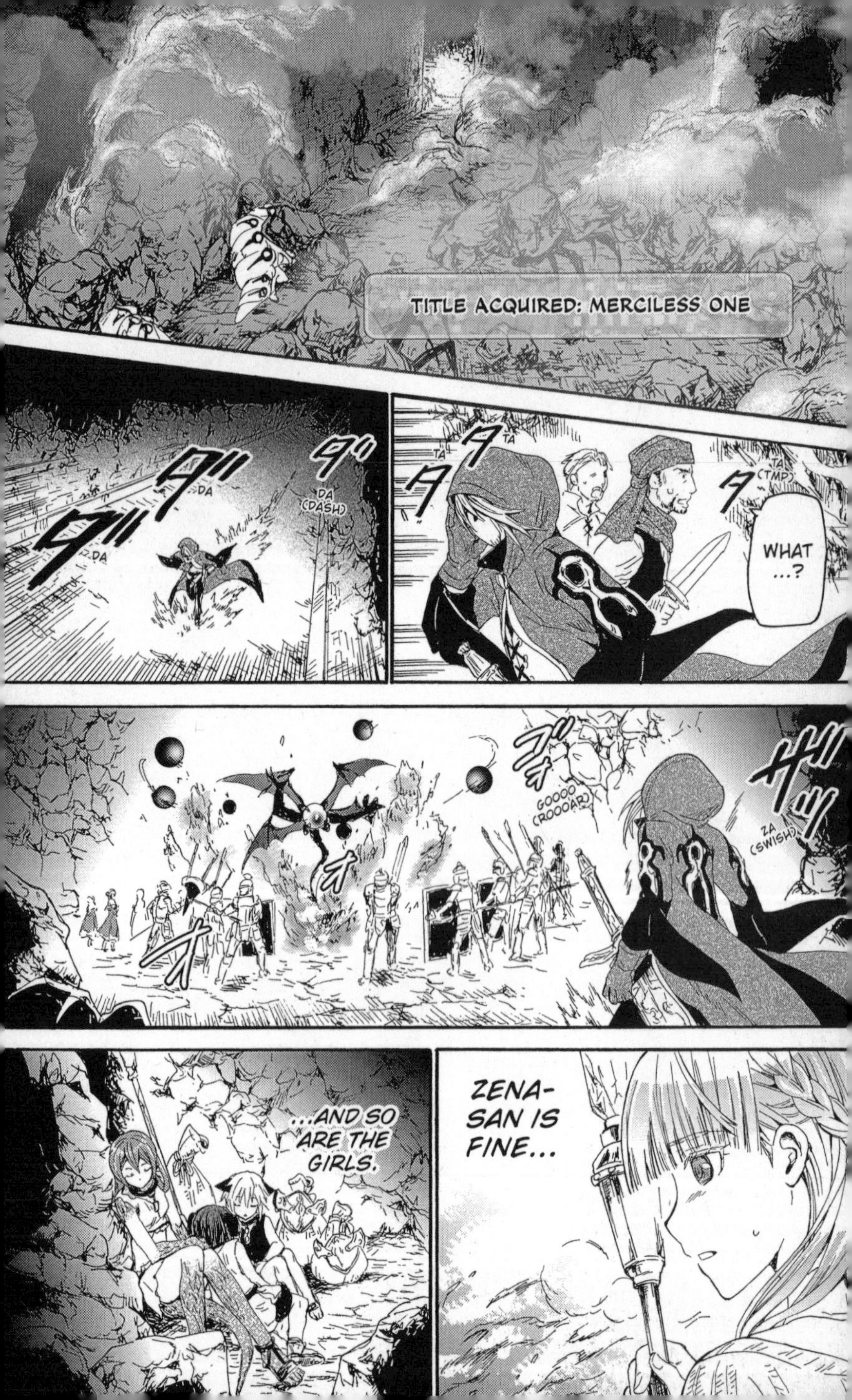
TITLE ACQUIRED: MERCILESS ONE
TA
TA
TA (TMP)
WHAT ...?
DA
DA
DA (DASH)
ZA (SWISH)
GOOOO (ROOOAR)
ZENA-SAN IS FINE...
...AND SO ARE THE GIRLS.

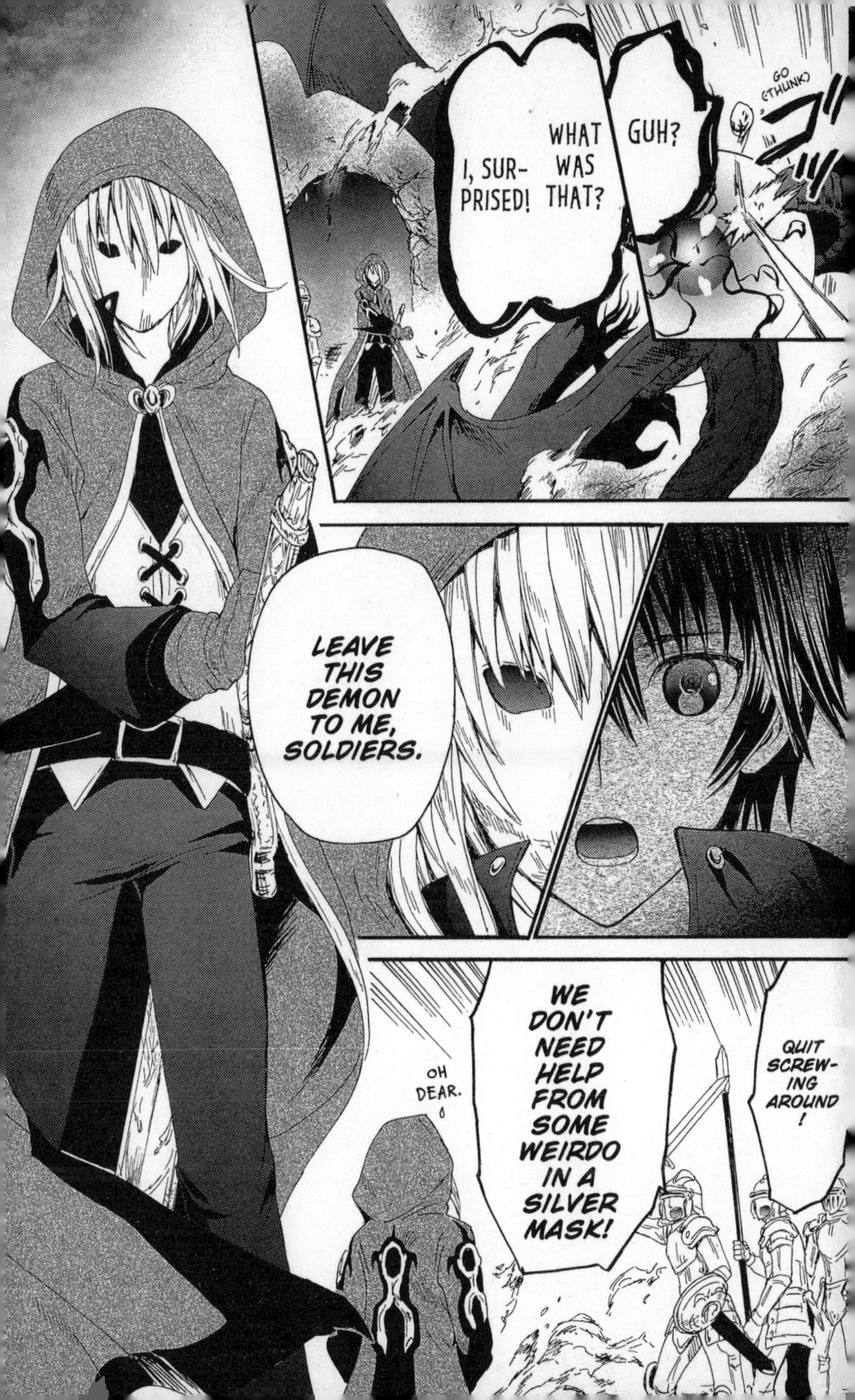
GO (THUNK)
GUH?
WHAT WAS THAT?
I, SURPRISED!
LEAVE THIS DEMON TO ME, SOLDIERS.
QUIT SCREWING AROUND!
WE DON'T NEED HELP FROM SOME WEIRDO IN A SILVER MASK!
OH DEAR.

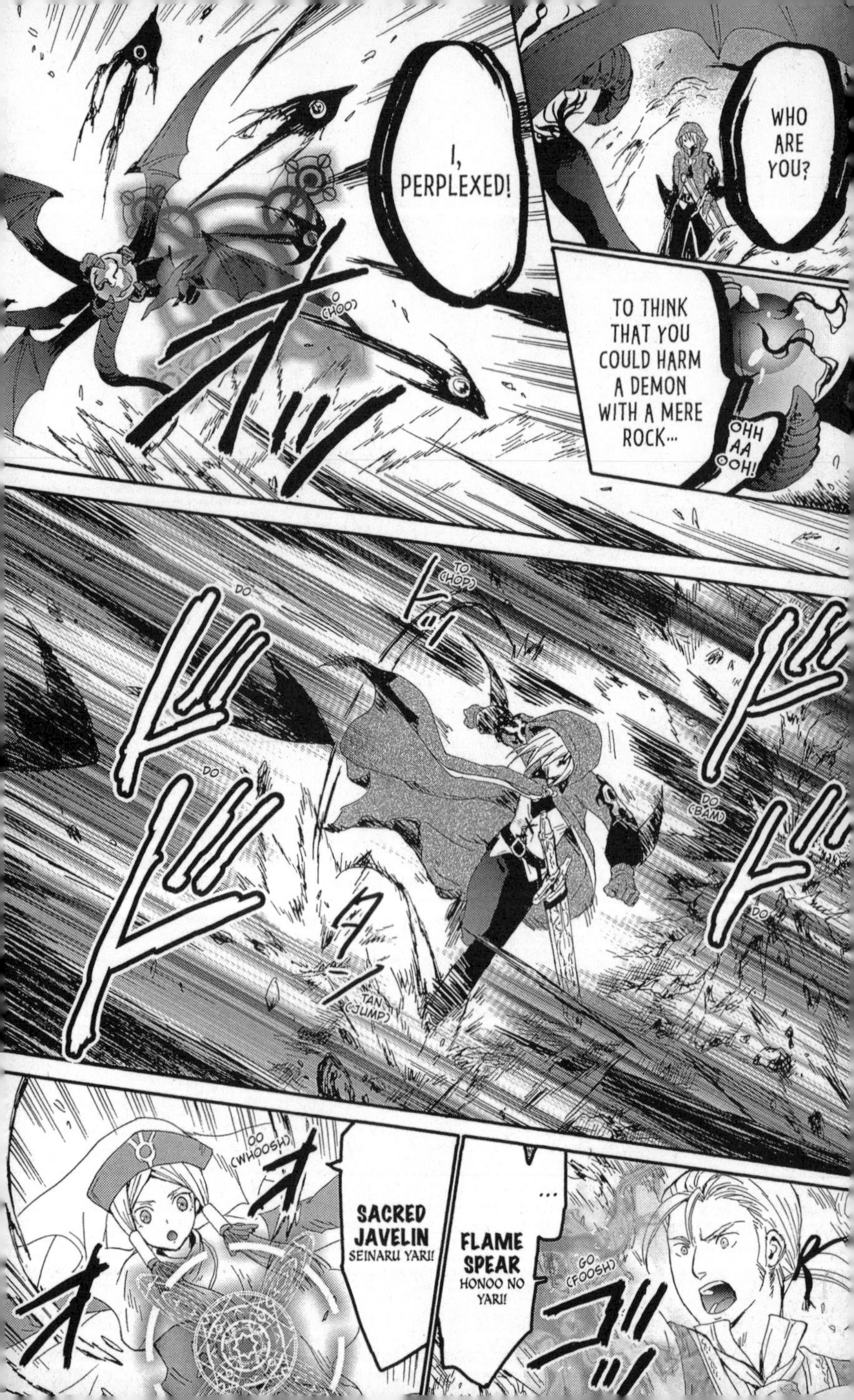
WHO ARE YOU?
TO THINK THAT YOU COULD HARM A DEMON WITH A MERE ROCK...
OHH AA OOH!
I, PERPLEXED!
O (HOO)
DO (BAM)
DO
TO (HOP)
DO
DO
TAN (JUMP)
...
FLAME SPEAR HONOO NO YARI!
GO (FOOSH)
SACRED JAVELIN SEINARU YARI!
OO (WHOOSH)

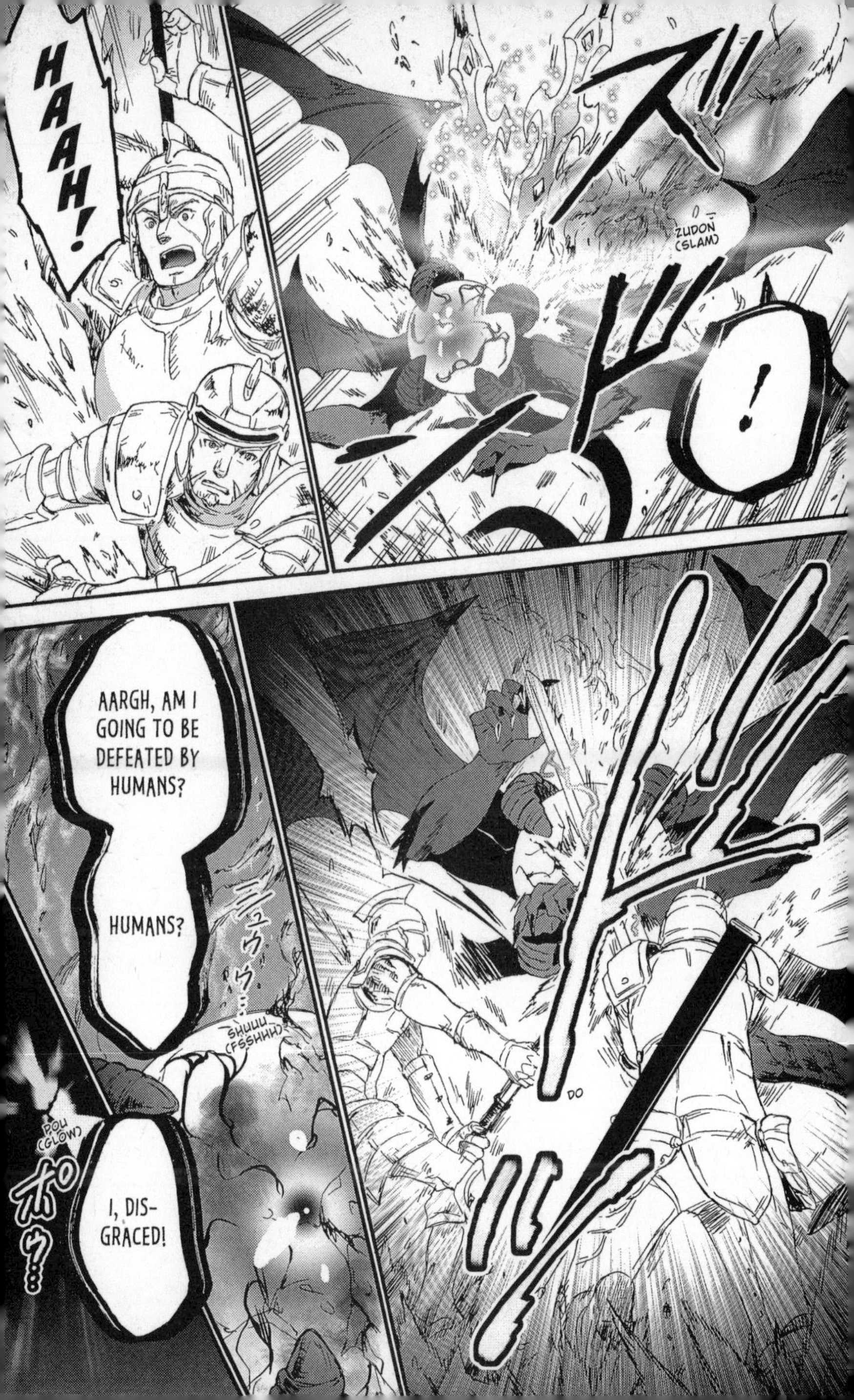
ZUDON (SLAM)
!
HAAAH!
DO
AARGH, AM I GOING TO BE DEFEATED BY HUMANS?
HUMANS?
SHUUU (FSSHHH)
I, DIS-GRACED!
POU (GLOW)

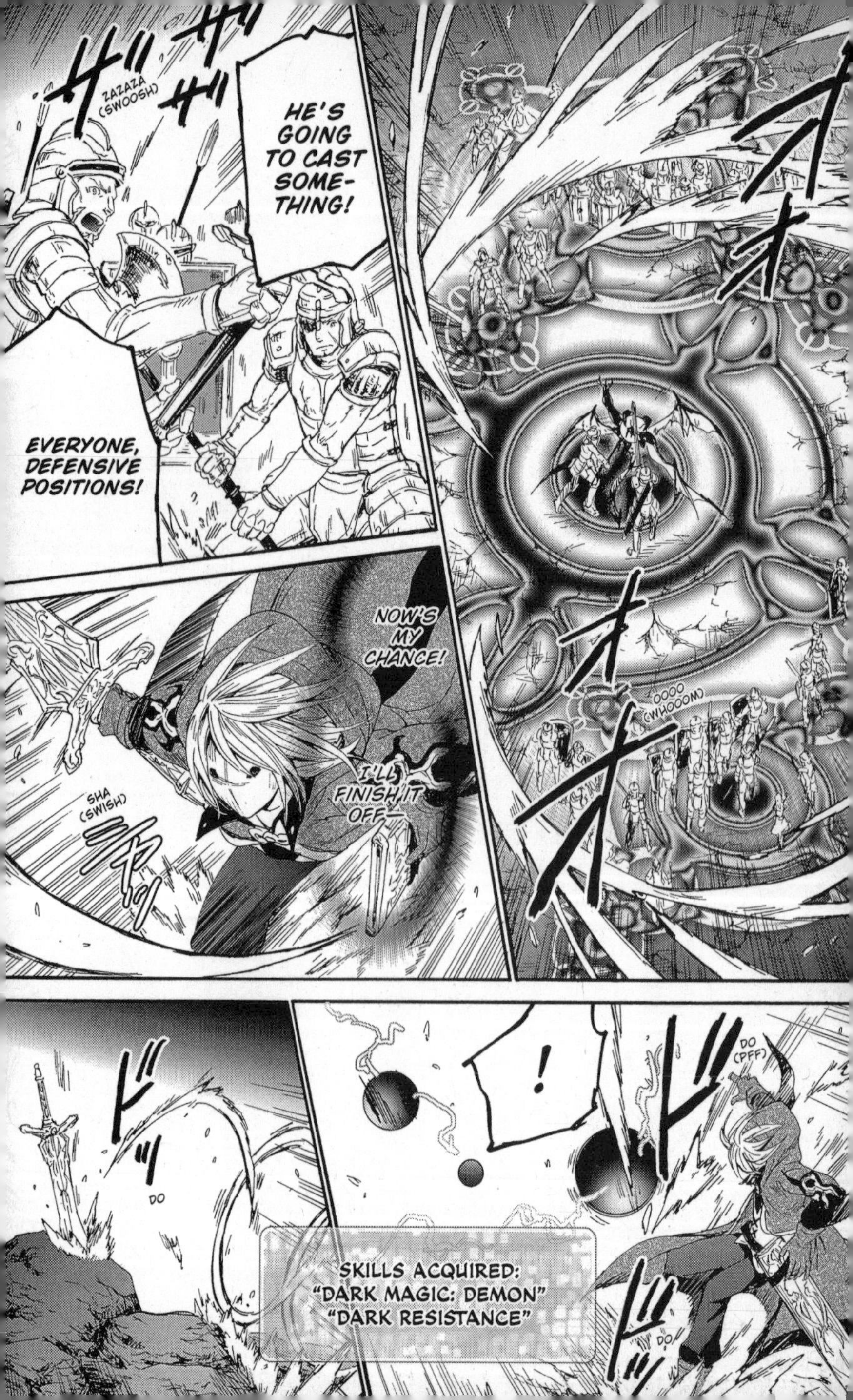
OOOO (WHOOOM)
ZAZAZA (SWOOSH)
HE'S GOING TO CAST SOME-THING!
EVERYONE, DEFENSIVE POSITIONS!
NOW'S MY CHANCE!
SHA (SWISH)
I'LL FINISH IT OFF—
!
DO (PFF)
DO
DO
SKILLS ACQUIRED:
"DARK MAGIC: DEMON"
"DARK RESISTANCE"

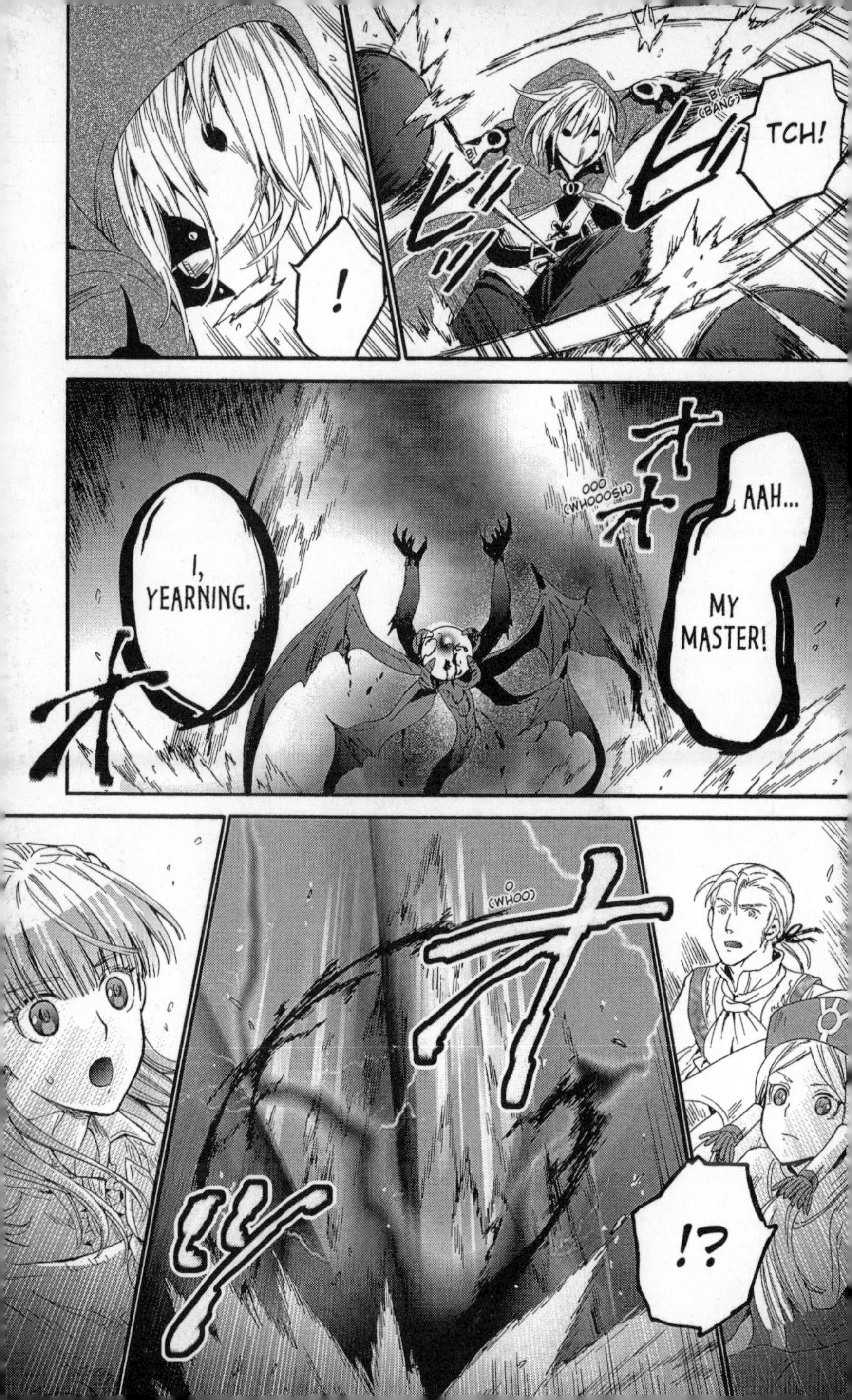
TCH!
BI (BANG)
BI
!
AAH... MY MASTER!
OOO (WHOOOSH)
I, YEARNING.
!?
O (WHOO)

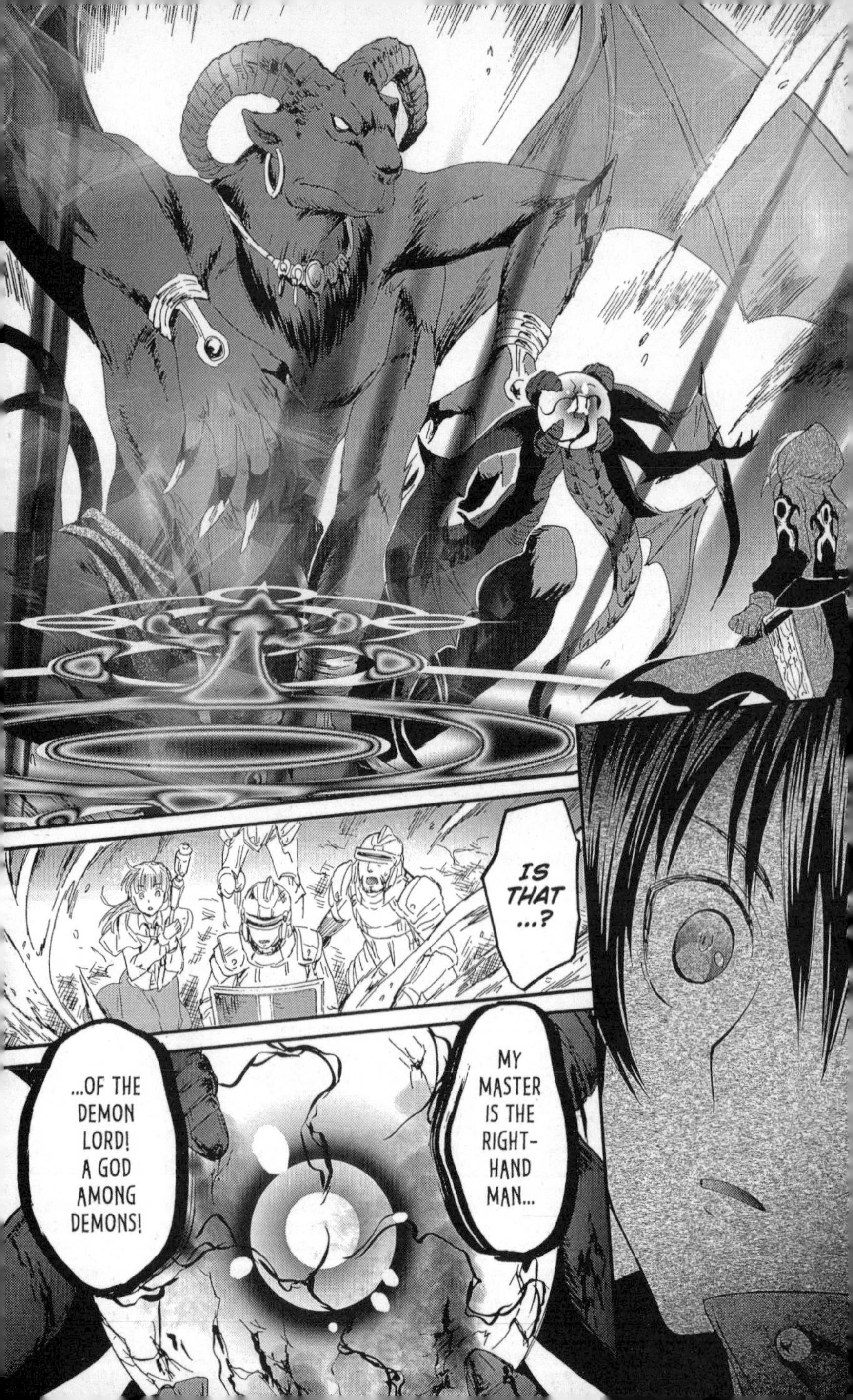
IS THAT ...?
MY MASTER IS THE RIGHT-HAND MAN...
...OF THE DEMON LORD! A GOD AMONG DEMONS!

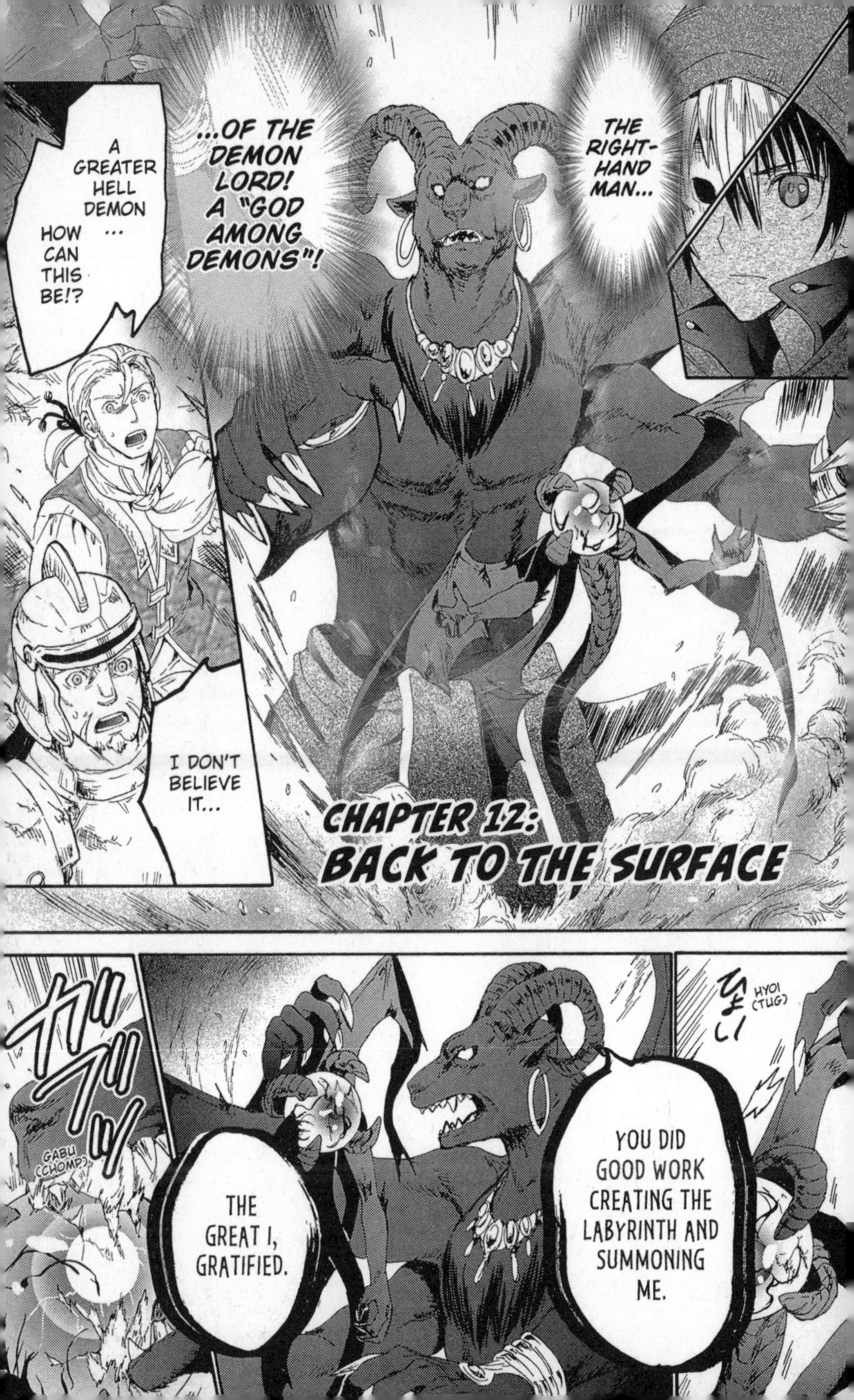
THE RIGHT-HAND MAN...
...OF THE DEMON LORD! A "GOD AMONG DEMONS"!
A GREATER HELL DEMON...
HOW CAN THIS BE!?
I DON'T BELIEVE IT...
CHAPTER 12: BACK TO THE SURFACE
HYOI (TUG)
YOU DID GOOD WORK CREATING THE LABYRINTH AND SUMMONING ME.
THE GREAT I, GRATIFIED.
GABU (CHOMP)

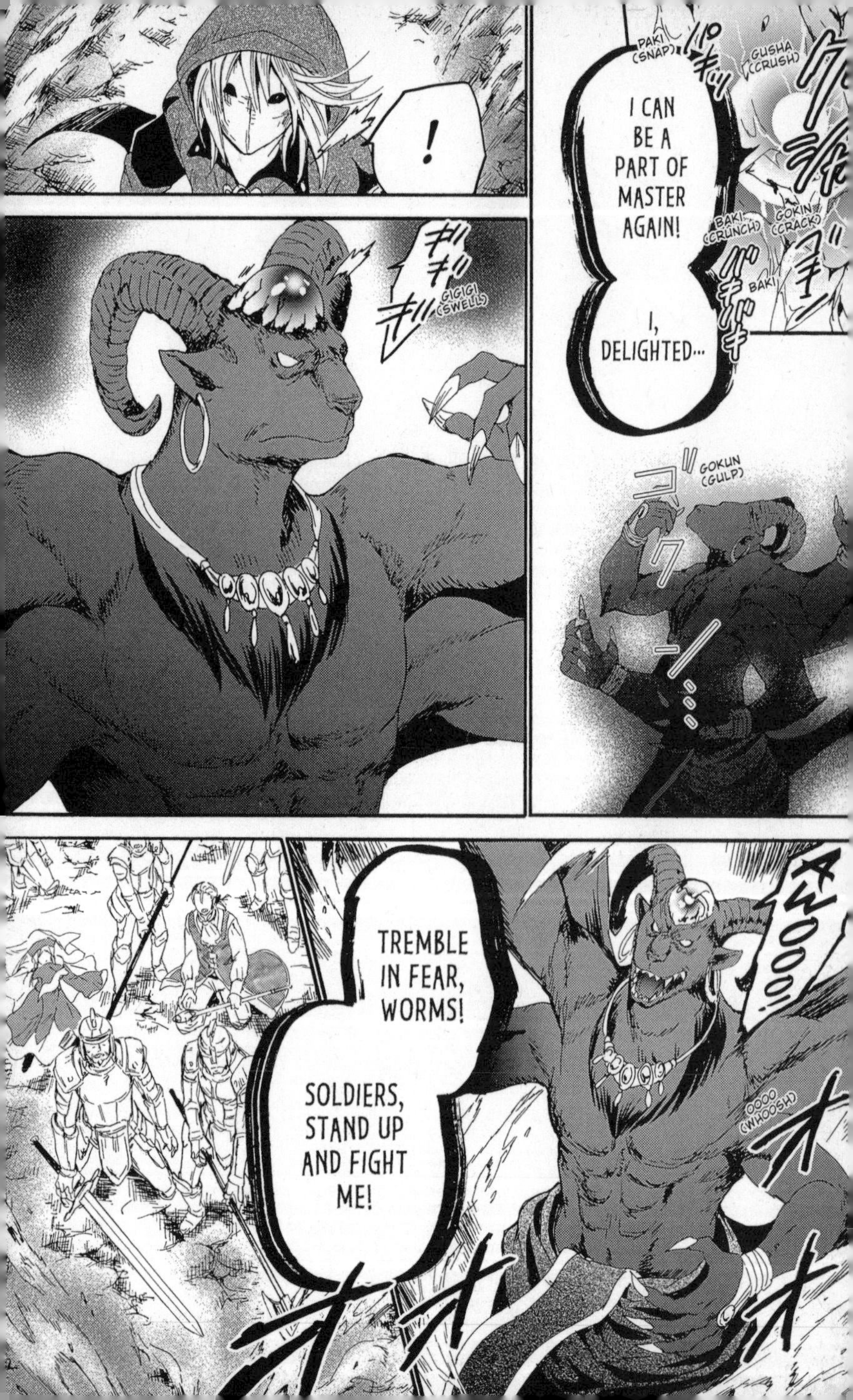
PAKI (SNAP)
GUSHA (CRUSH)
I CAN BE A PART OF MASTER AGAIN!
BAKI (CRUNCH)
GOKIN (CRACK)
BAKI
I, DELIGHTED...
!
GOKUN (GULP)
GIGIGI (SWELL)
AWOOOO!
OOOO (WHOOSH)
TREMBLE IN FEAR, WORMS!
SOLDIERS, STAND UP AND FIGHT ME!

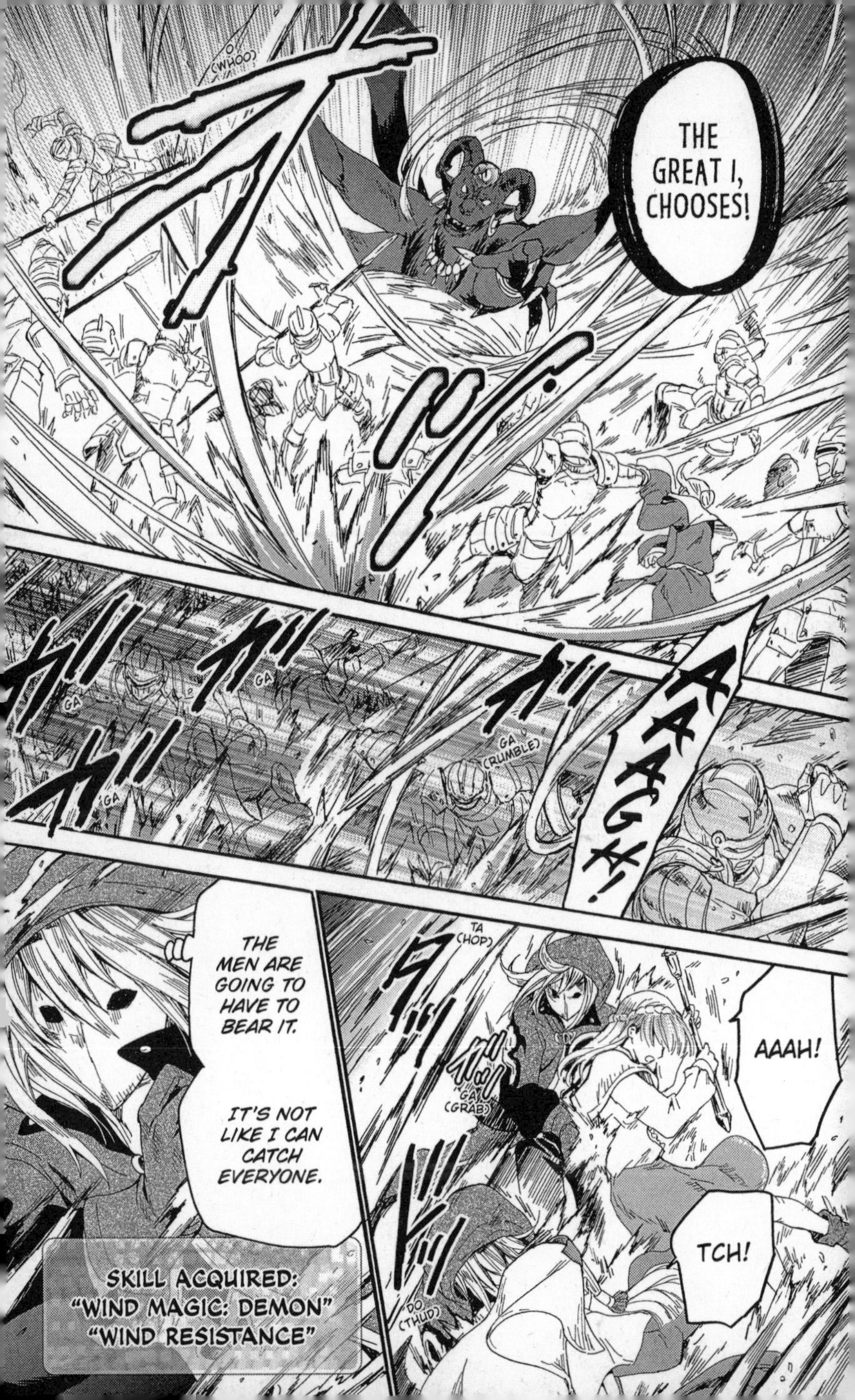
THE GREAT I, CHOOSES!
GA
GA
GA
GA (RUMBLE)
AAAGH!
TA (HOP)
AAAH!
GA (GRAB)
TCH!
DO (THUD)
THE MEN ARE GOING TO HAVE TO BEAR IT.
IT'S NOT LIKE I CAN CATCH EVERYONE.
SKILL ACQUIRED: "WIND MAGIC: DEMON" "WIND RESISTANCE"

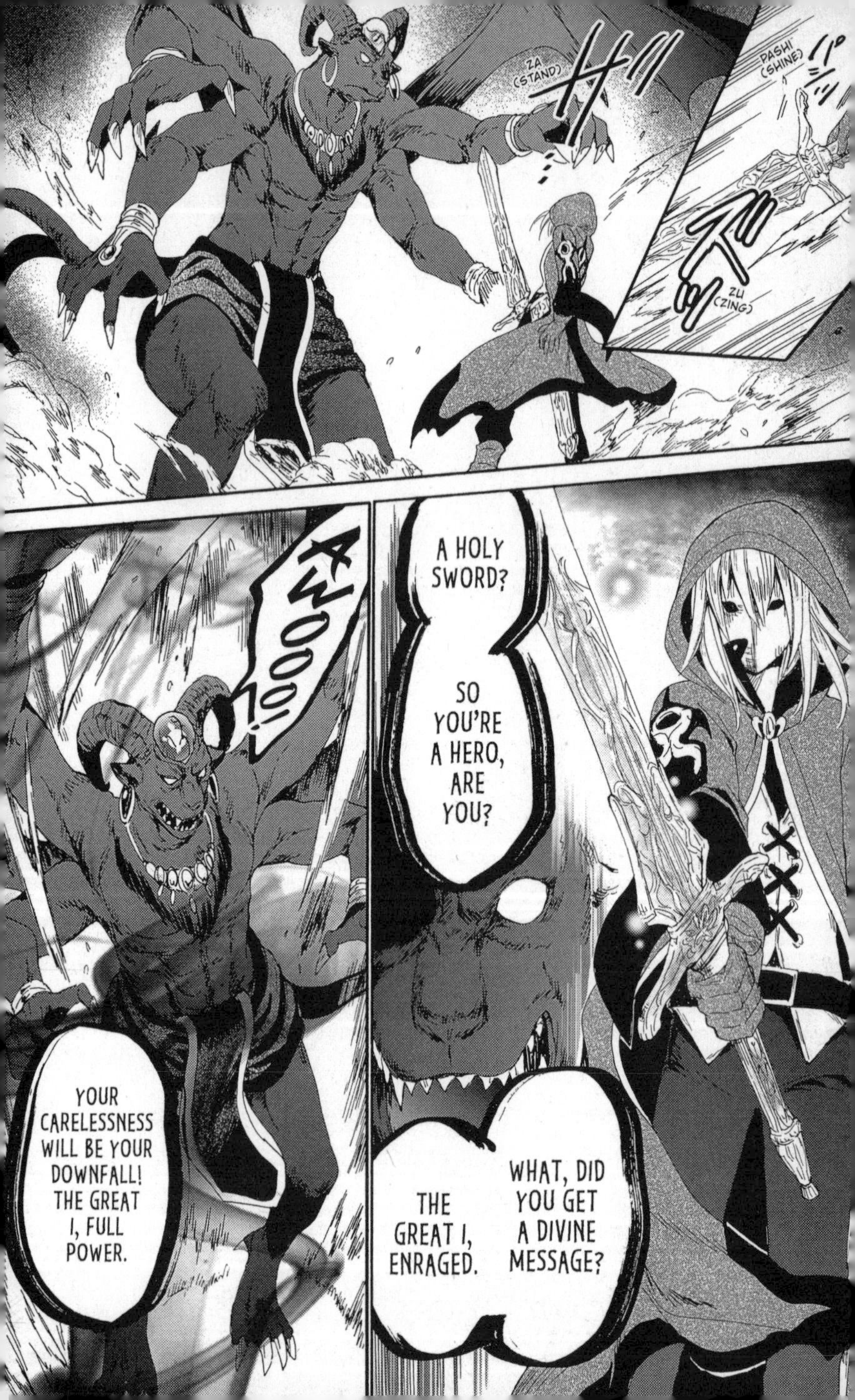
PASHI (SHINE)
ZU (ZING)
ZA (STAND)
A HOLY SWORD?
SO YOU'RE A HERO, ARE YOU?
WHAT, DID YOU GET A DIVINE MESSAGE?
THE GREAT I, ENRAGED.
AWOOOO!
YOUR CARELESSNESS WILL BE YOUR DOWNFALL! THE GREAT I, FULL POWER.

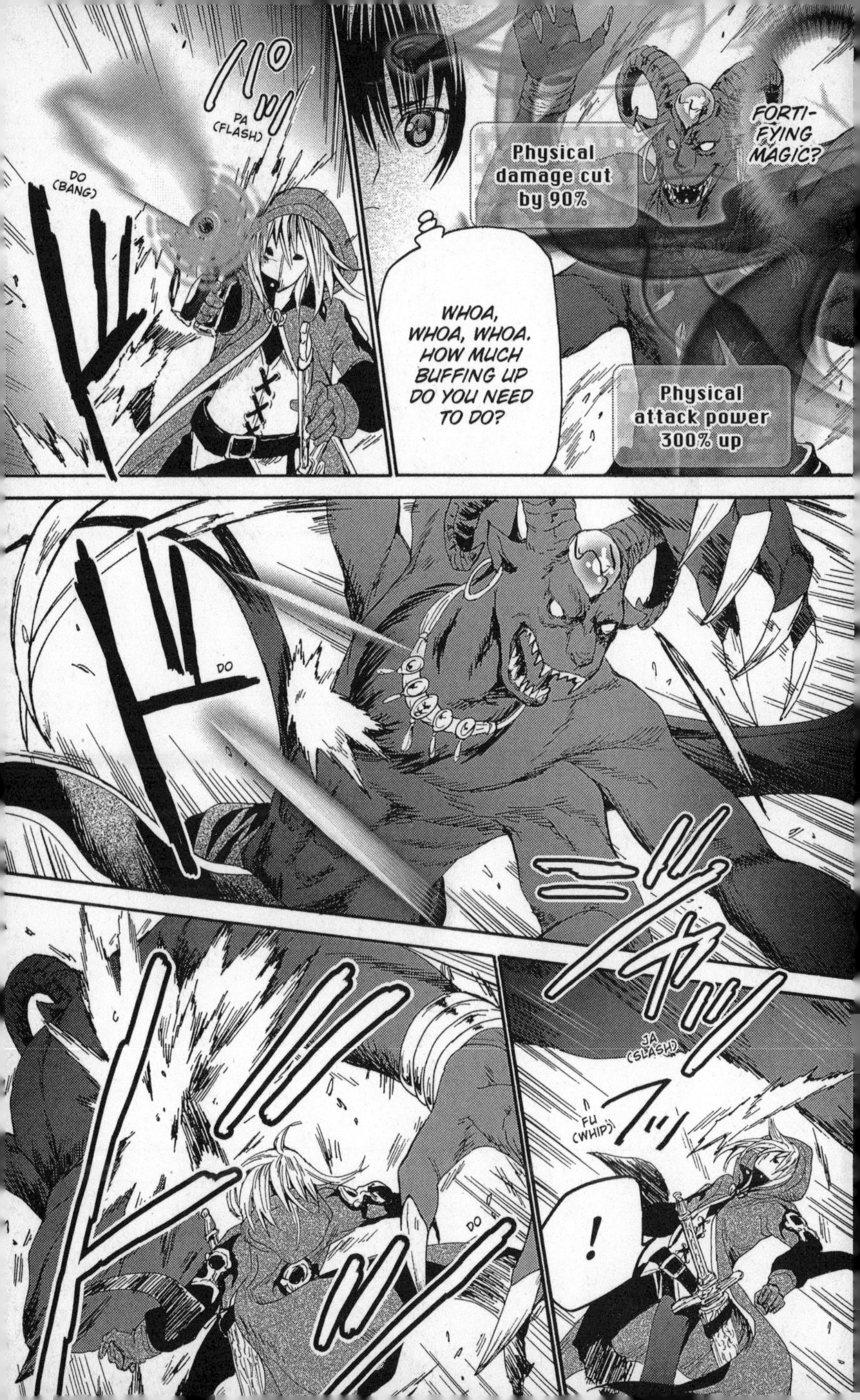
FORTI-FYING MAGIC?
Physical damage cut by 90%
WHOA, WHOA, WHOA. HOW MUCH BUFFING UP DO YOU NEED TO DO?
Physical attack power 300% up
PA (FLASH)
DO (BANG)
DO
JA (SLASH)
FU (WHIP)
!
DO

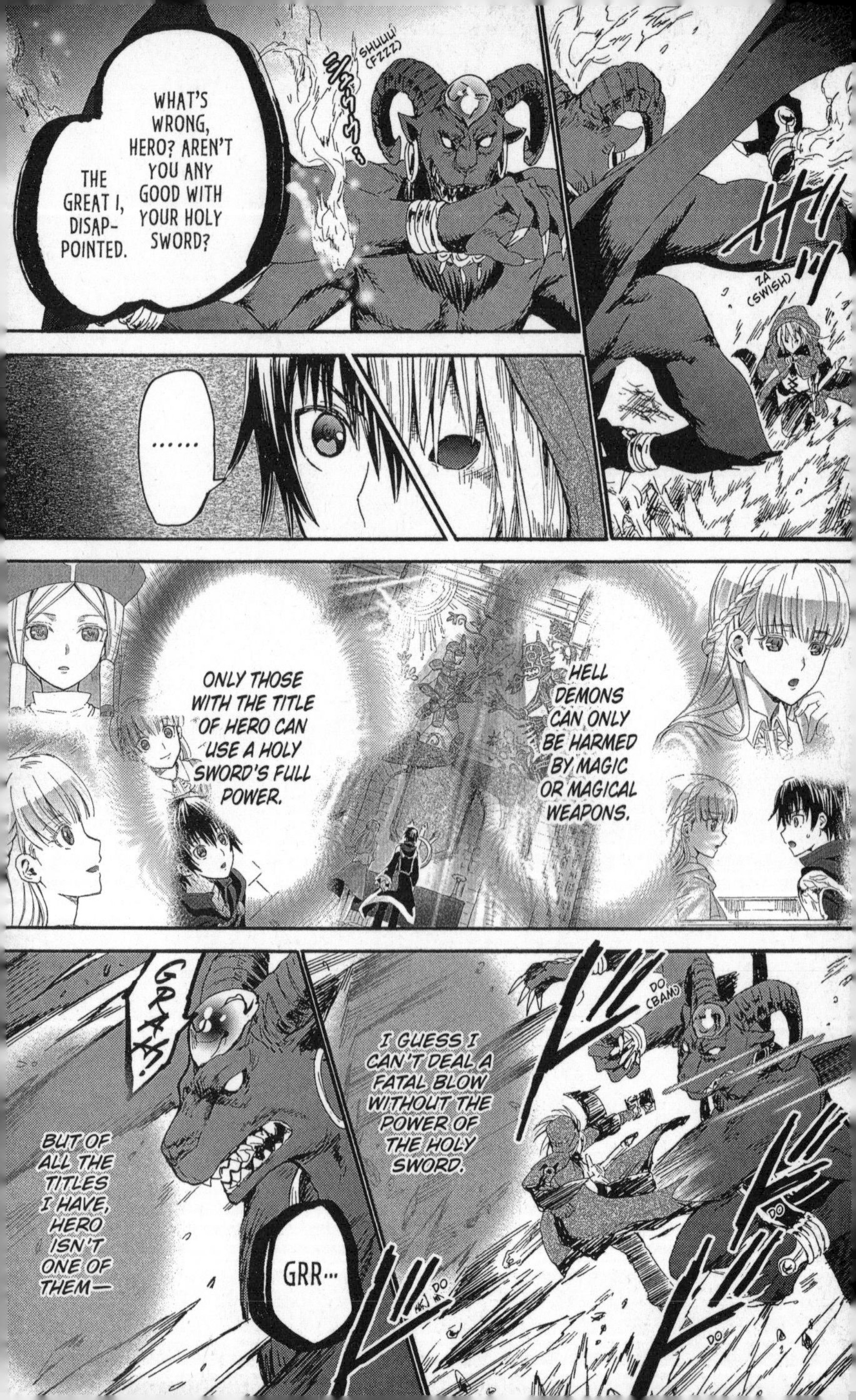
ZA (SWISH)
SHUUU (FZZZ)
WHAT'S WRONG, HERO? AREN'T YOU ANY GOOD WITH YOUR HOLY SWORD?
THE GREAT I, DISAP-POINTED.
......
HELL DEMONS CAN ONLY BE HARMED BY MAGIC OR MAGICAL WEAPONS.
ONLY THOSE WITH THE TITLE OF HERO CAN USE A HOLY SWORD'S FULL POWER.
DO (BAM)
I GUESS I CAN'T DEAL A FATAL BLOW WITHOUT THE POWER OF THE HOLY SWORD.
DO
DO
GRAAA!
BUT OF ALL THE TITLES I HAVE, HERO ISN'T ONE OF THEM—
GRR...
DO

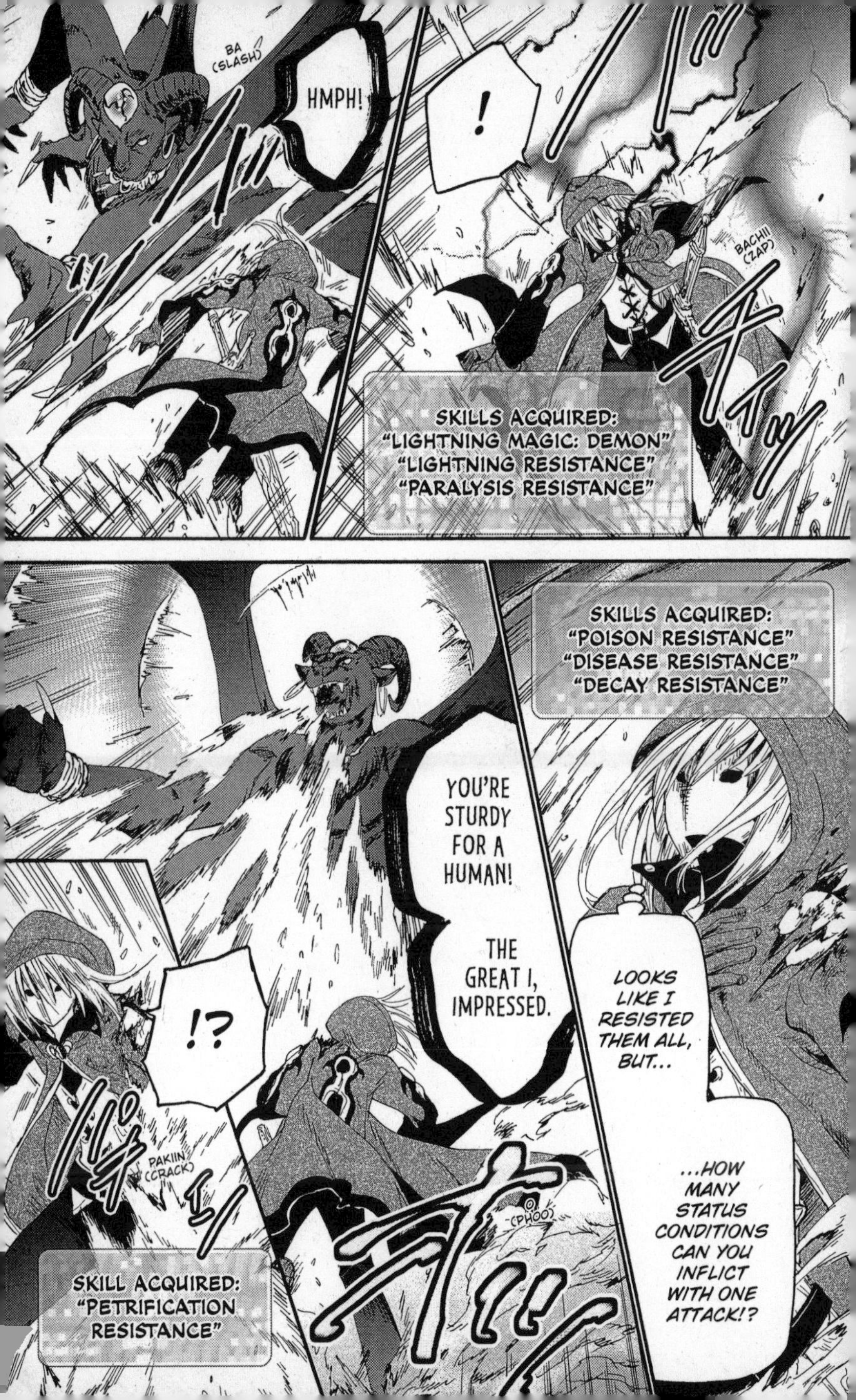
!
BACHII (ZAP)
SKILLS ACQUIRED: "LIGHTNING MAGIC: DEMON" "LIGHTNING RESISTANCE" "PARALYSIS RESISTANCE"
BA (SLASH)
HMPH!
SKILLS ACQUIRED: "POISON RESISTANCE" "DISEASE RESISTANCE" "DECAY RESISTANCE"
LOOKS LIKE I RESISTED THEM ALL, BUT...
...HOW MANY STATUS CONDITIONS CAN YOU INFLICT WITH ONE ATTACK!?
YOU'RE STURDY FOR A HUMAN!
THE GREAT I, IMPRESSED.
(PHOO)
!?
PAKIIN (CRACK)
SKILL ACQUIRED: "PETRIFICATION RESISTANCE"

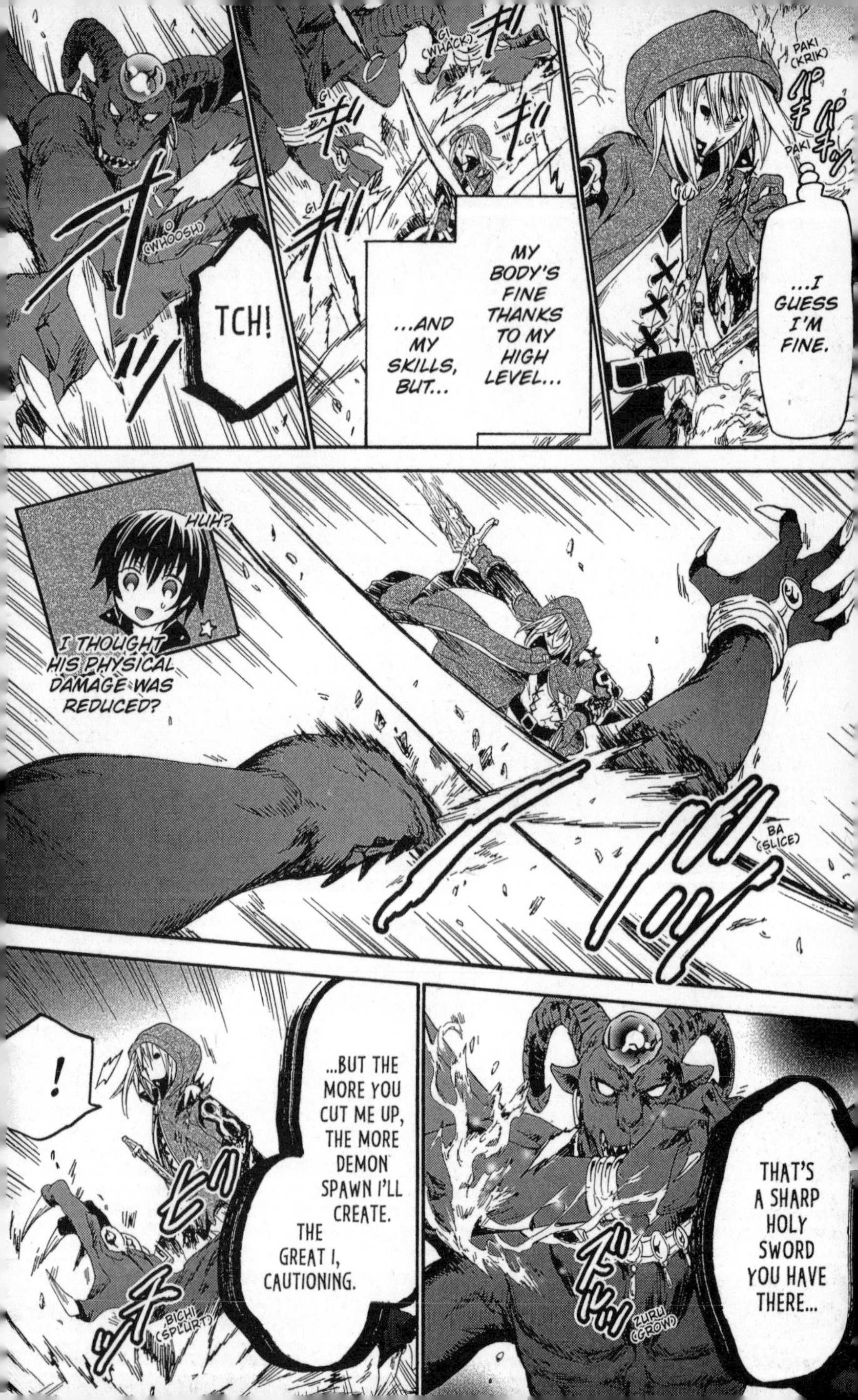
PAKI (KRIK)
PAKI
...I GUESS I'M FINE.
GI (WHACK)
GI
GI
GI
MY BODY'S FINE THANKS TO MY HIGH LEVEL...
...AND MY SKILLS, BUT...
O (WHOOSH)
TCH!
BA (SLICE)
HUH?
I THOUGHT HIS PHYSICAL DAMAGE WAS REDUCED?
THAT'S A SHARP HOLY SWORD YOU HAVE THERE...
ZURU (GROW)
...BUT THE MORE YOU CUT ME UP, THE MORE DEMON SPAWN I'LL CREATE.
THE GREAT I, CAUTIONING.
!
BICHI (SPLURT)

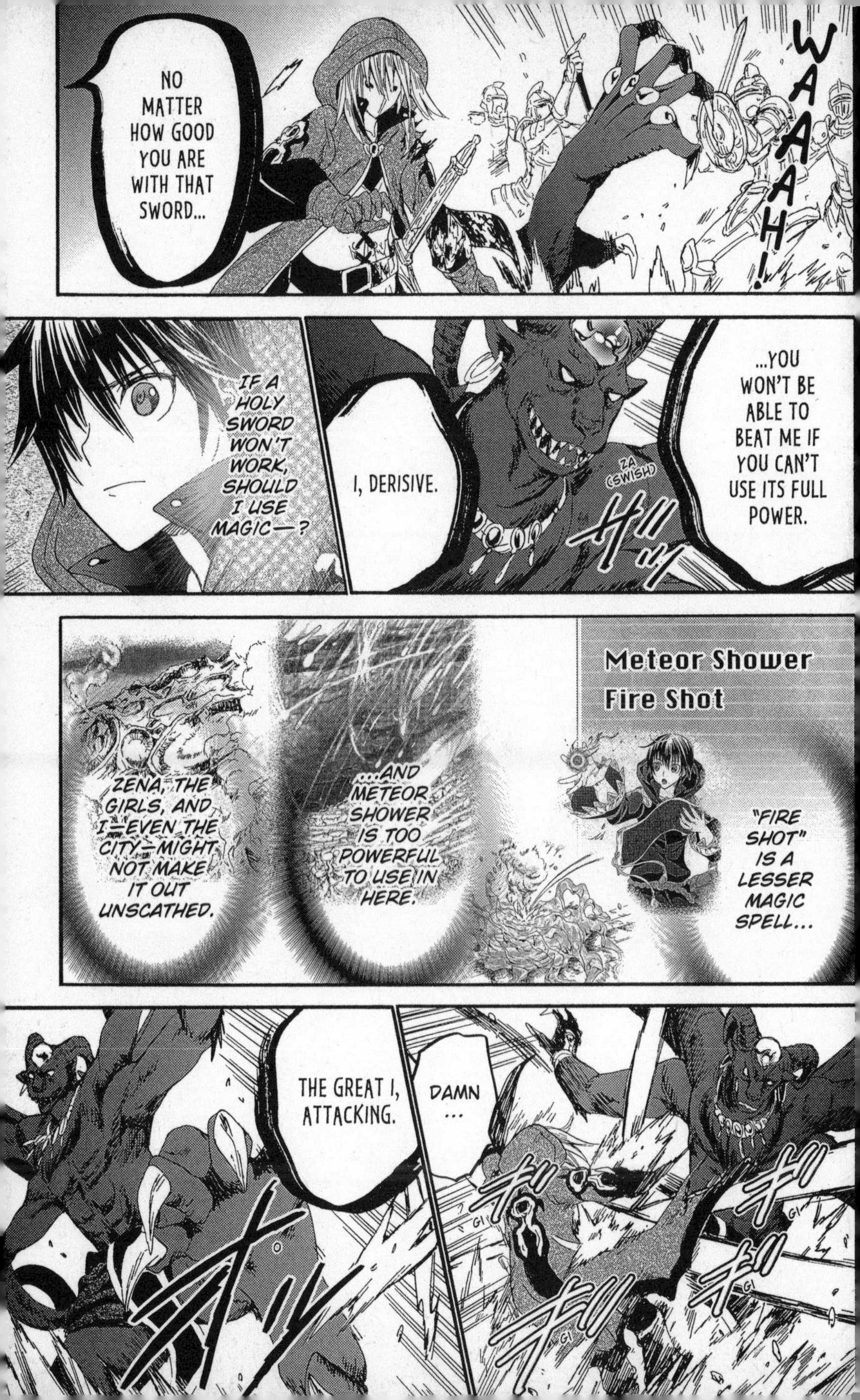
WAAAAH!
NO MATTER HOW GOOD YOU ARE WITH THAT SWORD...
...YOU WON'T BE ABLE TO BEAT ME IF YOU CAN'T USE ITS FULL POWER.
ZA (SWISH)
I, DERISIVE.
IF A HOLY SWORD WON'T WORK, SHOULD I USE MAGIC—?
Meteor Shower
Fire Shot
"FIRE SHOT" IS A LESSER MAGIC SPELL...
...AND METEOR SHOWER IS TOO POWERFUL TO USE IN HERE.
ZENA, THE GIRLS, AND I—EVEN THE CITY—MIGHT NOT MAKE IT OUT UNSCATHED.
GI
GI
GI
DAMN ...
THE GREAT I, ATTACKING.

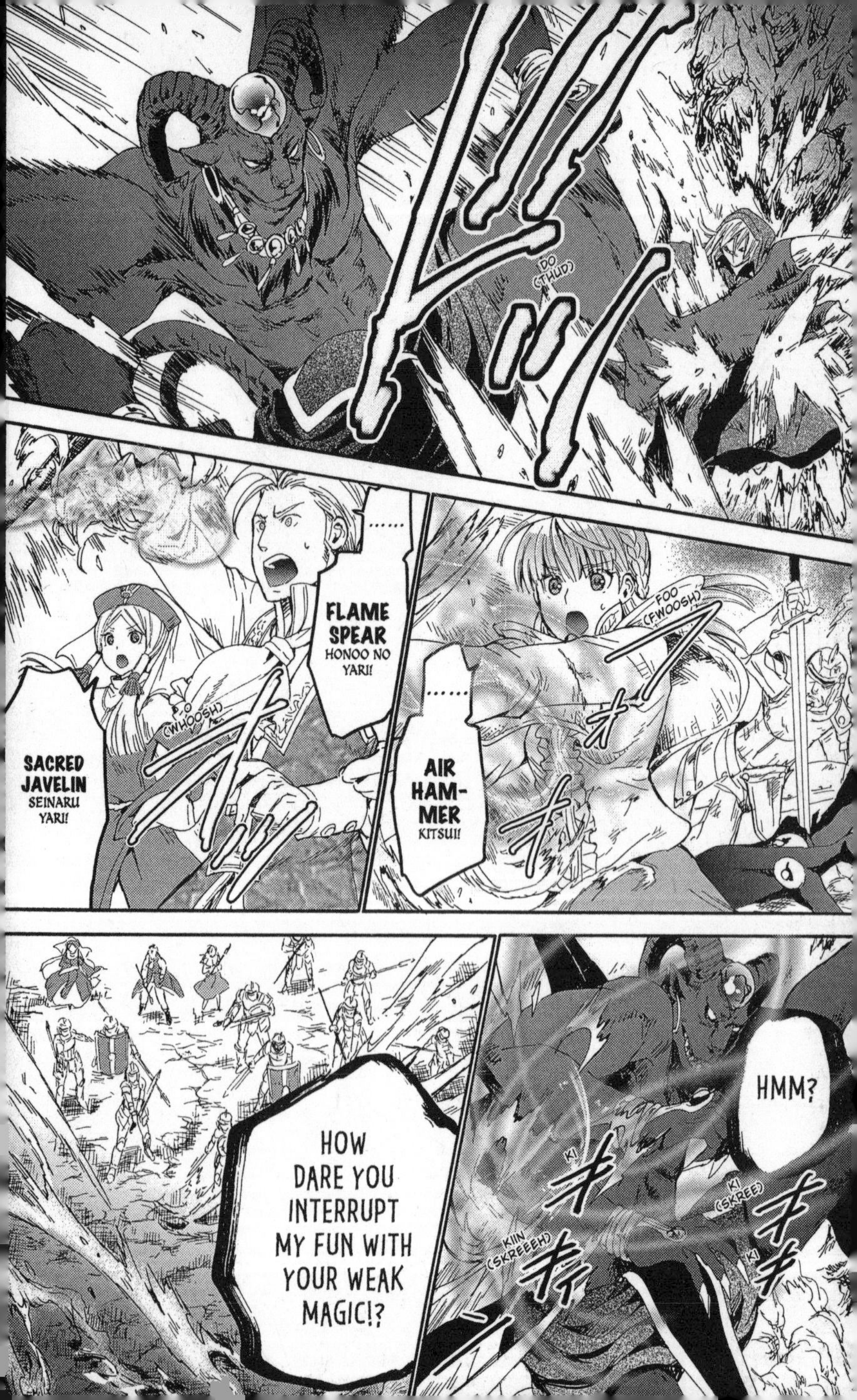
DO (THUD)
FOO (FWOOSH)
......
AIR HAM-MER
KITSUI!
......
FLAME SPEAR
HONOO NO YARI!
PO (WHOOSH)
SACRED JAVELIN
SEINARU YARI!
HMM?
KI
KI (SKREE)
KI
KIIN (SKREEEH)
HOW DARE YOU INTERRUPT MY FUN WITH YOUR WEAK MAGIC!?

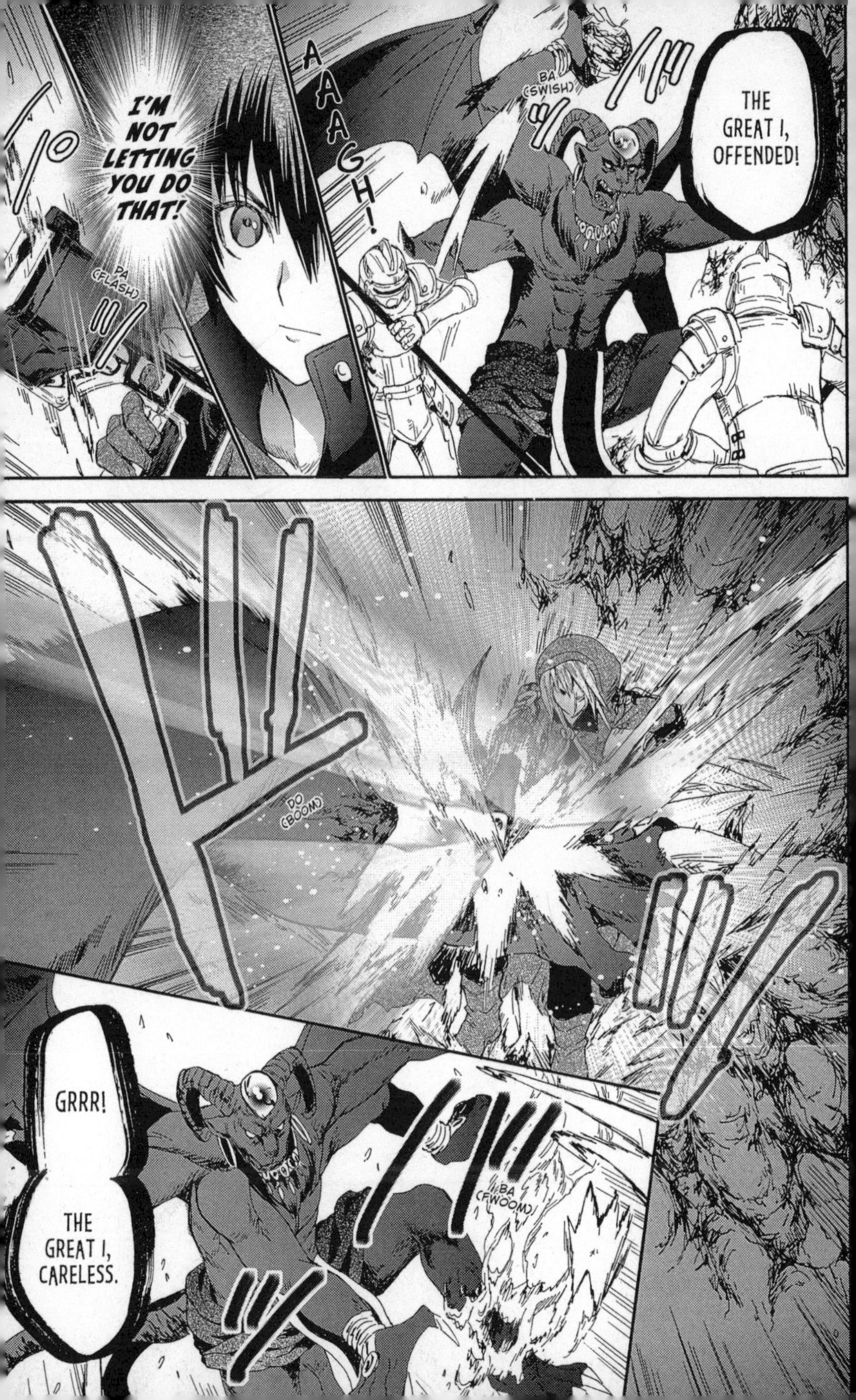
THE GREAT I, OFFENDED!
BA (SWISH)
AAAGH!
I'M NOT LETTING YOU DO THAT!
PA (FLASH)
DO (BOOM)
BA (FWOOM)
GRRR!
THE GREAT I, CARELESS.

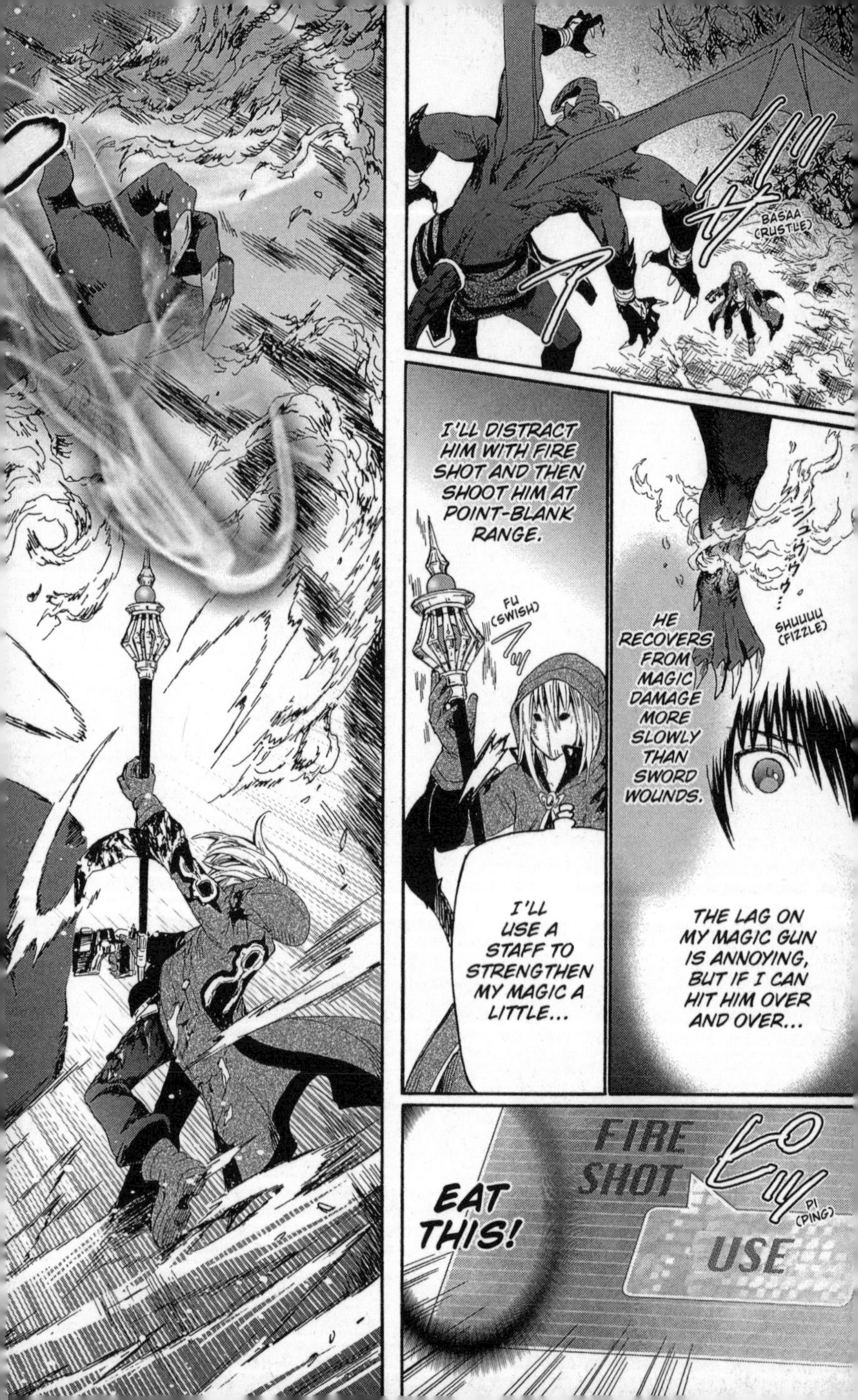
BASAA (RUSTLE)
HE RECOVERS FROM MAGIC DAMAGE MORE SLOWLY THAN SWORD WOUNDS.
SHUUUU (FIZZLE)
THE LAG ON MY MAGIC GUN IS ANNOYING, BUT IF I CAN HIT HIM OVER AND OVER...
I'LL DISTRACT HIM WITH FIRE SHOT AND THEN SHOOT HIM AT POINT-BLANK RANGE.
FU (SWISH)
I'LL USE A STAFF TO STRENGTHEN MY MAGIC A LITTLE...
FIRE SHOT
PI (PING)
USE
EAT THIS!

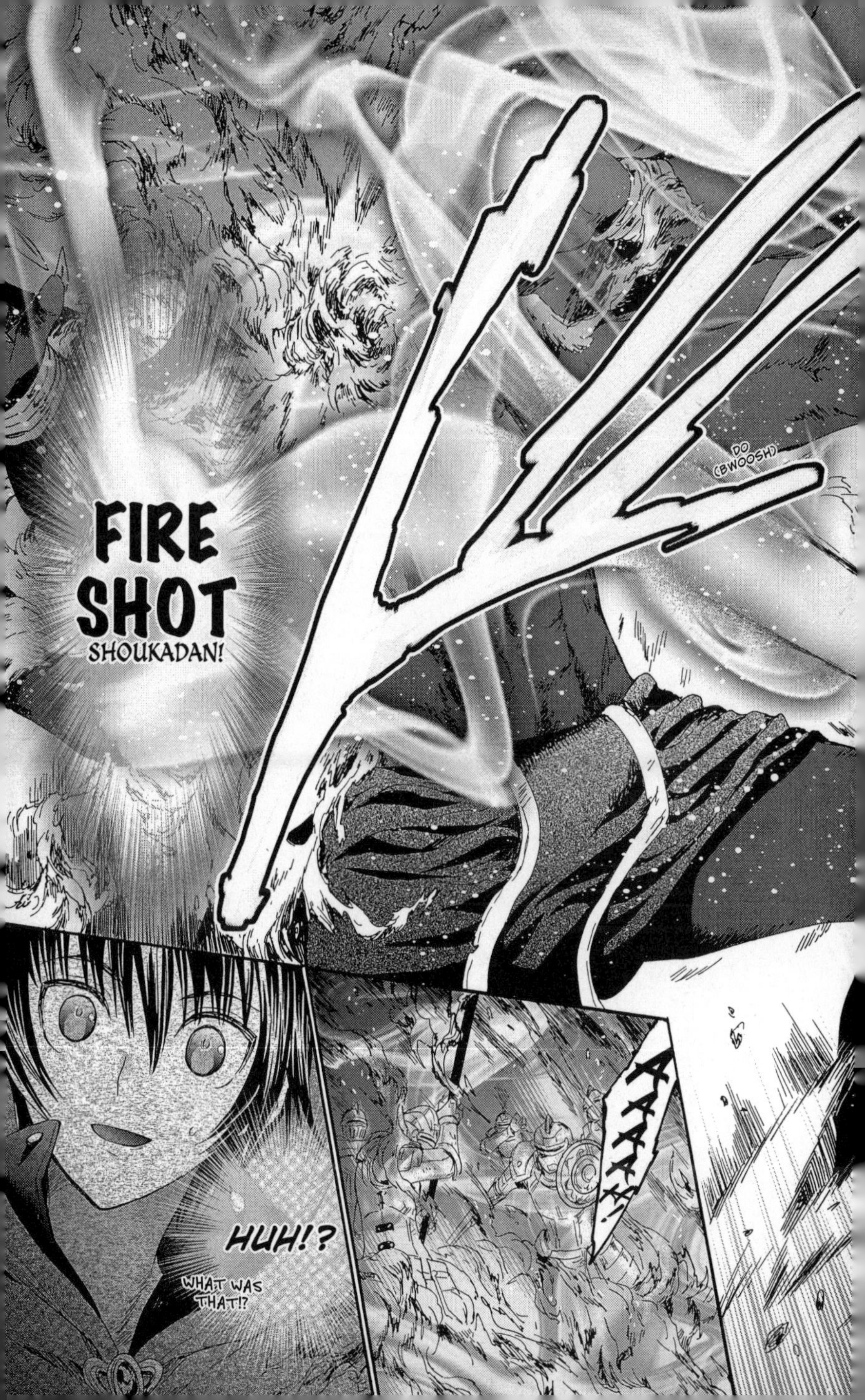
DO (BWOOSH)
FIRE SHOT
SHOUKADAN!
AAAAA!
HUH!?
WHAT WAS THAT!?

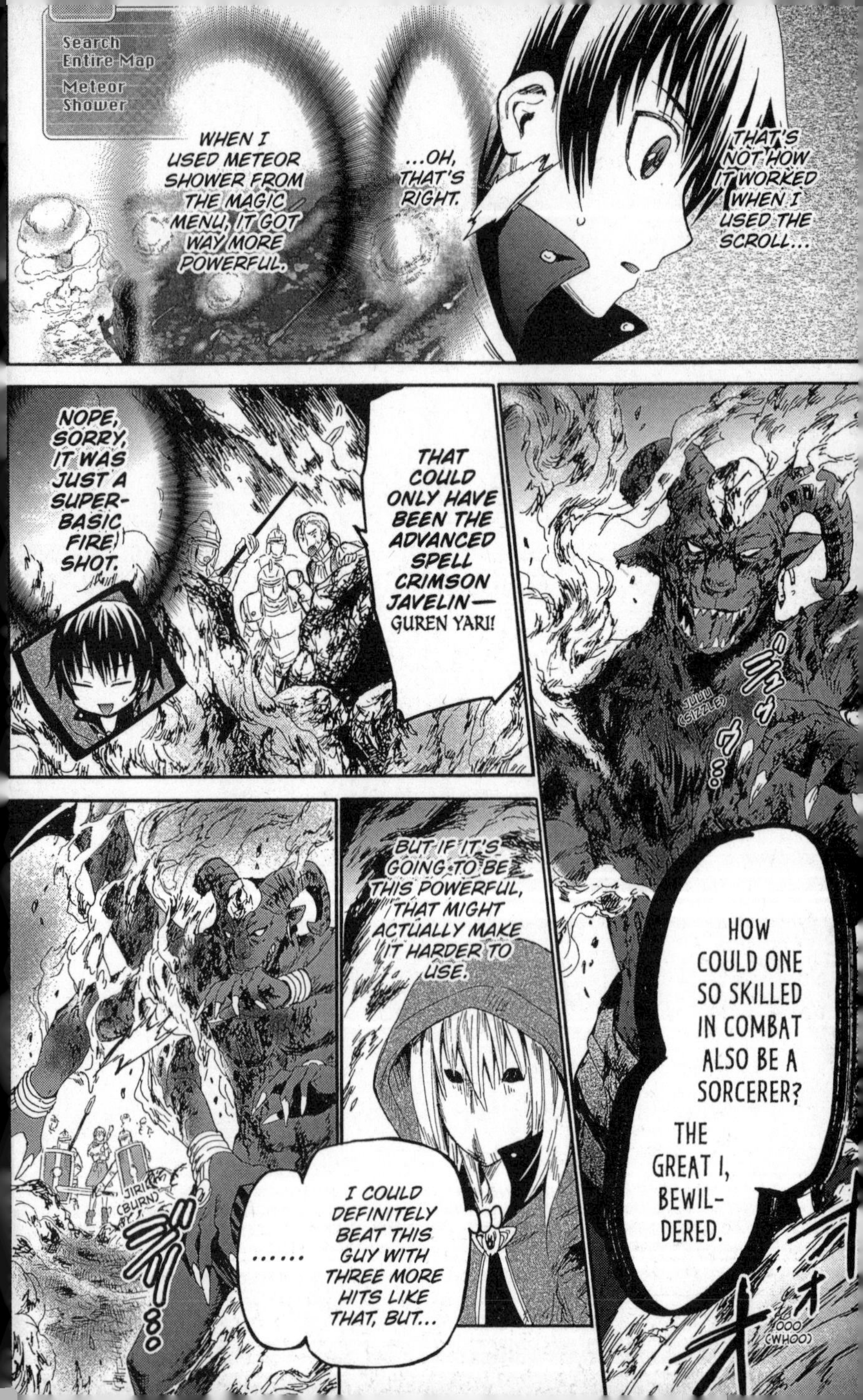
THAT'S NOT HOW IT WORKED WHEN I USED THE SCROLL...
...OH, THAT'S RIGHT.
WHEN I USED METEOR SHOWER FROM THE MAGIC MENU, IT GOT WAY MORE POWERFUL.
Search Entire Map
Meteor Shower
JUUU (SIZZLE)
HOW COULD ONE SO SKILLED IN COMBAT ALSO BE A SORCERER?
THE GREAT I, BEWILDERED.
OOO (WHOO)
THAT COULD ONLY HAVE BEEN THE ADVANCED SPELL CRIMSON JAVELIN— GUREN YARI!
NOPE, SORRY, IT WAS JUST A SUPER-BASIC FIRE SHOT.
BUT IF IT'S GOING TO BE THIS POWERFUL, THAT MIGHT ACTUALLY MAKE IT HARDER TO USE.
I COULD DEFINITELY BEAT THIS GUY WITH THREE MORE HITS LIKE THAT, BUT...
......
JIRI (BURN)

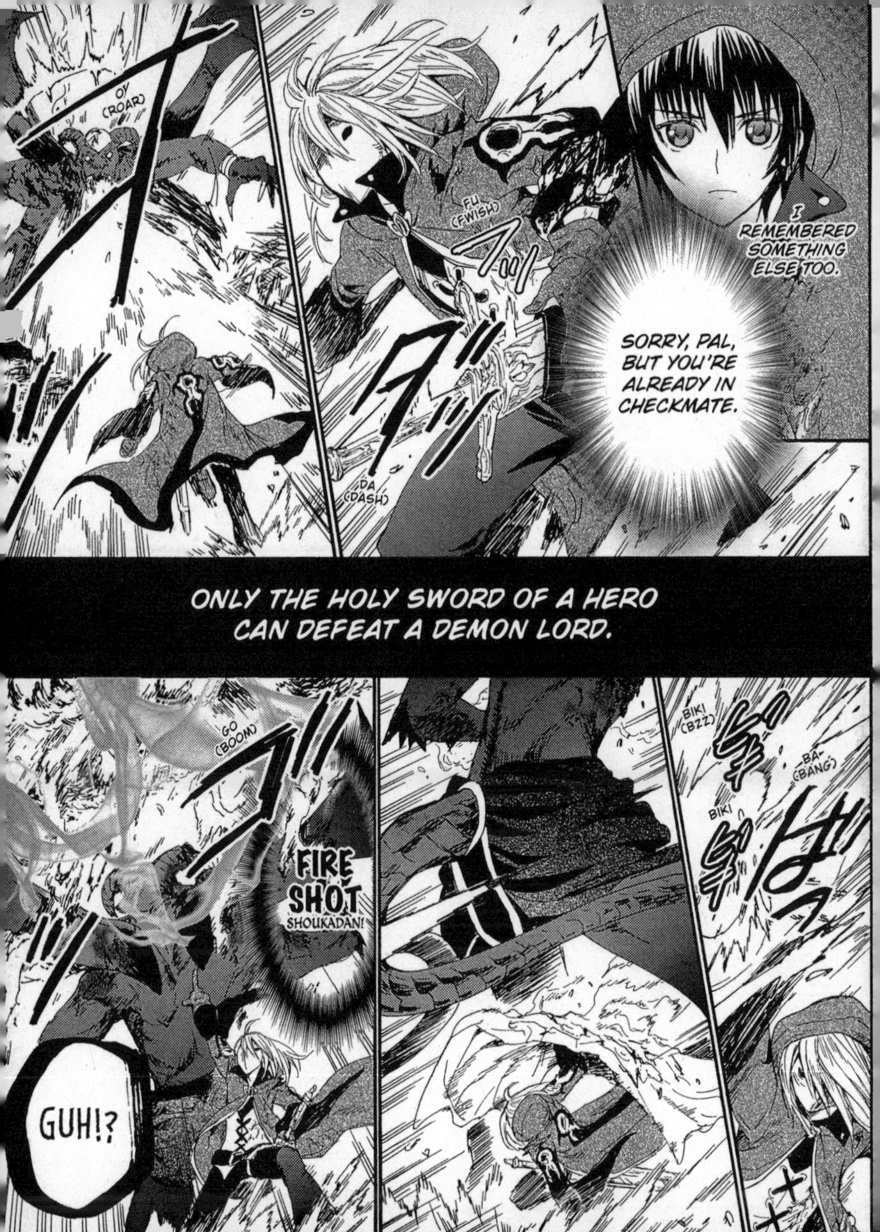
I REMEMBERED SOMETHING ELSE TOO.
SORRY, PAL, BUT YOU'RE ALREADY IN CHECKMATE.
FU (FWISH)
DA (DASH)
OY (ROAR)
ONLY THE HOLY SWORD OF A HERO CAN DEFEAT A DEMON LORD.
BIKI (BZZ)
BIKI
BA-BANG (BANG)
GO (BOOM)
FIRE SHOT SHOUKADAN!
GUH!?

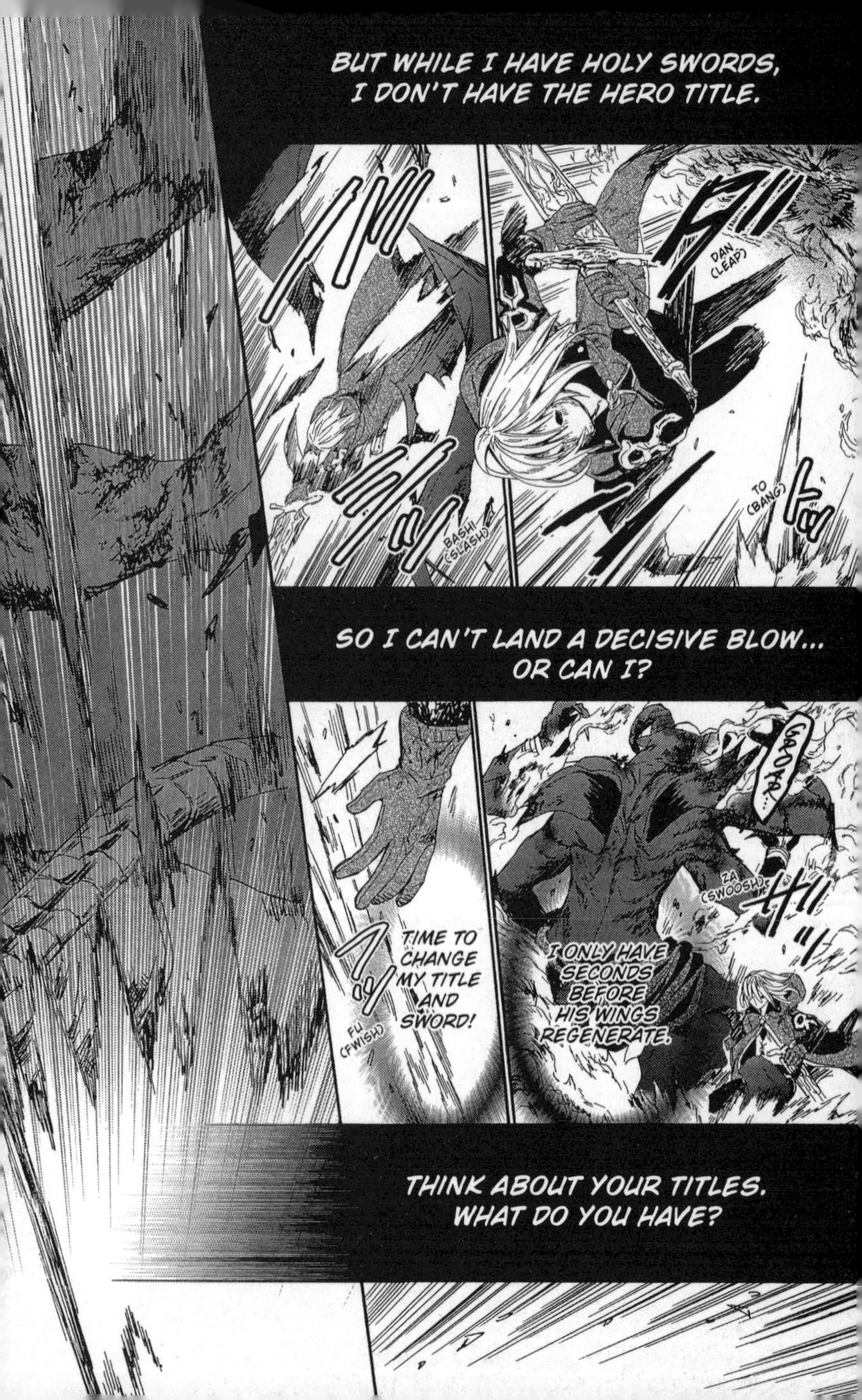
BUT WHILE I HAVE HOLY SWORDS, I DON'T HAVE THE HERO TITLE.
DAN (LEAP)
TO (BANG)
BASHI (SLASH)
SO I CAN'T LAND A DECISIVE BLOW... OR CAN I?
GROAR...
ZA (SWOOSH)
I ONLY HAVE SECONDS BEFORE HIS WINGS REGENERATE.
TIME TO CHANGE MY TITLE AND SWORD!
FU (FWISH)
THINK ABOUT YOUR TITLES. WHAT DO YOU HAVE?

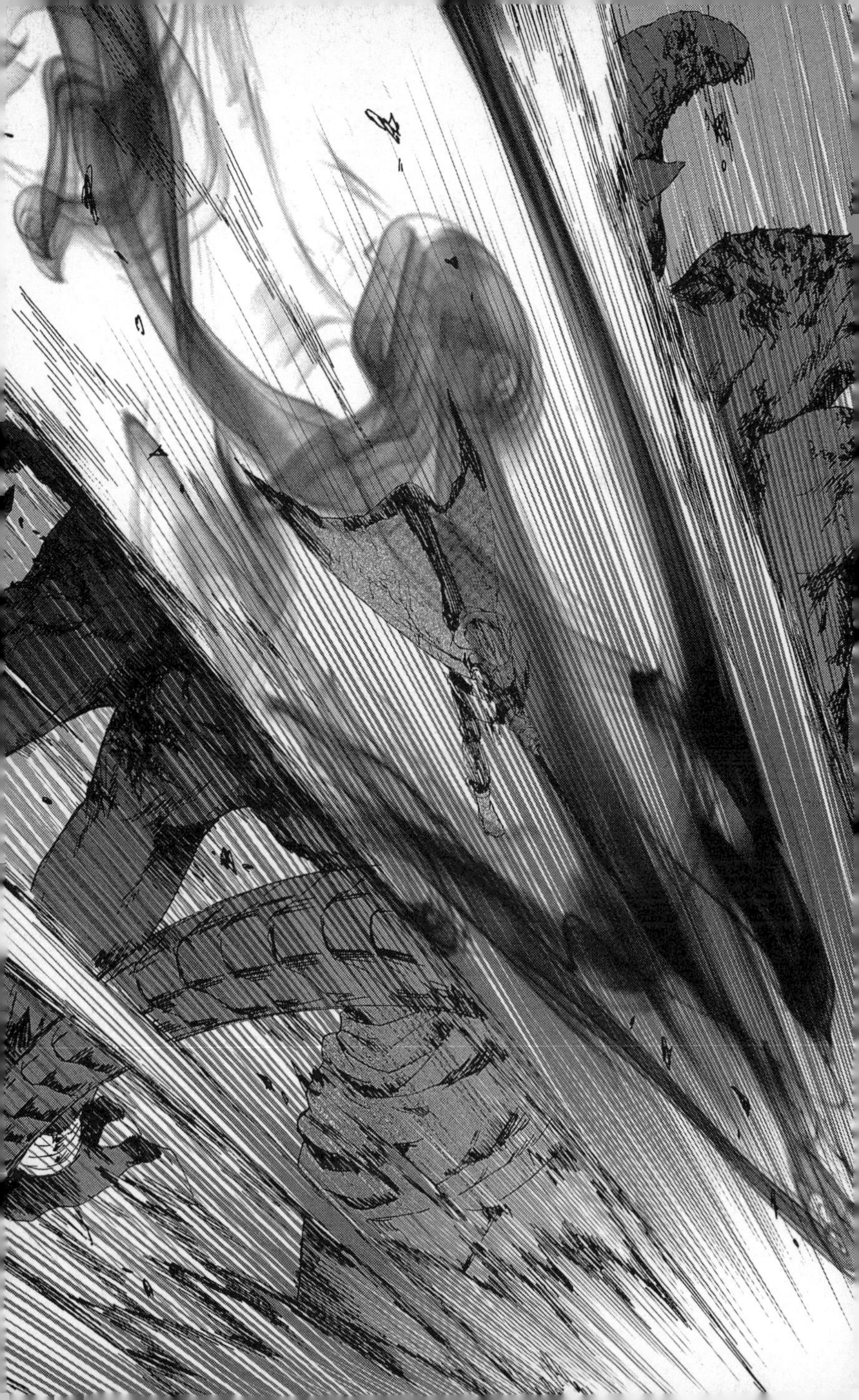

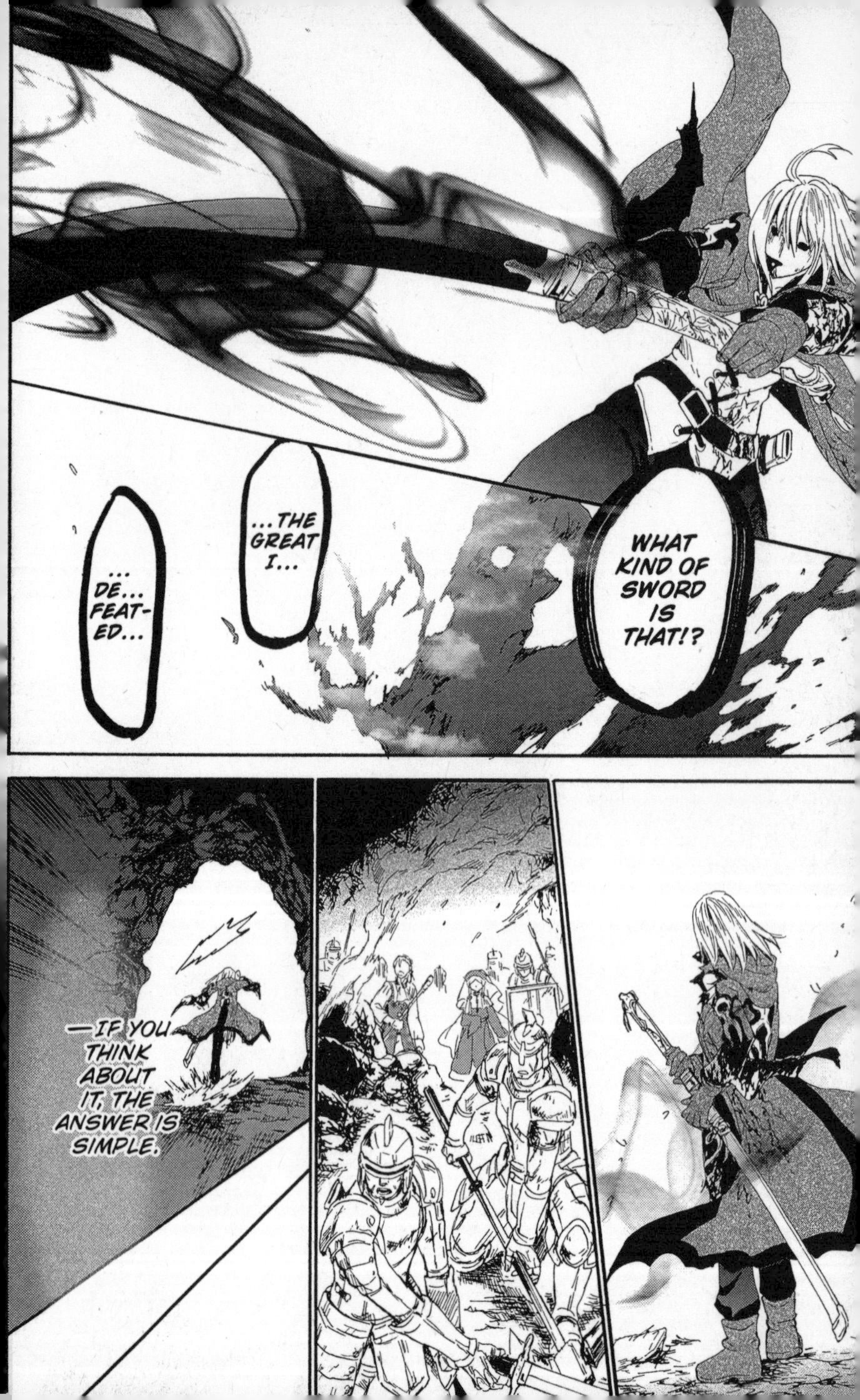

WHAT KIND OF SWORD IS THAT!?
...THE GREAT I...
...DE... FEAT-ED...
—IF YOU THINK ABOUT IT, THE ANSWER IS SIMPLE.

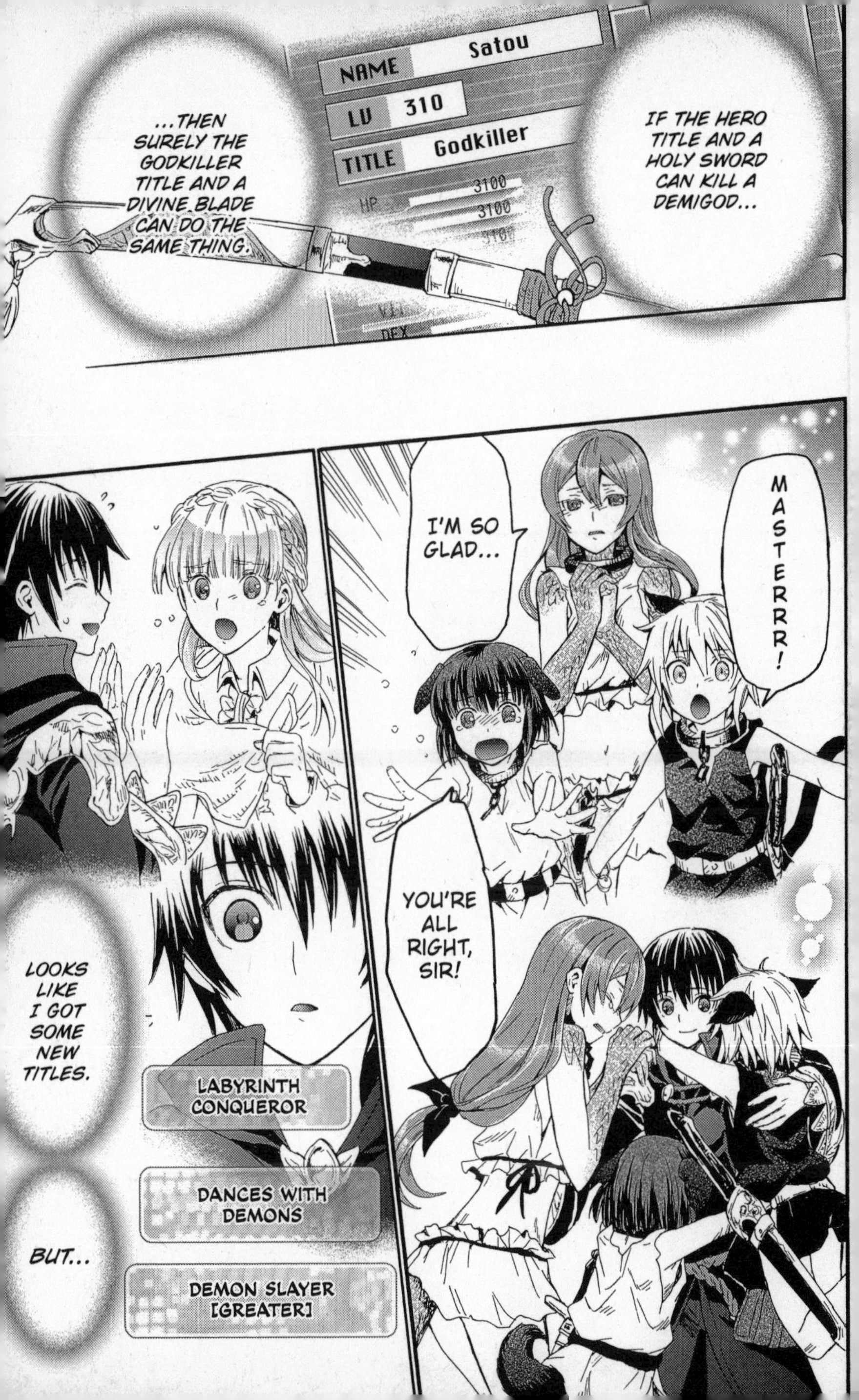
IF THE HERO TITLE AND A HOLY SWORD CAN KILL A DEMIGOD...
NAME
Satou
LV
310
TITLE
Godkiller
HP
3100
3100
...THEN SURELY THE GODKILLER TITLE AND A DIVINE BLADE CAN DO THE SAME THING.
MASTERRRR!
I'M SO GLAD...
YOU'RE ALL RIGHT, SIR!
LOOKS LIKE I GOT SOME NEW TITLES.
LABYRINTH CONQUEROR
DANCES WITH DEMONS
BUT...
DEMON SLAYER [GREATER]

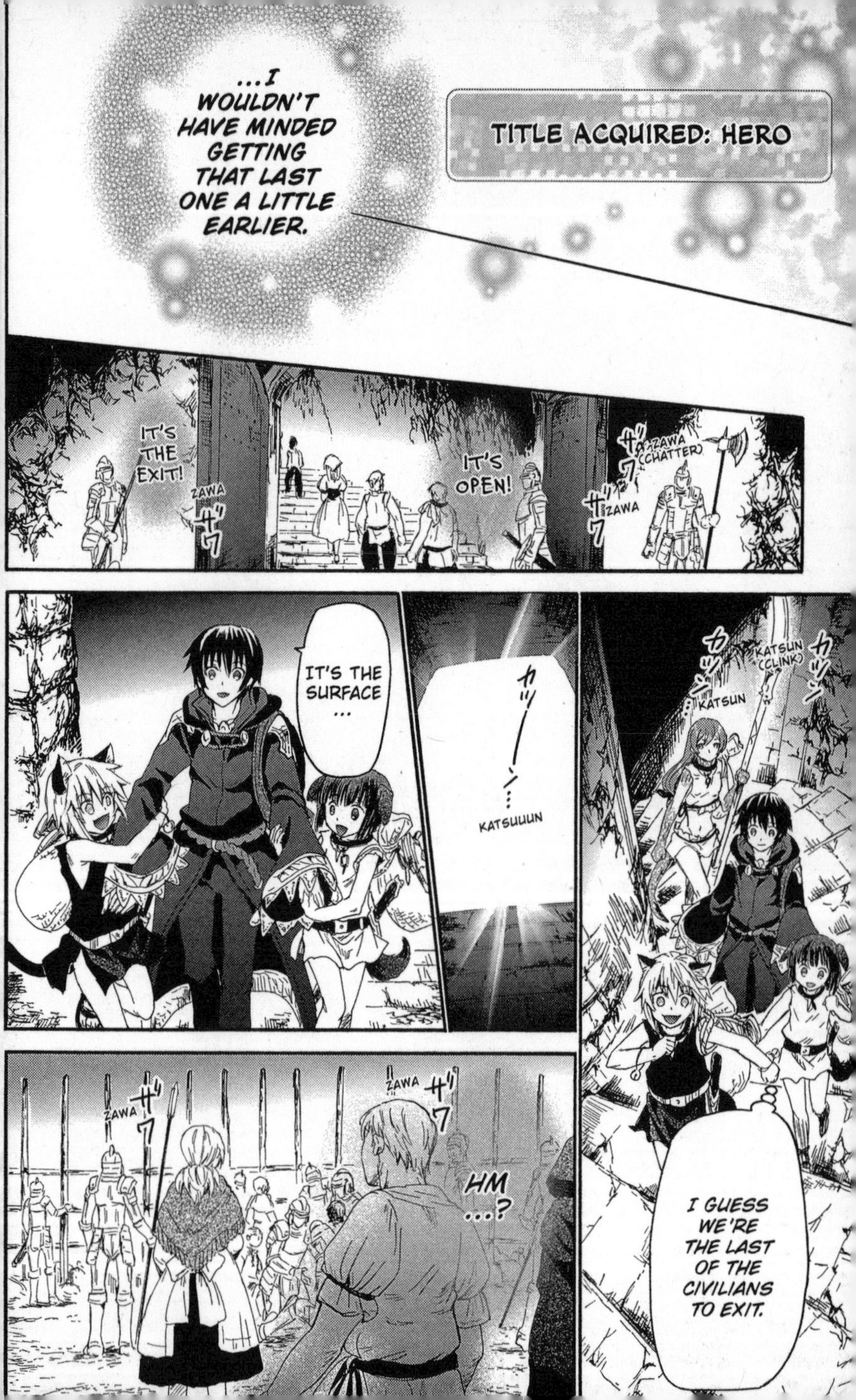
TITLE ACQUIRED: HERO
...I WOULDN'T HAVE MINDED GETTING THAT LAST ONE A LITTLE EARLIER.
ザワ ZAWA (CHATTER)
ザワ ZAWA
IT'S OPEN!
IT'S THE EXIT!
ZAWA ザワ
カツン KATSUN (CLINK)
カツン KATSUN
I GUESS WE'RE THE LAST OF THE CIVILIANS TO EXIT.
カツーン... KATSUUUN
IT'S THE SURFACE...
HM...?
ZAWA ザワ
ZAWA ザワ

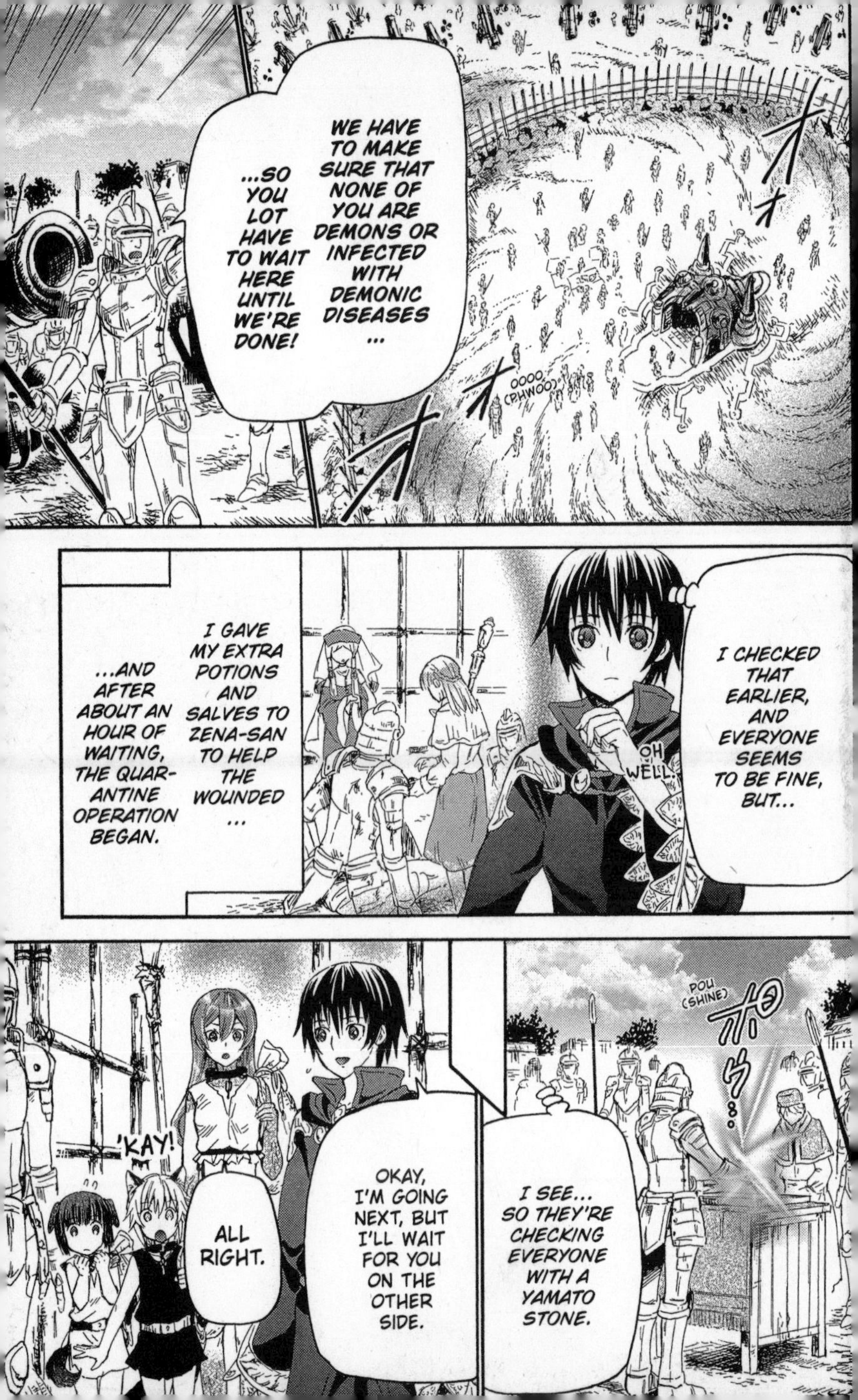
WE HAVE TO MAKE SURE THAT NONE OF YOU ARE DEMONS OR INFECTED WITH DEMONIC DISEASES...
...SO YOU LOT HAVE TO WAIT HERE UNTIL WE'RE DONE!
OOOO (PHWOO)
I CHECKED THAT EARLIER, AND EVERYONE SEEMS TO BE FINE, BUT...
OH WELL.
I GAVE MY EXTRA POTIONS AND SALVES TO ZENA-SAN TO HELP THE WOUNDED...
...AND AFTER ABOUT AN HOUR OF WAITING, THE QUAR-ANTINE OPERATION BEGAN.
POU (SHINE)
I SEE... SO THEY'RE CHECKING EVERYONE WITH A YAMATO STONE.
OKAY, I'M GOING NEXT, BUT I'LL WAIT FOR YOU ON THE OTHER SIDE.
ALL RIGHT.
'KAY!

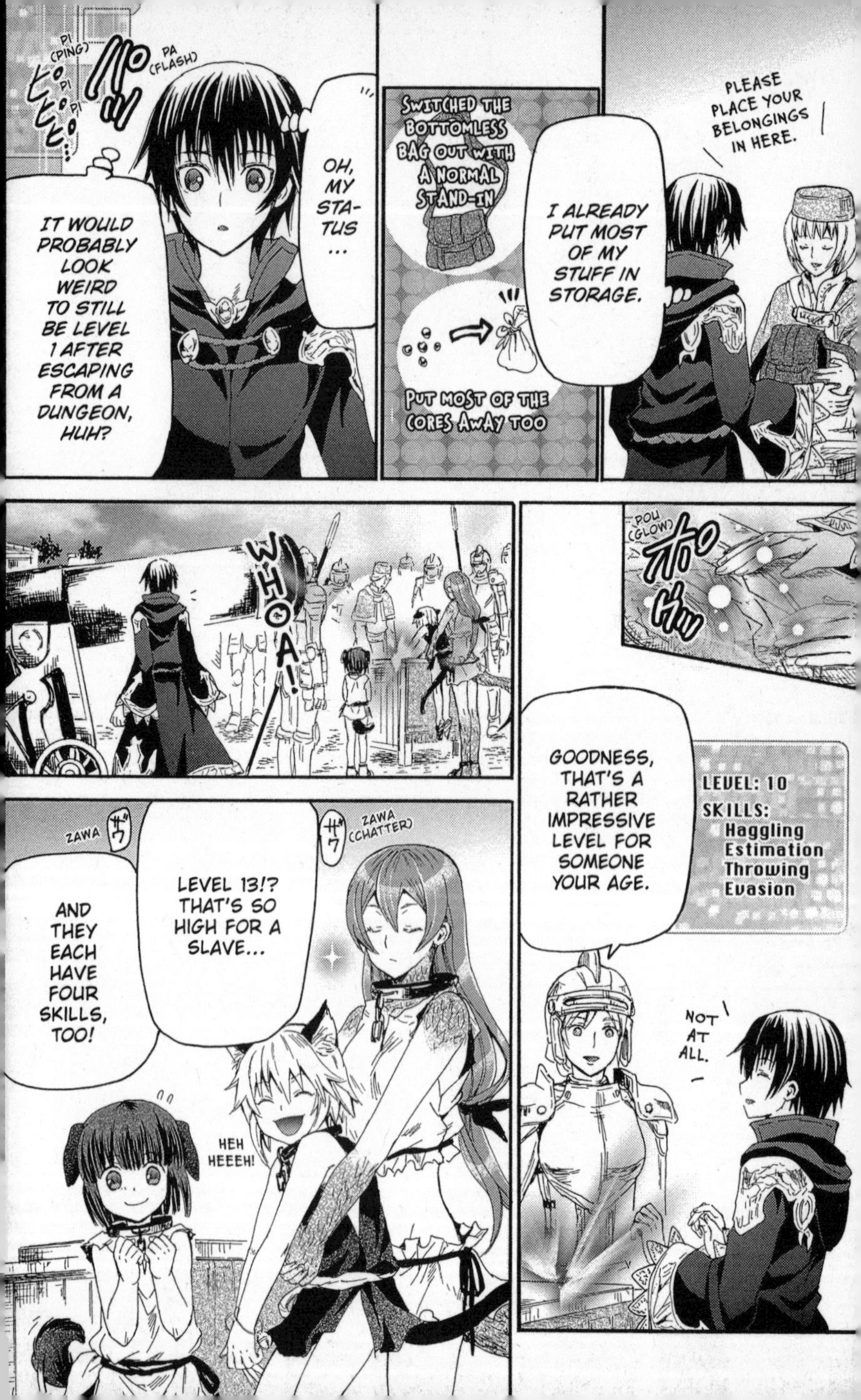
PLEASE PLACE YOUR BELONGINGS IN HERE.
I ALREADY PUT MOST OF MY STUFF IN STORAGE.
SWITCHED THE BOTTOMLESS BAG OUT WITH A NORMAL STAND-IN
PUT MOST OF THE CORES AWAY TOO
PA (FLASH)
PI (PING) PI PI PI
OH, MY STATUS...
IT WOULD PROBABLY LOOK WEIRD TO STILL BE LEVEL 1 AFTER ESCAPING FROM A DUNGEON, HUH?
POU (GLOW)
LEVEL: 10
SKILLS: Haggling Estimation Throwing Evasion
GOODNESS, THAT'S A RATHER IMPRESSIVE LEVEL FOR SOMEONE YOUR AGE.
NOT AT ALL.
WHOA!
ZAWA (CHATTER)
ZAWA
LEVEL 13!? THAT'S SO HIGH FOR A SLAVE...
AND THEY EACH HAVE FOUR SKILLS, TOO!
HEH HEEEH!

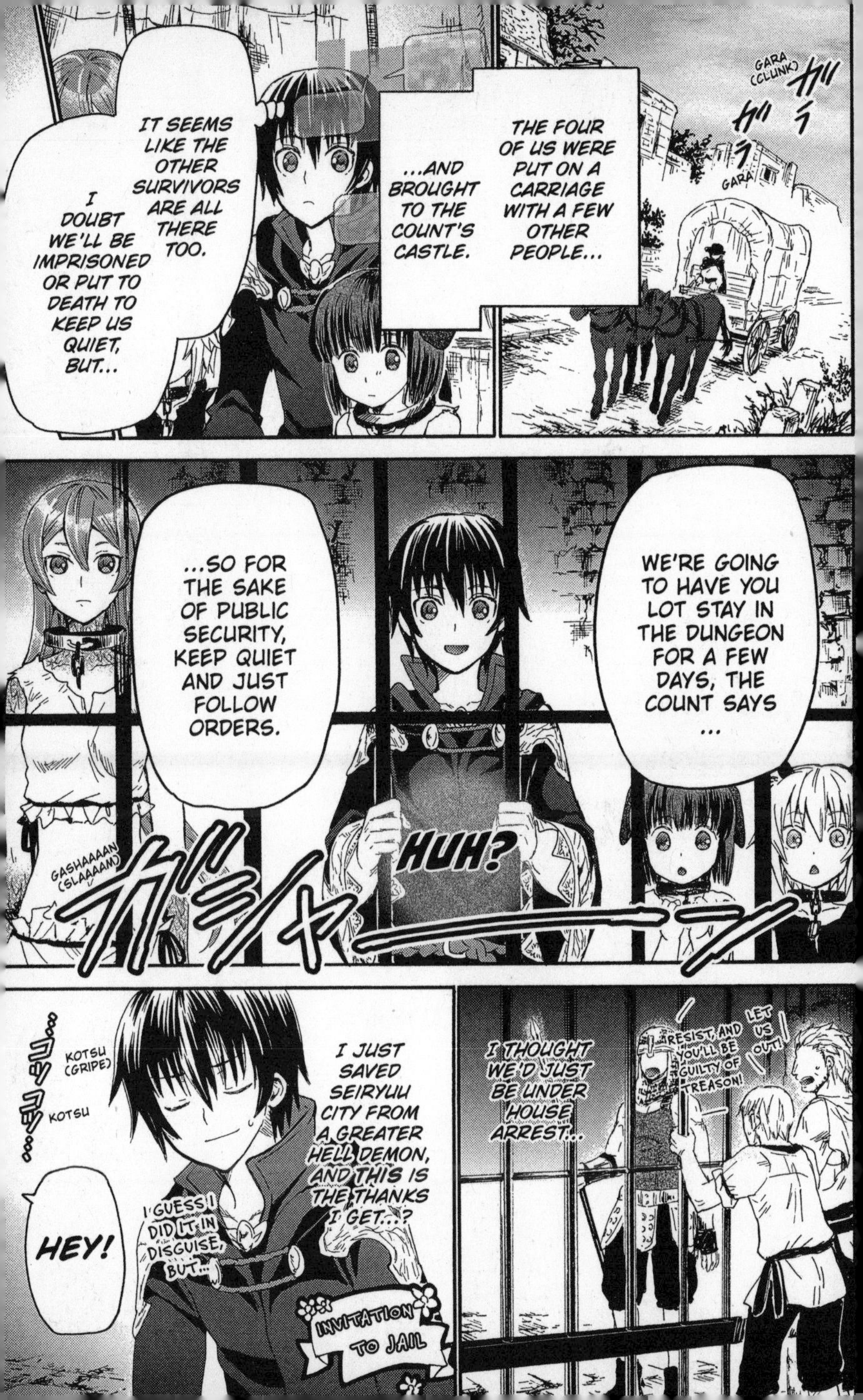
GARA (CLUNK)
GARA
THE FOUR OF US WERE PUT ON A CARRIAGE WITH A FEW OTHER PEOPLE...
...AND BROUGHT TO THE COUNT'S CASTLE.
IT SEEMS LIKE THE OTHER SURVIVORS ARE ALL THERE TOO.
I DOUBT WE'LL BE IMPRISONED OR PUT TO DEATH TO KEEP US QUIET, BUT...
WE'RE GOING TO HAVE YOU LOT STAY IN THE DUNGEON FOR A FEW DAYS, THE COUNT SAYS ...
...SO FOR THE SAKE OF PUBLIC SECURITY, KEEP QUIET AND JUST FOLLOW ORDERS.
HUH?
GASHAAAAN (SLAAAAM)
LET US OUT!
RESIST, AND YOU'LL BE GUILTY OF TREASON!
I THOUGHT WE'D JUST BE UNDER HOUSE ARREST...
I JUST SAVED SEIRYUU CITY FROM A GREATER HELL DEMON, AND THIS IS THE THANKS I GET...?
I GUESS I DID IT IN DISGUISE, BUT...
KOTSU (GRIPE)
KOTSU
HEY!
INVITATION TO JAIL

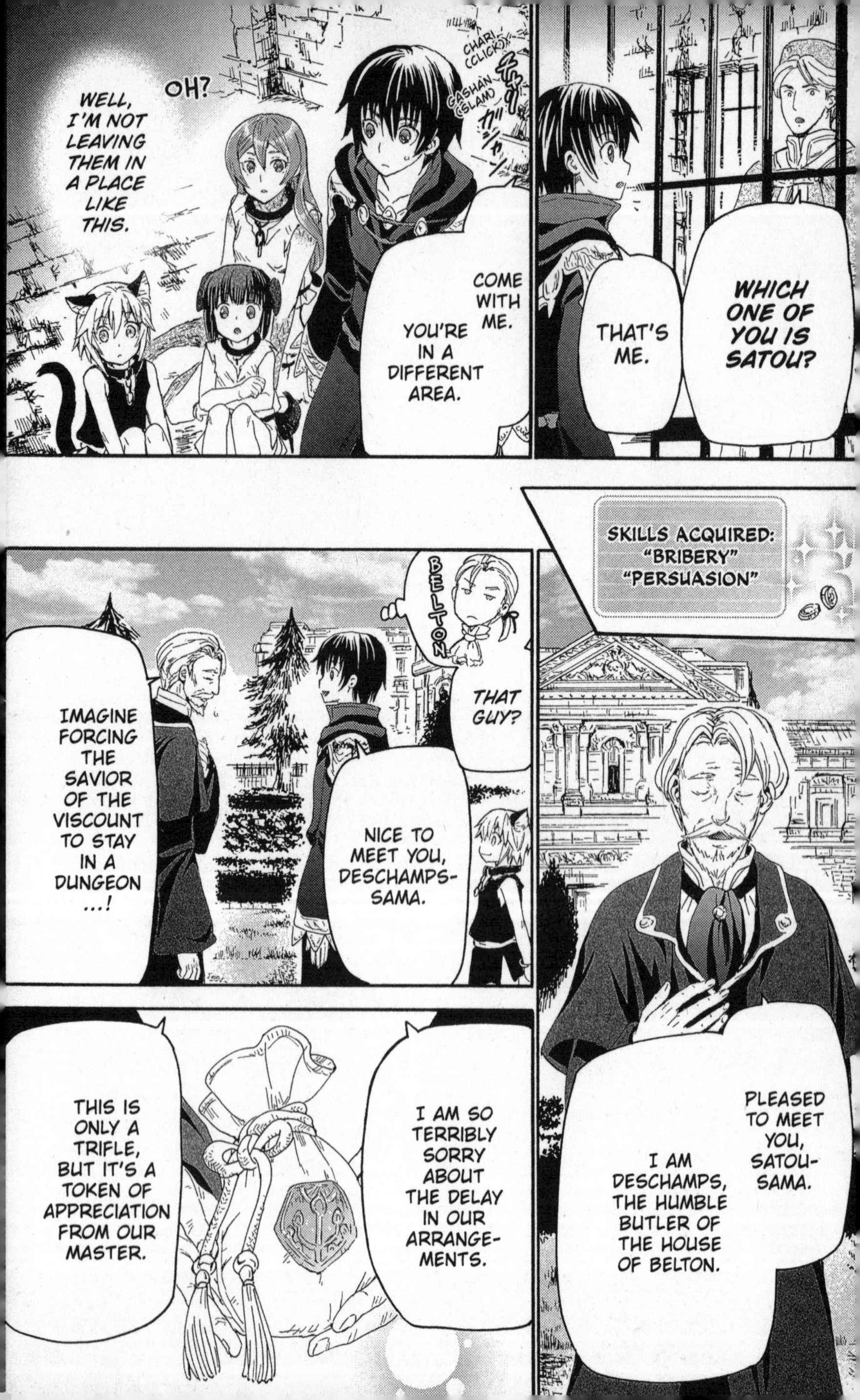

WHICH ONE OF YOU IS SATOU?
THAT'S ME.
CHARI (CLICK)
GASHAN (SLAM)
COME WITH ME.
YOU'RE IN A DIFFERENT AREA.
OH?
WELL, I'M NOT LEAVING THEM IN A PLACE LIKE THIS.
SKILLS ACQUIRED: "BRIBERY" "PERSUASION"
PLEASED TO MEET YOU, SATOU-SAMA.
I AM DESCHAMPS, THE HUMBLE BUTLER OF THE HOUSE OF BELTON.
BELTON
THAT GUY?
NICE TO MEET YOU, DESCHAMPS-SAMA.
IMAGINE FORCING THE SAVIOR OF THE VISCOUNT TO STAY IN A DUNGEON ...!
I AM SO TERRIBLY SORRY ABOUT THE DELAY IN OUR ARRANGE-MENTS.
THIS IS ONLY A TRIFLE, BUT IT'S A TOKEN OF APPRECIATION FROM OUR MASTER.

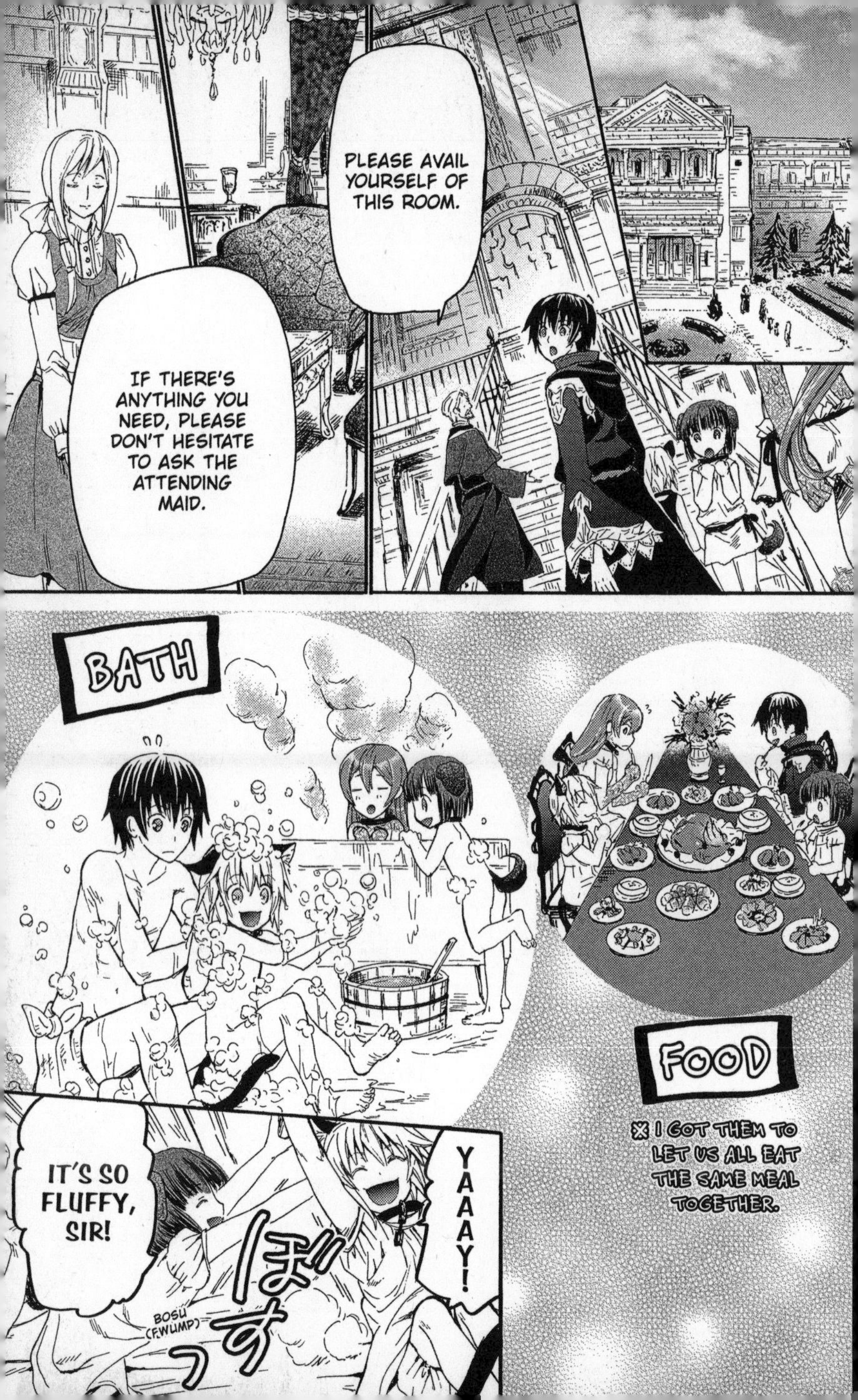
PLEASE AVAIL YOURSELF OF THIS ROOM.
IF THERE'S ANYTHING YOU NEED, PLEASE DON'T HESITATE TO ASK THE ATTENDING MAID.
FOOD
※ I GOT THEM TO LET US ALL EAT THE SAME MEAL TOGETHER.
BATH
YAAAY!
IT'S SO FLUFFY, SIR!
ぼすっ
BOSU (F.WUMP)

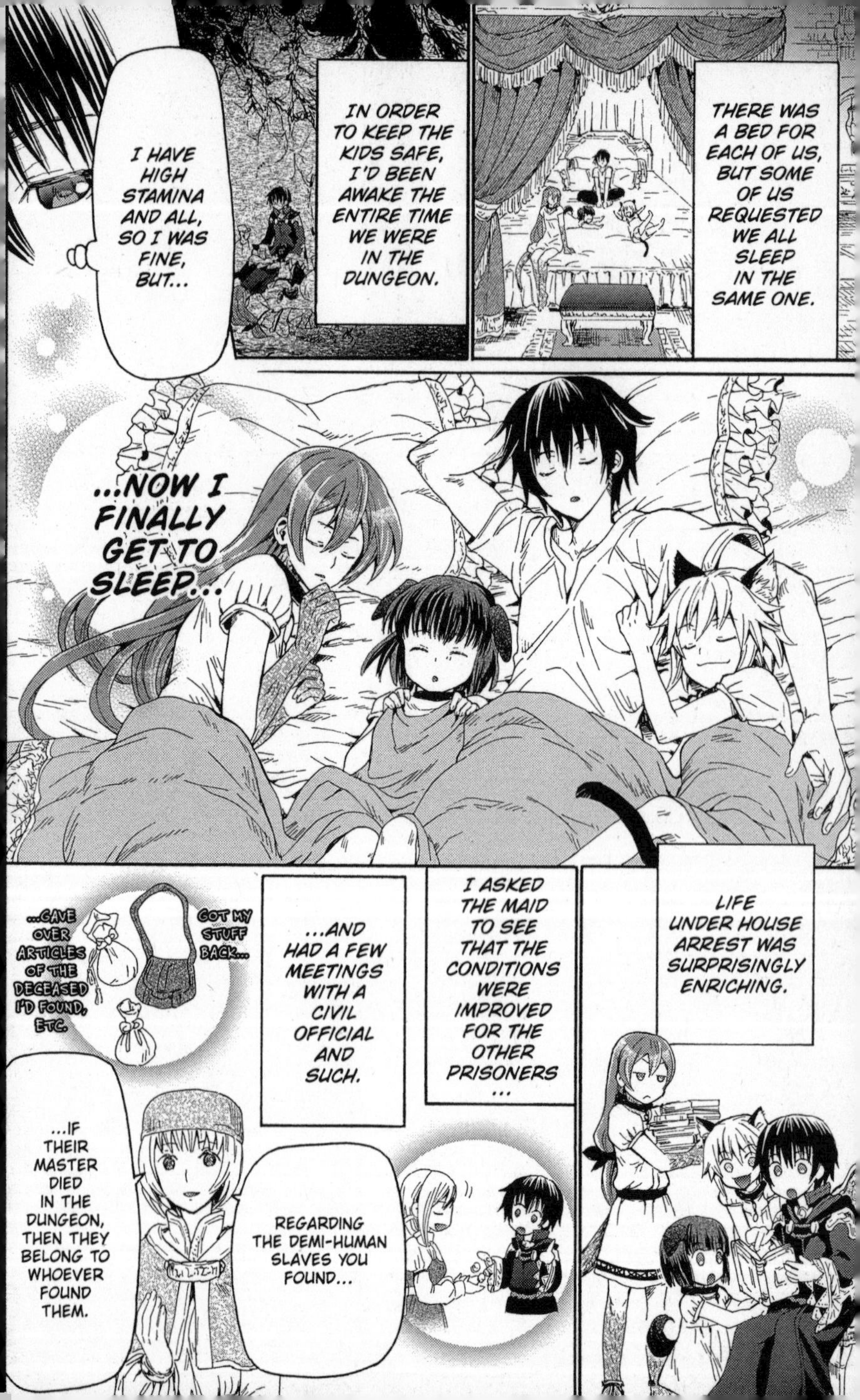
THERE WAS A BED FOR EACH OF US, BUT SOME OF US REQUESTED WE ALL SLEEP IN THE SAME ONE.
IN ORDER TO KEEP THE KIDS SAFE, I'D BEEN AWAKE THE ENTIRE TIME WE WERE IN THE DUNGEON.
I HAVE HIGH STAMINA AND ALL, SO I WAS FINE, BUT...
...NOW I FINALLY GET TO SLEEP...
LIFE UNDER HOUSE ARREST WAS SURPRISINGLY ENRICHING.
I ASKED THE MAID TO SEE THAT THE CONDITIONS WERE IMPROVED FOR THE OTHER PRISONERS...
...AND HAD A FEW MEETINGS WITH A CIVIL OFFICIAL AND SUCH.
GOT MY STUFF BACK...
...GAVE OVER ARTICLES OF THE DECEASED I'D FOUND, ETC.
REGARDING THE DEMI-HUMAN SLAVES YOU FOUND...
...IF THEIR MASTER DIED IN THE DUNGEON, THEN THEY BELONG TO WHOEVER FOUND THEM.

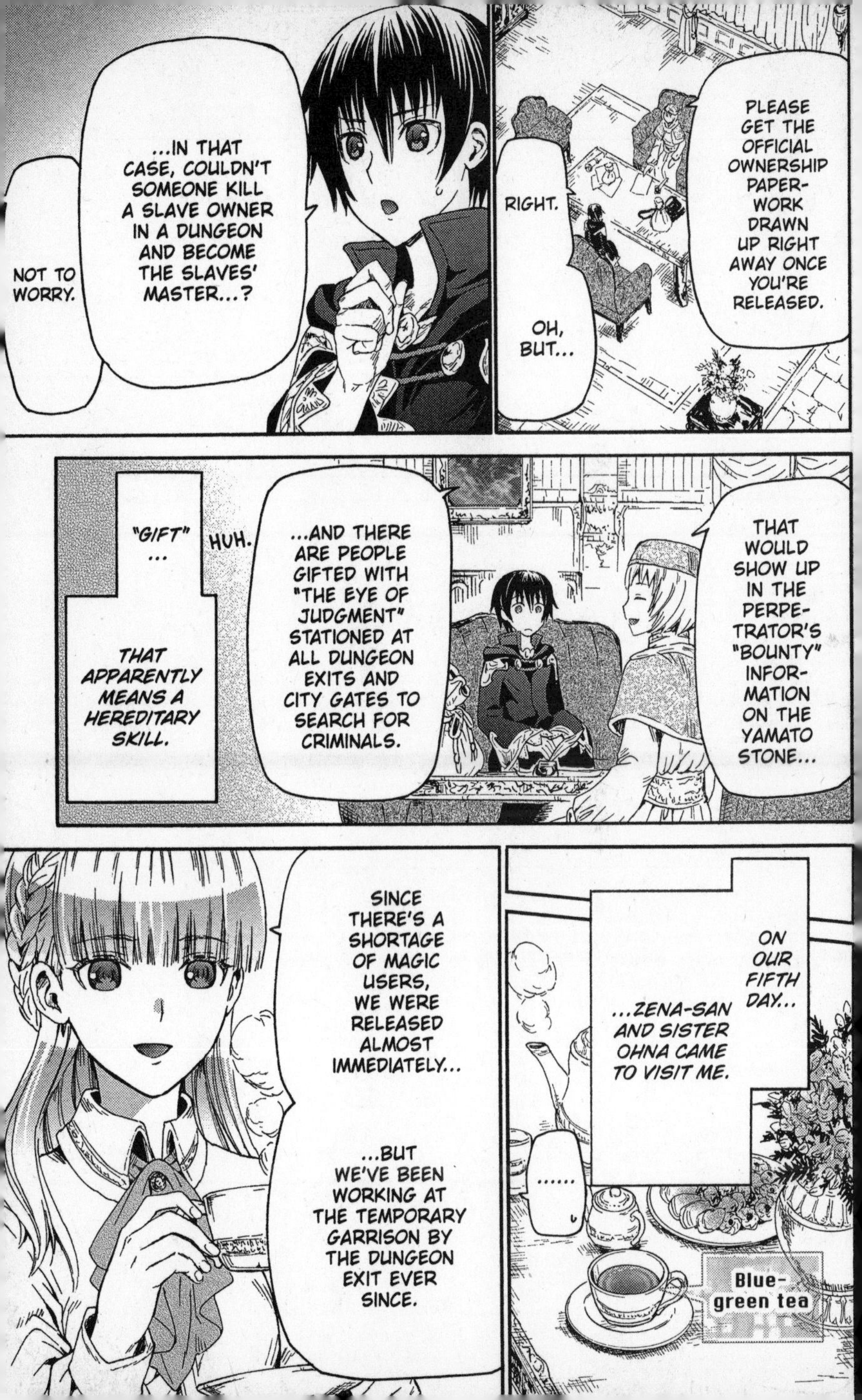
PLEASE GET THE OFFICIAL OWNERSHIP PAPERWORK DRAWN UP RIGHT AWAY ONCE YOU'RE RELEASED.
RIGHT.
OH, BUT...
...IN THAT CASE, COULDN'T SOMEONE KILL A SLAVE OWNER IN A DUNGEON AND BECOME THE SLAVES' MASTER...?
NOT TO WORRY.
THAT WOULD SHOW UP IN THE PERPETRATOR'S "BOUNTY" INFORMATION ON THE YAMATO STONE...
...AND THERE ARE PEOPLE GIFTED WITH "THE EYE OF JUDGMENT" STATIONED AT ALL DUNGEON EXITS AND CITY GATES TO SEARCH FOR CRIMINALS.
HUH.
"GIFT"...
THAT APPARENTLY MEANS A HEREDITARY SKILL.
ON OUR FIFTH DAY...
...ZENA-SAN AND SISTER OHNA CAME TO VISIT ME.
......
Blue-green tea
SINCE THERE'S A SHORTAGE OF MAGIC USERS, WE WERE RELEASED ALMOST IMMEDIATELY...
...BUT WE'VE BEEN WORKING AT THE TEMPORARY GARRISON BY THE DUNGEON EXIT EVER SINCE.

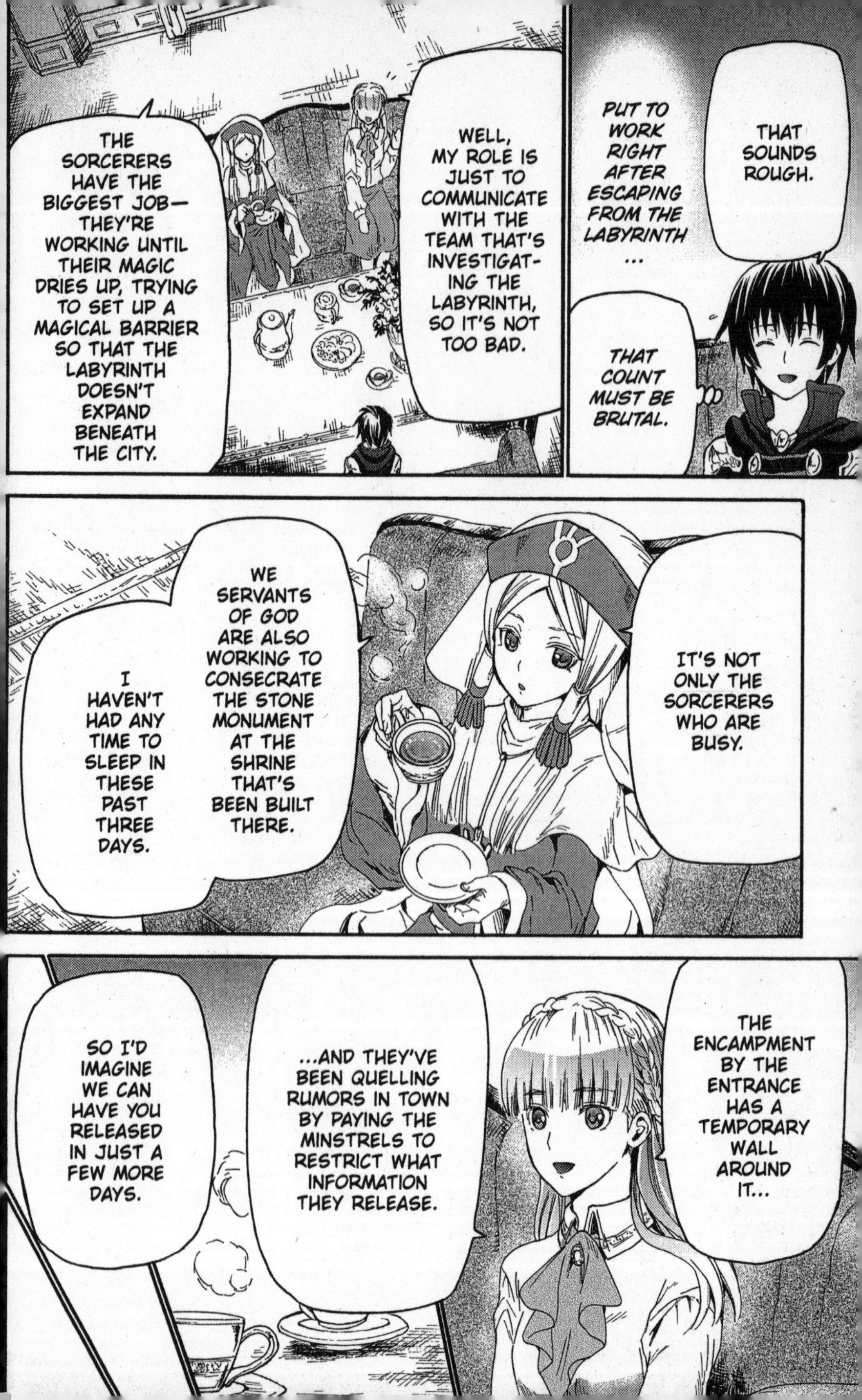
THAT SOUNDS ROUGH.
PUT TO WORK RIGHT AFTER ESCAPING FROM THE LABYRINTH...
THAT COUNT MUST BE BRUTAL.
WELL, MY ROLE IS JUST TO COMMUNICATE WITH THE TEAM THAT'S INVESTIGATING THE LABYRINTH, SO IT'S NOT TOO BAD.
THE SORCERERS HAVE THE BIGGEST JOB—THEY'RE WORKING UNTIL THEIR MAGIC DRIES UP, TRYING TO SET UP A MAGICAL BARRIER SO THAT THE LABYRINTH DOESN'T EXPAND BENEATH THE CITY.
IT'S NOT ONLY THE SORCERERS WHO ARE BUSY.
WE SERVANTS OF GOD ARE ALSO WORKING TO CONSECRATE THE STONE MONUMENT AT THE SHRINE THAT'S BEEN BUILT THERE.
I HAVEN'T HAD ANY TIME TO SLEEP IN THESE PAST THREE DAYS.
THE ENCAMPMENT BY THE ENTRANCE HAS A TEMPORARY WALL AROUND IT...
...AND THEY'VE BEEN QUELLING RUMORS IN TOWN BY PAYING THE MINSTRELS TO RESTRICT WHAT INFORMATION THEY RELEASE.
SO I'D IMAGINE WE CAN HAVE YOU RELEASED IN JUST A FEW MORE DAYS.

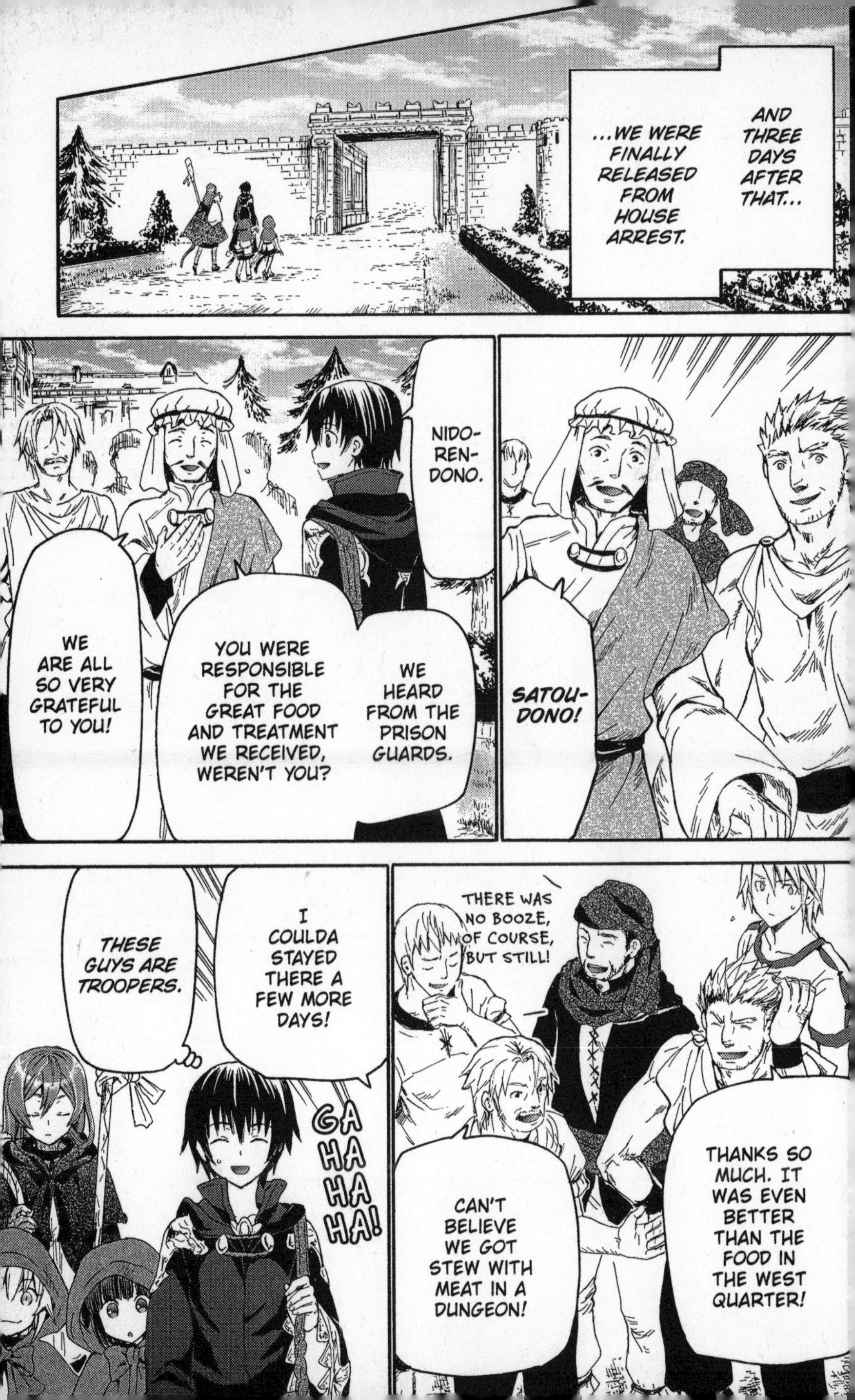
AND THREE DAYS AFTER THAT...
...WE WERE FINALLY RELEASED FROM HOUSE ARREST.
SATOU-DONO!
NIDO-REN-DONO.
WE HEARD FROM THE PRISON GUARDS.
YOU WERE RESPONSIBLE FOR THE GREAT FOOD AND TREATMENT WE RECEIVED, WEREN'T YOU?
WE ARE ALL SO VERY GRATEFUL TO YOU!
THANKS SO MUCH. IT WAS EVEN BETTER THAN THE FOOD IN THE WEST QUARTER!
CAN'T BELIEVE WE GOT STEW WITH MEAT IN A DUNGEON!
THERE WAS NO BOOZE, OF COURSE, BUT STILL!
I COULDA STAYED THERE A FEW MORE DAYS!
GAHAHAHA!
THESE GUYS ARE TROOPERS.

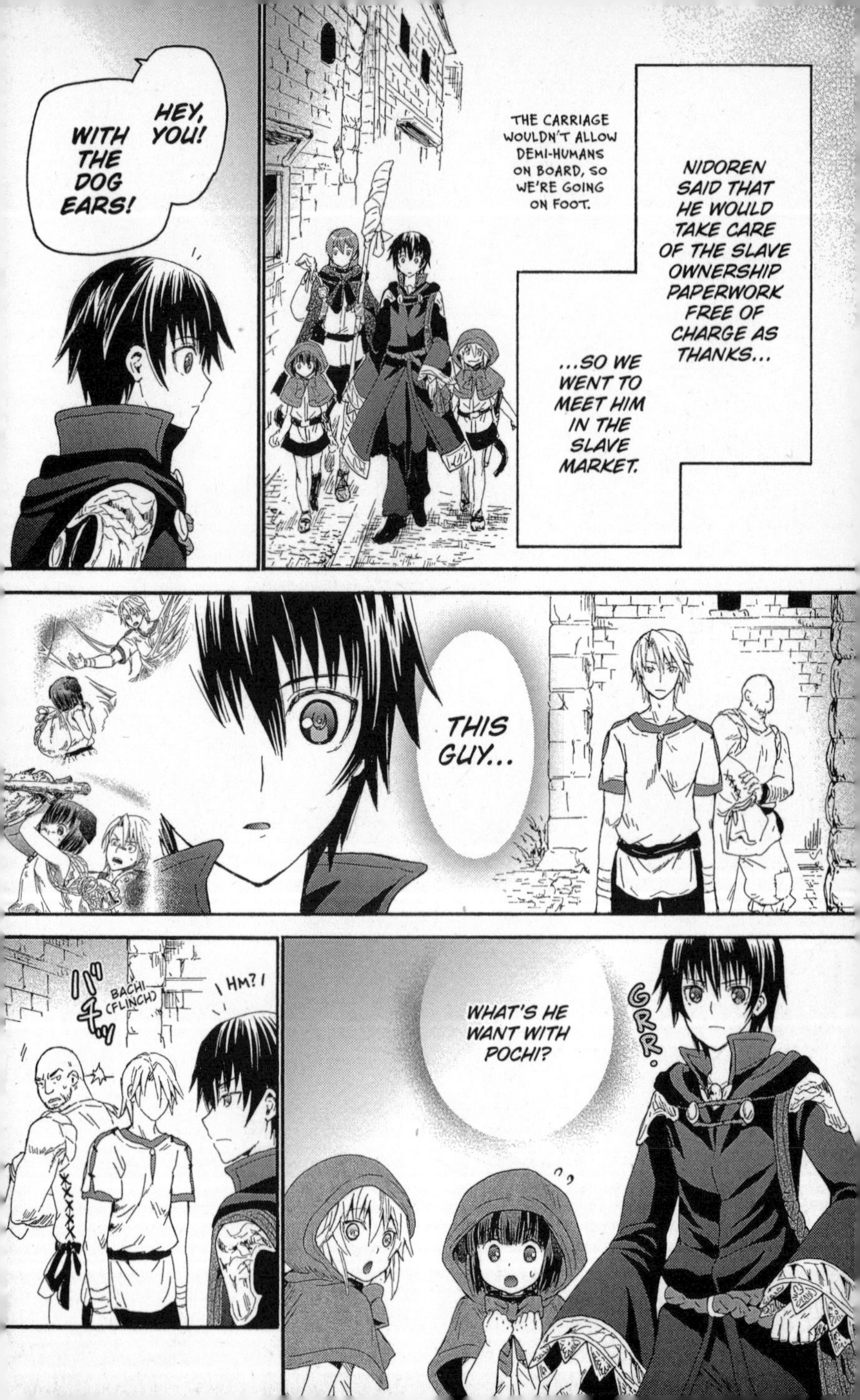
NIDOREN SAID THAT HE WOULD TAKE CARE OF THE SLAVE OWNERSHIP PAPERWORK FREE OF CHARGE AS THANKS...
...SO WE WENT TO MEET HIM IN THE SLAVE MARKET.
THE CARRIAGE WOULDN'T ALLOW DEMI-HUMANS ON BOARD, SO WE'RE GOING ON FOOT.
HEY, YOU! WITH THE DOG EARS!
THIS GUY...
GRR.
WHAT'S HE WANT WITH POCHI?
HM?!
BACHI (FLINCH)

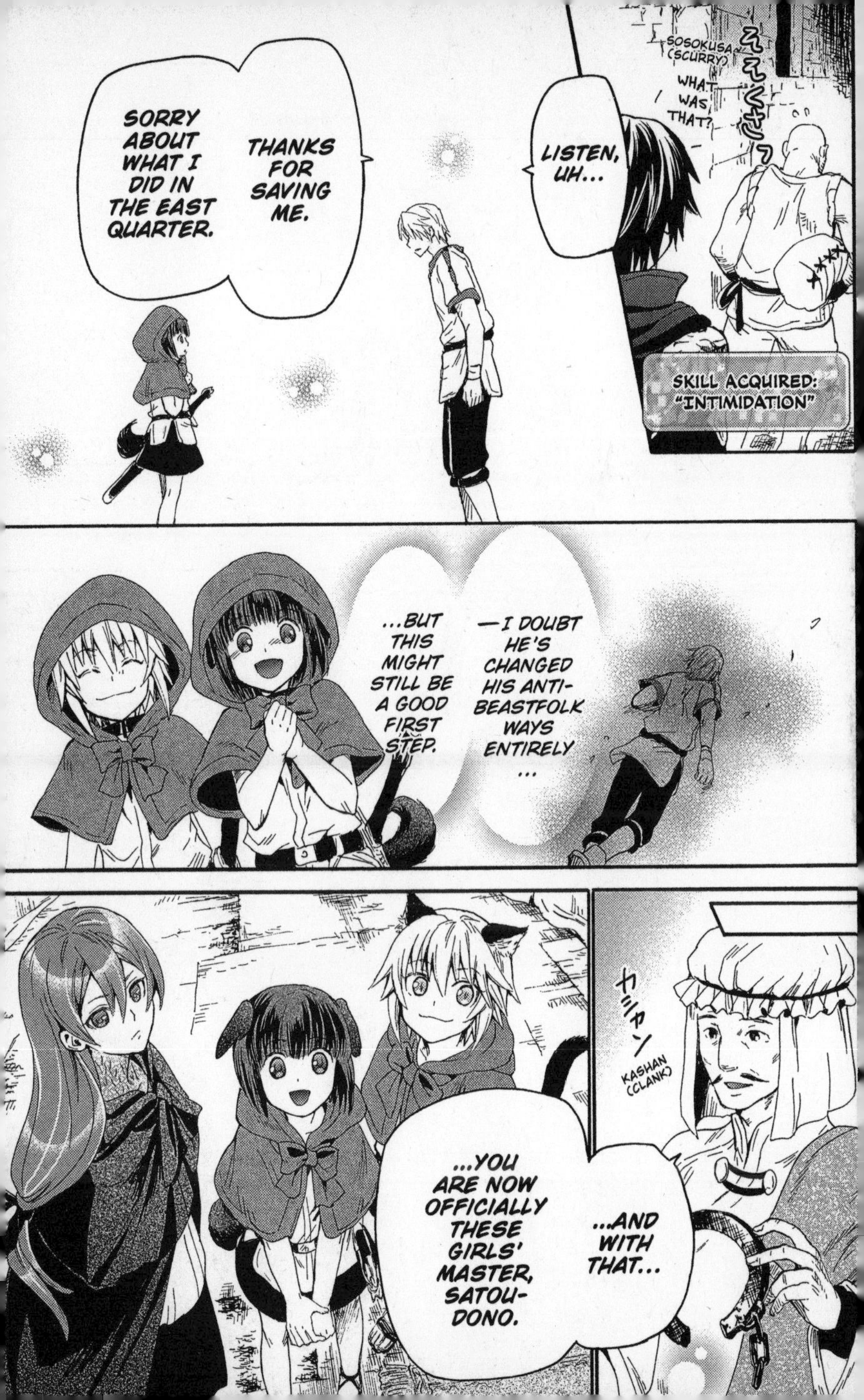
そそくさっ
SOSOKUSA (SCURRY)
WHAT WAS THAT?
LISTEN, UH...
SKILL ACQUIRED: "INTIMIDATION"
THANKS FOR SAVING ME.
SORRY ABOUT WHAT I DID IN THE EAST QUARTER.
—I DOUBT HE'S CHANGED HIS ANTI-BEASTFOLK WAYS ENTIRELY...
...BUT THIS MIGHT STILL BE A GOOD FIRST STEP.
カシャン
KASHAN (CLANK)
...AND WITH THAT...
...YOU ARE NOW OFFICIALLY THESE GIRLS' MASTER, SATOU-DONO.

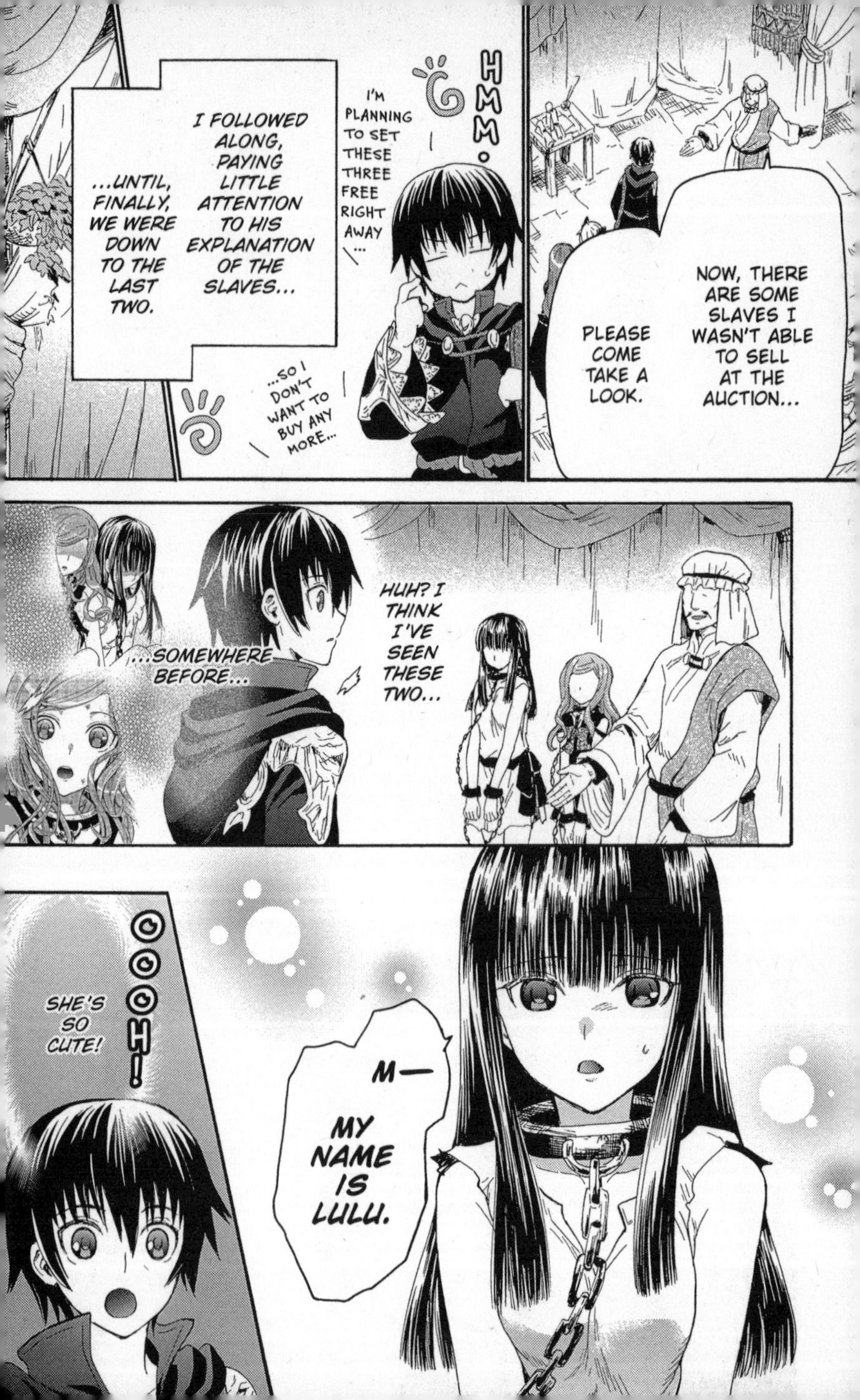
NOW, THERE ARE SOME SLAVES I WASN'T ABLE TO SELL AT THE AUCTION...
PLEASE COME TAKE A LOOK.
HMM.
I'M PLANNING TO SET THESE THREE FREE RIGHT AWAY...
...SO I DON'T WANT TO BUY ANY MORE...
I FOLLOWED ALONG, PAYING LITTLE ATTENTION TO HIS EXPLANATION OF THE SLAVES...
...UNTIL, FINALLY, WE WERE DOWN TO THE LAST TWO.
HUH? I THINK I'VE SEEN THESE TWO...
...SOMEWHERE BEFORE...
M—
MY NAME IS LULU.
OOOOH!
SHE'S SO CUTE!

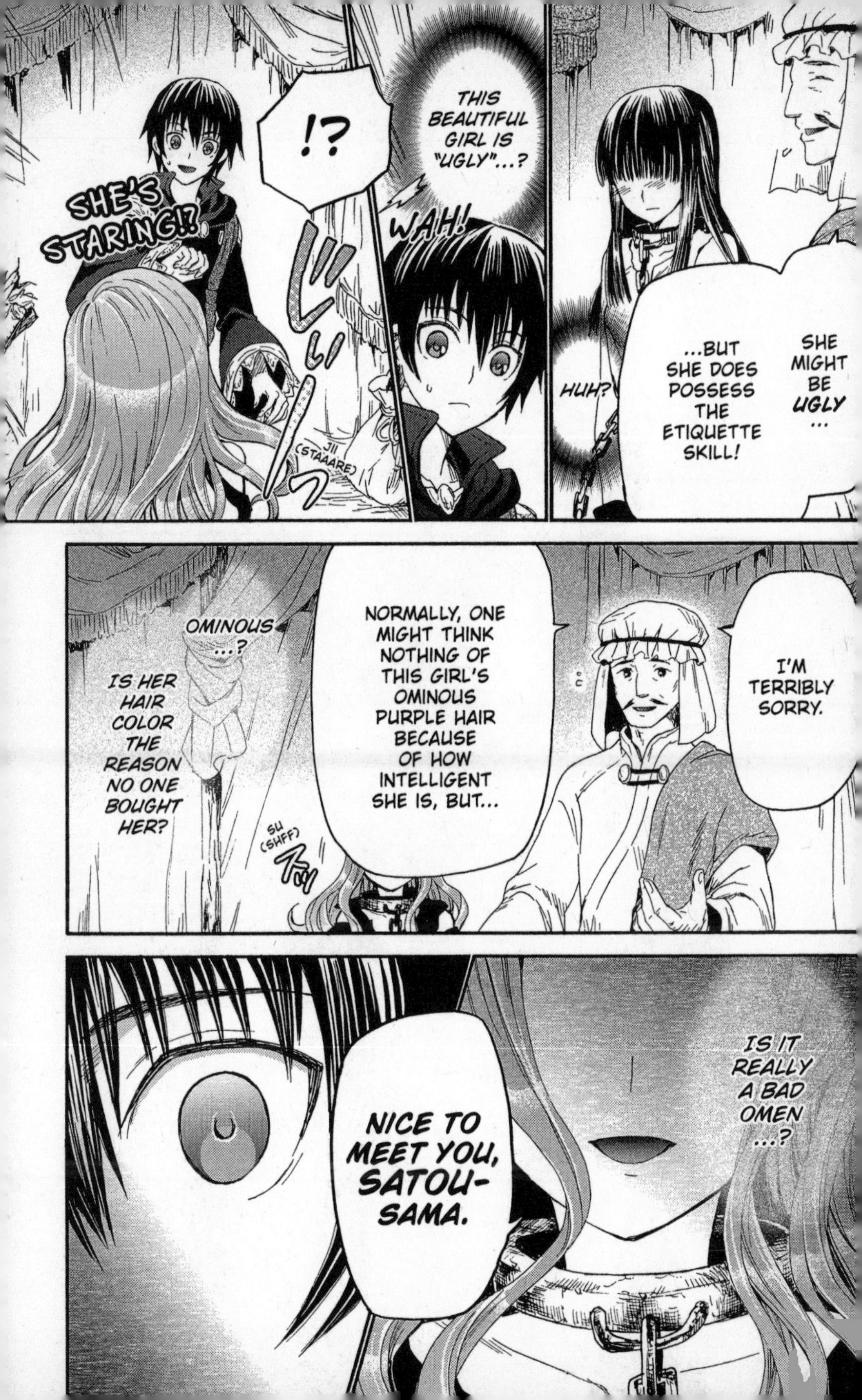
SHE MIGHT BE UGLY...
...BUT SHE DOES POSSESS THE ETIQUETTE SKILL!
HUH?
THIS BEAUTIFUL GIRL IS "UGLY"...?
WAH!
!?
SHE'S STARING!?
JII (STAAARE)
I'M TERRIBLY SORRY.
NORMALLY, ONE MIGHT THINK NOTHING OF THIS GIRL'S OMINOUS PURPLE HAIR BECAUSE OF HOW INTELLIGENT SHE IS, BUT...
OMINOUS...?
IS HER HAIR COLOR THE REASON NO ONE BOUGHT HER?
SU (SHFF)
IS IT REALLY A BAD OMEN...?
NICE TO MEET YOU, SATOU-SAMA.

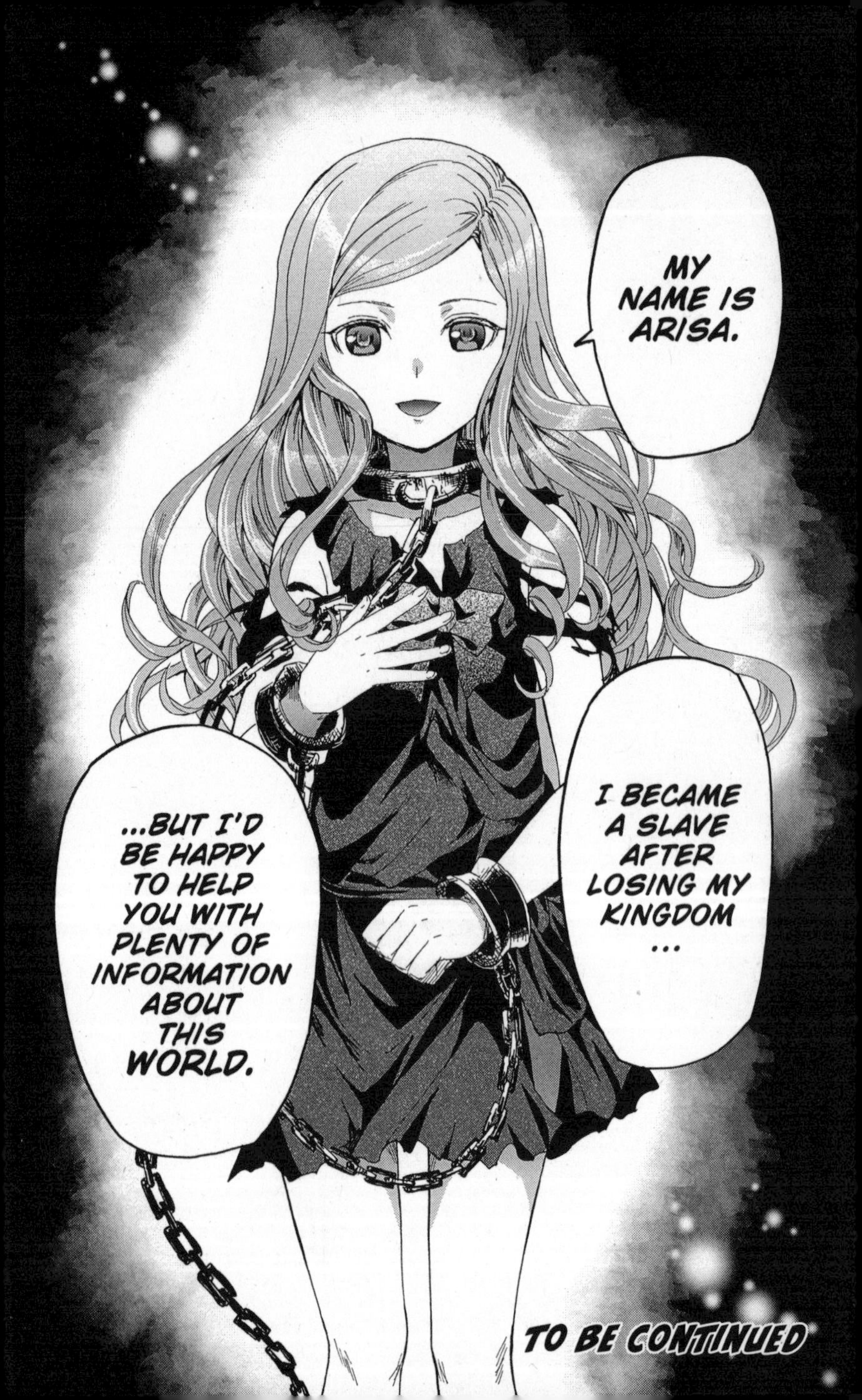
MY NAME IS ARISA.
I BECAME A SLAVE AFTER LOSING MY KINGDOM ...
...BUT I'D BE HAPPY TO HELP YOU WITH PLENTY OF INFORMATION ABOUT THIS WORLD.
TO BE CONTINUED

HIDDEN TREASURE

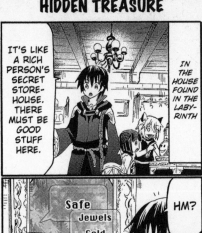

IN THE HOUSE FOUND IN THE LABYRINTH
IT'S LIKE A RICH PERSON'S SECRET STOREHOUSE. THERE MUST BE GOOD STUFF HERE.
HM?
Safe
Jewels
Gold coins
BEHIND A PAINTING? HOW CLICHÉ...
PA (POP)
"Treasure Hunting" skill
Treasure detected
!
ON THE BOOKSHELF TOO?
18+ art book
I GUESS THAT'S ONE KIND OF TREASURE, BUT COME ON!!
Portraits for adults only
IT'S FROM A FOREIGN CULTURE, SO I'M CURIOUS, BUT...

Hello, it's nice to meet you.

This is Volume 2.
I'm so relieved that we somehow made it this far.

As usual, I'm a mess on my own, so I'm very grateful to everyone involved in this project.

I hope we can meet again next time.

Thank you very much.

–Ayamegumu

...Special Thanks

● Manuscript production collaborators
Kaname Yukishiro-sama
Satoru Ezaki-sama
Yuna Kobayashi-sama
Hacchan-sama

● Editors
Toyohara-sama
Hagiwara-sama
Kuwazuru-sama

● Binding
coil-sama

● Supervision
Hiro Ainana-sama
shri-sama

● Everyone who helped with the production and publication of this book

And you!

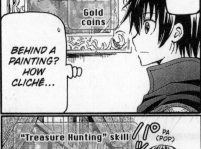

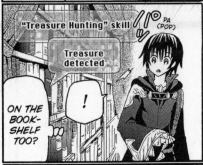

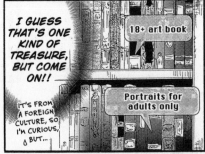

DEATH MARCH ②
TO THE
PARALLEL WORLD RHAPSODY

Original Story: Hiro Ainana
Art: AYAMEGUMU
Character Design: shri

Translation: Jenny McKeon ◆ **Lettering: Rochelle Gancio**

DEATH MARCHING TO THE PARALLEL WORLD RHAPSODY Vol. 2
©AYAMEGUMU 2015
©HIRO AINANA, shri 2015
First published in Japan in 2015 by KADOKAWA CORPORATION, Tokyo. English translation rights arranged with KADOKAWA CORPORATION, Tokyo through TUTTLE-MORI AGENCY, INC., Tokyo.

English translation © 2017 by Yen Press, LLC

Yen Press
1290 Avenue of the Americas
New York, NY 10104

Visit us at yenpress.com
facebook.com/yenpress
twitter.com/yenpress
yenpress.tumblr.com
instagram.com/yenpress

First Yen Press Edition: March 2017

Yen Press is an imprint of Yen Press, LLC.
The Yen Press name and logo are trademarks of Yen Press, LLC.

Library of Congress Control Number: 2016946043

ISBNs: 978-0-316-46923-4 (paperback)
978-0-316-47037-7 (ebook)

10 9 8 7 6 5 4 3 2 1

BVG

Printed in the United States of America